THE BOOK OF

ASHBURTON

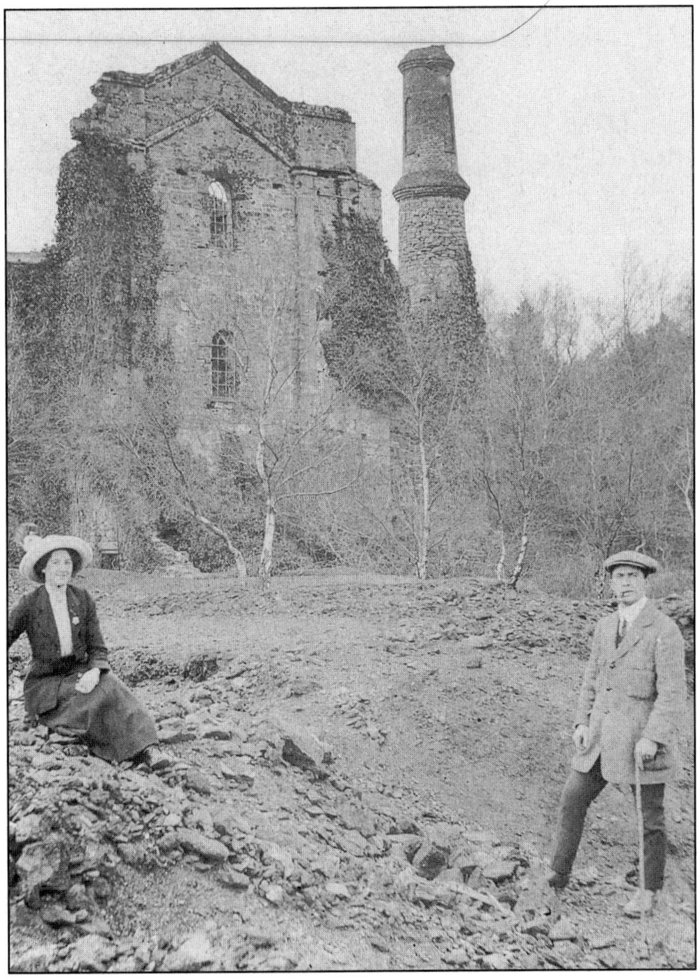

STUART HANDS AND PETE WEBB

HALSGROVE

First published in Great Britain in 2004

This book is dedicated to our wives, Margery and Viv, for their patience during the writing of this book and for their love at all times.
It is also dedicated to the people of Ashburton. Without them there could be no book.

British Library Cataloguing-in-Publication Data.
A CIP record for this title is available from the British Library.

ISBN 1 84114 347 2

HALSGROVE

Halsgrove House
Lower Moor Way
Tiverton, Devon EX16 6SS
Tel.: 01884 243242
Fax: 01884 243325
email: sales@halsgrove.com
website: www.halsgrove.com

Frontispiece photograph: *Druid Copper Mine, April 1913, photographed by Amy Satterley. Also called the Arundell Copper Mine, it was worked for brief periods in the 1850s and 1860s but was never successful. It had ceased working by 1870 and was a ruin even when the picture was taken, with nature rapidly covering it. It is now in the middle of a wood and even the chimney is dwarfed by trees. Sister Nellie and brother-in-law Norman Matthews appear in the picture.*
(PETE WEBB COLLECTION)

Printed and bound in Great Britain by CPI Bath Press, Bath.

Foreword

The Mayor and Portreeve of Ashburton work together in their different capacities for the good of the town. As somebody once said, Ashburton is a town with the heart of a village. We will see from this book how much history and tradition play an important part in its present.

We therefore wish this book every success and congratulate the writers, Pete and Stuart, together with the other contributors, for all the work and research in putting this publication together.

We hope you will all enjoy reading this fascinating pictorial history of Ashburton and learn a lot from the content. It is about the town's history and past. Today is Ashburton's history of tomorrow.

April 2004

Patricia Crook
1,183rd Portreeve of Ashburton

Wendy Gill
Mayor of Ashburton

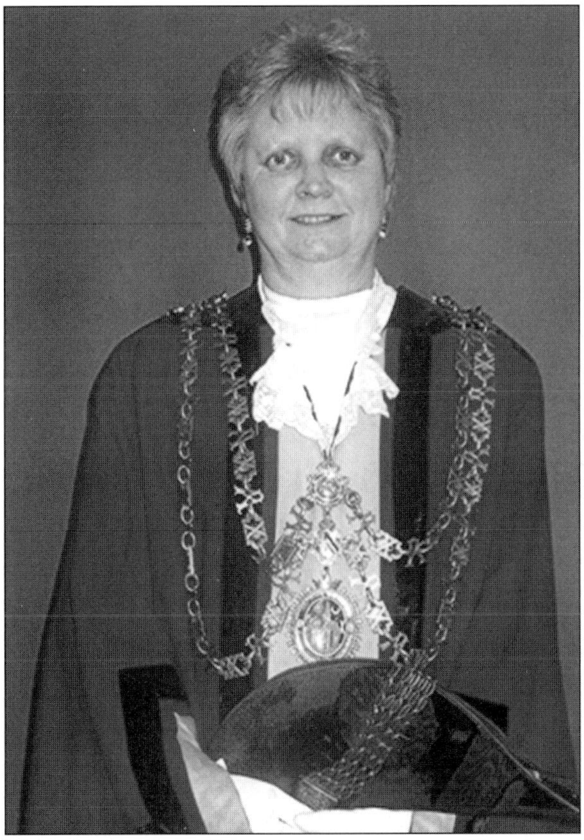

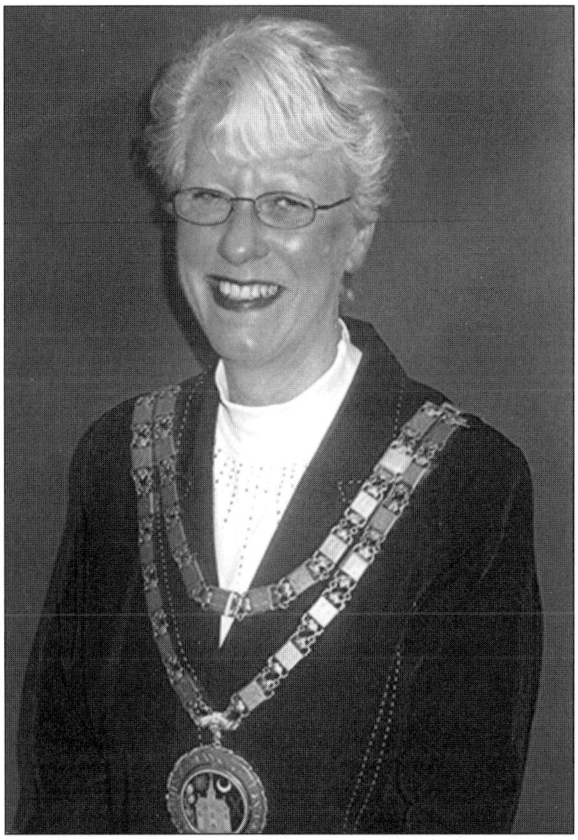

Preface

When approached to write one of the Halsgrove Community History Series the authors' first problem was how does one tackle a place such as Ashburton, which has already taken great care to record its past in one form or another? Not only this but published histories of the town and parish already exist either in part or whole.

It was decided therefore to make this a pictorial history, focusing on the place since the advent of photography. Even this was a task of selection from the wealth of photographs and material available. The nature of things is that events receive more attention from the photographer than the everyday life of the parish, for example pictures of the day-to-day life of farming, an important part of the parish, have been hard to come by. Whilst the focus of the book is the last 130 years, the earlier past has not been forgotten. This puts the late-Victorian era and twentieth century into context as not everyone who reads this book will have access to other published material. Ashburton of the early-twenty-first century recognises its past, whether this be institutions such as the office of Portreeve or the buildings which constitute the town centre. Yet it is also true to say that whilst the community spirit remains, the town is a different place. Until the 1960s, Ashburton had witnessed the decline of its traditional industries and population. Since then, however, Ashburton has discovered for itself a new role, primarily but not exclusively based on tourism. This has brought an influx of newcomers, as elsewhere in Devon. By and large these people have fitted into the community, bringing freshness yet without, in any way, destroying that essential spirit which is Ashburton. It is this change that the book hopes to illustrate.

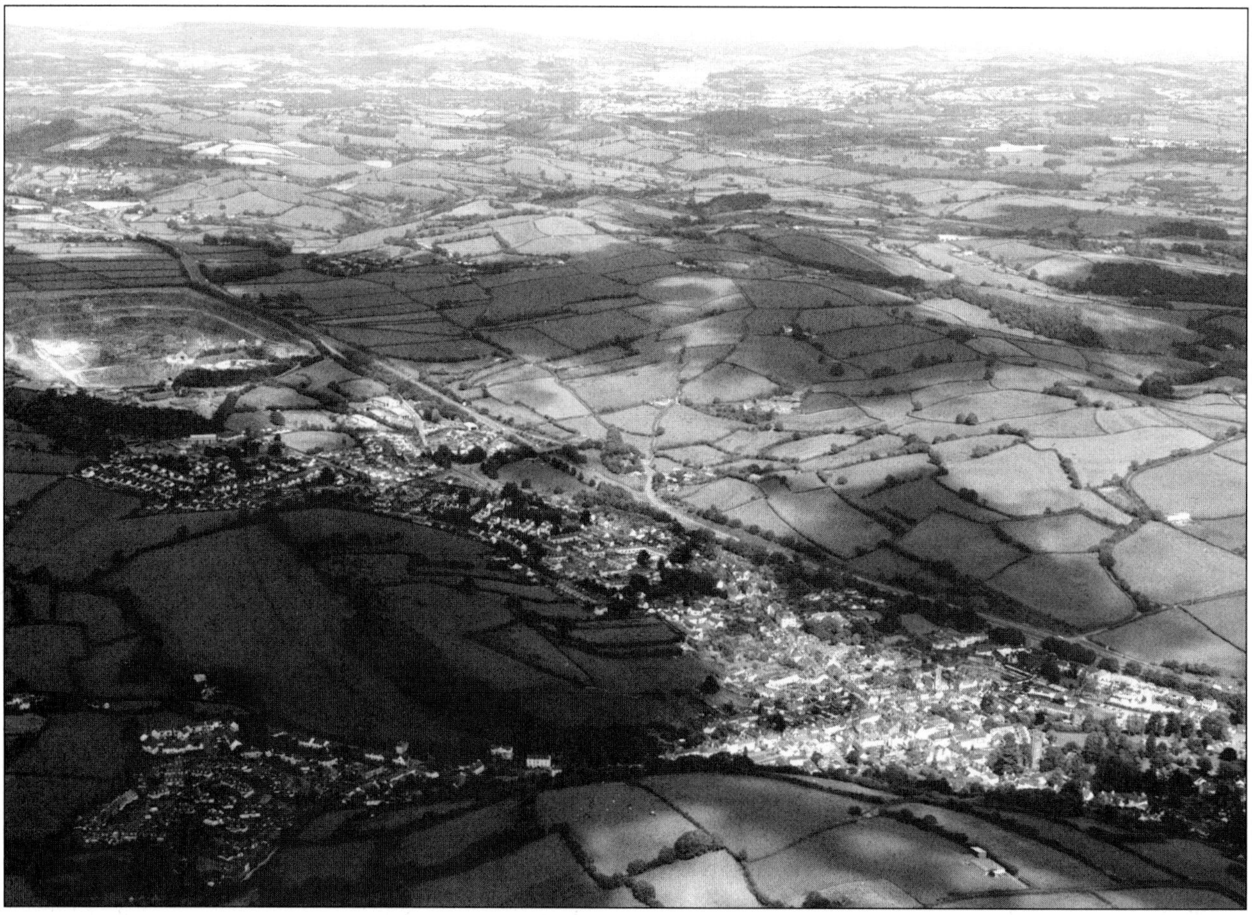

Aerial view of Ashburton.

Contents

Acknowledgements

This book could not have been written without the help we have received from so many people in Ashburton. An historic place such as this has a wealth of information which has been shared willingly with us. It is regrettable that we have been unable to include all the stories, facts and photographs either given or lent to us. The individual photographs are credited where it has been possible to trace the source. Where the name of the owner is known we have acknowledged it following the photograph.

It would be impossible to mention all those whom we would like to thank, we are however particularly grateful to the following people for sharing their personal recollections, or providing valuable information: Jean Allen, Ian Ashford (of Glendinnings), Peter Burden (Post Office information), Johnny and Sheila Chew, Fred Christophers, Joyce Coon (police information), PC Cluer of Ashburton Police, Adrian Daw, Eileen Egbeare, Wendy Gill, Garth Grose, Paddy Harding, Lorna Harvey, Peter and Mavis Head, Dr Klaus Hinst, Geoff Histed, Hilary King (Steiner School), Henry Lang, Maurice Mann, Pat and Fred Orsman, M. Pool (Torquay reference library), Paul Rendell, Ruby (Amy Satterley's daughter), Lincoln Shaw, Ken Watson (headmaster, Ashburton School, 1962–1971), Ruth Westall (Ashburton School), William West (tin mining), Mary Woollacott.

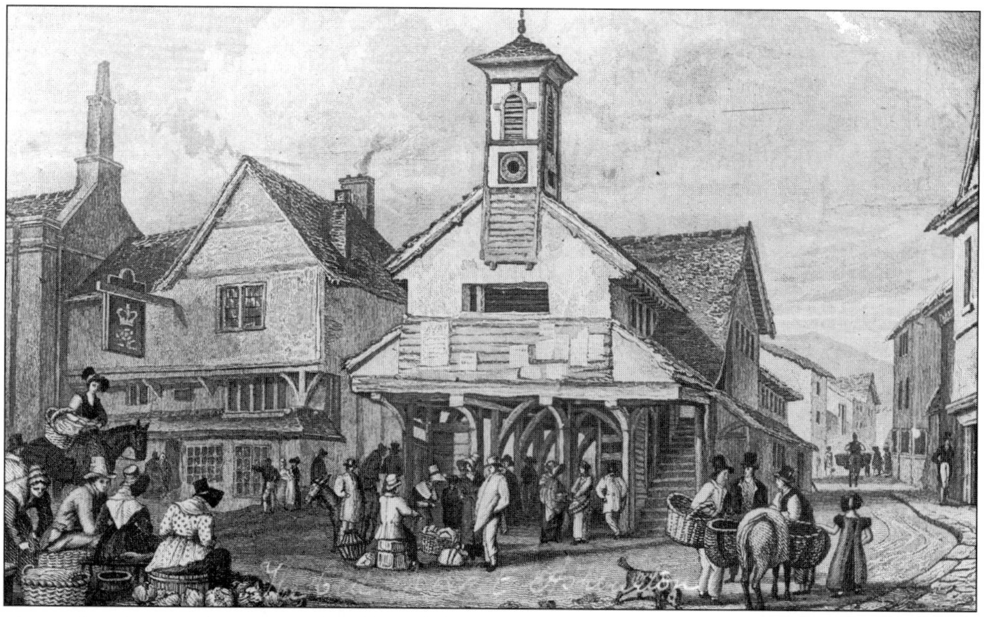

An early-nineteenth-century drawing of the town market. (PETE WEBB COLLECTION)

CHAPTER 1

Brief Outline of the History of Ashburton

Dr Francis Pilkington wrote a history of the parish which was first published in 1978. It is not the intention to go over in detail the same ground as covered in that excellent book. However, since that date research into the history of Devon has taken great strides and it would be appropriate to include some of this information in this publication.

There will be those who, for one reason or another, have not read Pilkington's book. It therefore seems appropriate to include a summary of the history of the parish before the advent of photography in the nineteenth century, the remainder of this volume being dedicated to providing a photographic record of the parish. Other aspects of Ashburton's history are dealt with in the appropriate chapters.

Long before Ashburton became Ashburton, people lived in the area. Some of the earliest human artefacts were found in Tornewton Caves, just south of the parish. Whilst there is little or no trace of succeeding peoples, we have no reason to believe that they were not present at least for some of the time. It is not until we come to the Bronze Age, about 3,000 years ago, that we have more tangible evidence of people's presence. The Dartmoor reave systems have been well documented. Part of the Ripon Tor system fell within what was to become Ashburton. At Goodstone, to the left of the road leading up to Stormsdown, there are a number of small, oblong fields. These may follow the same pattern as Bronze-Age fields. The Iron-Age people left a number of hill settlements within the parish. These are often referred to as hill-forts. The surrounding bank and ditch provided some protection in times of trouble, but this may have been a secondary function in the smaller settlements we find on the south-east Dartmoor fringe. Two of these sites disappeared in early-Victorian times, namely Ashburton Down and Stormsdown. These were on the left and right of the Goodstone to Stormsdown road. Place Wood or Tower Hill Castle and Boro Wood Camp are still discernible. As times became more settled these Celtic peoples settled in the valleys – some of the farms of the parish started life as Celtic farms.

Whilst it is true that the Celtic peoples probably determined the farm settlement of the parish, Ashburton as an administrative area can be traced to Saxon times, although there is a possibility that they themselves used pre-existing boundaries. They gave most of the places within the parish their names.

Names within the Parish

The name Ashburton has been variously spelt over the centuries:

Below are listed the earliest recorded names of various places in the parish and what they might mean. These are dates appearing in documents – the origin of the name could be much earlier.

Present Name	*Earliest Recorded Name*	*Date*	*Meaning*
Alston	*Alston*	*1504*	
Ausewell	*Ausewellwode*	*1553*	*possibly Aspen spring*
Blackmoor	*Blackmoor*	*1579*	*Black Moor*
Boro' Wood	*Boroughwod*	*1553*	*from beorg, fortified settlement – there is an ancient earthwork here*
Bowdley	*Bogedelegh*	*1330*	*clearing by the curved wood*
Brownswell	*Brunswell*	*1238*	*Brun's spring*
Byland	*Bilond*	*1604*	*curve may be shape of land here*
Caton	*Cadetone*	*1330*	*Cada's farm*
Chuley Cross	*Chiuelege*	*1228*	*a personal name*
Dolbeare	*Dollebeare*	*1333*	*Dola's grove (beare meaning grove)*
Furzeleigh	*Furslegh*	*1304*	*furze clearing*
Gages	*Gades*	*1413*	
Halsanger	*Halsangre*	*1244*	*hazel wooded slope*
Lurgecombe Mill	*Loryggecombe*	*1504*	
Owlacombe	*Hulecombe*	*1244*	
Summerhill	*Sumerhill*	*1238*	*hill used for summer pastureage*
Welstor	*Welestorre*	*1281*	*spring by the tor*

Other names in the parish are also of an early date.

Aesburnan lande (1088–1012)
Essebretona (1086 Domesday Book)
Aisbernatonam (1150)
Eispreton (1185)
Asperton (1238)
Ashperton (1313)
Aysshpertone (1356)
Ayssberton (1483)

The origin of the name is generally given as the farm by the Ashburn stream. The stream, once called the Yeo and now Ashburn again, flows through the centre of the town, where much damage has been caused by flooding in the past.

Even today the way the name is pronounced varies, the stress being put on different syllables.

A study of farm and other names, too, is a complex one; some in the parish are easy to understand, others are misleading and yet more defy interpretation.

Geology

Ashburton owes its existence, or at least its status as a town of some importance, to its underlying geology. The parish is on the edge of the Dartmoor granite. Where this borders on the older, mainly upper carboniferous, rocks through which Dartmoor arose is the area known as the metamorphic aureole, an area where intense heat occurred. This is where the greatest concentration of metals such as tin are found, giving rise to the creation of Ashburton as a stannary town. The moor has always provided grazing for sheep, as has the lower ground of the parish. From the slopes of the moor run fast-flowing streams providing power to the mills processing the wool. Limestone is found in the parish as a band of rock running parallel to the A38 trunk road. This valuable material is the basis of the present quarrying industry. The production of umber, a brown dyestuff, was formerly a thriving industry in the town. Between the moor and the Devonian slate hills to the south of the parish lies the corridor through which passes the A38 on its way from Plymouth to Exeter. The various inns of Ashburton bear testimony to the trade created to meet the needs of travellers along this route. Finally, this is a beautiful part of the country – the lovely juxtaposition of hills, moor and valley much prized by the tourist industry. As the traditional industries have declined, so tourism has provided employment for many.

Creation of the Parish

Looking at a parish map of South Devon one immediately notices two things. Firstly there is a variation in the size of the parishes. Compare Ashburton to its neighbour, Buckland in the Moor, for example. Secondly, around the central parishes of Dartmoor there are many parishes with a 'foot' on the moor.

So why was Ashburton parish created as it is? We cannot know for certain. Evidence from elsewhere indicates that boundaries can be very old. How old are Ashburton's?

When the Saxons came to Devon, they probably either took over pre-existing estates or created new ones. A clue to how this may have happened can be found in the neighbouring parish of Bickington. Until the mid-fourteenth century the land now forming Bickington was part of Ashburton parish. Ashburton at that time was both a borough and a parish, the borough not being coterminous with the parish. At some time before the Norman Conquest a number of smaller estates were probably combined to form Peadington. We know this from a boundary clause which is undated, though a copy we have of it is dated to about AD1000. This copy is itself believed to be a copy of an earlier document.

His (whoever or whatever Peadington was) estate embraced the whole of what is now Ashburton parish. The boundary can be traced from the juncture of Ashburton with Woodland. It then follows the course of the Ashburn (spelt Aescburne) until its confluence with the Dart. The clause boundary then embraces sections of other parishes until Ramshorn Down and follows the boundary of what became Ashburton (later Bickington) until it again departs, taking in parts or all of Torbryan and Denbury. So we know that the boundaries of the parish, at least those in the east and west, were fixed by AD1000.

By 1089 the Bishop of Exeter held the manor, as recorded in the Domesday Book. There were other smaller manors – Halsanger, Bagtor and later Sigford and Love Lane (now Bickington).

In all probability these lands were held by the bishops as part of the Paignton Manor to provide summer grazing for these lowland manors. The bishops kept the manor here until the time of James I.

Creation of the Town

So much for what we know about the creation of the parish. What about the creation of the town? By the end of the eleventh century the bishops had created a market in the town – it was in their interests to do so as, being lords of the manor, they collected tolls from any markets. Before 1238 the town received borough status and was administered largely through the guilds. We know very little about these Ashburton guilds other than they were collectively part of the Guild of St Lawrence. This chantry, from which Ashburton Grammar School developed, was overseen by laymen who paid for a chantry priest to look after the religious aspects of the chantry. The Guild, through its officers, controlled most of the affairs of the borough. The Chapel of St Lawrence

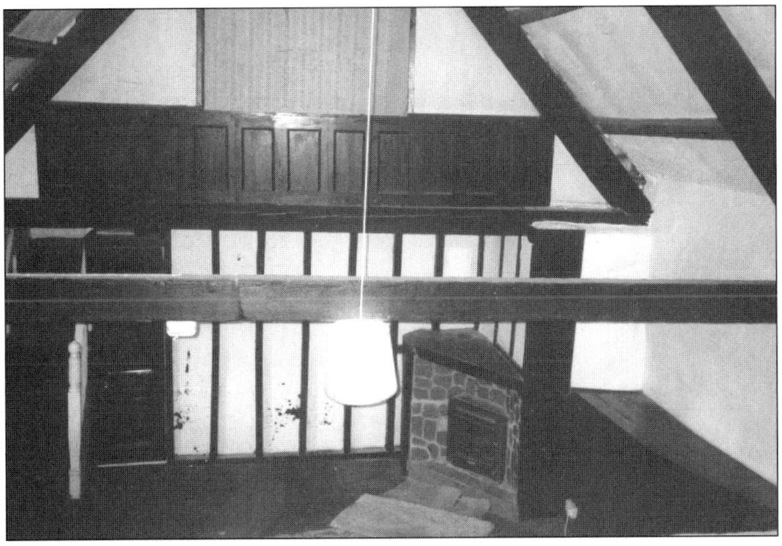

Cockpit behind Sparnham House. This was where the 'sport' of cock-fighting was held until made illegal. It was a very large room and a balcony overlooking the pit could be seen behind the modern lighting fixture.

(PETE WEBB)

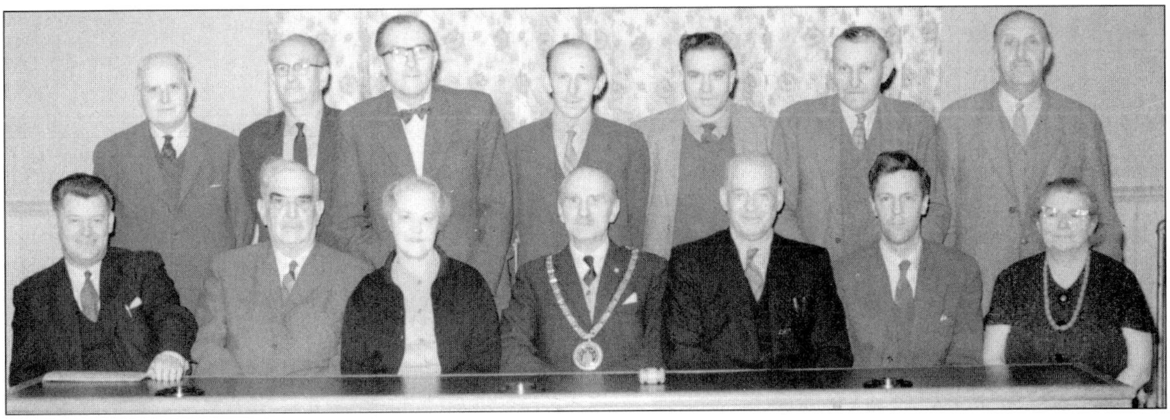

Ashburton UDC, 1964. Left to right, back row: *Charlie Paul, Bill Davies, Mr Hatch, Owen Tucker, Mr Stacey (postmaster), Sid Baker, Harry Bennett;* front: *Vic Counter, Dick Arscott, Margorie Morris (Clerk), Mr Underhill (Mayor), Bill Cartwright, Bob West, Mrs Parker.*

(PETE WEBB COLLECTION)

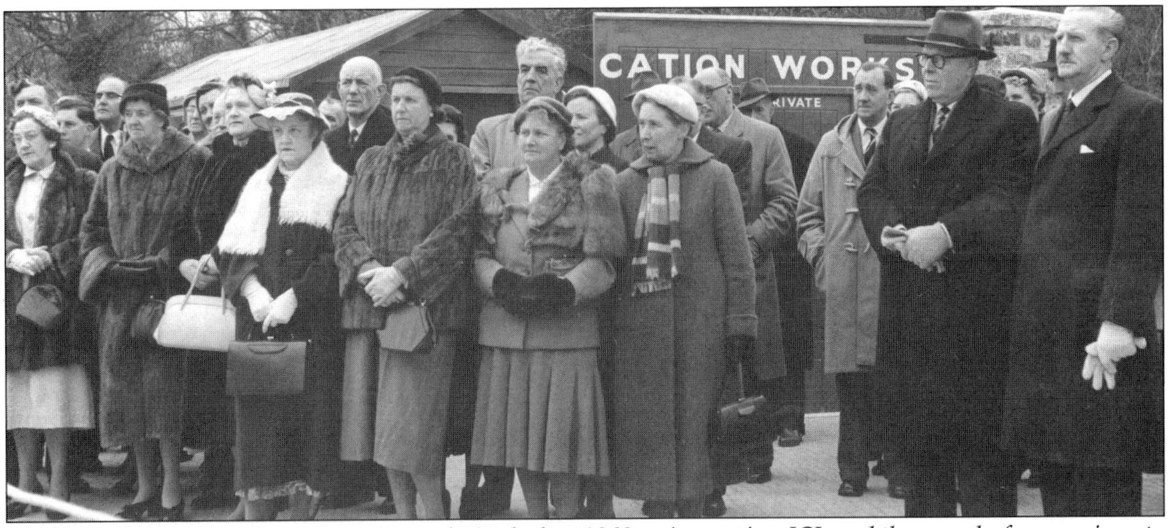

Opening of Kilbury sewage treatment works in the late 1960s. At one time ICI used these works for experiments as the incoming material was the 'strongest' in the UK. Pictured are dignitaries from Ashburton and Buckfastleigh. Picture includes: *Mrs Margorie Morris (Clerk to Ashburton UDC), ?, Joan Underhill, Mrs Hubbard, Richard Arscott* (behind)*, Dr McVicar (Chairman of Newton Abbot RDC), Robert Garner and Bill Underhill.*

(PETE WEBB COLLECTION GIVEN BY BOB WEST)

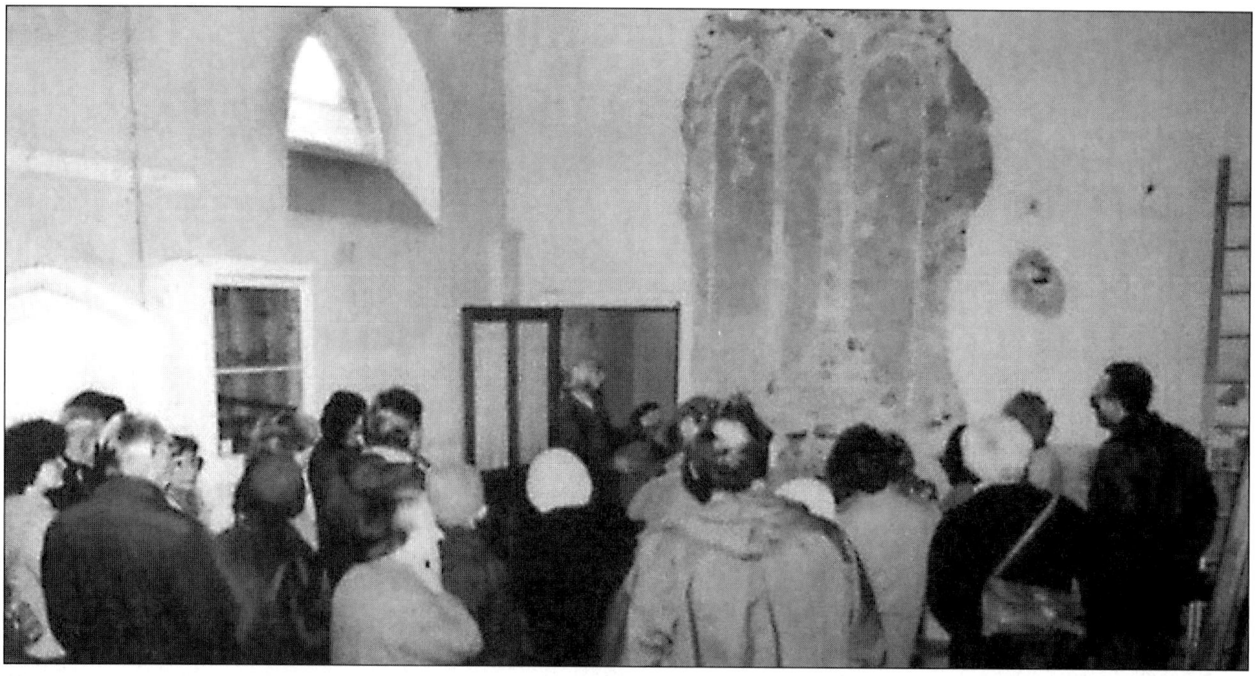

A group of interested Ashburton residents at the first public airing of the thirteenth-century window in 1987. It was uncovered during the renovation work carried out by Dartmoor National Park under the direction of Eric Blatchford, who is here outlining its discovery. (ST LAWRENCE CHAPEL)

was granted to the town by Bishop Stapledon in 1314 and the town attached its own seal to this grant. The fact that by 1314 the town was important enough to have its own seal was a sign of its developing status. The presence of burgesses was a further indication of this status. Two of these were in Parliament in 1298. There was a distinct possibility of Ashburton receiving incorporation, that is freedom from a lord of the manor. In the event the development of an incorporated borough didn't materialise and Ashburton remained a seigneurial borough and, whilst having some privileges, remained under the control of the Bishops of Exeter. Many bishops took little interest in the town and by the beginning of the sixteenth century only the fraternity of St Lawrence was functioning and thus effectively the only organisation capable of leading the town, though even this Guild was poor. Hugh Oldham, Bishop of Exeter from 1505 to 1519, was the exception. He, together with the wealthier burgesses in the town, put together a package of resources which made possible a reliable source of income for the Guild. Unfortunately the Reformation and the Dissolution of the Monasteries followed shortly after.

Of greater importance to the town were the Chantries Acts of 1545 and 1547/48. These Acts meant that all chantries were, because of their religious nature, forfeited to the Crown. In Ashburton's case the whole governance of the town was, as we have seen, bound up in the Guild of St Lawrence. Forfeiture spelt disruption for the corporate life of the town. The Acts were enforced by the Devonshire Commissioners. Over the next few years much wheeling and dealing took place in an attempt to preserve the market and the school. The school, as a secular organisation, was saved largely through being overlooked amongst all the other matters requiring the Commissioners' attention.

Except for the Civil War, Ashburton got on with its affairs with the Portreeve as its chief citizen for the next 300 years. In 1848 Ashburton lost its second Member of Parliament, the remaining Member covering a larger area.

In 1895 the governance of the town was passed to the newly created Ashburton Urban District Council, this being disbanded in 1974 with the formation of Teignbridge District Council. A town council functioning as a parish council now (2004) represents the interests of the parish. Lemonford was transferred to Bickington in 1935. There have also been other minor boundary changes.

CHAPTER 2

Wars

Civil War

Towards the end of 1645 the Civil War was entering its final phase. That phase consisted largely of bringing the West of England under Parliamentary control.

Cornwall had been staunchly Royalist throughout the wars – or at least those who had any say were. The majority of the people understood few of the finer points of the argument and just wanted to get on with their lives. They were the ones who suffered, as is often the case in conflict. Devon was, to a large extent, Royalist, the exception being Plymouth which was under siege for the latter part of the war. To maintain this siege demanded considerable numbers of troops.

Having been freed up by victories elsewhere Cromwell, Fairfax and Waller all converged on Devon in the autumn of 1645. Their plan was to engage Grenville, who was defending the gateway to Cornwall at Okehampton. Following the success of this mission, Cromwell and Fairfax moved south to Moretonhamptstead and on to Bovey. On 9 January 1646 they surprised a detachment of Wentworth forces on Bovey Heath. Wentworth had spent the previous night in Ashburton. This skirmish successfully completed, the next objective was to relieve Dartmouth. The Royalists in Plymouth, having heard of the Bovey 'battle', lost most of their troops, who retreated to Cornwall to protect their homes. Thus Plymouth was relieved without a fight. Prior to the journey west Fairfax spent the next two nights in Ashburton, his troops encamped nearby. A plaque marks the house in North Street where Fairfax stayed. That was Ashburton's contribution to the Civil War.

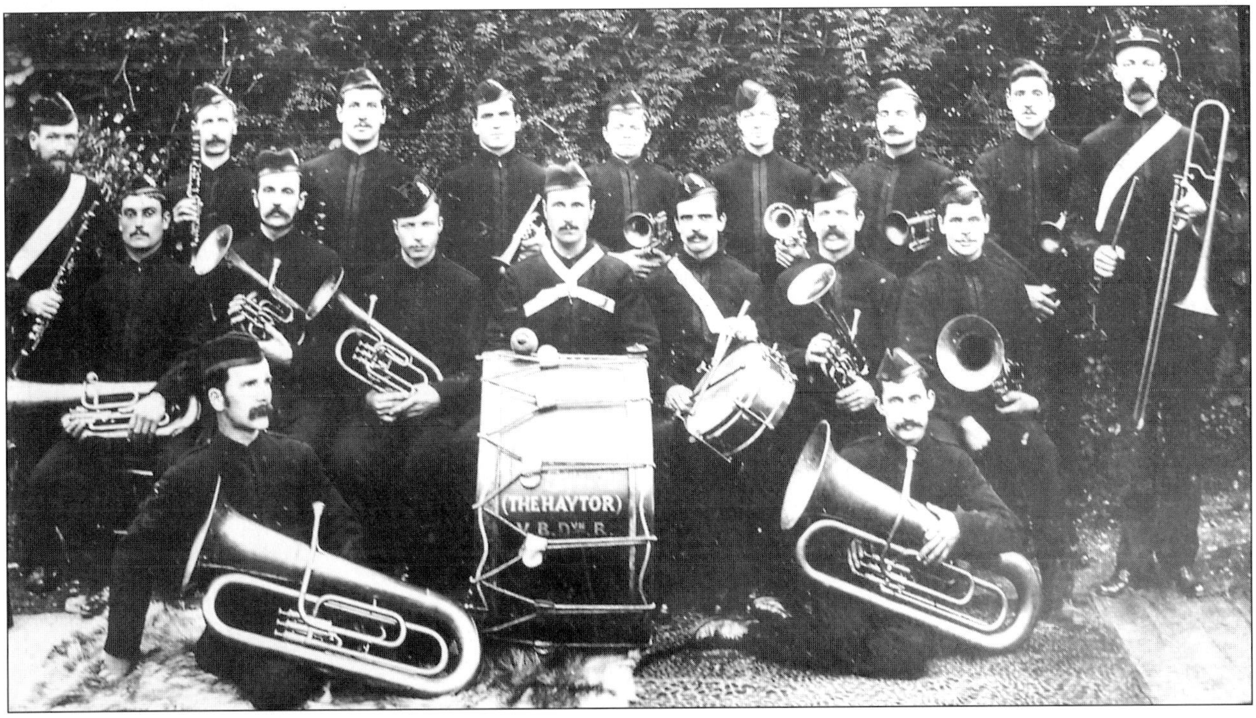

Fifth Volunteers band, formed in 1891 under Sgt H.H. Eggbear. At their final march-past on 28 February 1908 they finished with 'Widecombe Fair'. (St Lawrence Chapel)

Parole Prisoners of War in Ashburton

Around Ashburton are a series of parole stones. These date from the Napoleonic Wars when French prisoners of war were held at Dartmoor Prison. Rather than being incarcerated in the prison, officers were billeted in eight towns around Devon, Ashburton being one such town. Officers from the American War of Independence were also billeted in Ashburton.

In general, the inhabitants welcomed their presence. This was partly due to the money paid by the British Government for their lodgings and also

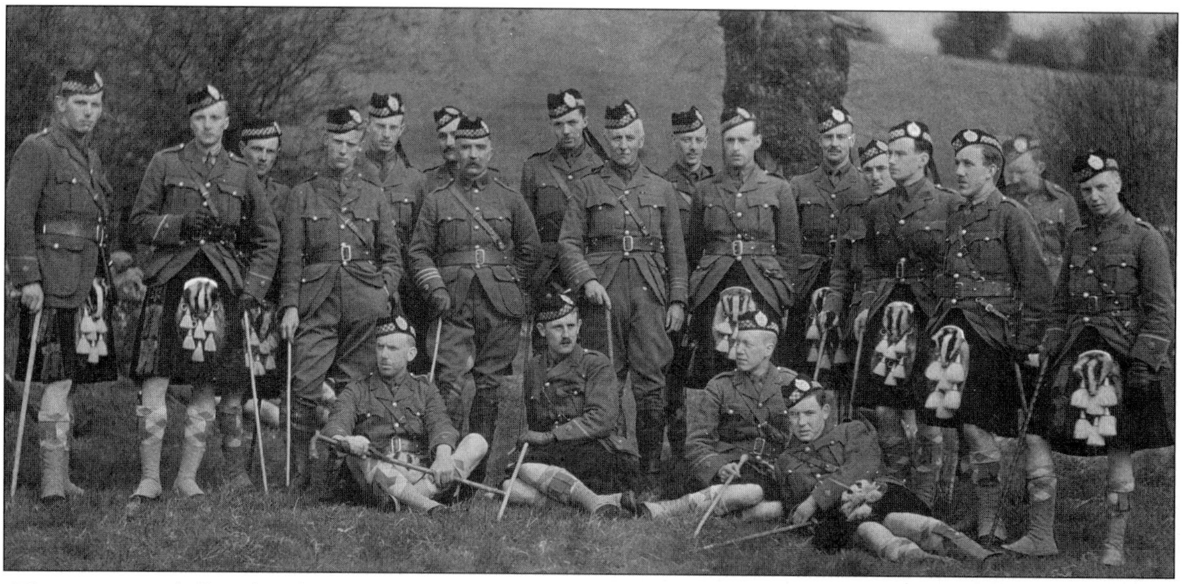

These men are believed to be some of the King's Own Scottish Borderers stationed in town during the First World War. (WILFRED 'TAFFY' EVANS, WHO WAS KILLED IN THE TRENCHES; PETE WEBB COLLECTION)

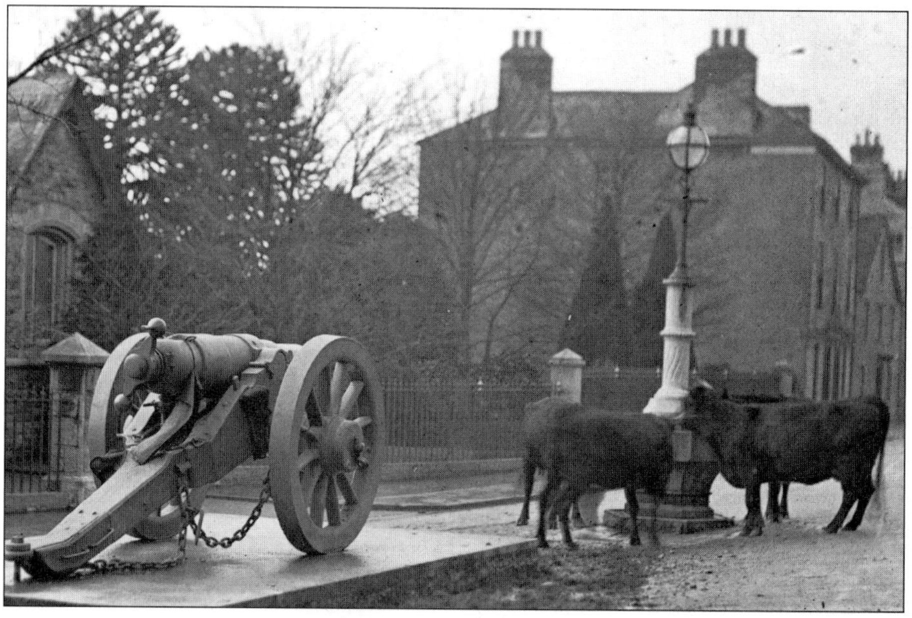

Col Tucker's Boer War gun and Bovey Memorial (fountain). The fountain now stands beside the Bay Horse in North Street. Note the cattle free to roam the streets of Ashburton at the turn of the nineteenth and twentieth centuries. (PETE WEBB COLLECTION)

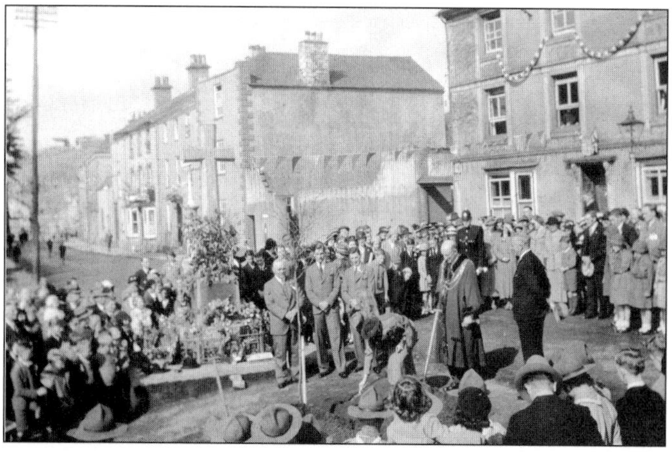

Planting the May tree beside the War Memorial in 1937 for the coronation of George VI. Mrs Joyce (the Portreveen) is bending over with her husband (with the shovel) *standing behind her.* (PETE WEBB COLLECTION)

because such a large number of cultivated and, in most cases, unattached officers enhanced the social life of the town. Generally they behaved well but occasional friction arose between them and the populace. Their quality of life depended on the parole agent's character and in 1756 the Compte de Gramont, who was paroled in Ashburton,

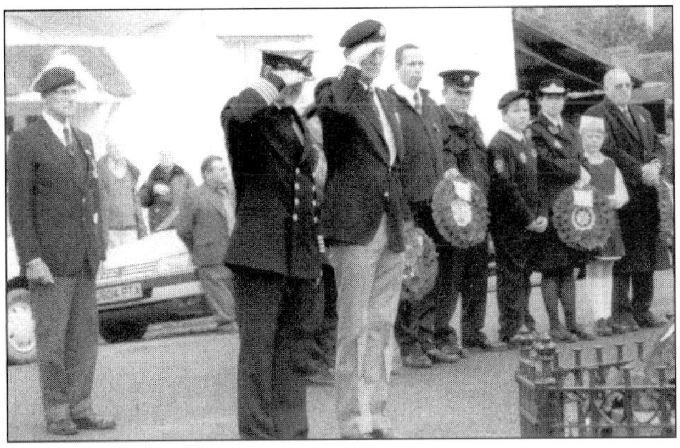

Royal British Legion (Ashburton Branch), Remembrance Sunday 2002, at the War Memorial. Behind: *Cecil Woods;* left to right, front: *Captain Mike Jamieson, Maurice Mann, Mike Billington.*

(MAURICE MANN COLLECTION)

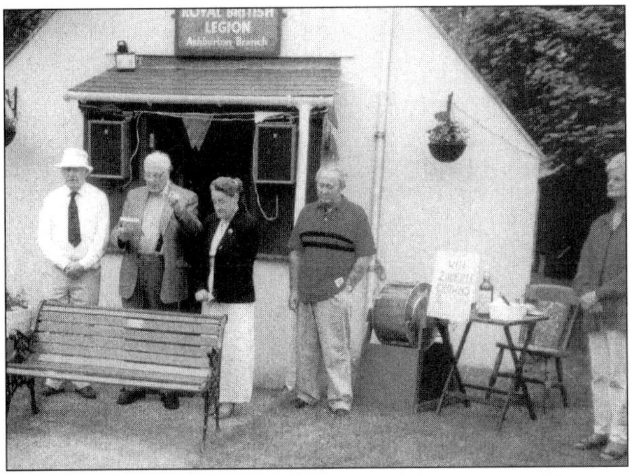

Presentation of bench by Mrs Adnitt to RBL (Ashburton Branch) in memory of her husband, 12 September 2002. Left to right: *Henry Bradford, Revd J. Brown, Mrs Adnitt, Ernest Smerdon (Chairman), Mrs Golding (Treasurer).* (MAURICE MANN COLLECTION)

complained about inhabitants who had stoned, insulted and hissed at him. He also ridiculed the local agent. Many parole agents were inferior tradesmen, and Ashburton's agent seems to have been unwilling to take the part of the prisoners against local business interests.

Many prisoners formed masonic lodges and Ashburton had separate lodges for the Americans and the French. Sometimes the officers' wives accompanied them and others had no difficulty finding admirers from among the local ladies. Many officers took a relaxed view of their parole obligation which was not go beyond the parole stones – still visible, one mile from the centre, in eight of the small lanes leading out of Ashburton. Escapes, especially by senior officers, were not uncommon and were often funded by French money, escapees being smuggled or returned by other means to France.

Ashburton's streets would have been crowded with over 100 foreign officers billeted there, some of them quite famous. General Canbronne, wounded while at the head of the Imperial Guard at Waterloo, was here in 1815 and the town's doctor successfully treated his wounds. Lt Francois Guidon never left. He died of his wounds in 1815 and his gravestone, near the base of St Andrew's Church tower, is reputed to have a branch of willow from St Helena, the island to which Napoleon was exiled, planted beside it.

First World War

A total of 72 brave men are remembered on Ashburton's War Memorial as having fallen in the Great War of 1914–18.

Royal British Legion

The Ashburton Branch of the British Legion was founded in 1927. The first president was Major Varwell, followed by Colonel Fosbrook. Meetings were held in various public houses until approximately 1945–6 when an old Nissen hut was purchased. Land next to the recreation ground, which was then the bowling green, was purchased and became the site for the RBL (Ashburton) HQ. Suitably modernised over the years, it still admirably serves its purpose at the time of writing. In 1955 the Poppy Appeal raised a then all-time record of £114.14s.8d. (£114.73). In 2003/4 the sum raised was in excess of £6,000. The membership has remained at around 80 for several years. Branch meetings are held on the second Monday of each month. During the year several events are held to raise funds both for maintenance of the HQ and garden and towards the Poppy Appeal. Remembrance Sunday is commemorated with a short service at the War Memorial, the laying of wreaths and a march through the town to a remembrance service in the parish church.

Second World War

A number of the townspeople went to war and some became celebrities due to their experiences, including:

Gunner Jack 'Shorty' Leaman of the Queen's Own Rgt was captured at Dunkirk in 1940. He was the first Ashburton prisoner of war to reach home and was given an official welcome at the town's railway station. For many years he paraded in the town's carnival parade in military uniform.

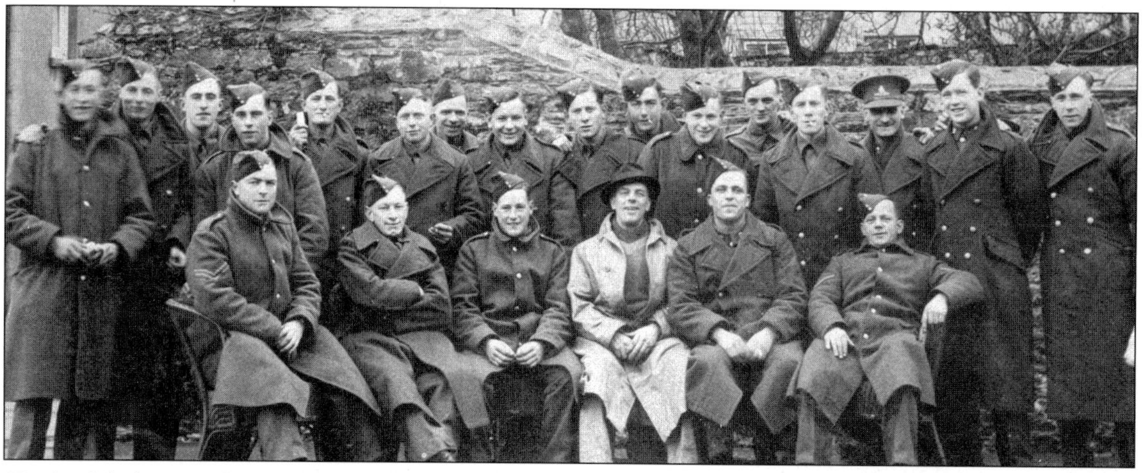

Territorials leaving for the Second World War. Back row includes: *Harold Frost, George Penuilly, John Germon senr, Percy Aplin, Ernest Carpenter, Reginald Estwick, William Hamlyn, William Cross, Frederick Carpenter, Harold Rogers, James Keast, an unknown 'peaked capped regular', Henry Bradford, Reginald Bellworthy;* front: *Charles Bowen, William Heathman, Reginald Keat, Sgt Frank Ryall* (in civvies), *Sidney Woodgates, William Waldron.* (PETE WEBB COLLECTION)

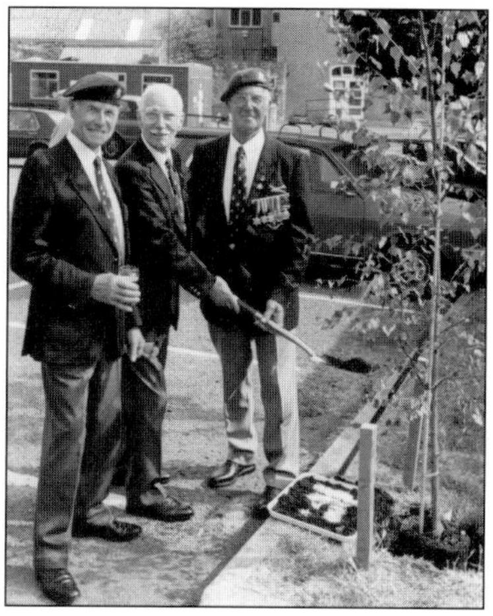

Left: *Three old soldiers planting a tree on the edge of Ashburton's car park to commemorate the 50th anniversary of VJ Day, 1995.* Left to right: *Alf Anderson, Tom Heyward and Stuart Brooking.* (PETE WEBB COLLECTION)

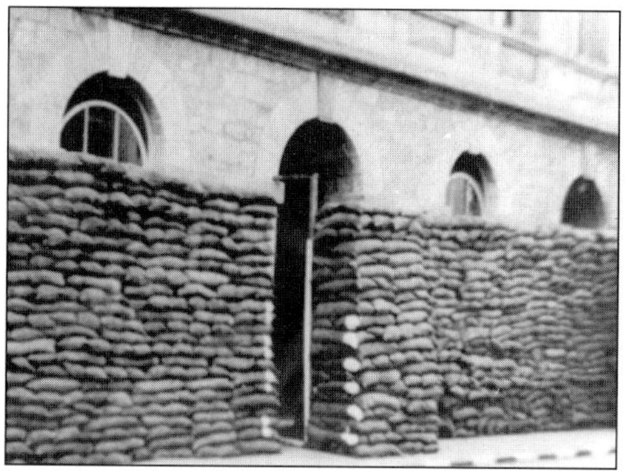

Above: *Second World War sandbags outside Ashburton town hall – photo by the then Town Clerk Mr Leslie Smith.* (PETE WEBB COLLECTION)

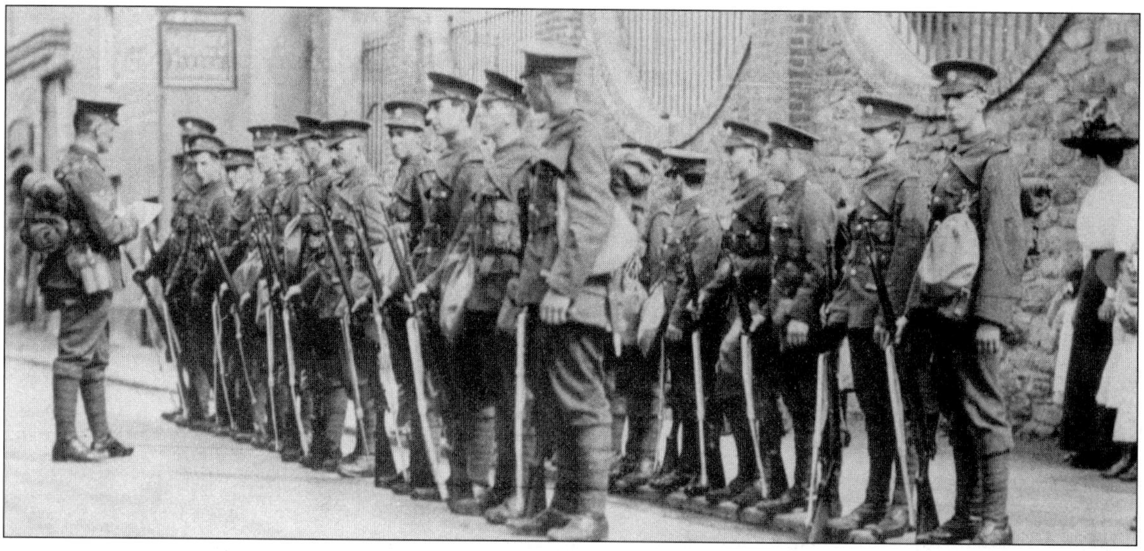

Mobilisation parade in St Lawrence Lane, 1914. Ashburton Company 5th Territorials ready to march to the railway station for the train to Aldershot with Sgt Nicks inspecting. Front row includes: *F. Pascoe, Aubrey Mann, and Jack Bovey.* (ASHBURTON MUSEUM)

Andy Dent was an RAF pilot who flew a Halifax for 138 Sqdn out of Tempsford Airfield. He mainly flew over France to drop agents and supplies to the Resistance. The plane had a special hole cut in the fuselage from which cargo was dropped. There was a barn on the airfield inside which was a brick building in which the 'spies' kitted themselves out before take-off. The pilots never knew (except by rumour) who they were flying. On one mission to the Massif Central in France Andy was shot down over enemy-occupied territory. The crew walked across France for three months until they reached Gibraltar. As they flew to freedom, Winston Churchill flew into Gibraltar on his way to Malta.

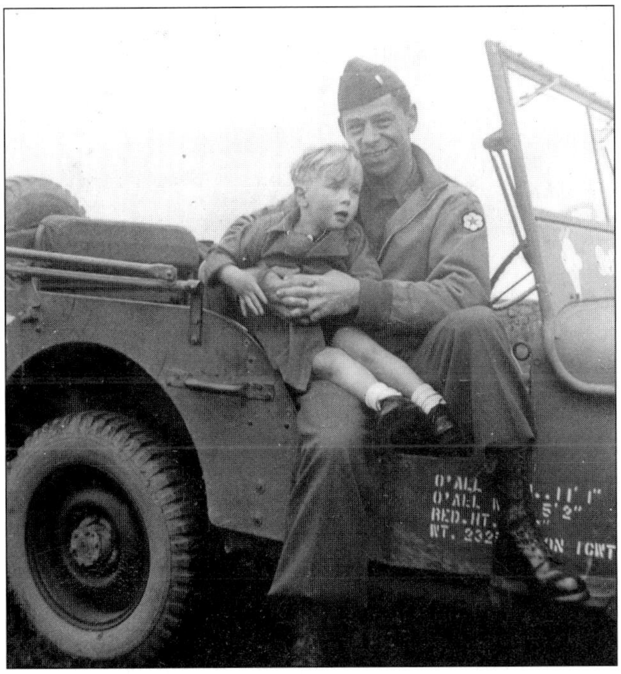

An American serviceman named Joe. Engaged to a local girl, Joan Brooking, sadly Joe was killed during D-Day. On his lap, Martin Daw. (PAT ORSMAN COLLECTION)

These two must represent those from the town who served in the war. Many went, sadly not all came home.

D-Day

It has been estimated that up to 50,000 troops were in the Ashburton and Buckfastleigh areas at the time of the preparations for the D-Day landings. On the 50th anniversary local residents, many of whom still remembered the many American and other troops in the town, gave an insight into how the town fared.

The first arrivals were thought to have been the Oxford and Buckinghamshire Light Infantry, who were billeted both with families in the town and in some of the bigger houses on the outskirts. They had a cookhouse behind Bank House, now the Indian restaurant (2004), a 'glasshouse' next to the Exeter Inn and their Bren carriers were garaged behind the Somerfield shop (in Stapledon Lane).

By 1941, Holne Park (now the River Dart Country Park) was the HQ of the RAF with WAAFs billeted with Ashburton families (Eileen Egbeare remembers her mother had four). When the RAF left, thousands of Americans moved in. Large 'cities' of tents covered the surrounding fields and also Spitchwick Common, Lower Hannaford and anywhere else there was a flat field along the River Dart. Buckfastleigh Racecourse was a large storage depot. Most of the fields from Buckfastleigh to Totnes were also occupied and the road between the towns closed to regular traffic.

The American troops were well remembered

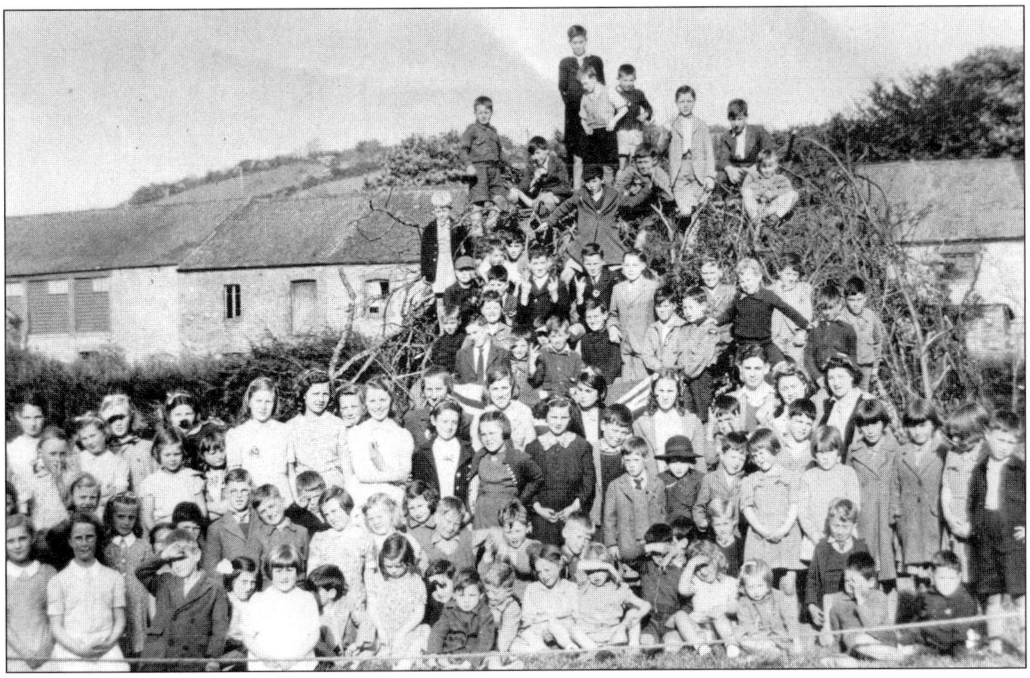

VE Day bonfire, 1945. (RUTH BROTHERS; PETE WEBB COLLECTION)

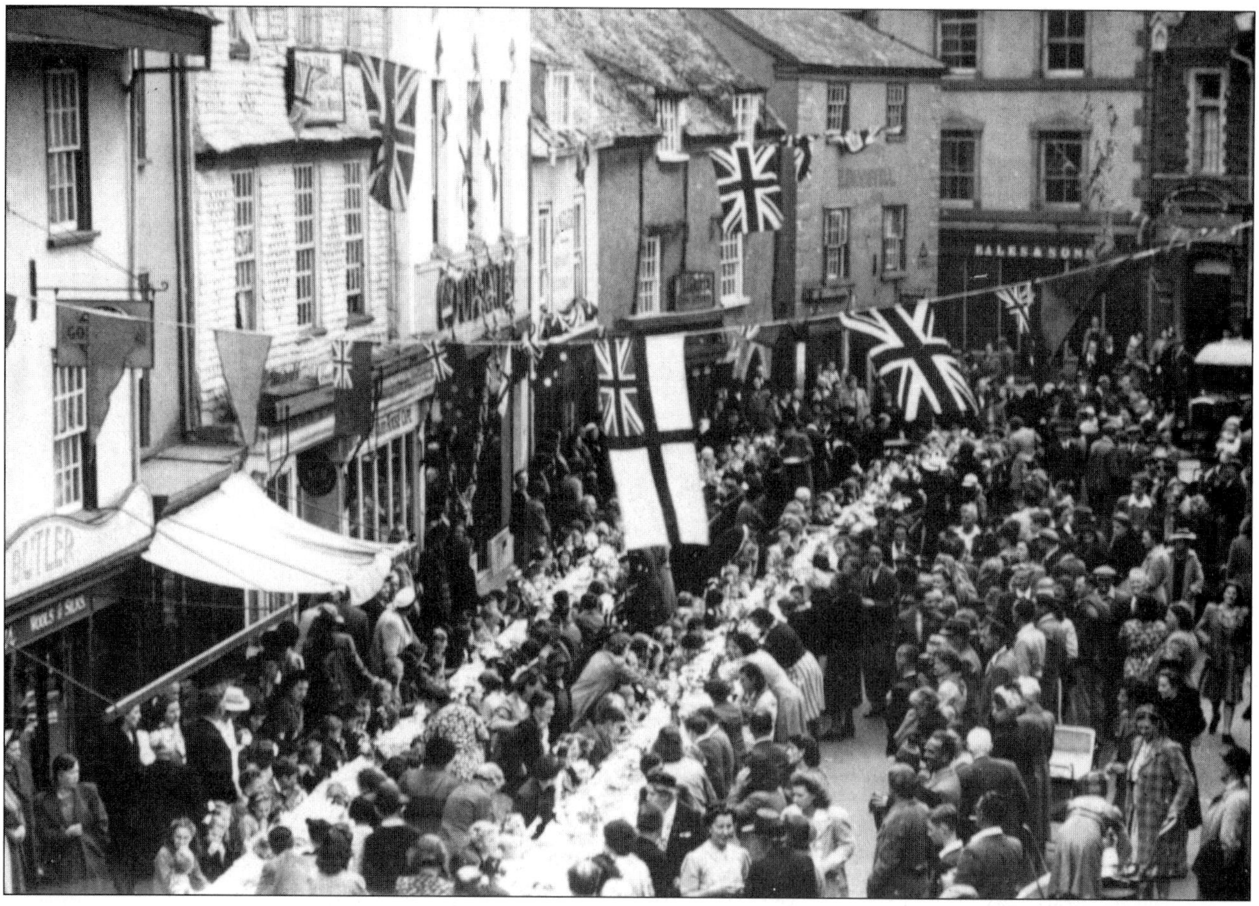

VE Day street party in North Street, May 1945. (Pete Webb collection)

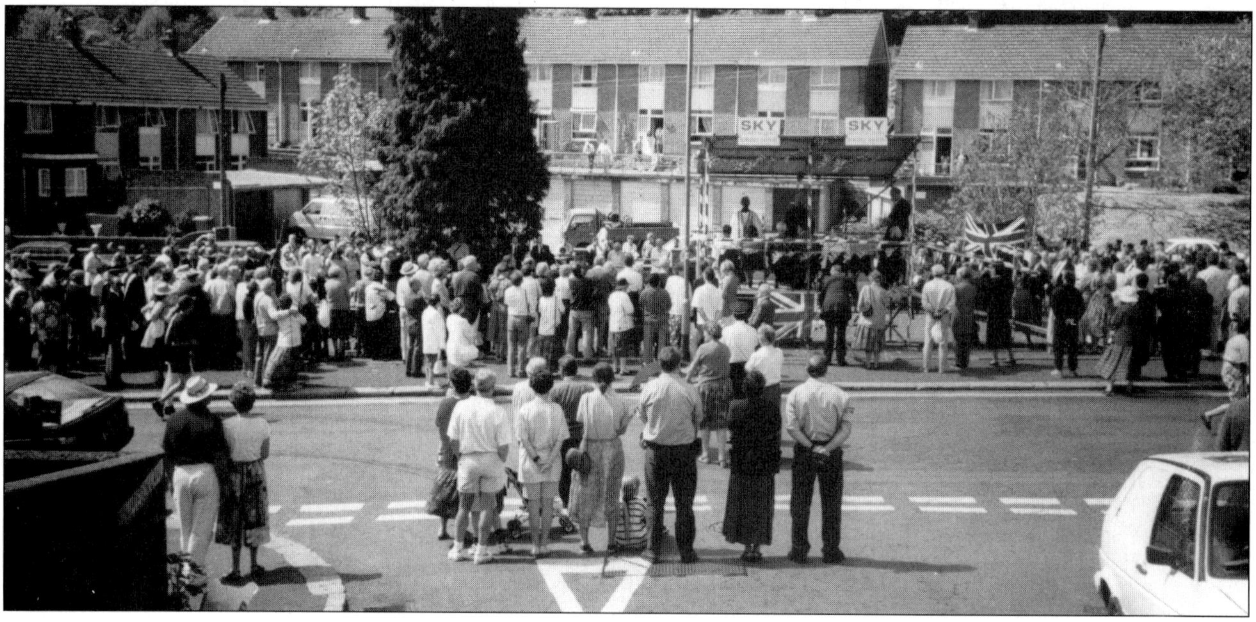

Interdenominational service, Cleder Place, 50th Anniversay VE Day celebrations, May 1995. (Pete Webb)

for their generosity and for taking part in local activities. Fund-raising activities such as 'Wings for Victory' and 'War Weapons Week' were supported and sweets and oranges thrown from passing lorries carrying troops to any children they passed. They are also said to have been astonished by the primitive activities of farmers. Horses were still used for transport and Daw's Dairy walked their cattle through the town every day for milking.

Ashburton fared better than the South Hams, where large areas were evacuated, but in the period immediately leading up to the landings, troops and vehicles began to move. The old bypass (now the

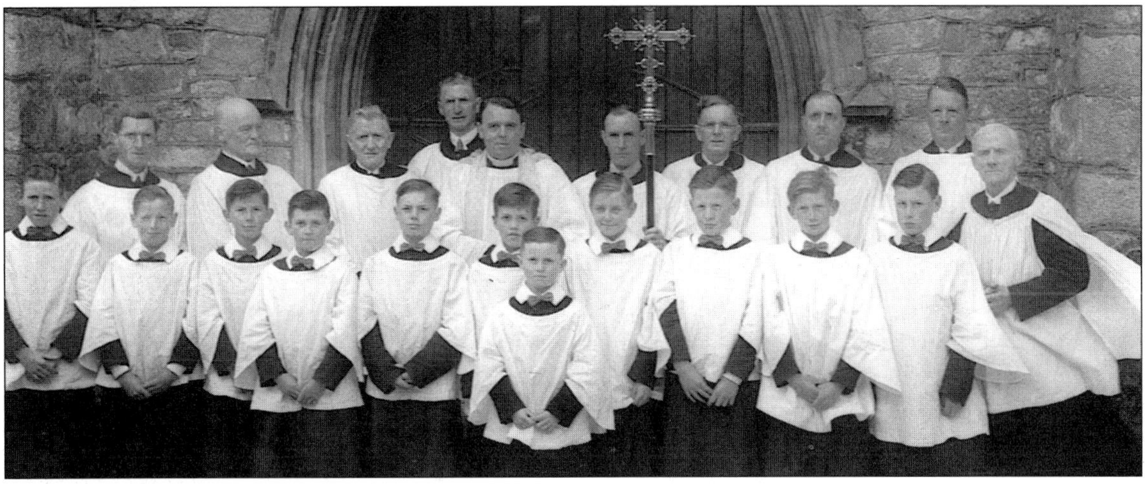

Church Choir, 1948. Left to right, back row: *Reg Andrews, Mr Edgecombe, Dave Cowls, Fred Turner, Revd G.A.B. Jones, Jack Bray, Bill Eales, Harry (Henry) Bennet, Mr Caws (organist), Dick Jones;* front: *Alfie Goodwin, Edward Matthews, Ken Widden, Terry Baker, Neil Bligh, ?, David Woodley, Tony Pugh, Henry Lang, ?, Michael Kiff.* (MICHAEL KIFF COLLECTION)

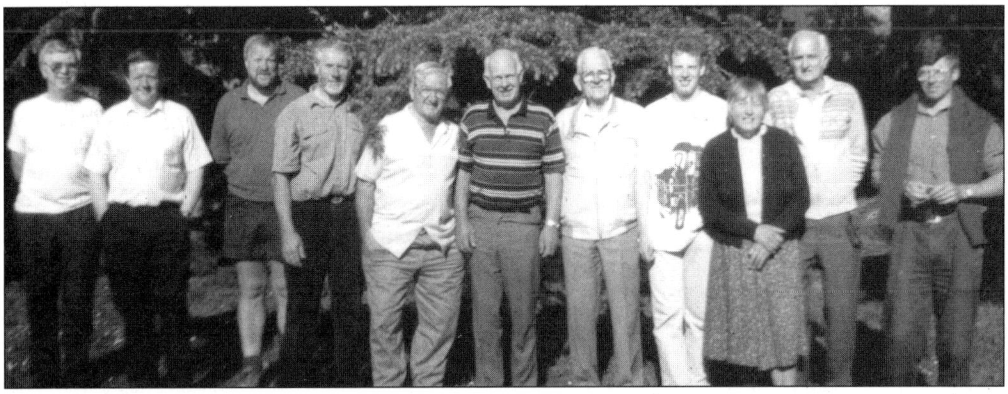

St Andrew's Church bellringers in May 1995. Left to right: *Adrian Jackson, John Germon, Andrew Hamlyn, Geoff Histed, George Edwards, Bernard Miners, Henry Pascoe (captain), Alan Brown, Pam Lodder, John Caunter, Rupert Baker.* (PETE WEBB COLLECTION)

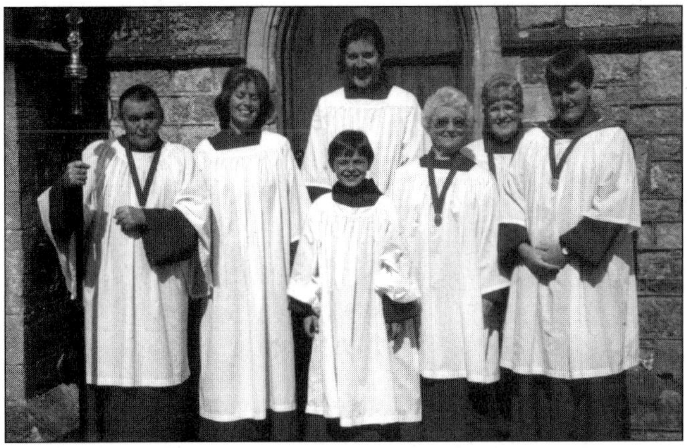

St Andrew's Church Choir, 2001. Pictured are left to right: *Denis Gill, Penny Smith, George Gotleib, Pete Webb* (behind), *Val Jones, Wyn Warwick and Sandra Gill. (Missing Julia, as it was the occasion of her marriage to Alan Brown, and Geoff Histed who took the photo).* (PETE WEBB COLLECTION)

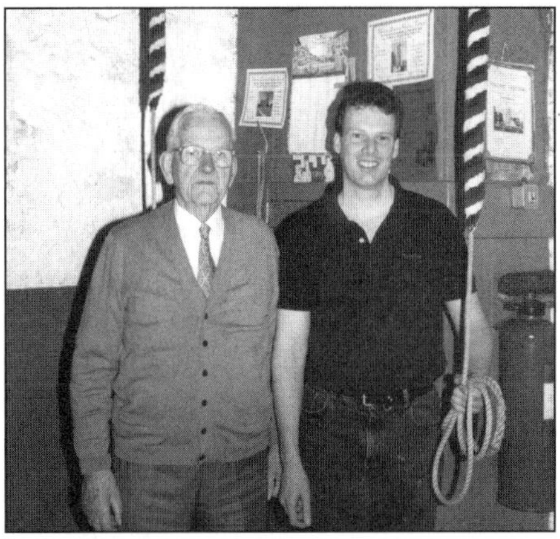

Above: *Bellringers. Retiring tower captain Henry Pascoe and incoming captain Alan Brown who took over the ropes in 2002. Henry first started ringing in 1928.* (PETE WEBB COLLECTION)

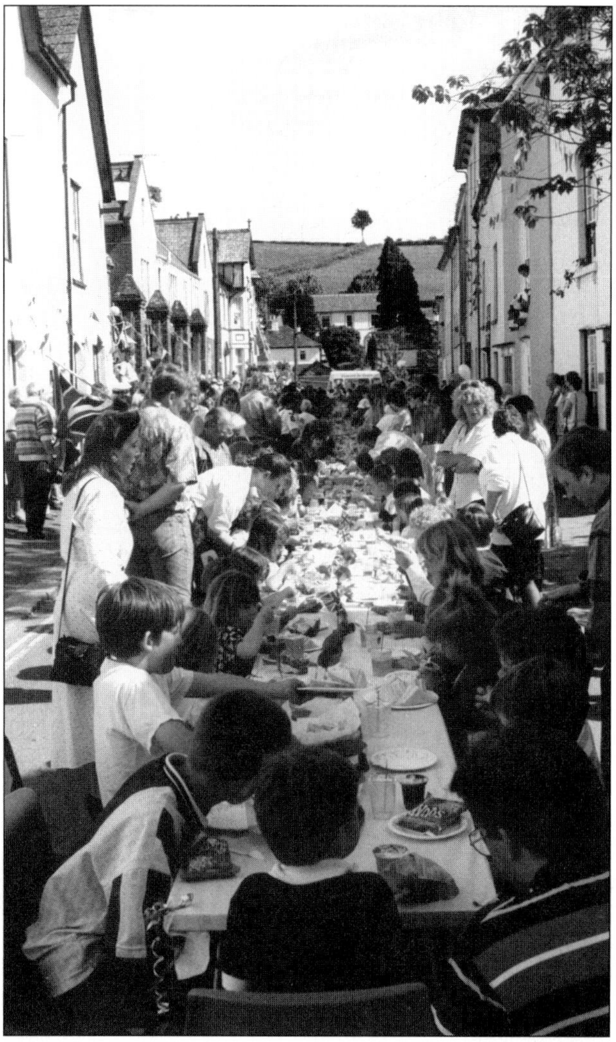

Left: *VE Day celebrations, May 1995 – street party in St Lawrence Lane in full swing.* (JOHN MITCHELL)

Below: Left to right: *Portreeve R.G. Robertson, Sgt Widger of Ashburton Police, Jack French.* (PETE WEBB COLLECTION)

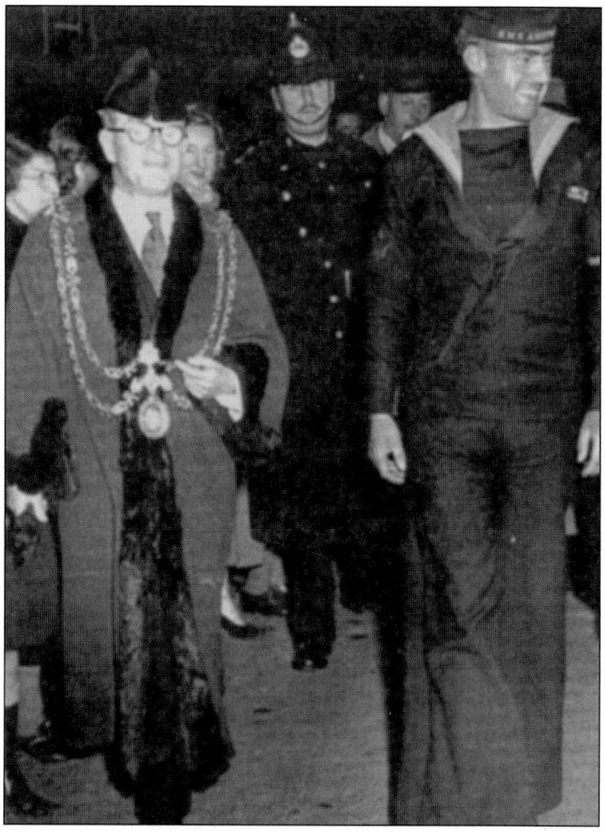

A38 dual carriageway) and all the roads leading through to Totnes were nose-to-tail with military traffic. The service at Buckland Church on Sunday 4 June 1944 was completely drowned out by the roar of passing tank engines. Within a week the town had returned to normal and Holne Park in particular, after a short period (1946–7) when it was used by displaced Poles, became an outward bound school.

The end of the war was celebrated, as it was across the country, with bonfires and street parties as well as floodlit buildings and a 'furry dance' through the town's streets.

On the town's War Memorial are recorded 19 men and one woman who lost their lives in the war of 1939–45.

Jack French

Jack French was Radio Operator on HMS *Amethyst* during the Yangtze Incident. The ship was trapped in the Yangtze when the communists over-ran China in 1949. The ship made a daring run for it under cover of darkness. Jack returned to Ashburton where he was fêted as a hero.

✥ CHAPTER 3 ✥

Faiths

St Andrew's Parish Church

St Andrew's Parish Church, with its imposing 92-foot high tower, can be seen from most of the town. It is likely that it was rebuilt on the site of an earlier Saxon church which would probably have been of English oak. Accurate records only date from the end of the twelfth century when John Caunter was Bishop of Exeter from 1186 to 1191. The church is alleged to have been founded by William de Pomeroy in about 1137 and some earlier records date from the eleventh century. The church was restored several times up until the year 1314, when Bishop Stapledon made a formal visitation on April 3 and found the building in need of much work. In the fifteenth century a much finer church was built with some features of the original retained, the tower being finished between 1430 and 1440. Also in the latter part of the fifteenth century the church house was first used to brew ale, which was sold at a profit for the upkeep of the church. When not in use the building was let out for meetings.

The main fabric of St Andrew's dates from the middle of the fifteenth century but further additions were made in the sixteenth. In 1518 a fine rood screen was erected but by 1537, during the Reformation, images were frowned upon and it was removed. It was forbidden to place candles before any image except the crucifix. A Bible was set up in the church in 1541 by edict of Parliament and further work was carried out, such as the demolition of the rood loft in 1578. By 1580 St Andrew's Church had an annual income of almost £11 from land, tithes and other sources. Unfortunately much of this was 'taxed' by the Crown. There is a unique record of this period, with the Churchwarden's accounts from 1479 to 1580 furnishing an almost unbroken record of this time. Alison Hanham edited a reprinted version of these in 1970 through the Cornwall & Devon Record Society.

In Tudor times, the people of Ashburton seem to have had a special flair for woodcarving, with a fine screen and much other work being done between 1515 and 1525. Much of it was removed and passed into private hands – initially in a house in West Street – then was lost to the town completely in the 1960s. Religious plays were also enacted in the church with records in the accounts of clothes for various 'pleers' (players) and even 'Robyn Whode' (Robin Hood).

Samuel Tidball, vicar of Ashburton, was dispossessed of his living before the Reformation, and his successor, Alexander Crosse, died in 1654. Crosse was followed by Joshua Bowden, who refused to conform to the Act of Uniformity in 1662, whereby the State dictated the form of worship, and so was deprived of his living. There was a particularly high incidence of Nonconformity in Devon and in particular in the diocese of Exeter. A Presbyterian meeting house was established in Ashburton in 1689 and in 1698 Celia Fiennes noted that many of the most important people were Dissenters.

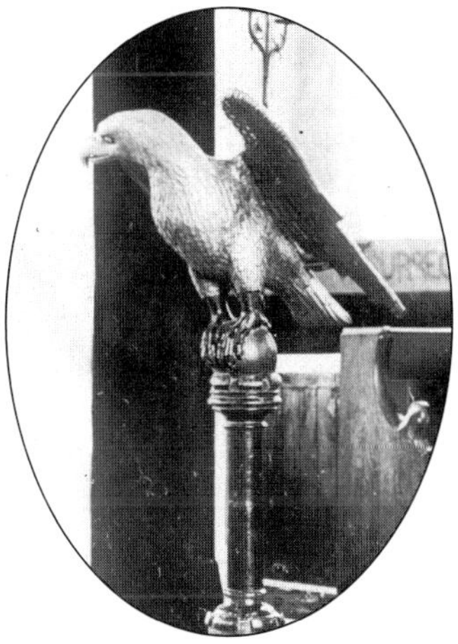

Lectern formerly at St Andrew's Church, now at Bigbury (moved in 1977). Originally this had an owl's head but the new parishioners replaced it with an eagle. It had originally been carved by John Mayne in the sixteenth century. (Amy Satterley; Pete Webb collection)

Rich merchants, who owed their wealth to the wool and tin trade, paid for much of the work, giving thanks to God for their good fortune. It is widely believed that the north transept, called the Thomas à Beckett Chapel, was the guild chapel of the wool-workers. In the Victorian era many 'improvements' were made to the interior. Some of the historical and architectural splendour of St Andrew's has been lost but much remains. It is a much-loved building, not only by worshippers but by the town itself and also by its many visitors. A good example of this was the money raised for the 1989 restoration of the bells by the town and the sums raised for the new heating system in 1993 and other work in the 1990s.

United Reform/Great Meeting

Ashburton's Congregational or United Reformed

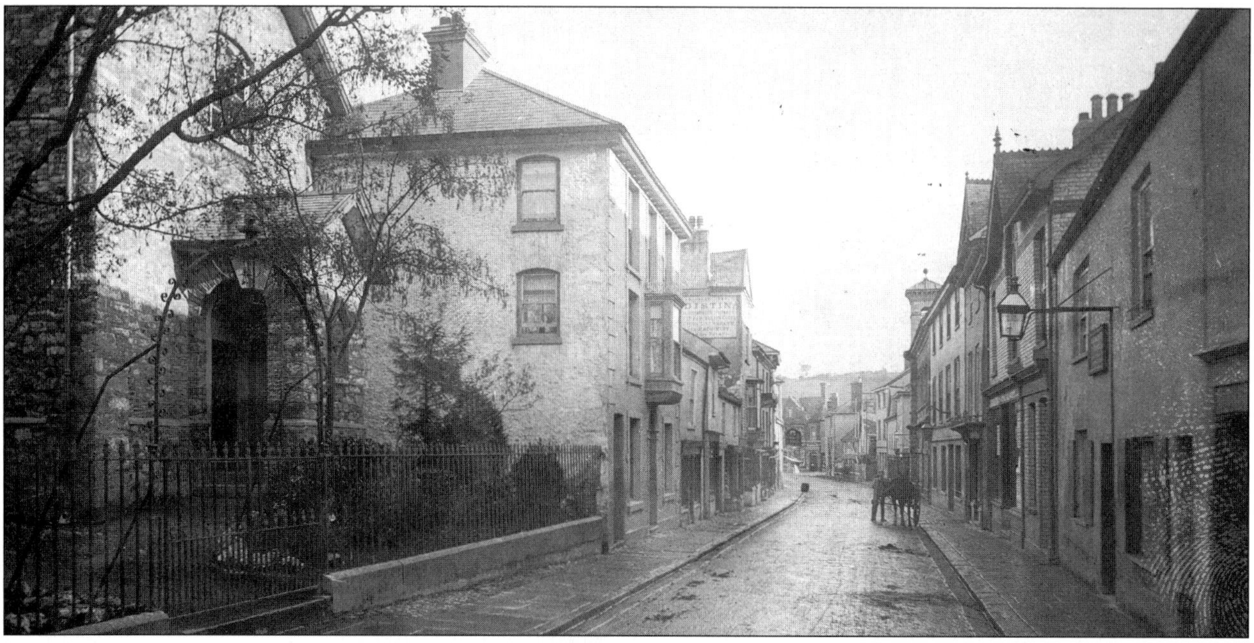

Exterior view of North Street c.1905 showing Great Meeting (railings on left). *This is now Adrian Agar's Ashburton Marbles. The buildings on the right were the last few to be demolished on what is now Cleder Place. The building with a lamp is the former Engineers' Arms.* (PETE WEBB COLLECTION)

Church existed in North Street until 1985. It doubtlessly originated when several ministers were ejected from neighbouring parishes around the period 1659–62. It started out as a barn behind the North Star Inn, where the Revd John Nosworthy gathered his congregation in 1665, having been ejected from Manaton in 1660 and Ipplepen in 1662. He suffered at the hands of the lord of the borough, William Stawell MP, and William Bogan. Mr Nosworthy died in 1677. Later, during the ministry of the Revd William Pearse, the building was converted to a meeting-house. Mr Pearse had been ejected from Dunsford, where he was vicar, and suffered severe persecution at the hands of the then lord of the manor and MP for Ashburton, Mr Hugh Stowell. Pearse died in 1690 and was succeeded by another pioneer, the Revd John Syms.

The first Trust was made in 1739, when a church was first erected on the site. Originally two barns standing side by side, each had a separate 'meeting'. The connecting wall was demolished to form one church which became 'Great Meeting'.

Sir Robert Palk, on returning from India in 1785, presented the Parliament Clock as a gift to the church. (This was restored in the 1960s and has been housed in the museum since the church finally closed.) In 1791, major works of reconstruction were carried out at a cost of £218, with further works in 1818 including the present limestone frontage.

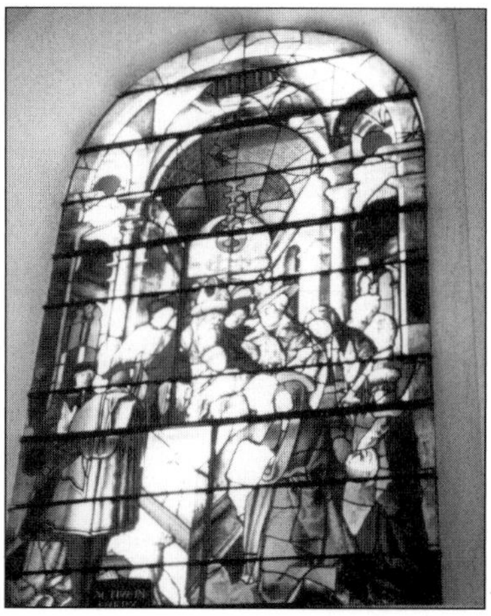

In 1850 a building was added on the right-hand side to house the expanding Sunday school and at the same time the former inn, the North Star, was demolished. Tradition has it that in the church's early 'secret' days, worshippers passed along the alley to the pub, but instead of going in carried on to the barns behind. The owner of the site at this time was Lord Clinton, who granted a lease on the old inn and gave permission for the works and extensions. The Sunday school, started in 1815, was the first in Ashburton. The organ was installed in 1875, moved in 1892 and electric blowers were fitted in 1938.

This was possibly the most popular church in Ashburton around this time, and records show that the Sunday congregation sometimes comprised 400 worshippers in the latter part of the nineteenth century.

In 1934 the Right Honourable L.S. Amery presented the Flemish stained-glass window (left), which dates from 1610–20, in memory of his two cousins, Fabyan and John Sparke Amery. It can still be seen and depicts the Presentation of the Child Jesus in the Temple. Originally purchased by public subscription in 1805, the window was placed in the Chapel of the Royal Female Orphanage in Westminster Bridge Road, London. It was then stored in a shed when the institution moved to Beddington, Surrey, and was purchased and brought to Ashburton by L.S. Amery.

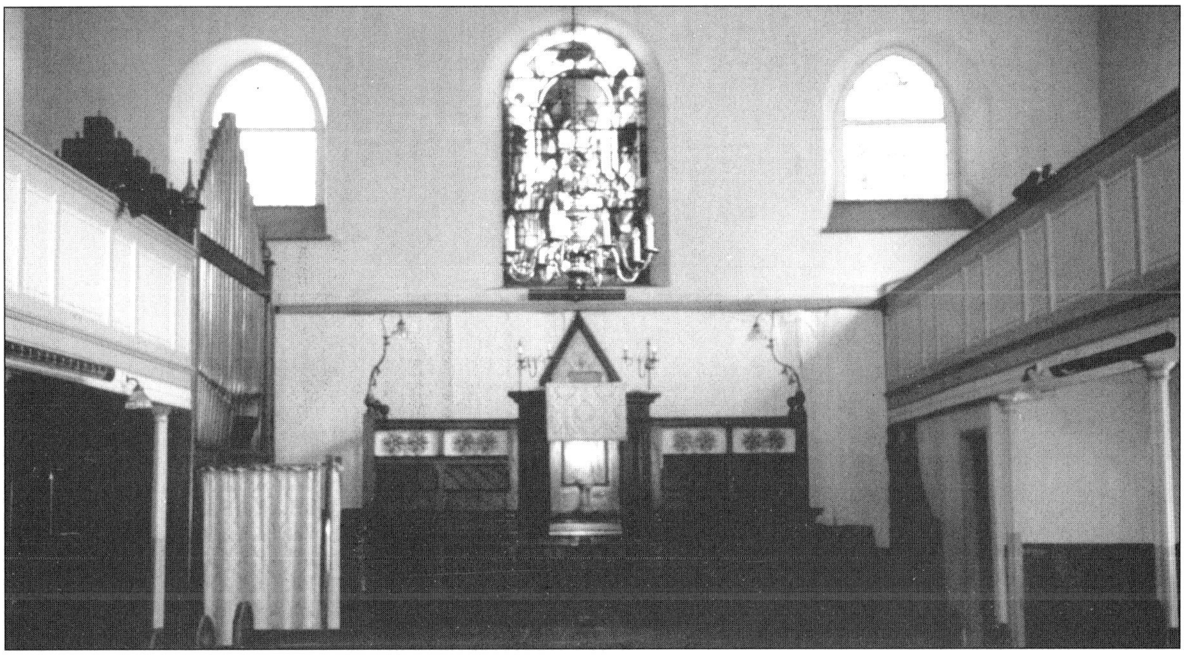

Great Meeting just prior to closure, 1986. (RUTH WESTALL)

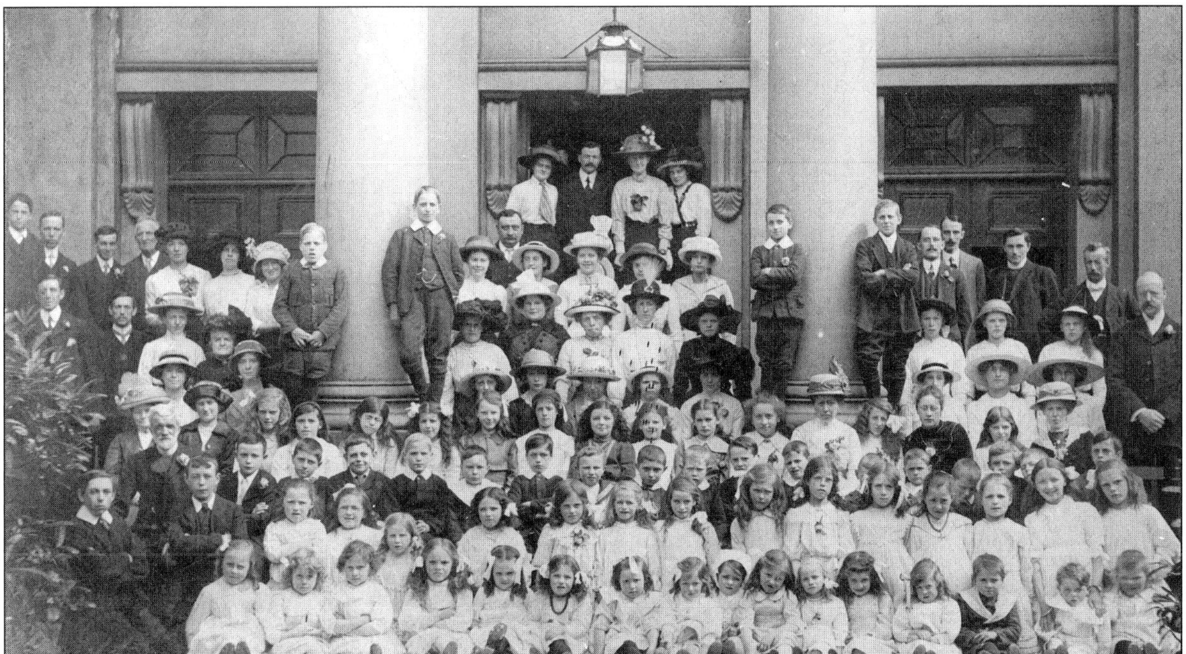

Methodist church, late 1914. Photo includes: *William (Bill) Tucker (blacksmith), Miss Lilian Bowden (later Mrs Boon), Mrs Betty Pascoe, Miss Eveline Boon (daughter of Horace Boon), Miss Annie Mann, Charles Eales (saddler), Mrs Eales, Miss Eva Mann, Mr W. Beer, Horace Boon, T.W. Mann (local preacher), Sophia Boon (wife of Horace), Frederick Boon (younger son) and Wilfred Owen (who died in the trenches).*

(ASHBURTON METHODIST CHURCH)

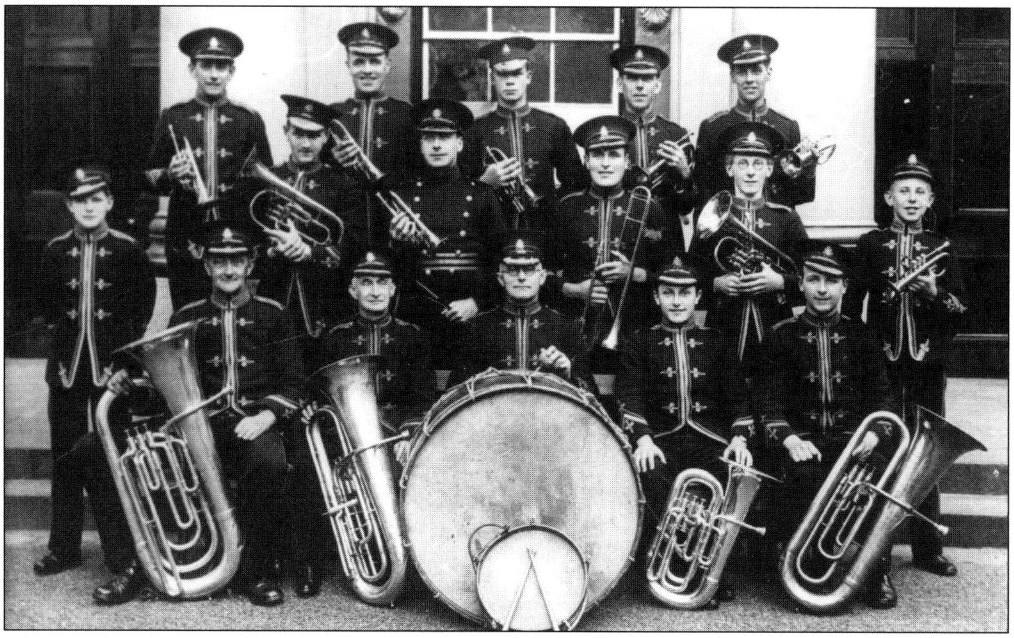

Methodist brass band, 1935. (PETE WEBB COLLECTION)

Great Meeting closed in 1985. At the time of writing it houses Ashburton Marble.

Methodist Church

Until the rise of Methodism in Ashburton in the early nineteenth century, Great Meeting was the choice of Protestant Dissenters. Ashburton appears to have been one of the earliest strongholds of this faith in South Devon. John Wesley preached at Ashburton in August 1766 but was not pleased with the reception he got. It was 31 August and Wesley was 63 years of age. He came back in 1785, 1787 and yet again two years before his death in 1791. On his final visit he met with a linen draper called William Bickford, a pioneer of Methodism in Ashburton. William Thorensby came in 1802 with missionary zeal but it was not until 1808 that the first Wesleyan Chapel opened. Some 27 years later, in 1835, the present church was built in West Street. In 1957 a new roof was needed and further major works were carried out in 1980. At the time of writing it still housed a strong congregation.

Our Lady and St Petrock's Roman Catholic Church

Two centuries ago, only 300 Roman Catholics worshipped in the whole of the Exeter Diocese. When the monks returned to Buckfast in 1882, not a single Roman Catholic lived in Ashburton. Revival was slow and it was 1902 before a small barn in Roborough Lane was first used and in 1911 Mass was restored. In 1914 a corrugated iron hut was erected on the opposite side of the lane and continued to be used until the present church, Our Lady and St Petrock's, was constructed, from 1933–35, at the junction of East Street, Eastern Road and Dolbeare Road. The new church was opened in November 1935 but building work continued until 1976, with the church in its present form opening the week before Christmas, 1977.

Baptist and Plymouth Brethren Places of Worship

A Baptist church existed in Woodland Road, or Heavyhead Lane as it was formerly called. There seem to be no central records of this church but it is certainly marked on older maps and was probably an entirely independent group. It was not recorded in 1744 when a survey was done. The building was later used by the Grammar School with the gymnasium floor supposedly being built over the baptism pool in 1912.

The Plymouth Brethren founded an assembly in Ashburton in 1880. Originally in Foals Court, they moved to the Gospel Hall in East Street and very recently, when the group had dwindled to only a few, this became the home of C.J.'s Bakery.

✦ CHAPTER 4 ✦

Trades

In past times Ashburton was far more self-sufficient than it is today. Reference to trade directories or to the chapter in this book on nineteenth-century Ashburton will illustrate this fact. People only occasionally travelled outside the town to purchase goods. It was usually a case of folk from the outlying districts coming into market, doing their trading and taking home their requirement which could be bought locally. In 1850 there were sixteen boot and shoe makers, seven milliners, nine butchers, fifteen bakers, three chemists and numerous other trades. Until the late 1800s all the shops were locally owned – the Co-op was the first store to have a manager.

From the earliest records, Ashburton had bankers with Browne, Winsor and Cuming in East Street in 1823, and Nathan Beck was for many years an agent for the Devon and Exeter Savings Bank in North Street. The first banks as we recognise them were both built on the sites of pubs. The present (2004) Lloyds-TSB was built on the site of the old Duke's Head in the centre of town and the National Westminster in East Street on the site of the Golden Lion. The town also had a branch of the Midland Bank and the Devon and Exeter Savings Bank (TSB) which only closed in the 1980s. It was 1994 before the first cash-point appeared, after a long battle by the Chamber of Trade (first formed in the 1930s and still going strong at the time of writing).

Many of the shops seen in these photographs will be recognisable, yet the type of goods sold were very different. One of the biggest differences is there were no antique shops!

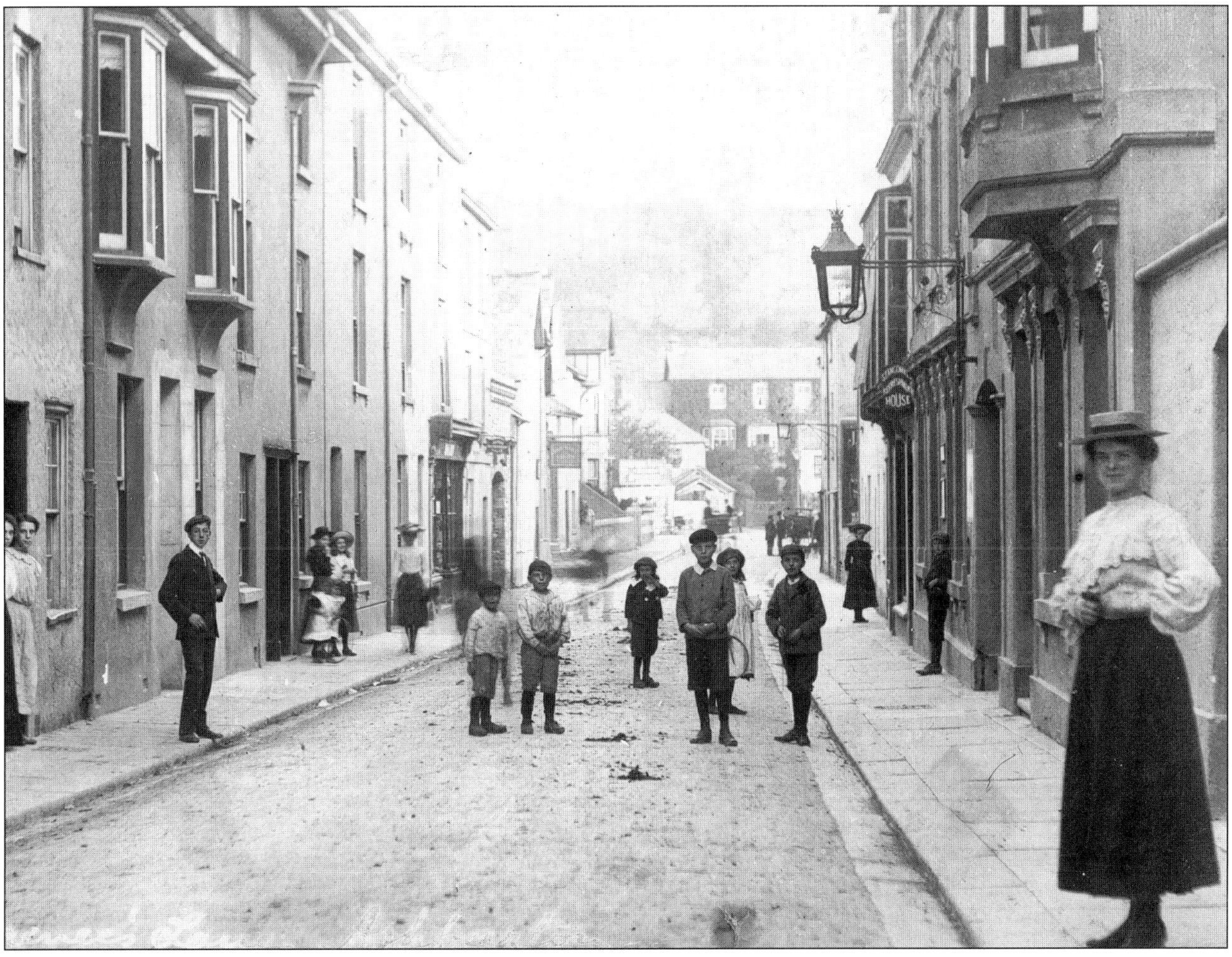

St Lawrence Lane, 1905. Daw's shop is first on the left (a fish and chip shop in 2004), the Post Office and Stancombe Refreshment Room are on the right. Note the dung on the road! (AMY SATTERLEY; PETE WEBB COLLECTION)

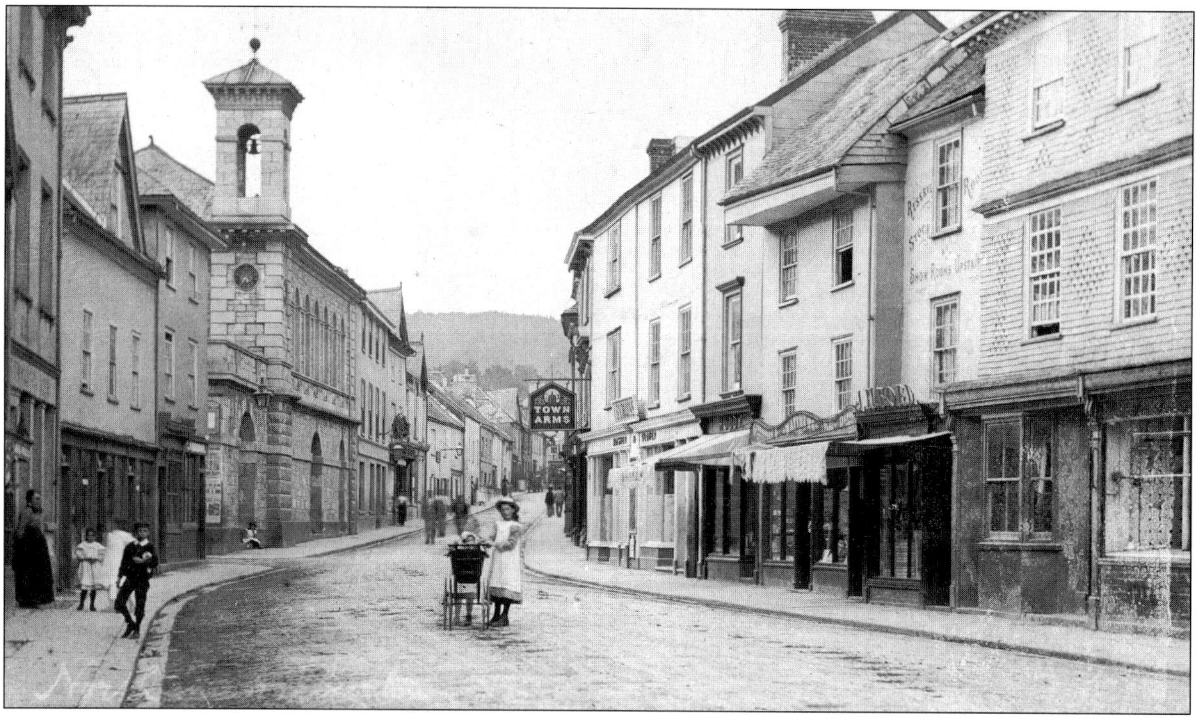

An early picture of North Street, c.1905. Mr Ford's shop next to 'House of Cards' is now the off-licence (2004). Note the sign for the Town Arms. (AMY SATTERLEY; PETE WEBB COLLECTION)

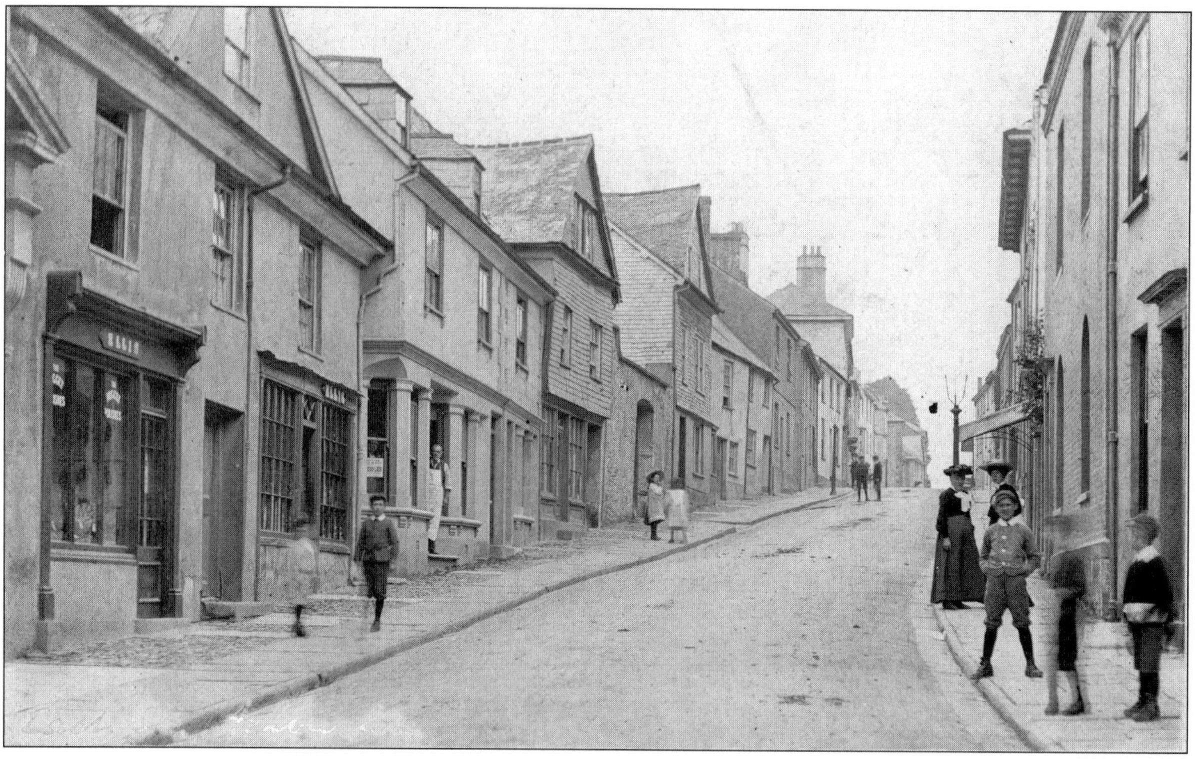

An early picture of East Street, 1905. Ellis Bootmaker is the first shop on the left (now Nos.21–23). In the next doorway, with apron, is Henry Foot, the town's returning officer. (AMY SATTERLEY; PETE WEBB COLLECTION)

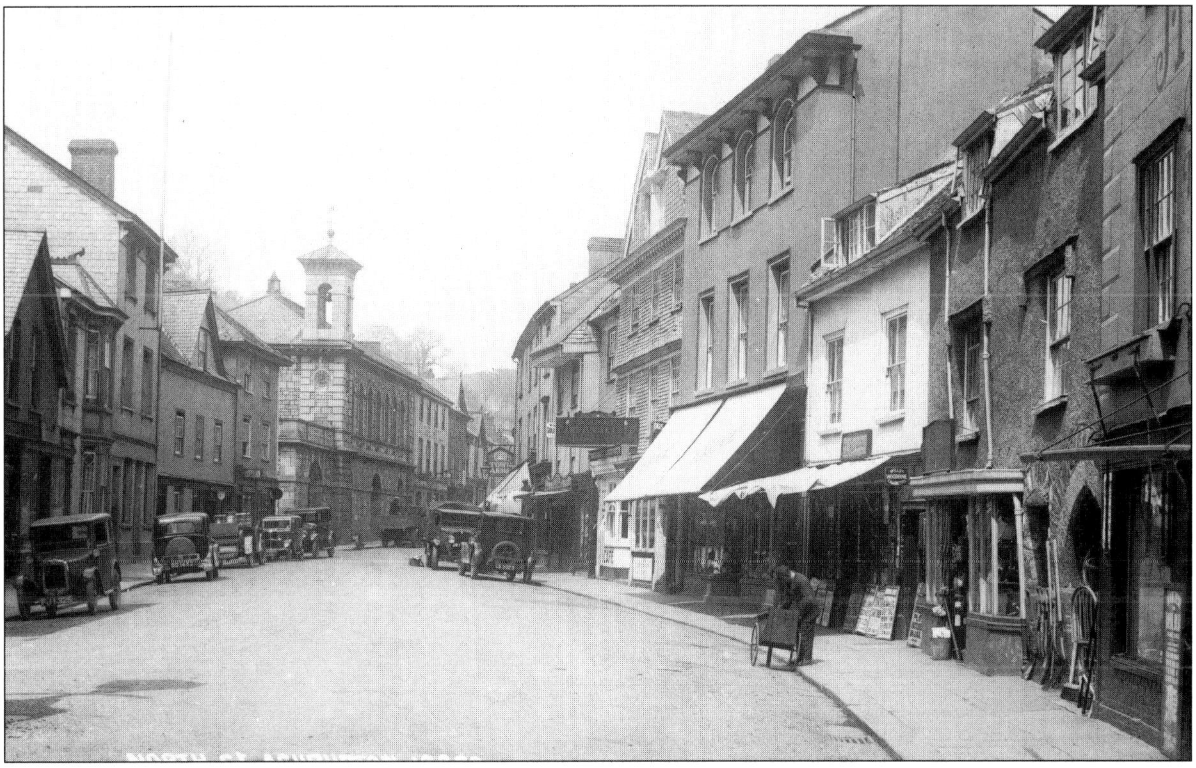

View of North Street in the late 1940s. (PETE WEBB COLLECTION)

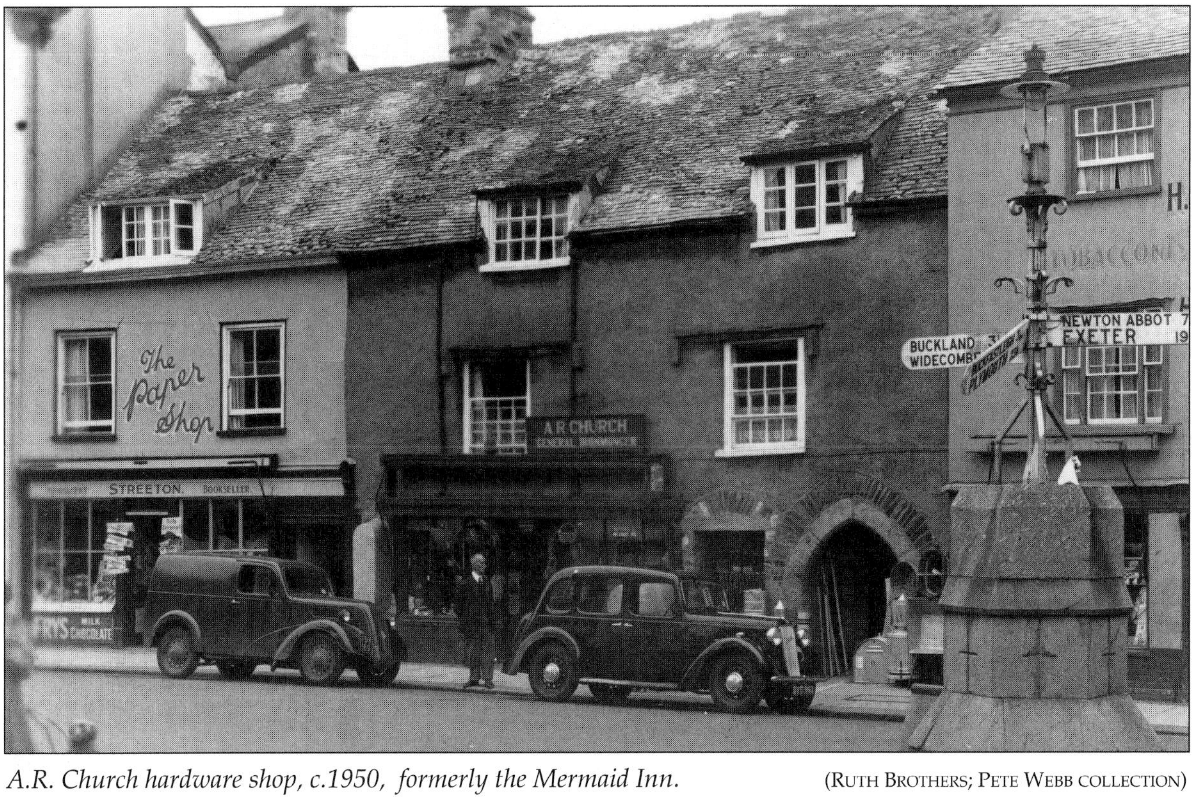

A.R. Church hardware shop, c.1950, formerly the Mermaid Inn. (RUTH BROTHERS; PETE WEBB COLLECTION)

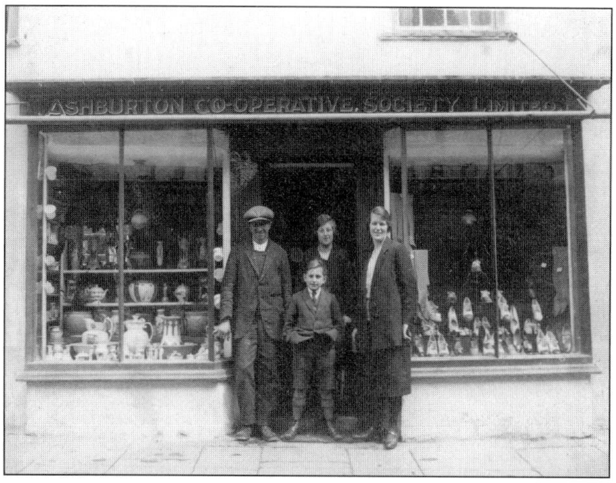

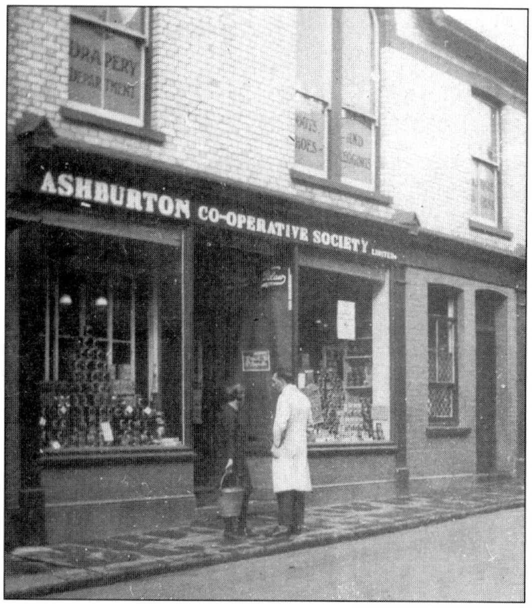

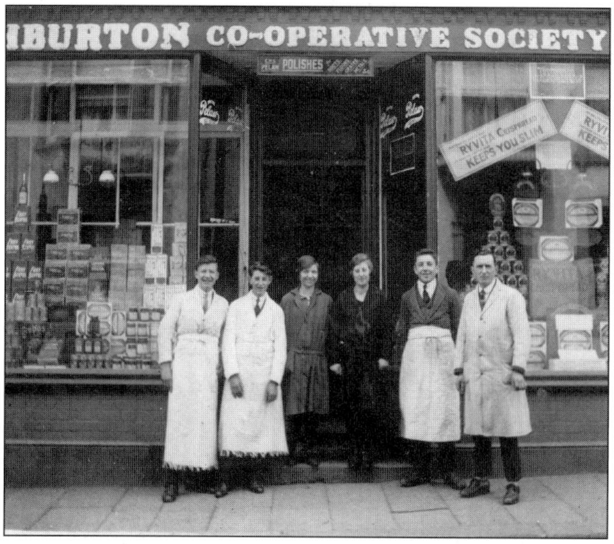

Three views of Ashburton Co-op taken through the years – the last building before what is now (2004) the open space of Cleder Place on North Street.
(Pete Webb collection)

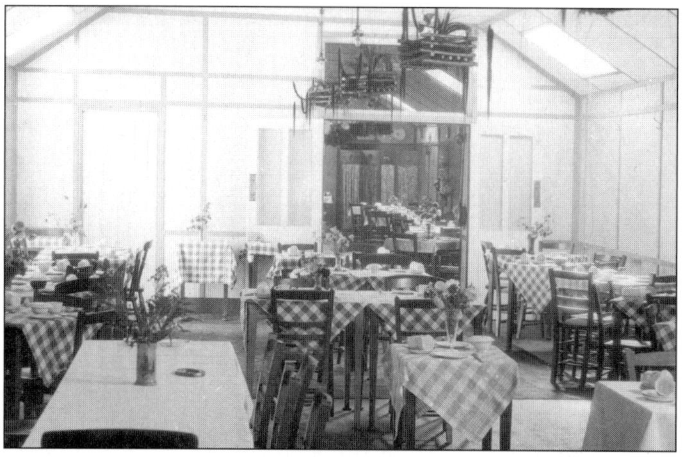

Interior of Barnes' tea rooms, postwar. (Pete Webb collection)

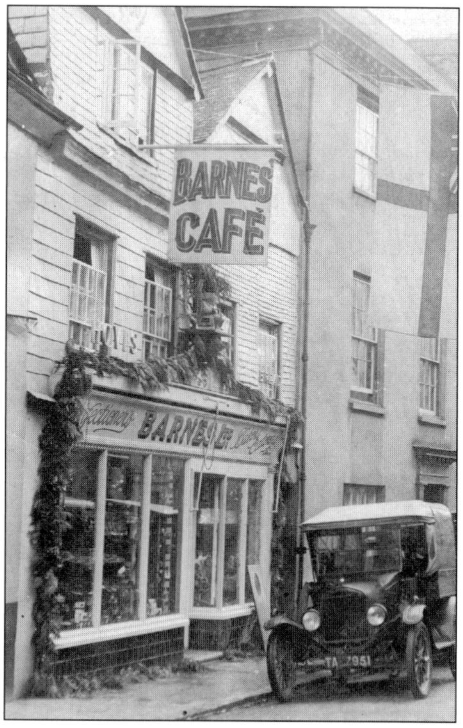

Exterior of Barnes', c.1925. Note the van – the first commercial vehicle in Ashburton.
(Pete Webb collection)

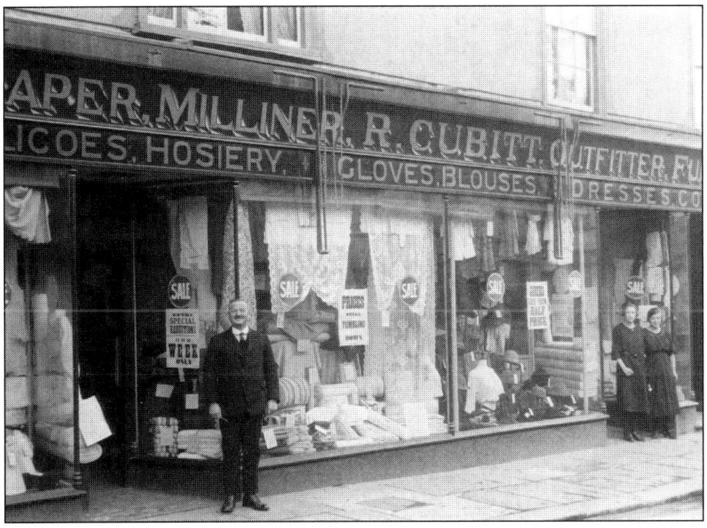

Cubitt's – drapers in Clinton House, North Street, 1940s. Mr Cubitt moved to Ashburton from Newton Abbot around 1911/12. He is pictured here with the Misses Sergent and Loader, shop girls. The shop closed in the late 1970s. J.H. Ford occupied the same premises before Mr Cubitt. (PETE WEBB COLLECTION)

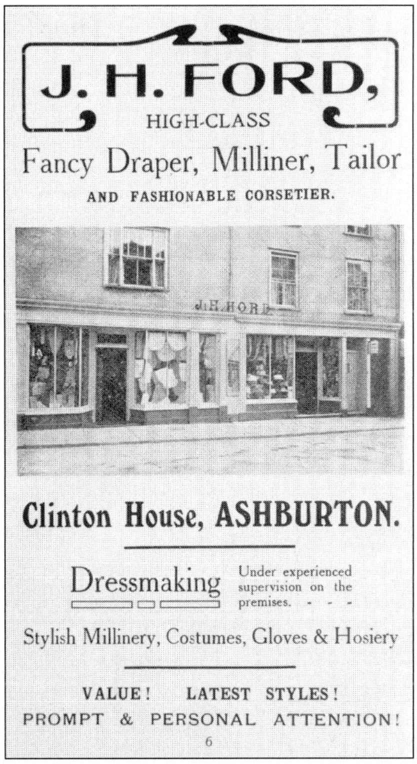

Ford's advert for the 1905 Town Guide
(PETE WEBB COLLECTION)

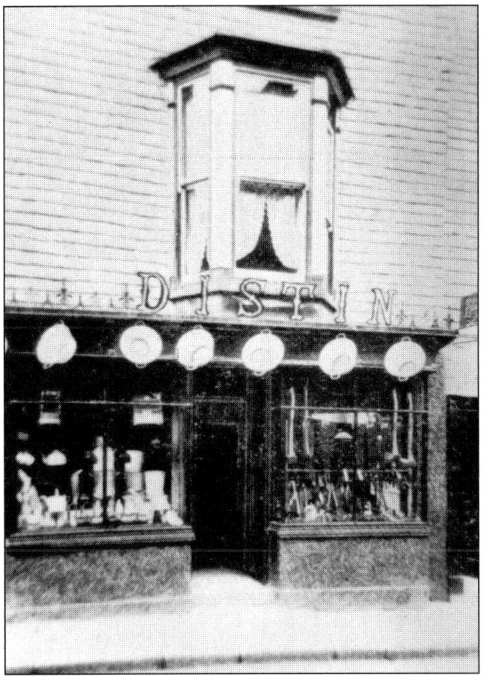

Distin's ironmongers in North Street, 1905.
(PETE WEBB COLLECTION)

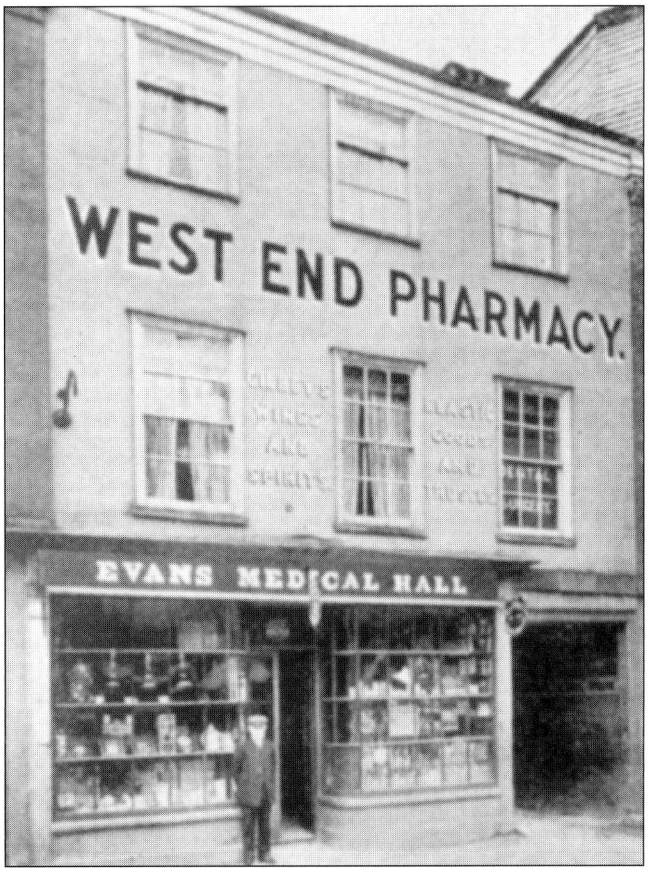

West End Pharmacy in West Street, 1905.
(PETE WEBB COLLECTION)

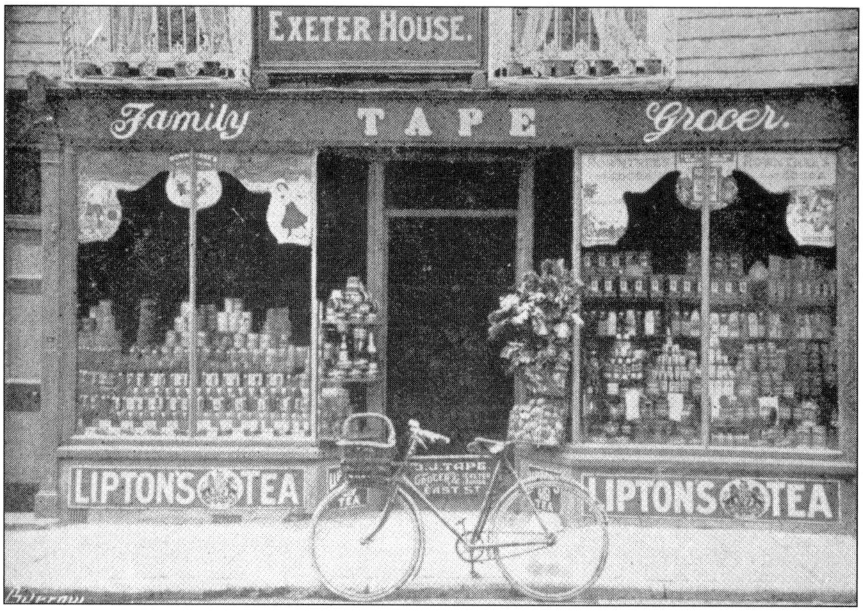

John Tape's grocery shop, Exeter House, East Street, from the 1905 Town Guide. (PETE WEBB COLLECTION)

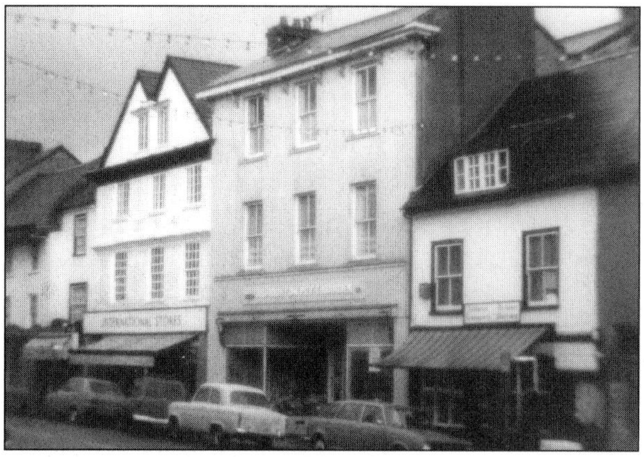

North Street shops, 1987 – note Ashburton Pet & Garden, which swapped premises with the chemist's. (PETE WEBB)

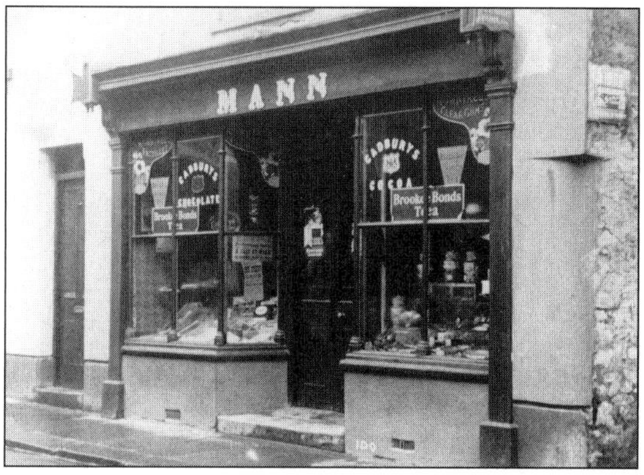

The Misses Mann's sweet shop, 13 St Lawrence Lane. (PETE WEBB COLLECTION)

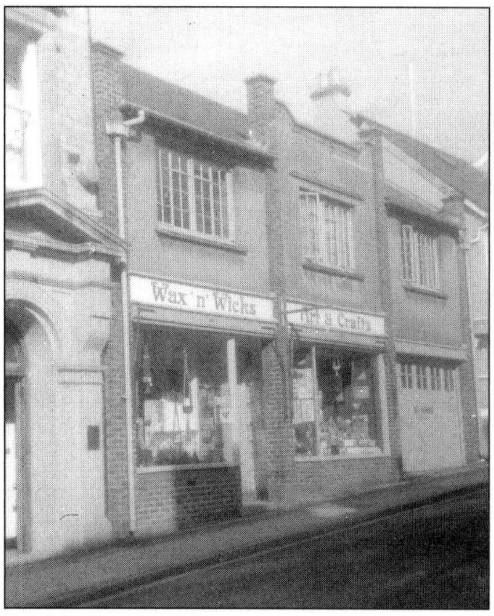

Wax 'n' Wicks, Pete Webb's art and craft shop for eight years in the 1970s. (PETE WEBB)

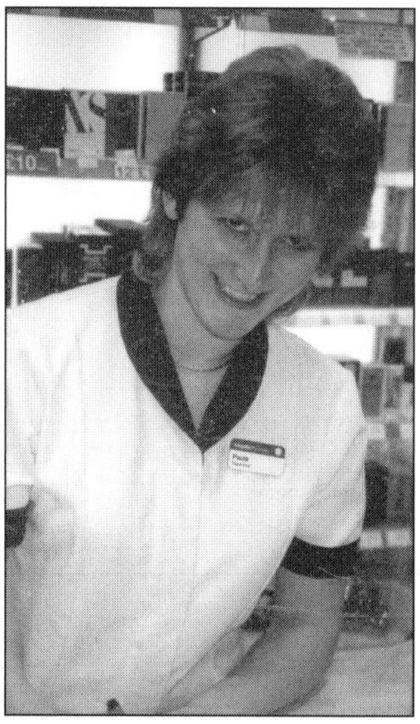

Paula Foley, Lloyd's the Chemist, North Street, 2003. (STUART HANDS)

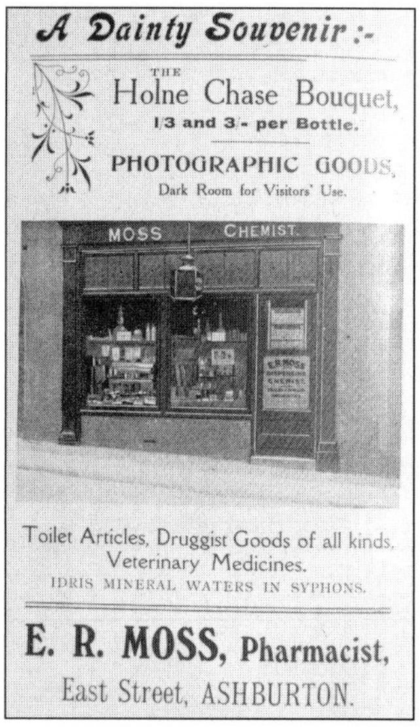

Moss Chemist's advert, East Street, 1905. This shop was unchanged until the 1980s. (PETE WEBB COLLECTION)

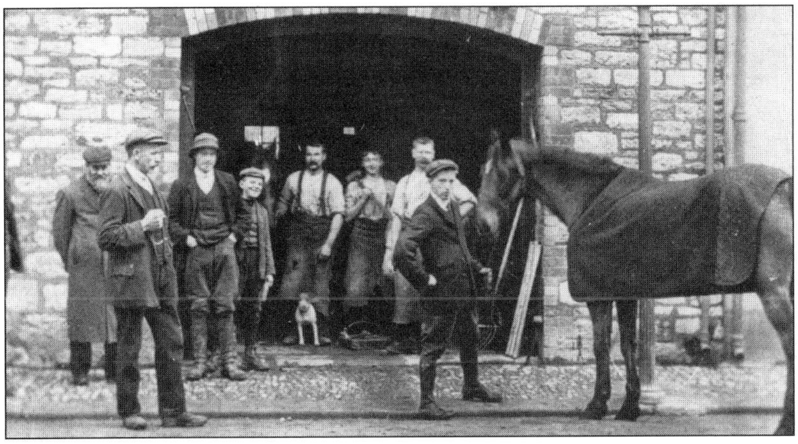

French & Sons, blacksmiths in St Lawrence Lane, c.1915 (there from around 1906 to 1935). From left: *man with beard unknown, chap in road George French (brother of smith), ? Satterley* (in hat), *unknown lad, Symons* (moustache and apron), *Richard (Dick) Northway (lad who later took over business), James (Jimmy) French (blacksmith), unknown lad holding horse in road.* (PETE WEBB COLLECTION)

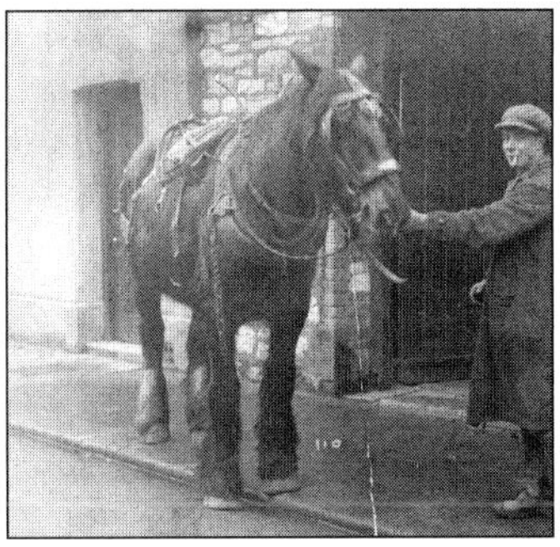

Above: *Archie Brailey with horse outside the blacksmith's in St Lawrence Lane, c.1940.* (ASHBURTON MUSEUM & PETE WEBB COLLECTION)

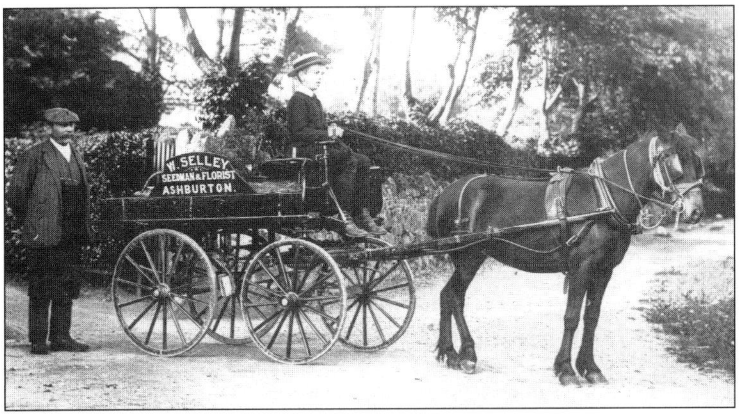

Above: *Selley the seedsman. This was a card sent to his daughter in Brussels. He had a business in Staverton Gardens off Old Totnes Road, where this picture was taken around 1914.* (PETE WEBB COLLECTION)

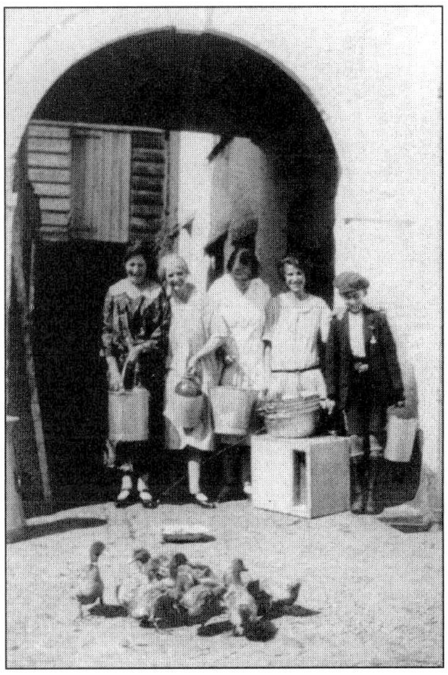

Above: *Kingsbridge Dairy, early 1940s.* Left to right: *?, Connie Osbourne, Louie Daw, Nora Knapman, ?. Note that the cobbles on the earlier picture have by this time been replaced.* (PAT ORSMAN COLLECTION)

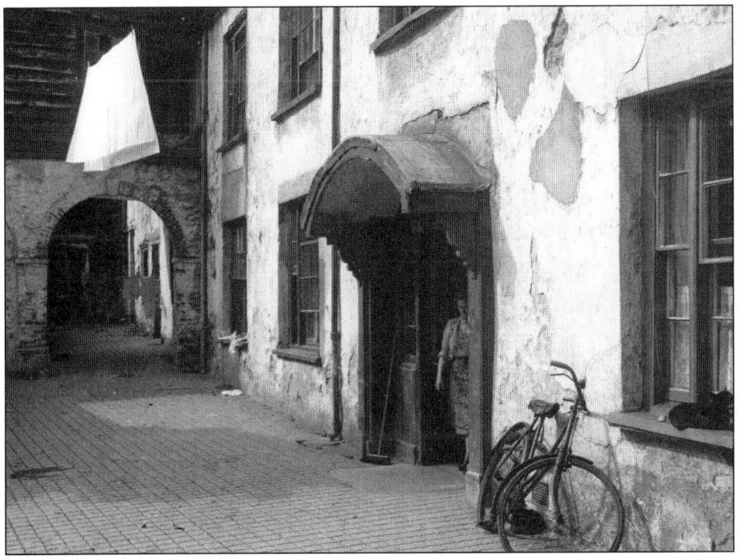

Left: *Daw's Kingsbridge Dairy.* (PAT ORSMAN COLLECTION)

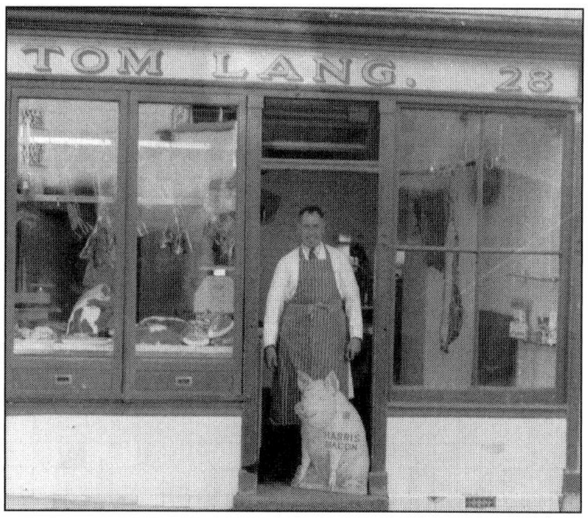

Tom Lang, butcher, 28 East Street, 1950s.
(HENRY LANG COLLECTION)

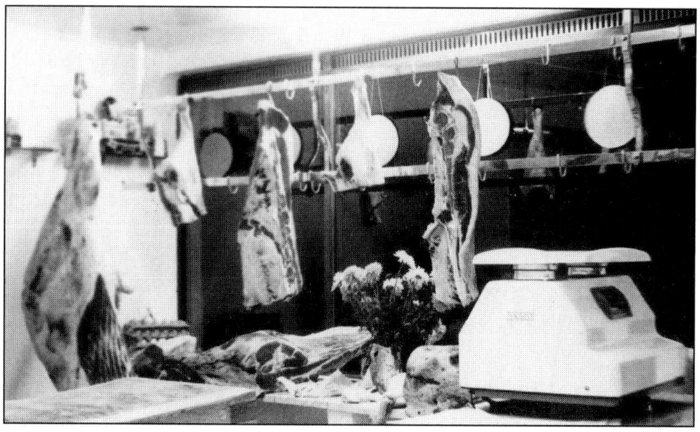

Interior of Lang's butcher's in the 1960s.
(HENRY LANG COLLECTION)

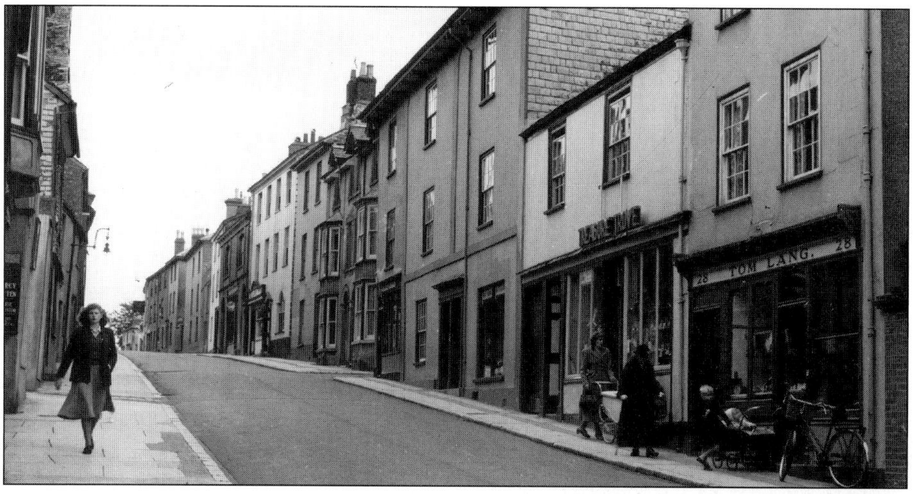

Left: *Lang's, East Street, 1950s.*
(RUTH BROTHERS; PETE WEBB COLLECTION)

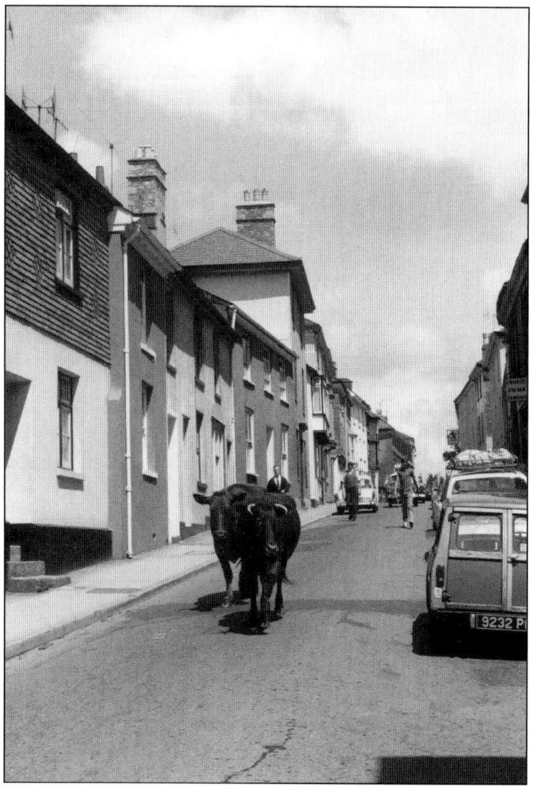

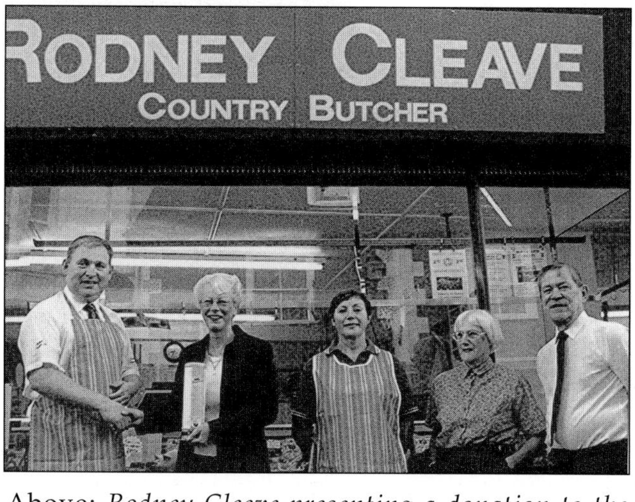

Above: *Rodney Cleeve presenting a donation to the museum.* From left: *Rodney Cleeve, Wendy Gill (chair of trustees), Carol Cleeve, Alison Burden, Jamie Broughton (curator). This was Lang's shop.* (JOHN GERMON)

Left: *East Street, c.1968. Cattle being driven to Lang's by Andrew Pedrick.*
(HENRY LANG COLLECTION)

CHAPTER 5

Ashburton's Pubs and Inns

Ashburton, like many other small market towns around the country, had a lot of pubs, inns and hotels. In 2004 it also still retained an historical event connected with them that is not so common. The ancient Ale Tasting and Bread Weighing Ceremony visits every pub and bakery each year. This is a re-enactment of what originally would have been weights and measures or customs and excise checks on the quality of produce sold in the town. There were more pubs to visit in the past and, even though they were not all open at the same time, there were over 30 at one time or another in the town's past. This may seem rather a lot but the town had a steady stream of customers from the local tin mines, farms and general population, as well as the occasional punter from the weekly markets and annual fair, and any passing stagecoach and packhorse trade.

Some of the names are long forgotten whilst others have closed only in the recent past. Many of the landlords, and in some cases landladies, were larger-than-life characters – a fuller history on the subject can be found in *The Pubs and Inns of Ashburton,* by Pete Webb.

The **Anchor Inn**, or **Blue Anchor**, was on the south side of East Street near the junction with St Lawrence Lane. It was listed in the 1820s with Christopher Preston as the landlord and as the residence of John Caunter, who was also a tin miner, in the 1851 census. It was most likely in the same premises as the Anchor Café, which was in the building next to what was formerly Bradford's printers and is now (2004) a photographer's shop.

The **Barnstaple Inn**, now known as **The Bay Horse**, is in North Street. It was probably originally named for the packhorse route which passed its doors en route to Barnstaple from Brixham. The name didn't appear in trade directories as it was a beerhouse and only later became an inn – although it no longer provides accommodation. James Wills was the landlord in October 1886, when he was summoned to keep the peace by his wife Lavinia. John Cooper was there from around 1900 until the Short family took over in 1928. Mabel will be well remembered by many and she took over when her husband Ernie died in November 1953. Ernie was a hard working and fair landlord who did not believe in the practice of 'buying custom' whereby certain landlords would visit other pubs and buy a round for the regulars in the hope of poaching a few. Ernie would also call out the back for a hunk of bread and cheese if a 'milestone inspector' (tramp) called in. Mabel used to bring out lemonade for the kiddies during ale tasting and would also tell off any regular who stayed too long if his Sunday lunch was waiting at home. Originally a Starkey, Knight and Ford house, it was taken over by Whitbread and sold in 1974 when Mabel retired. It is now a free house.

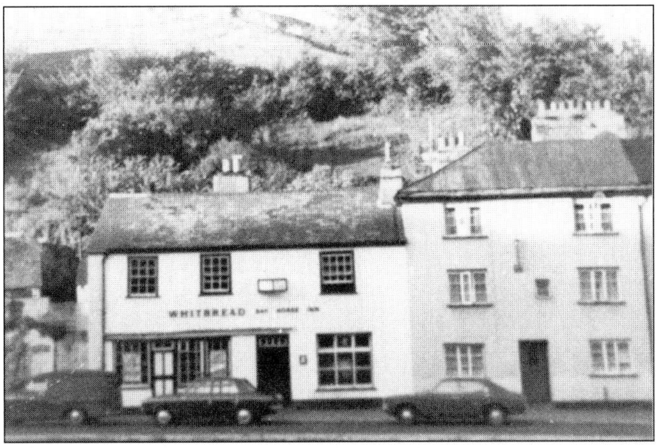

Bay Horse Inn (c.1970). Photo given to Pete Webb by Derek (Dinky), the then landlady Mabel Short's son.

The **Commercial Inn** was situated in North Street opposite the card house (Somerfield). It closed in 1911 when it was stated in the licensing review that there were no less than seven licensed houses within 20yds. The Liberal Club bought it in 1912 and spent some months making improvements before opening in April 1913. It had billiards and card rooms, a reading room and caretaker's accommodation. It was used by the Forces in the 1940s and closed in the 1960s. Mr Roberts used it in the 1970s as an office for his coal merchants and it was then used as an accountant's for many years. It is now the premises of the outdoor equipment firm Trailventure.

Crispin's Arms is listed as being in North Street in the 1823 and 1830 trade directories with Alice Husson as landlady, but its exact position is unknown.

The **Culloden Inn** was in the green space of Cleder Place, almost opposite the entrance to Stapledon Lane. It had a distinctive packhorse door, shaped to allow the passage of the animals without the need to unload. In 1892 it was purchased for £480 by the brewer W.H. Mortimer from the retiring landlord Joseph Winsor. It had its licence revoked at

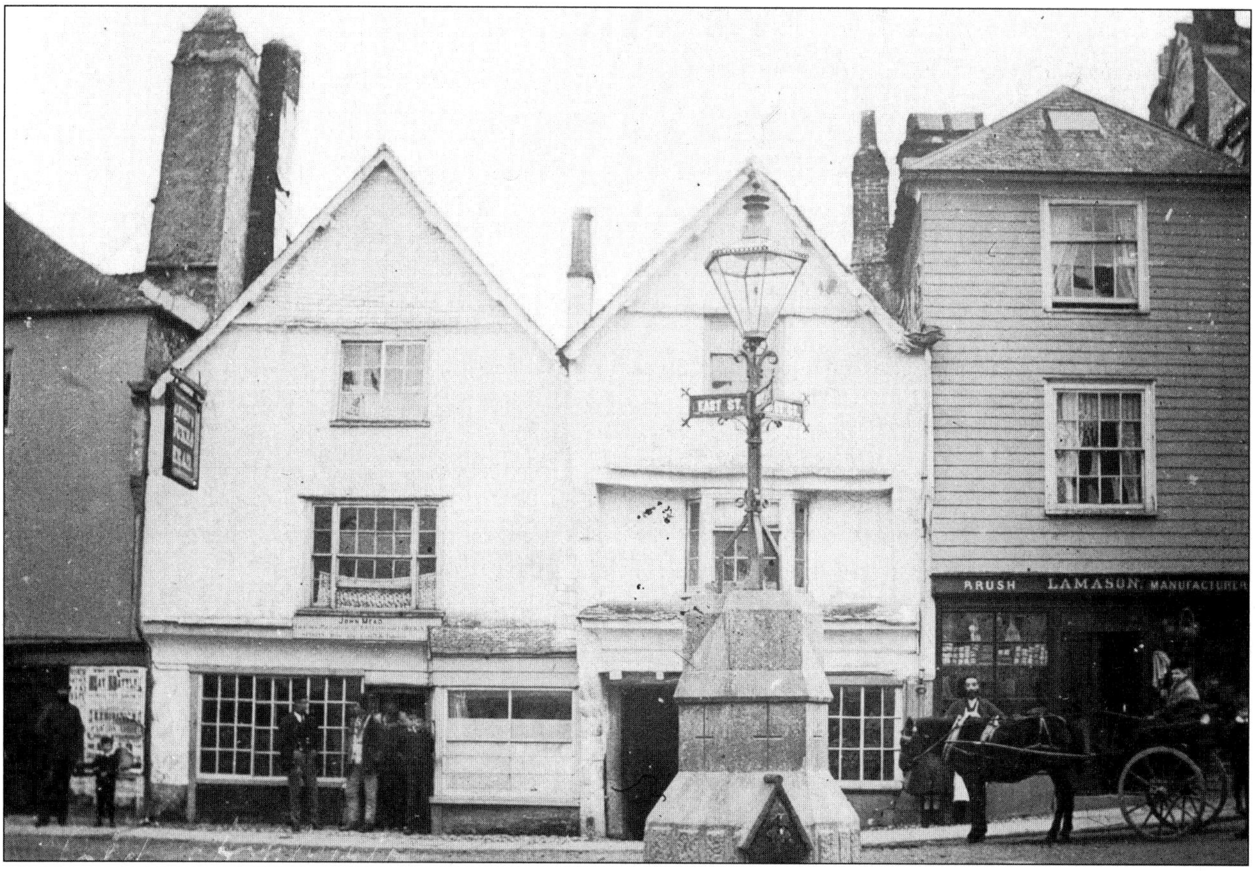

The Duke's Head, c.1890, around the time John Mead was landlord. It closed in 1891 when it was sold to the Capital and Counties Bank. The lease remained with the owner, Sir L.V. Palk. Lamson's Brush Manufactory is on its right and is now the town's museum. Amy Hannaford produced this as a postcard around 1920 and lived in the building during the 1950s. Note also the 'Bull Ring', or water conduit, taken away in the early 1960s. (PETE WEBB COLLECTION)

the same time as the Commercial, in 1911.

The **Dartmoor Lodge Motel**, as its name suggests, is not really a pub but it does have a bar for non-residents. Originally the Pear Tree Café, it is pictured in Chapter 17, on p.125.

The **Duke's Head** was situated where the present Lloyds TSB Bank stands. It was mentioned in the will of Mr Jeffreys in 1706, purchased by Thomas Abraham in May 1814 and a lease was granted to Soloman Tozer in June 1814. It closed in 1891 when Messrs Tozer and Abrahams founded the Capital and Counties Bank. They leased the building along with the solicitors Wollacombe and Watts until November 1906 when the bank obtained the release of the leasehold.

Opposite the Golden Lion was the **Eagle** or **Spread Eagle** Inn. It was a coaching inn and notorious bawdy-house and closed with the decline of the coaching trade. The Eagle Dairy was in the same premises until the 1970s when it became a private dwelling.

The **Engineers Arms** stood opposite Great Meeting and was also closed in 1911. It once stood next to the last building on the west side of North Street where the children's playground is on Cleder Place (see photo on p.20).

The **Exeter Inn** in West Street is probably the oldest public house in Ashburton. It was mainly rebuilt in the seventeenth century but dates from the mid-twelfth century when the church opposite was built. It was thought to have been erected to house the church builders and was later used to brew ale for church funds. It benefited from the passing coach trade – Sir Walter Raleigh had just left the building when he was arrested in 1603 and taken to the Tower of London. It has a long history with a long list of landlords. John Stentiford (1823), Joseph Bowden (1830), James Burnett (1850), Henry Mugford (1857), followed by Richard Luscombe in the 1870s, then Richard Merryfield until around 1890. The Merryfields were followed by the Denny family, then William Halse. William was the tenant until October 1927 when he bought the Inn for £1,000 and remained until the 1930s. A further succession of landlords occurred until

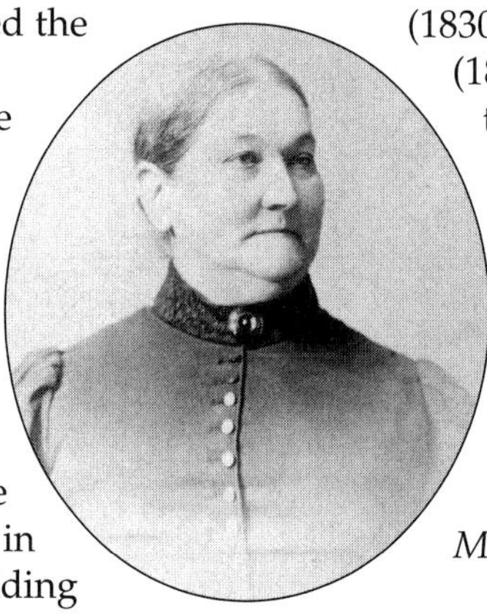

Mrs Merryfield of the Exeter Inn.
(PETE WEBB COLLECTION)

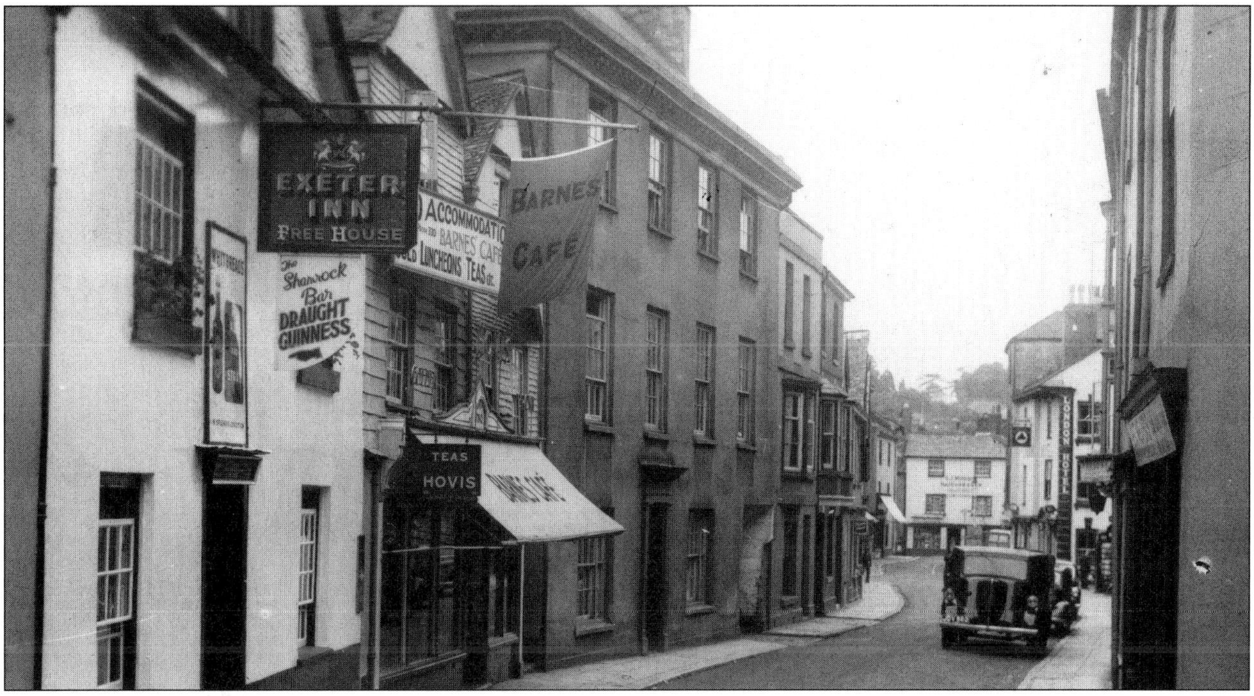

The Exeter Inn, c.1950 (note the Shamrock Bar). (PETE WEBB COLLECTION)

1986 when the present family, Jim and Carol McNichol and mother, Pam Billington, took over

The **Globe Inn** or **Globe Hotel** was one of the town's better establishments for most of the twentieth century until it closed after the war (in the late 1940s). From the late 1880s it was called the Edwards Globe Hotel, after James Edwards and then his daughter Sarah. Many balls and social occasions were held there and it was sold as part of Sarah's estate for £1,700 in April 1921 to Mr Taylor of Chudleigh. It seems to have changed landlords often, with Charlie Waterfield in the 1940s remembered by many. Like many pubs it was used by the Armed Forces during the war and Charlie was fined for serving an American serviceman after hours in January 1944. It was well used by the businessmen of the town and Charlie was still there in 1949 when it closed. There are now three antique shops and an optician on the ground floor and flats upstairs.

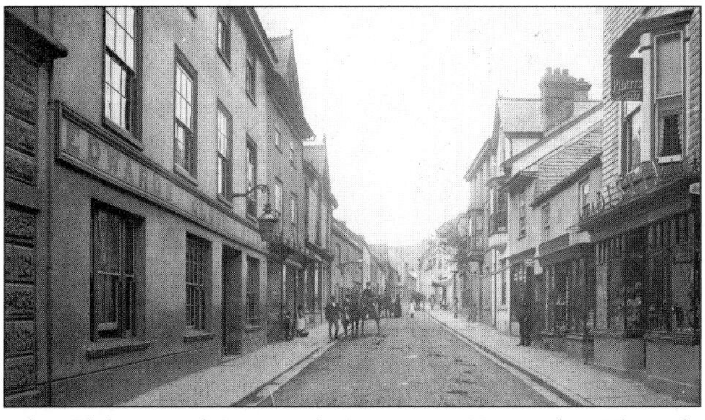

The Globe Hotel in North Street, c.1920. The Edwards family ran this – first Mr Edwards then, on his death, his daughter Sarah for a further 20 years. (PETE WEBB COLLECTION)

The **Golden Fleece** was in St Lawrence Lane next to the Grammar School. It is believed to have occupied the site of Bishop Stapledon's palace. It is most likely that it was named after the town's thriving woollen trade but there is a story that it was named after the Golden Hind's sister ship, the Golden Fleece. This is supposed to have foundered in Lannacombe Bay and its salvaged timbers were said to have been used to build the pub. Elizabeth Perkins followed on from her husband George in 1856 and when she died in 1886 she had been there for over 50 years. The Knapmans, then William Stagg and Samuel Lock followed them. Samuel was summonsed in July 1914 for selling intoxicating liquor to a drunken person. This was none other than one Frederick Eggbear, the great uncle of Eileen Egbeare's late husband Fred.

The Fleece closed as a public house in 1939 and was used from 1962 to 1969 by the local Girl Guides. It was converted into two houses in the early 1970s.

The **Golden Lion** in East Street was built in 1768 as the mansion of Nicholas Tripe, a surgeon of the town. He was also the owner of the original Golden Lion, which was further down East Street where the National Westminster Bank now stands. In 1795 he converted his mansion into an inn, closing the original Golden Lion in 1797. The new inn was on the main coaching route and quickly became the premier coaching inn, taking over as the posting house from the London Inn in 1825. William Barons was responsible for the London Inn when his mother-in-law, Mary Lloyd, retired as landlady.

William was also a strong supporter of the Tory party and held regular meetings on the premises. In the summer of 1837, during a local election, he

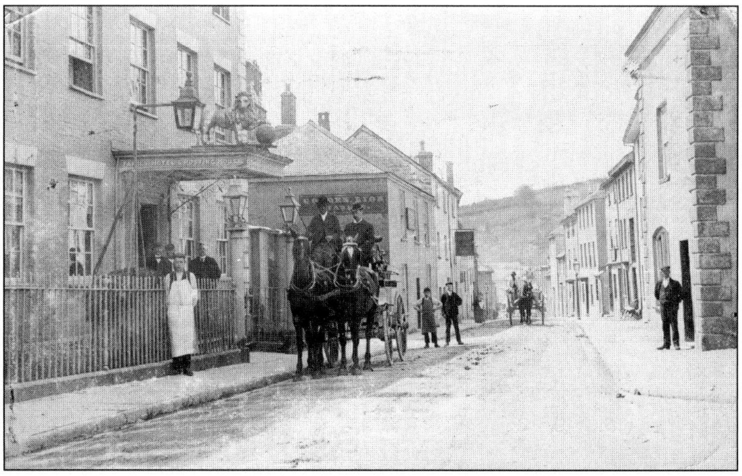

The Golden Lion c.1910. Note the Golden Lion Tap. The carriage would have possibly just collected guests from the railway station.
(PETE WEBB COLLECTION)

enticed a Liberal rival, George Knowling, into the inn and drugged him with a spiked drink. Barons' heavies then carried him out onto Dartmoor and dumped him there. Mr Knowling's friends, having followed at a safe distance, then rescued him and brought him back to Ashburton. They then taunted the Tories in the Golden Lion by parading him outside, causing a well-documented riot.

Mr Barons left in 1842 and was succeeded by George Bate, the inn then becoming a hotel. James Clymo followed and Arthur Conan Doyle is reputed to have stayed here during research for his book *The Hound of the Baskervilles* (see Chapter 12, p.90). This seems unlikely as the Robertson family only lived in Ipplepen. It is more probable that they stayed at the Duchy Inn in Princetown, which also makes the claim.

The hotel was used by Cambridge-based St Faith's Preparatory School during the Second World War and the Old Boys' Association held a reunion in Ashburton in 2003. Run by W.T. Lovegrove after the war and then the Greenwoods until 1955, there were a further twelve landlords until Alan and Norma Hope took over in 1978. It became the headquarters of the Monster Raving Loony Party in 1990 under the leadership of Screaming Lord Sutch. Their Annual Party Conferences were occasions to remember, not only in the Golden Lion but also in the town, and attracted large numbers of gaily-dressed visitors. Norma became ill in the 1990s and moved back to Hampshire. Alan sold the Golden Lion to a developer in 1999, the same year that David Sutch died, and now runs the Dog and Partridge in Yateley. The Golden Lion building now houses two large apartments, one of which has a 42ft drawing room in the former ballroom, while another eight houses have been built in the car park.

The **Golden Lion Tap** existed between the Golden Lion and the Red Lion. It was probably an annexe to the main pub and had stabling in the rear for the next-door hotel. Aaron Bickham, there at the time of the 1851 census, was listed as an ostler, but was listed in the trade directory of the period as landlord. The building was demolished in the early 1900s and replaced with the town's fire station which, in 1949, was used in the film *Guilt is my Shadow* as a garage. This was itself demolished in the early 1970s, a new fire station and police station having been built in 1965.

Lavender House Hotel on the outskirts of town started life as a house called **Betweenways**, built by James Pearce Foaden as his residence. It later became a hotel of the same name and was renamed **The Grasshopper** in the early 1970s. In 1990 it was renamed **Lanterns** before taking its present name. This inn has been renowned variously for its night life (and trouble), for being home to one of the biggest music venues in Devon, for its food and now for its wedding receptions, complete with fireworks.

The **London Inn/Hotel** was a fifteenth-century coaching house on the main London to Plymouth turnpike. Until the recent building work the stables were still visible at the rear. The Angel family were there in 1866, with William Hill, whose name can still be seen carved above the former windows on the side, following on until 1894. Arthur Cove followed until 1919. A well-respected couple, the Coves were helped by the town to celebrate their Golden Wedding in February 1929. Boxing took place here in the 1930s and it was used as an officer's mess during the Second World War. In the 1950s the inn held a music licence for handbell ringing.

The custom was for an apprentice to have a pint in every pub on completion of his indentures. With eleven pubs, plus starting and finishing in the London, the lad would have had to down a dozen pints (although often word had got round and instead of the final pint there would be a whole row of them on the bar).

Once part of the Symons brewery chain, the

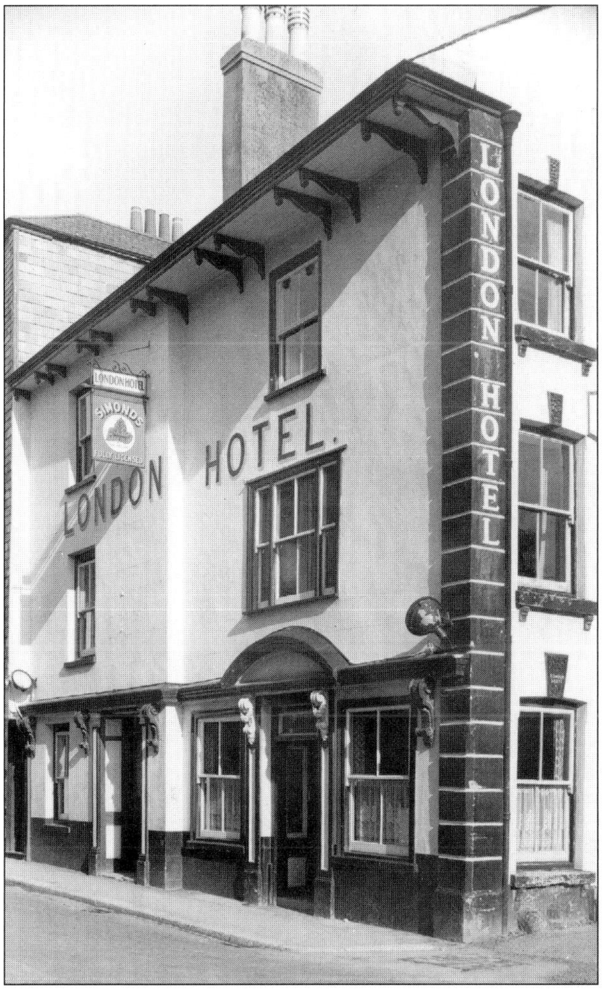

The London Hotel, c.1950. (PETE WEBB COLLECTION)

London Inn was auctioned in 1958 and became a free house. The Thompson family were there from 1979 until 1997, when it closed after a disastrous fire. As well as the brewery in the stable (set up in 1981) there was also a popular restaurant. The building now has flats upstairs, houses behind and a 'Moorish' restaurant on the ground floor.

The **Mermaid Inn** in North Street was the building which now houses the A.R. Church hardware shop. Some authorities regard it as having been an early church house inn and it certainly dates from the first half of the fifteenth century with sixteenth-century additions and served as General Fairfax's headquarters during the Civil War. It has been a hardware shop since before the 1850s.

The **New Bottle** stood somewhere in North Street. Its position is not known but it appeared in trade directories between 1823 and 1873.

The **New Inn** as a pub name appears in two places. There was a New Inn in North Street next to the Card House (Somerfield in 2004), which is seen in the picture by Foot of the old market (see p.77). It also appeared in trade directory entries between 1823 and 1850. It is now Lloyd's chemist's shop and has its own ghost or poltergeist probably dating from the pub's era.

The other **New Inn** or **New House Inn** was near the northern boundary of the parish out on Dartmoor near Rippon Tor. It had a tradition of being burned down by tin miners' wives fed up with their husbands stopping there on their way down off the moor and spending all their wages. It is mentioned in Hemery's *High Dartmoor* as being run by a Mrs Hannaford. She remarried and, as Mrs Follet, moved down to the Rugglestone in Widecombe where Mrs Audrey Lamb (a member of the fourth generation of the same family) retired about ten years ago.

The **North Star** was next to the Great Meeting (now Ashburton Marbles) in North Street. It is mentioned in 1739 when a trust was set up to rebuild the chapel, and purchased by them in 1829, being demolished to extend the building in 1850. Tradition has it that the entrance to the chapel was along the same alley that served the pub and that during times of religious persecution the congregation could pretend to be visiting the pub.

The **Plymouth Inn** was in West Street near the

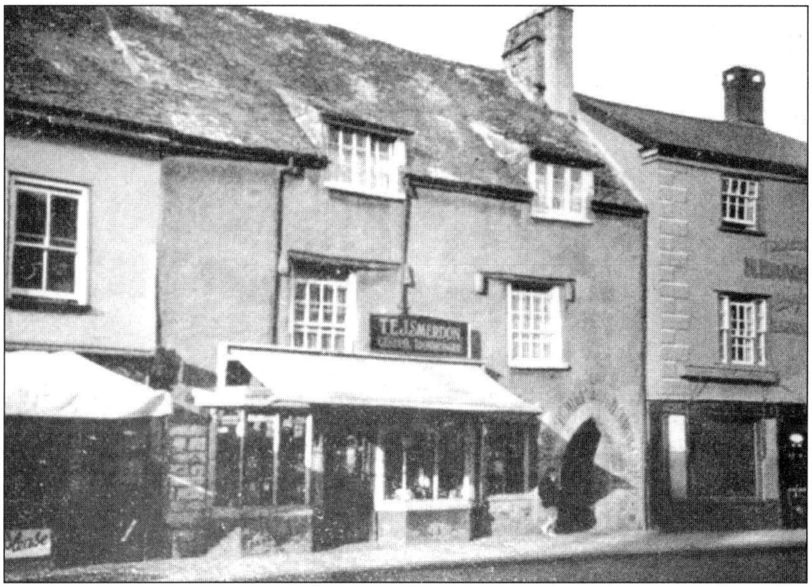

The former Mermaid Inn (Smerdon's hardware shop) in the 1930s. (PETE WEBB COLLECTION)

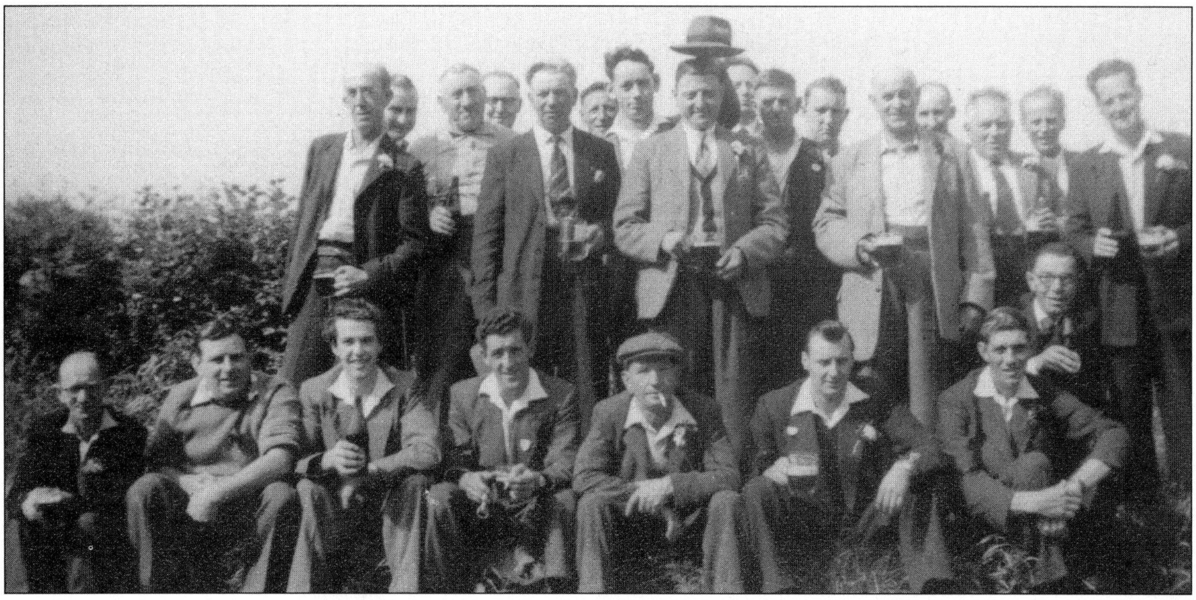

Red Lion Inn pub outing, 1954. Back row includes: *George Endacott, Bill Sergent, 'Buckie', Jack Couch, Les Underhill, ?, Bill Hext, Edgar Pedrick* (with hat above his head*), ?, Charlie Harvey, Sam Steer, George Wyatt, ?, Bill Sergent senr, ?;* left to right, front: *Reg Steer, Bert from Bovey, David Putt, Garth Grose, Ernie Knapman, Reg Pedrick, Richard Elliot.* (GARTH GROSE COLLECTION)

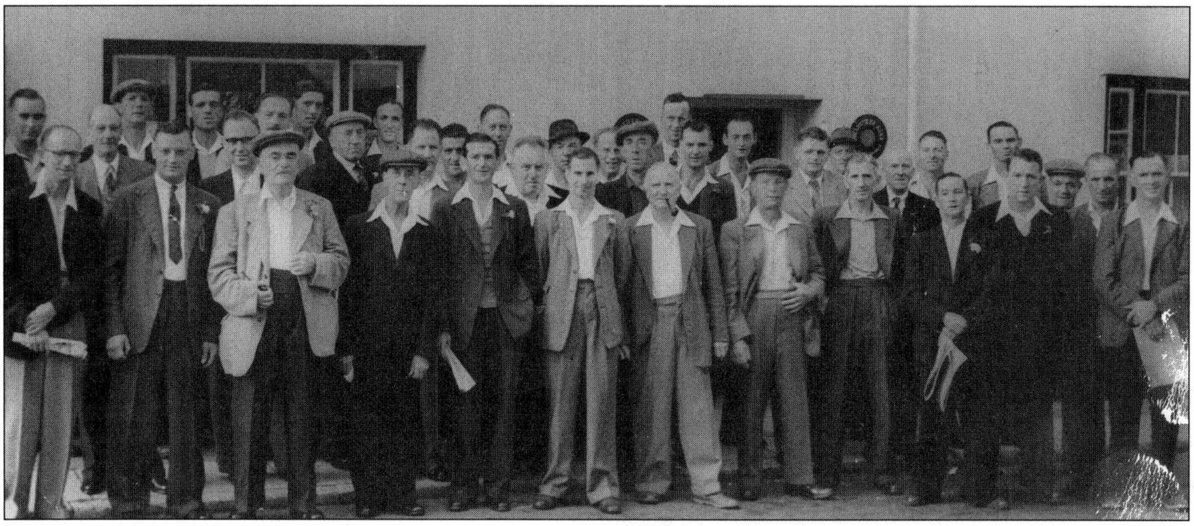

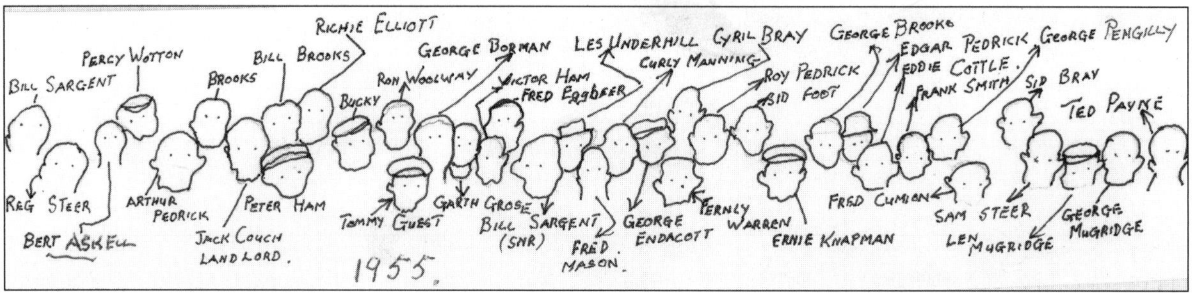

Red Lion Inn pub outing, 1955. (DETAILS GARTH GROSE)

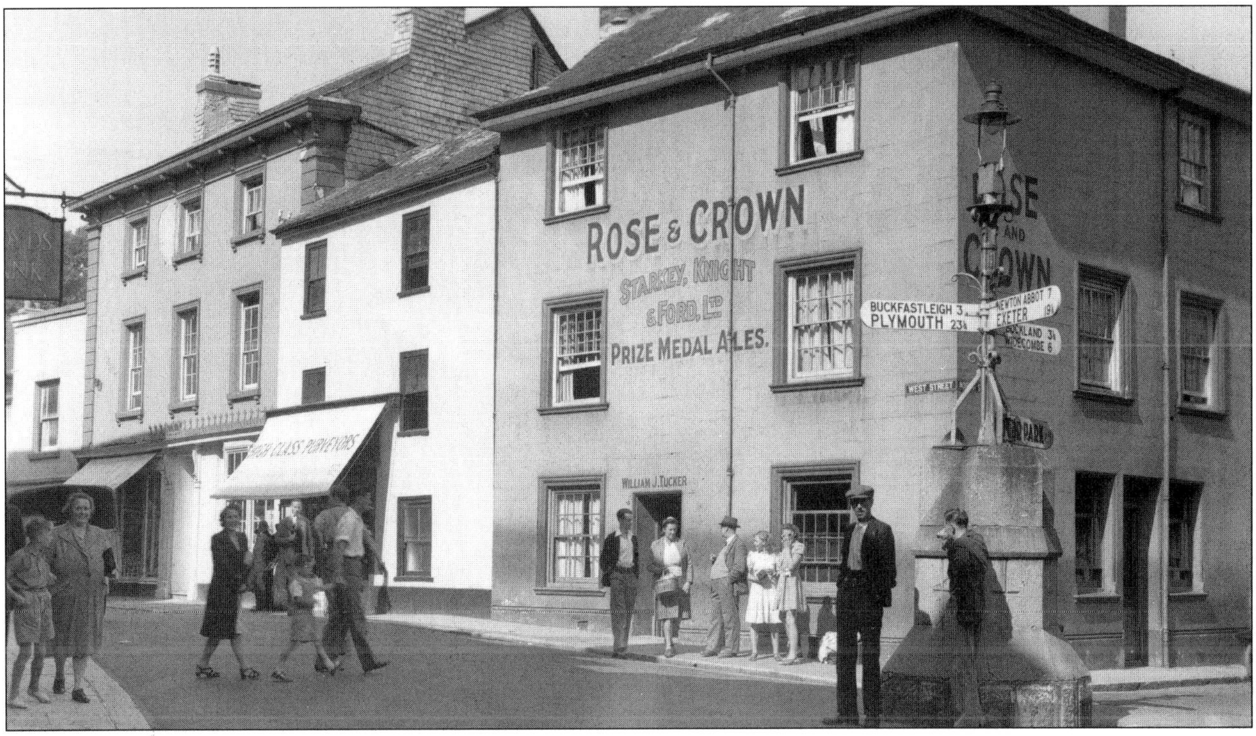

The Rose and Crown on the corner of North Street and West Street. Bill Tucker was the landlord when this 1950s photo was taken by one of the Ruth brothers. Cyril Bray and Nipper Warren have been identified standing next to the conduit. Mrs Binmore is thought to be the lady on the far left. (PETE WEBB COLLECTION)

bottom of Bowden Hill. It stood at the other end of the row of raised cottages from Mayflower House and mention is madc of it on the owner's house deeds. It was possibly the same inn as the beerhouse on Bowden Hill, mentioned in nineteenth-century trade directories.

The **Red Lion** is in East Street and affectionately known as the Red Dog by locals. It is probably eighteenth century and also had stabling to the rear to serve the passing coaching trade. A succession of landlords from 1830 included William Bowden, William Lukey, Thomas Trunan, William Stevens, Richard Preston and Frederick Loveys in the 1890s. John Robert Hern followed until the late 1930s with the Couch family there during the Second World War. Mike and Peggy Roberts were there from the 1950s until 1964 when Tom and Gwen Heywood arrived. They were there until they retired in 1989 and Gwen told many stories for the book *The Pubs and Inns of Ashburton*. She remembered the church choir calling in for a drink after Sunday service and the youngsters being told off by the local bobby, who thought they were drinking not Daw's apple juice but cider. There were onion and bean-growing competitions to raise funds for the Church or for local charities. It has been a Heavitree house since the 1920s.

The **Rose and Crown**, on the junction of North and West Streets, will be remembered by many. It is shown in paintings of the old market, demolished in 1850, as a very different building. Captain John Cooke was born there in 1765 and became a bodyguard for the Exeter Crown Court judges, a post he held for 70 years. He was known to proclaim the virtues of 'Ashburton pop' from the top of a coach. This same area was also the site of the former Bull Ring, used for bull baiting until outlawed by an Act of Parliament in 1835. (The centre of Ashburton gets its name from this practice.) It was the traditional meeting place for wool-staplers during the nineteenth-century Tuesday wool market. It closed in 1969 and was taken over by the Churchward family to extend their grocer's shop with what was previously the Sun Inn next door. It has been the Spar shop for nearly 15 years.

The **Royal Oak** in East Street is another early travellers' inn with a 300-year history. It was used during the Civil War and in the early part of the twentieth century was a St Annes Ales house. During renovations in the summer of June 1990 a large number of relics of the Civil War were found, as well as a series of medieval roof trusses. These arch-braced trusses date to the fourteenth and fifteenth centuries and there are drawings of them on the wall. Lionel and Lynne Goodman have been there since 1992.

The **Seven Stars** was in East Street on the upper corner of Woodland Road. It certainly appears in the 1850s trade directories but does not appear after 1857. It was destroyed by fire possibly at about this time and rebuilt by John Hannibal Foaden around the turn of the century as two grand houses. William Edgecombe lived in one of the two houses and was the local postmaster while his wife was a milliner

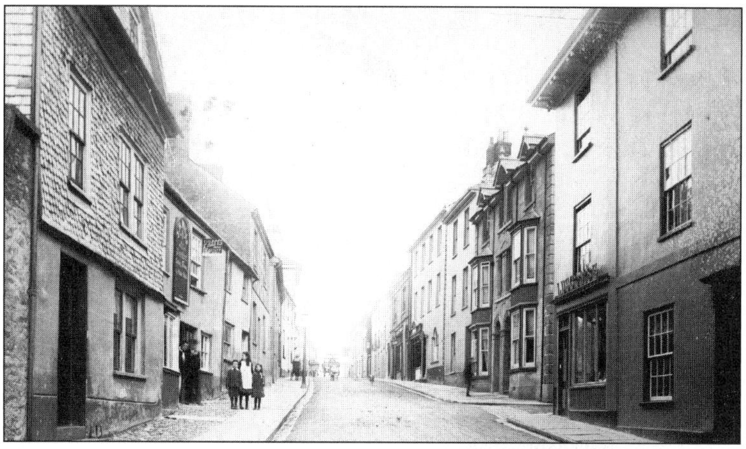

The Seven Stars in East Street. This view, c.1940, shows the building, now the Ark, which replaced the original Seven Stars around 1910.
(PETE WEBB COLLECTION)

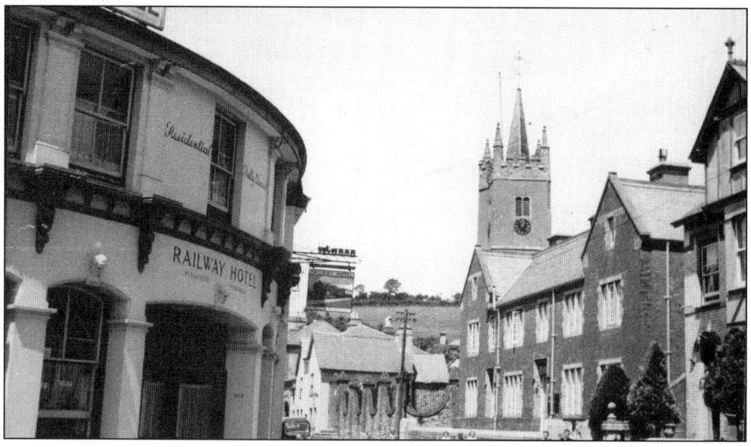

The Railway Hotel in the 1950s. Note the long building on the right – the police station and the Golden Fleece after the chapel.
(PETE WEBB COLLECTION)

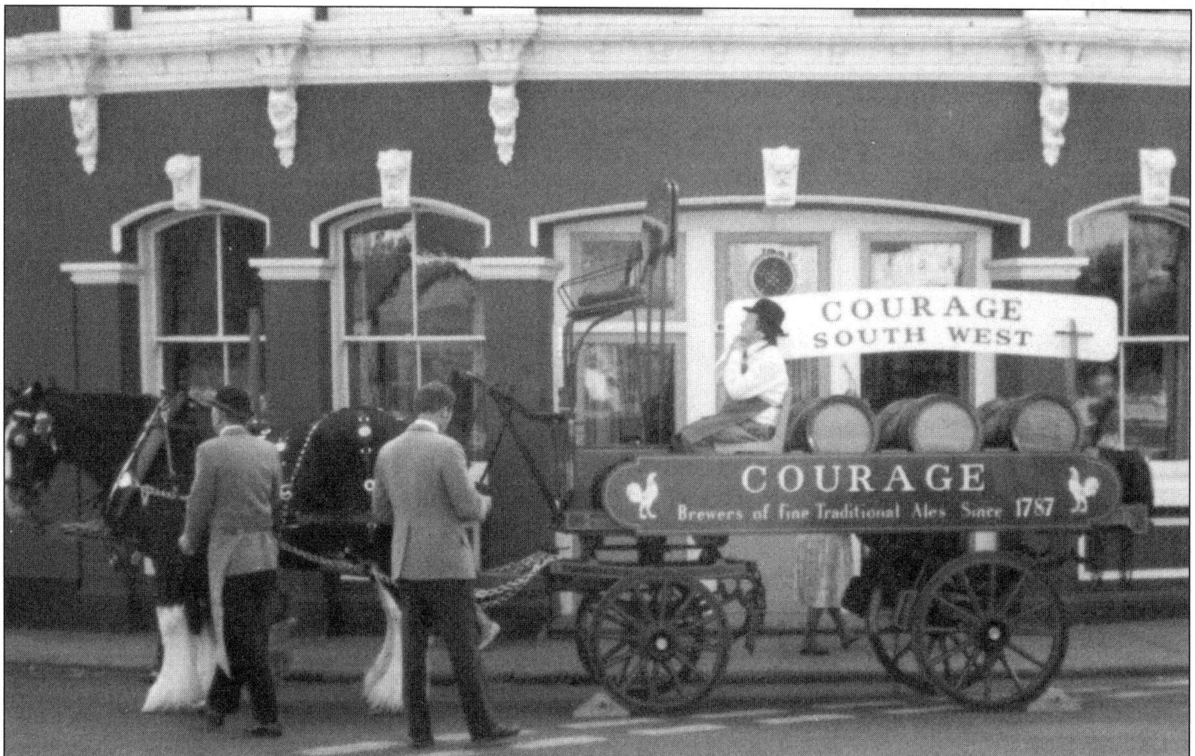

A brewer's dray from Courage Brewery outside the Silent Whistle, 1984. It was used by Douglas Edwards in the carnival procession as the Portreeve's transport.
(PETE WEBB)

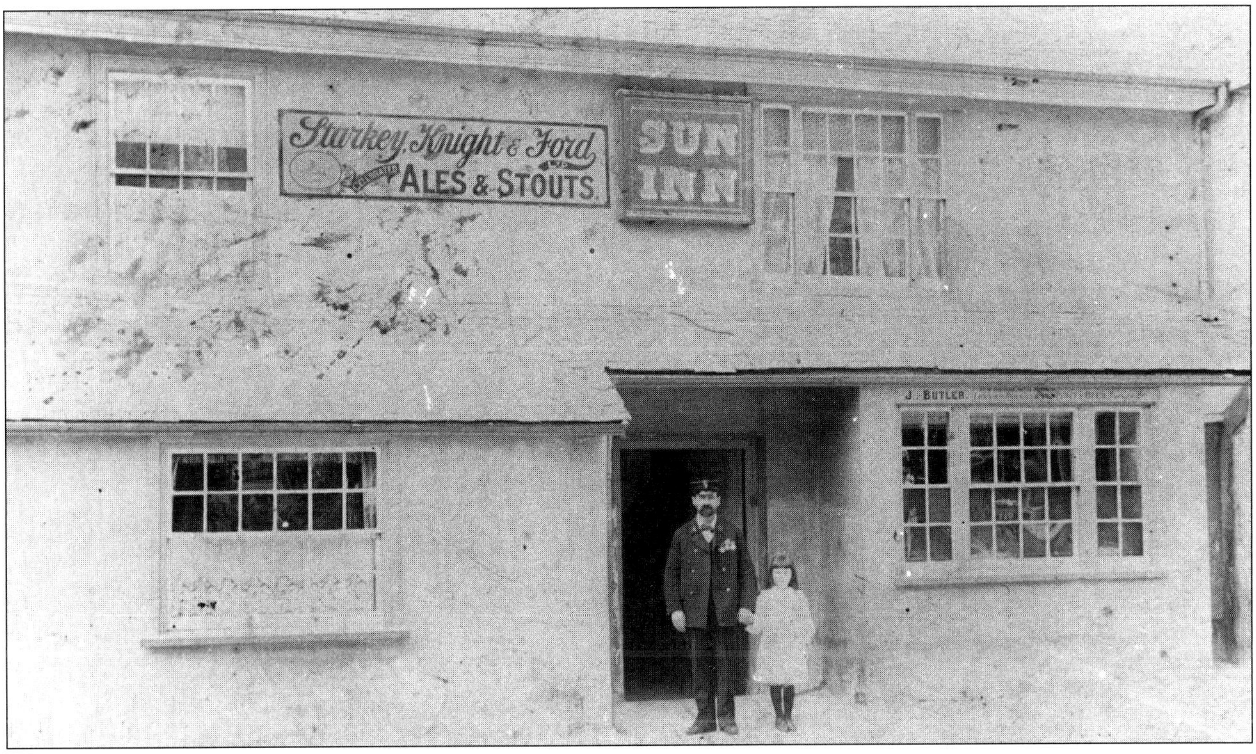

Mr Butler's Sun Inn in North Street, c.1900. John Butler is here pictured with one of his two daughters (Mabel or Minnie). They were very well known in the town and ran a shop on the site of the present Bishop's tearooms for many years, as well as running the Sunday school. (DARTINGTON RURAL ARCHIVE – STAN GILL'S COLLECTION)

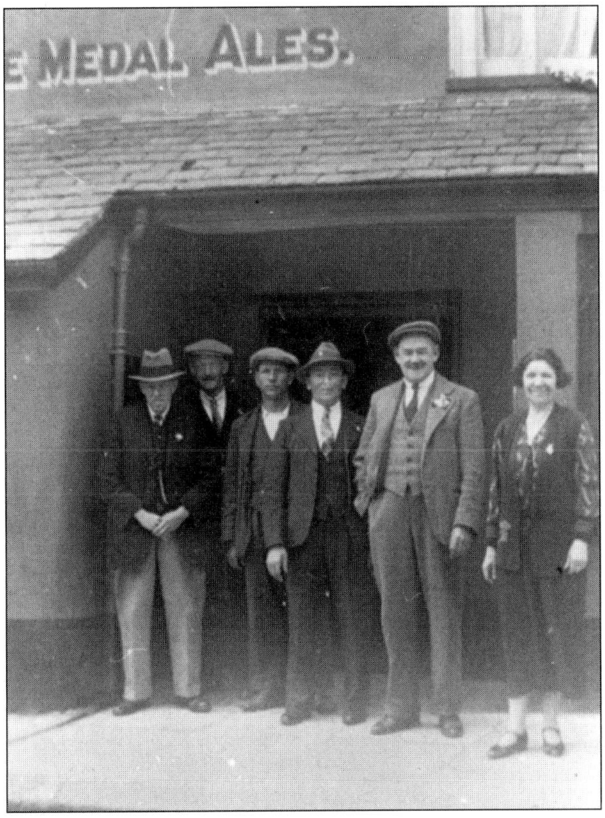

The Sun Inn in 1930. Left to right: *George Foot, Herbert Pengilly, Ern Knapman, Jack Worthington, Arthur Lakin (landlord) and Sarah Lakin (landlady).* (PETE WEBB COLLECTION)

making fine hats.

The **Silent Whistle** in St Lawrence Lane has had a succession of names. It started life as **The Old Bottle** and became the **Railway Hotel** when the railway arrived in 1872. A notable family here were the Joneses, parents of Amy, the town's first lady Portreeve and an MBE. A well-known regular was James French, who worked his thirsty trade as a blacksmith near the chapel. At the first stroke of eleven he would down tools, walk to the pub, down a pint of cider, put down his money and be back at his anvil by the time the clock had finished striking.

The railway station closed in 1962 and soon after the dual carriageway was built over the line in 1971 the pub was renamed the **Silent Whistle**. Jack and Phil Billing left in 1985 after 15 years and the then owners, Courage, closed the pub for over a year for a major revamp. It has had a succession of landlords since then and was briefly named the **Fleece and Firkin** before reverting to the Silent Whistle when Ushers took it over in 1994.

The **Sun Inn** in North Street was another of the town's Starkey, Knight and Ford houses. It seems to have been briefly called the **Swan** in 1879, the best-known landlord probably being John Butler. He took over from his father when he left the Navy in 1901 and was there for over 25 years. His two daughters, Mabel and Minny, who had a shop opposite until it was rebuilt in the 1970s, are also well remembered. The Sun Inn closed in 1936 to become the

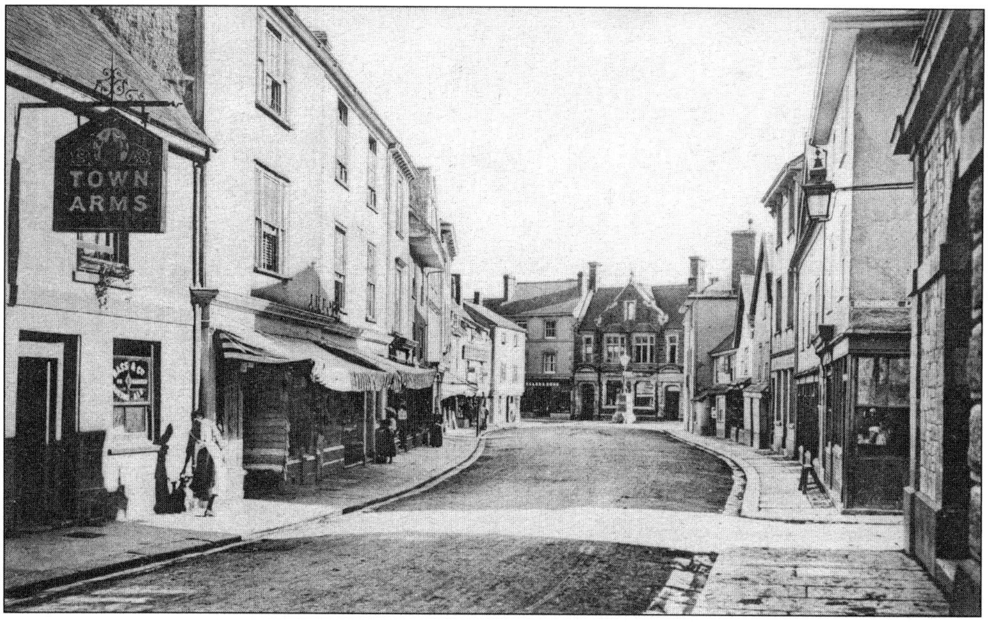

The Town Arms in North Street, c.1915 – Mr Dunstan was the landlord around this time. The pub, which had special permission to use the town's crest, closed in 1939 (along with the Golden Fleece). It is now the bookshop. (PETE WEBB COLLECTION)

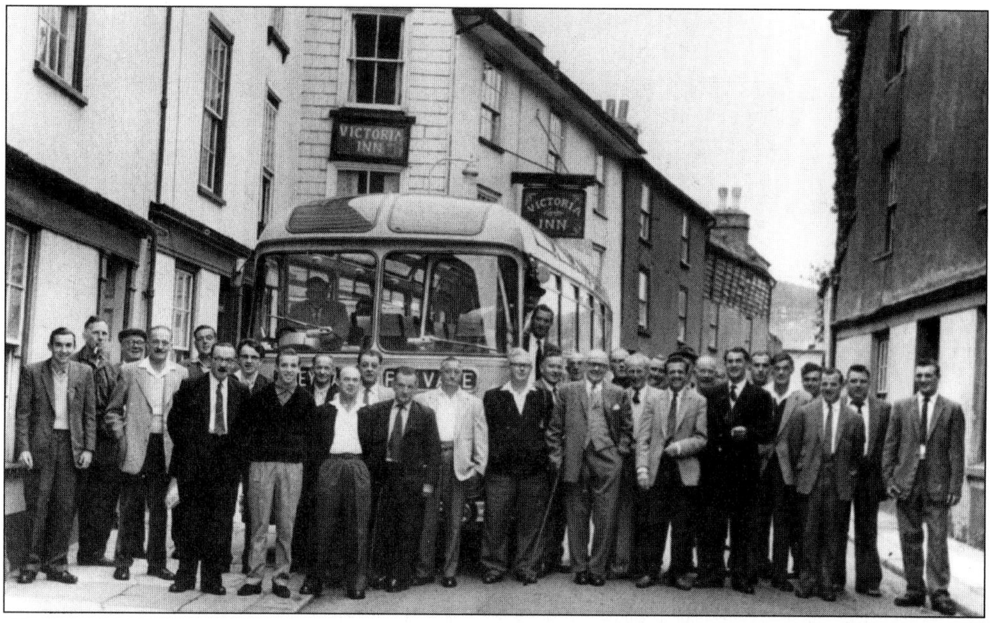

Victoria Inn coach outing, 1969. Some of the 30-odd regulars are well remembered and easily recognised. The inn can be seen behind the coach, and the buildings on the right have long since been demolished. This section of the road is now the small lay-by in front of the pub. (PETE WEBB COLLECTION)

Churchward family's Sun Stores. They also extended into the Rose and Crown when it closed in 1969.

The **Three Tuns** was listed briefly in the 1823 and 1830 trade directories as being in West Street.

The **Town Arms** was a well-known pub in North Street opposite the entrance to Kingsbridge Lane. It is listed in trade directory entries from 1823 to 1939 when it closed, along with the Golden Fleece and the Globe. At one time it opened early to serve cider to miners on their way to Owlacombe and had special permission to use the town crest. It is now a bookshop.

The **Two Sawyers** was lost with other buildings in the eighteenth-century fire, the only clue to its existence being a painting at The Wilderness, now on the site.

The **Victoria Inn** is also known as the **First and Last** and was originally a number of weavers' cottages. The 1851 census has one John Luscombe living there as an innkeeper and wheelwright but it does not appear in trade directories until 1870. John was still landlord then but Mrs Luscombe had taken over by 1878. The Victoria was acquired by Heavitree, along with the Red Lion, from Pinsetts Brewery.

CHAPTER 6

Schools

The earliest known school in Ashburton was what became the Grammar School.

Bishop Stapledon, in the early fourteenth century, granted his private chapel to the town of Ashburton – he had a home in the town. The condition of this grant was that prayers should be said for his soul – and for all those Bishops of Exeter who followed him.

For this purpose a chantry priest was appointed and the Guild of St Lawrence founded to administer the chapel. There is no evidence that a school existed at this early period. However, the teaching of the children was usually initiated by the local parish priest. Few records exist of the school from earlier centuries, just passing reference in church wardens' accounts, and these are mainly concerned with the paying of the priest of the chapel for services rendered to the parish church. In 1546 it was reported that the priest responsible for education received a salary of £6.66 (£6.13s.4d.).

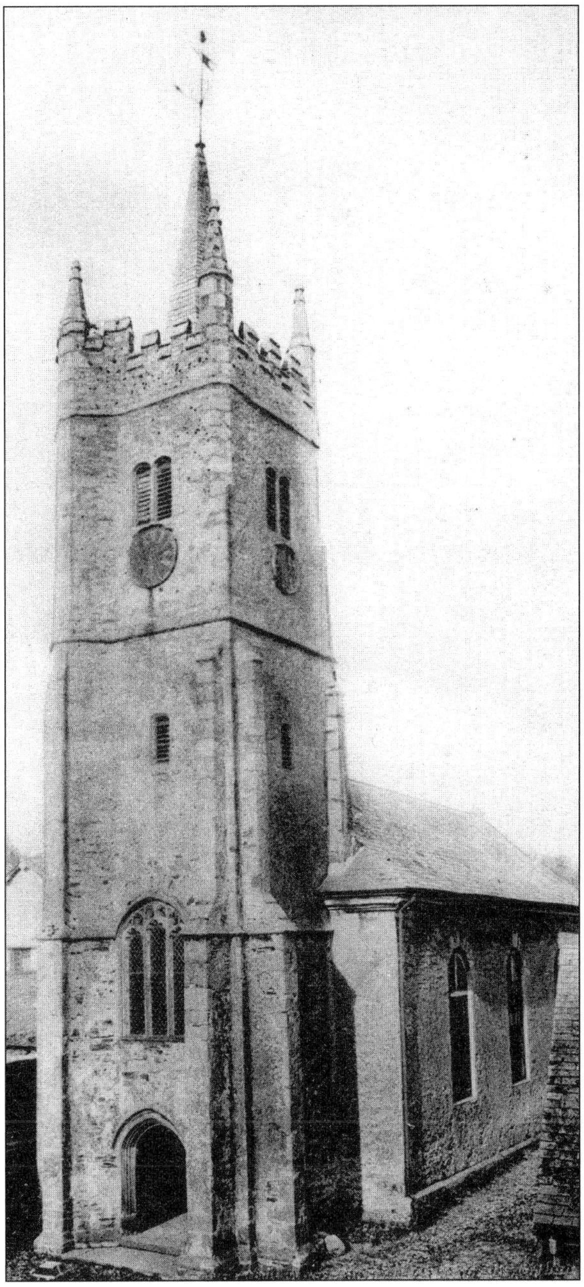

St Lawrence Chapel, Ashburton Grammar School.

At the time of the Reformation most chantry chapels were forfeited to the Crown, but as St Lawrence was by then a school it was saved from this fate. The records are not clear on this matter – some suggest that the school was forfeited to the Crown but purchased by local people so that it might continue. This was much to the benefit of the town, the names of those purchasing the chantry being Hugh Pomeroy, John Blundell, George Knowle and John Rewell. However, on 27 December 1594 ownership passed to John Caunter. These records mention that the school was supported by income from lands owned by the Guild. In 1596 the site was purchased by the parish. A parish rate of 1d. was levied to maintain the work.

Endowments were gradually made to ensure the continuance of the school.

It must be remembered that until Victorian times education for the masses was not considered. Any place which was fortunate enough to possess a 'grammar school', as schools of this type were called, were fortunate indeed.

Whilst prominence has been given to those ex-pupils who made a name for themselves in the world, the vast majority of pupils never hit the headlines but must still have added immeasurably to the intellectual wealth of the town.

It is, however, to the recollections of the great and the good that we must turn if we are to obtain a glimpse into life at the school over the centuries.

William Gifford was born in Ashburton (see p.86 for a brief biography). When young, William was more interested in learning than in work – he was an apprentice shoemaker. It is said he used to work out algebraic problems with his awl on the leather. The master did not take kindly to this. Eventually a subscription of £6 was raised among the townsfolk to enable him to attend the Grammar School where, with his background, he did

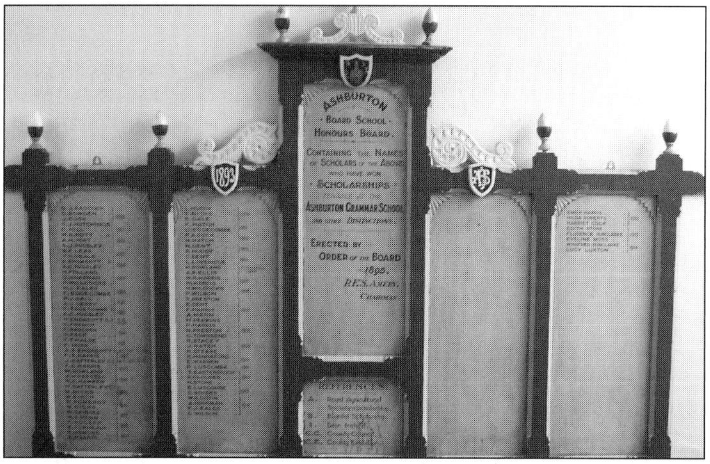

Ashburton Grammar School honours board (St Lawrence Chapel). (STUART HANDS)

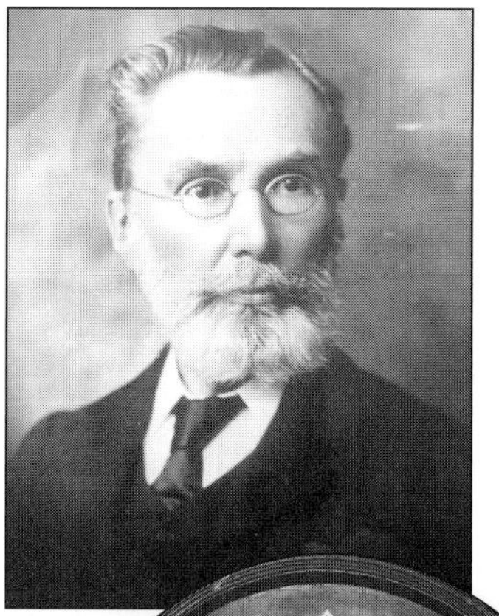

James Mortimore (ST LAWRENCE CHAPEL)

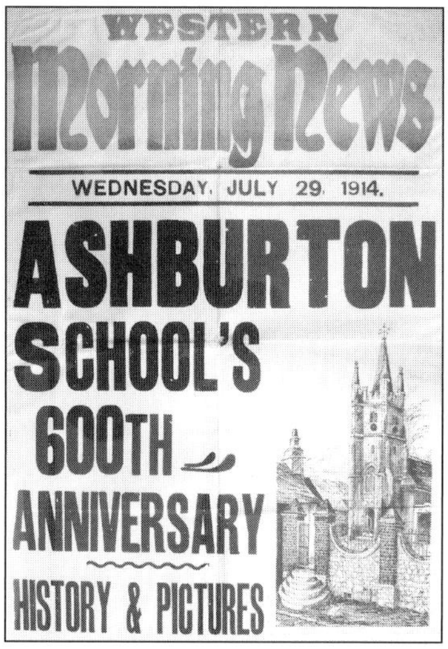

The Western Morning News *features the school's 600th Anniversary.* (ST LAWRENCE CHAPEL; STUART HANDS)

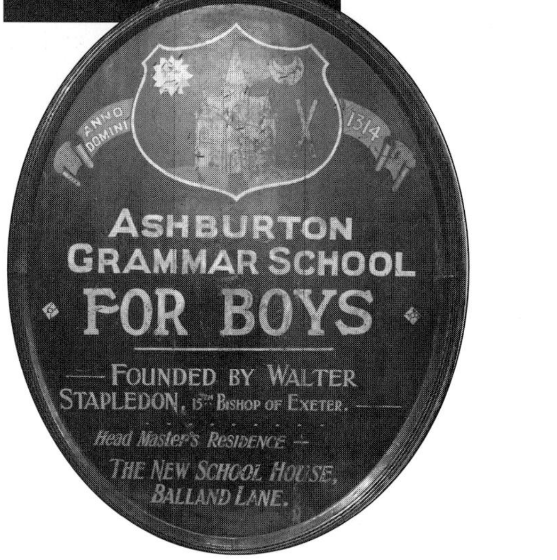

Ashburton Grammar School for Boys. The board, rescued when the school closed in 1938 after over 600 years, is now in the Stanley Gill Room of St Lawrence Chapel (on loan from Ashburton Museum). (STUART HANDS)

not easily fit in. He wrote a poem for his headmaster, Mr Furlong:

Though my name is cloudy,
Yet cast me not away,
For many a cloudy morning,
Brings forth a sunny day.

And so it proved to be. He writes:

After Holydays I returned to my darling pursuit – arithmetic; my progrees [sic] *was now so rapid that in a few months I was Head of the School, and qualified to assist my new master, Mr E. Furlong on any ordinary emergency.*

After two years he was able to go to Exeter College, Oxford. In 1798 he was appointed editor of the *Anti Jacobin* – the beginning of his work in journalism.

The irony of William's story is that a near contemporary of his at the school was Richard Carlile. Carlile also became a 'journalist', taking the diametrically opposed view to Gifford. Thus, in the turbulent time of the late-eighteenth and early-nineteenth centuries, two pupils from the Grammar School were at the cutting edge of the intellectual milieu of the day.

Ireland House was a boarding-house from 1845 to 1928, when the present secondary school main block was built.

A report of prize-giving day in the local paper of 24 July 1911 gives us a flavour of life at the school at that time.

Religious knowledge was high on the agenda. Mr Lamshead reported that for practical work they had well-equipped workshops and a garden. Boys went through a course of training in how to use tools, which stood them in good stead for life. The garden work helped in the understanding of botany. A prize was awarded to the pupil obtaining the best collection of plants. On this occasion it was awarded to F.W.S. Abbott.

Science was not neglected either. Dr Clayton Davies emphasised the value of a scientific training to any boy or girl. (In an example of forward thinking, in February 1914 girls were admitted to the school and in future, the report stated, ladies would be appointed to the board of governors.) The school did not aim to instil as many facts as possible into

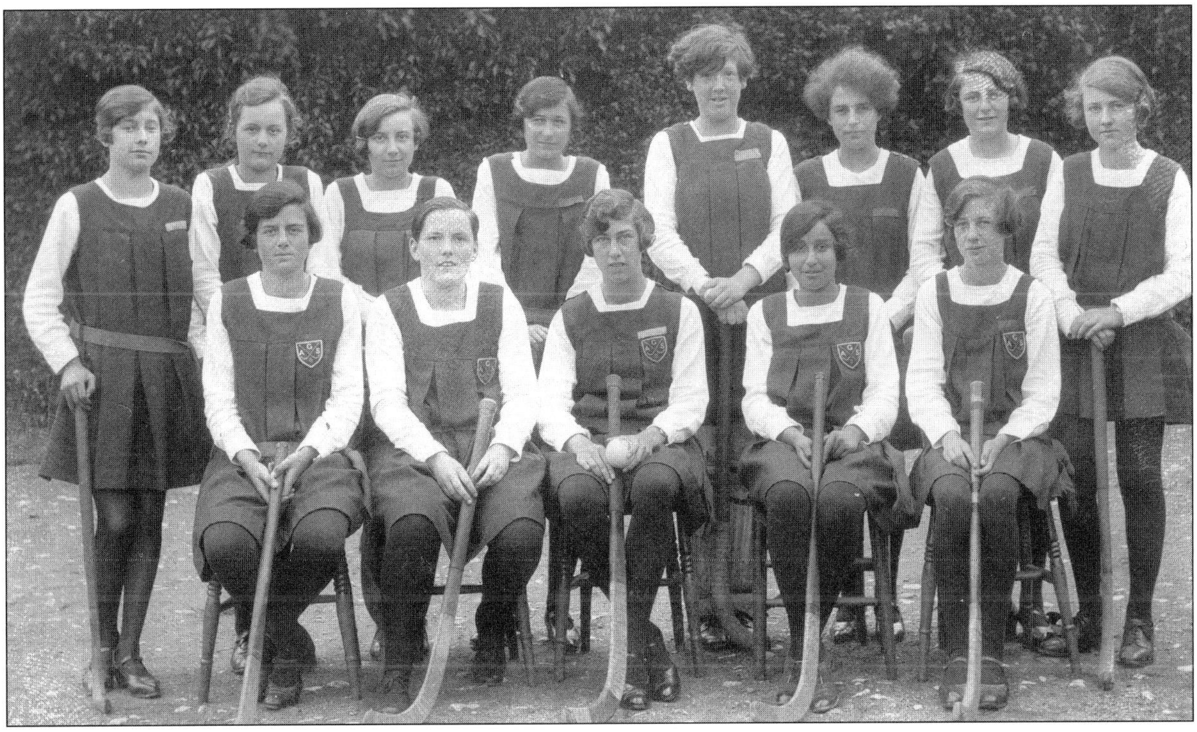

Ashburton School Hockey Team, 1927/28. Back row, left to right: *Ruth Penny, ?, ?, ?, Lorna Ayres, Ruth Prowse, Amy Oldrieve, Barbara Jones;* front: *Dorothy Rodick, Suzanne ?, Doris Head (head girl), Kathleen Banerjee, Dorothy Distin.*

(PETE WEBB COLLECTION)

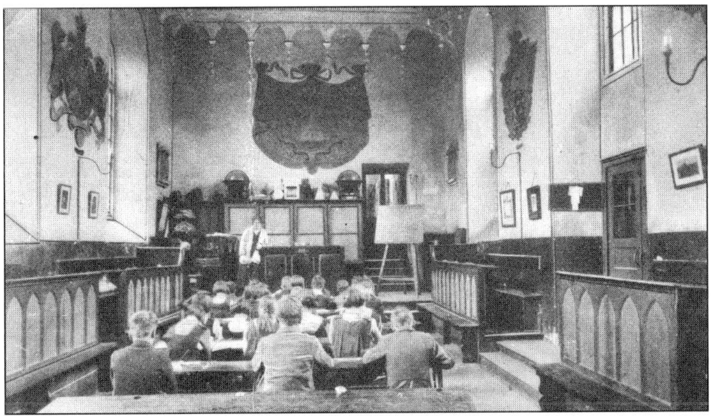

Left: *Ashburton Grammar School class in the main room of the chapel, c.1930.* (PETE WEBB COLLECTION)

Right: *Girls in Ashburton Grammar School gym (the old Baptist chapel), 1930s.* (PETE WEBB COLLECTION)

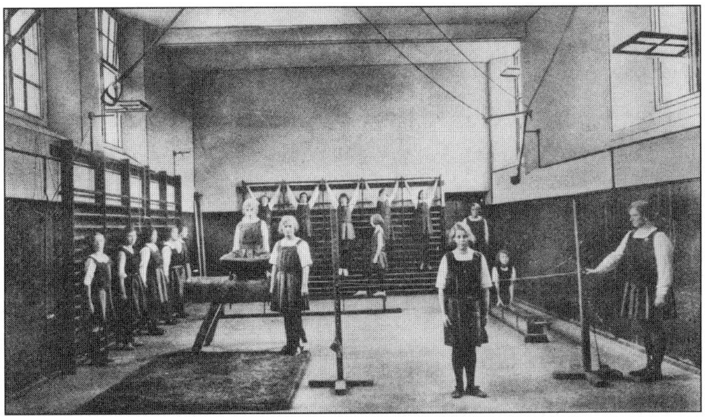

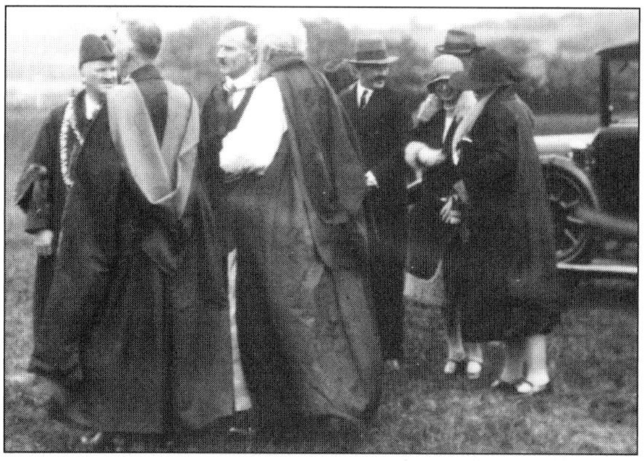

The opening of the Grammar School boarding-house, Balland Land, 1928. Photo includes: *Portreeve Robert Cubit, Jonathan Cock (Chairman of the Governors) and Lord Eustace Percy. This building is now part of South Dartmoor Community College.* (ST LAWRENCE CHAPEL)

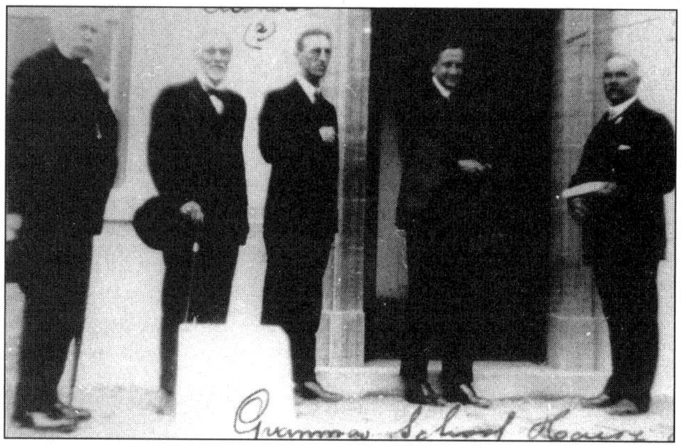

Grammar School, opening of new buildings, 1928. From left: *Mr Parker, C. Wallis (architect), ?, Lord Eustace Percy (MP), Jonathan Cock (Chairman of Governors).* (ASHBURTON MUSEUM)

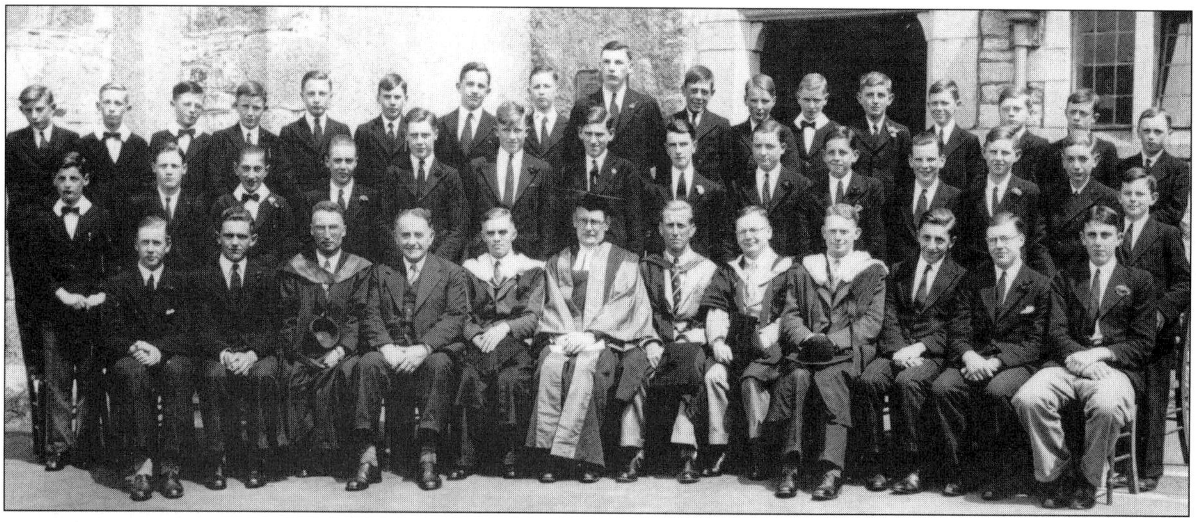

Ashburton Grammar School, 1930s. (GARTH GROSE)

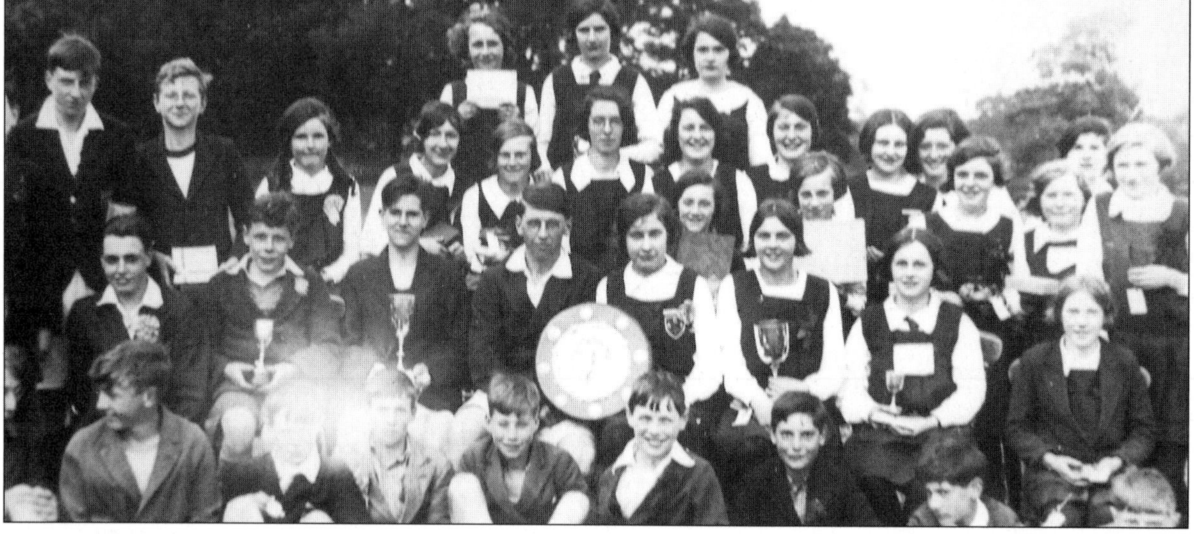

Ireland House, Ashburton Grammar School – winners of the sports trophy, 1928. (ST LAWRENCE CHAPEL)

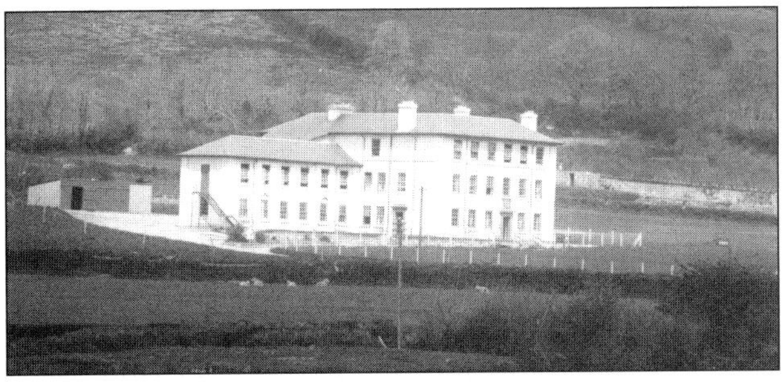

Ashburton Grammar School boarding-house, c.1930, newly constructed – now the main building of the South Dartmoor Community College (2004).

(PETE WEBB COLLECTION)

the children's minds but to lead them into correct habits of thinking and acting so that the greatest good might accrue not only to themselves but also to the community in which they found themselves placed. In sport, too, the school had done particularly well at cricket.

Sadly, as the twentieth century progressed, it became increasingly difficult to maintain the numbers attending the school, despite the provision of a new boarding-house opened in 1928. This building now forms part of South Dartmoor Community College. The situation was exacerbated by the opening of schools at Newton Abbot and Totnes. Although the press at the time reported that overcrowding existed in both schools, the County Council took the decision to close the Grammar School following an enquiry in 1937.

So ended a tradition of some six centuries of learning. Had the decision been delayed until the Butler Act of 1944 introduced universal secondary education, things might have been different; the County Council may have shelved the decision and Ashburton may still have had its Grammar School.

After the Grammar School closed in 1938 it was used by the County School until 1958, when the older children moved to Balland Lane. The Primary School continued to use it right up to the 1980s. It was also used as the town's library for over 40 years and for many other community purposes.

The second Guild of St Lawrence evolved in 1984 to protect and preserve this ancient building, which was in danger of collapse through neglect. Uncertainty over the then ownership (it is now owned by the Guild) did nothing to help. The Dartmoor National Park Authority (DNPA) stepped in and major renovation was carried out with

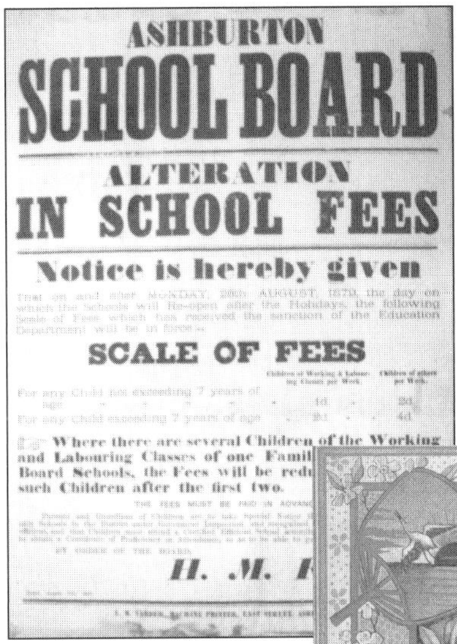

An 1879 notice of school fees alteration.

(ASHBURTON MUSEUM)

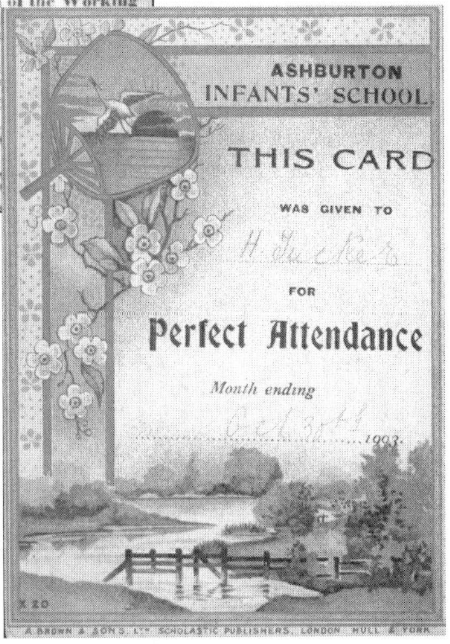

A card given to Master Tucker for perfect attendance at Ashburton Infants School in 1903.

(PETE WEBB COLLECTION)

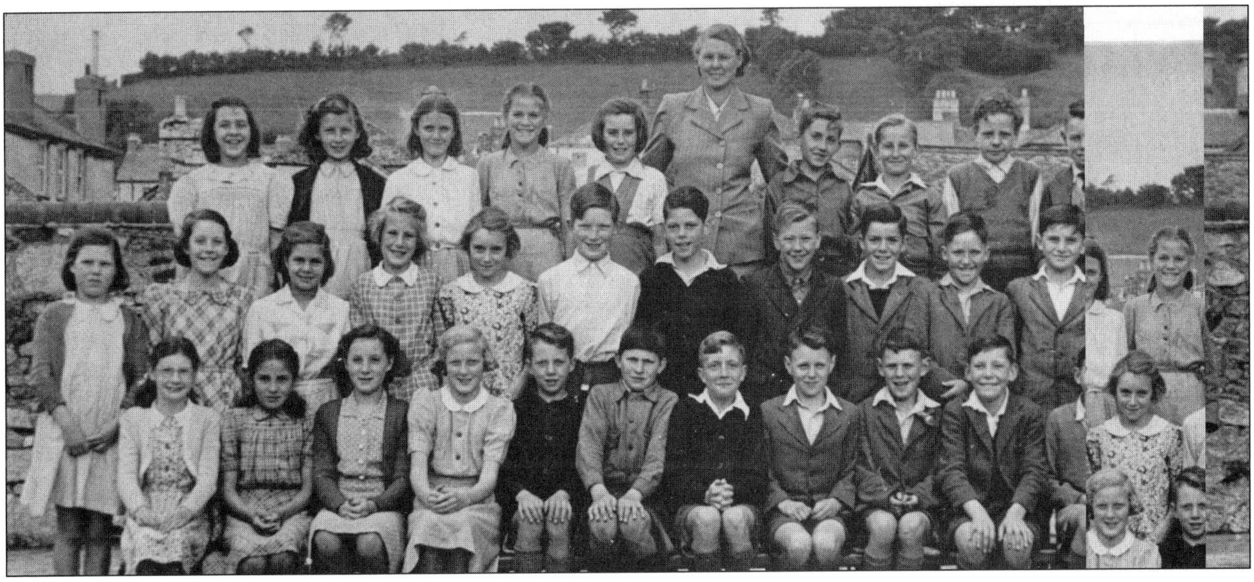

Council School pupils from the 1940s with teacher Miss Lucy Luxton.

(PETE WEBB COLLECTION)

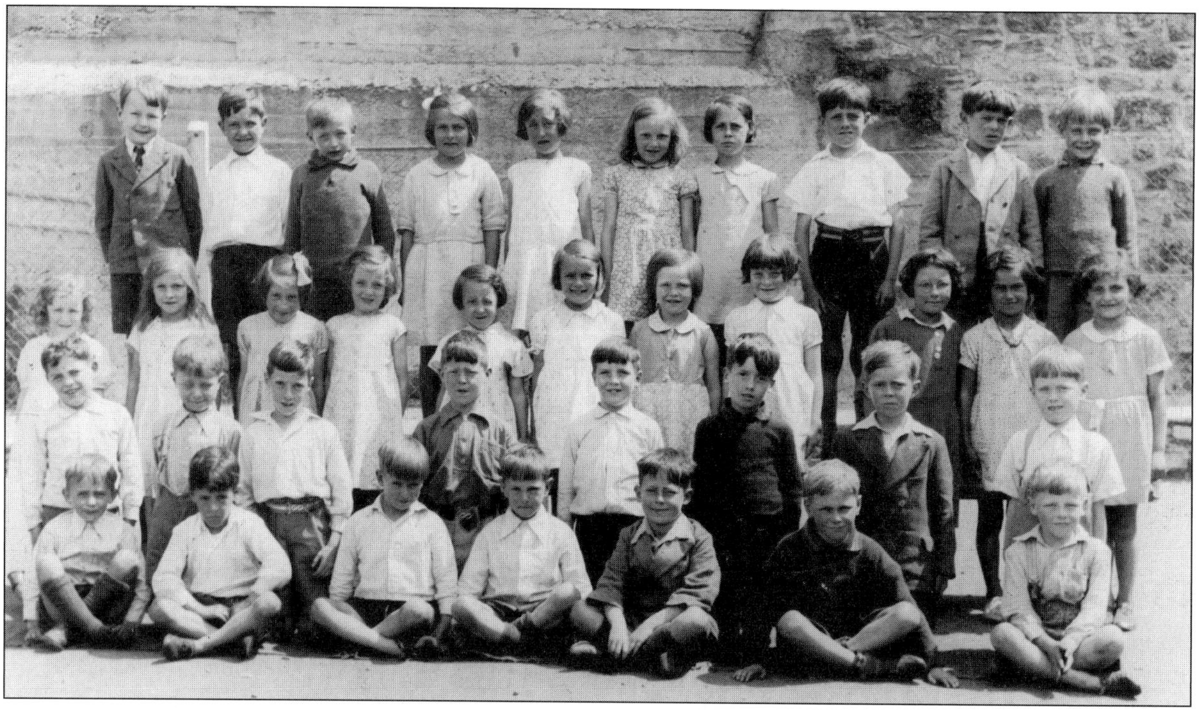

Ashburton Council School, 1936. Left to right, back row: *John Villas, Tom Guest, John Harvey, Mary Vooght, Pat Eales, ?, Dorothy Bray, Richard Elliot, Edgar Ellis, ?;* third row: *Betty Coaker, ?, Mary Baker, Doreen Brooks, Elsie Carpenter, May Bishop, Frances Davis, ?, Kathleen Lewis, Joan Palmer, Edith Langworthy;* second row: *Alfred Horton, ?, D. Cox, Roy Finch, Fred Barnet, ?, Jim Eales, J. Warren;* front: *N. Dennis, Garth Grose, John Desland, Ken Hext, Eddie King, Stanley Warren, David Ryall. Some teachers at the time were Miss Simpson, Miss Holwell, Mr Shepheard, Miss Blackler, Mr Matthews, Mr Bawden and Mr Evans (carpentry). The Headmaster was Mr Green.* (GARTH GROSE COLLECTION)

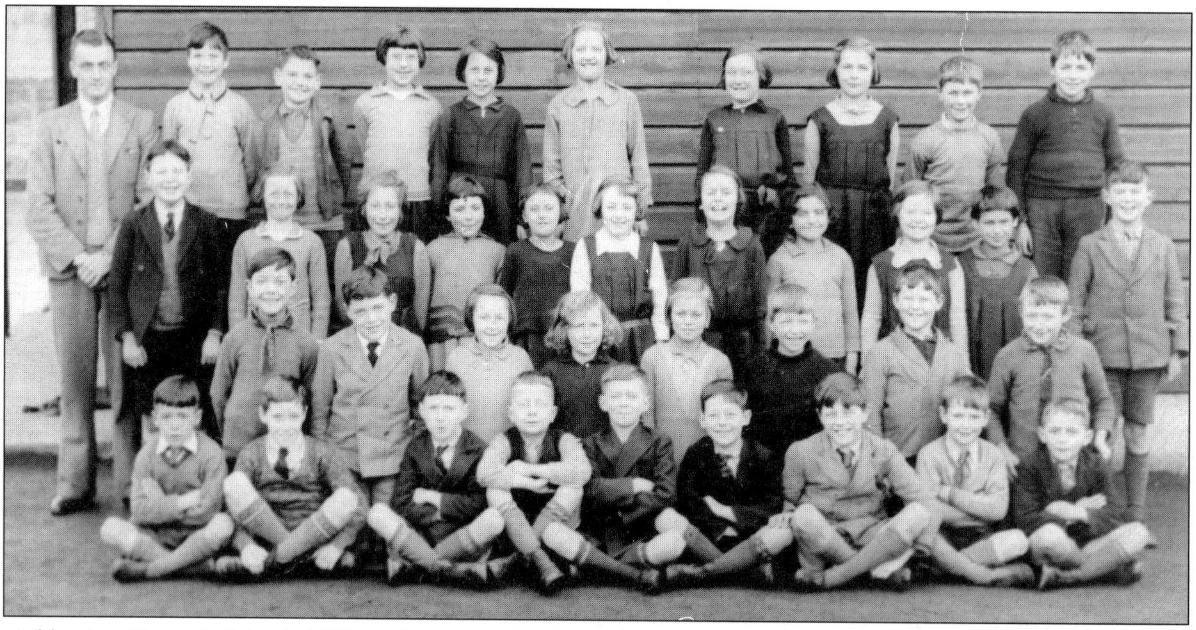

Ashburton Council School, 1937, and teacher Lloyd Matthews. Left to right, back row: *Fred Barnet, Victor Ham, Sylvia Smith, Dorothy Bray, Ida Pedrick, Pat Eales, Mary Vooght, Stanley Warren, Fred Wallace;* third row: *Bob Pascoe, Bertha Eales, Mary Baker, Kathleen Lewis, Alice Bartlett, Doreen Brooks, May Eales, Edith Langworthy, Frances Davis, Joan Palmer, Edgar Ellis;* second row: *Tom Guest, Alfred Horton, Elsie Carpenter, Betty Coaker, Joan Martin, Fred Webb, Roy Finch, John Harvey;* front: *Garth Grose, Douglas Cock, Michael Whiteway, Dennis Sargent, Jim Eales, Eddie King, Richard Elliot, John Desland, Norman Denn.*

(GARTH GROSE COLLECTION)

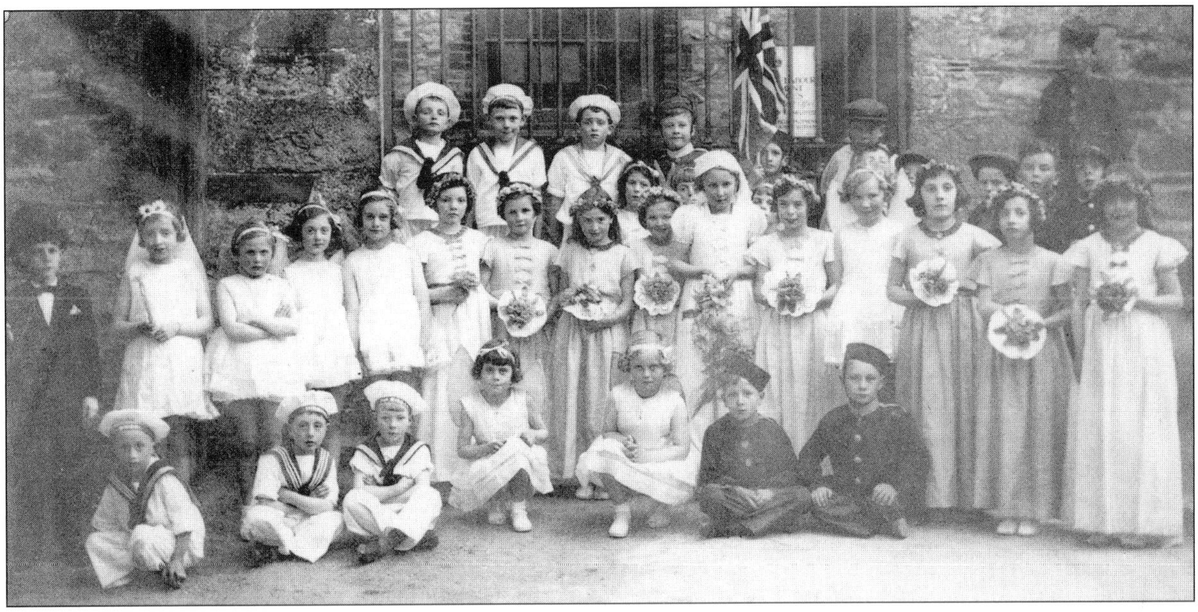

Ashburton Council School concert (c.1937 or '38), lent by Christine Dickens. Left to right, back row: *Ivor Powell, ?, Arthur Townsend, John Baker, Jim Guest, ?,?,?,?, Bernard Hooper, Bernard German (policeman);* centre: *? (top hat), Christine Lawrence (now Dickens), Louie Hearn, Betty Peck, ?, Kathleen Mann, Edna Papworth, Rosemary Beavis, Gwennie Bartlett (*behind Rosemary*), Josephine Davies, Barbara Binmore (bride), Mary Down, Hazel Warren (now in New Zealand), Doris Horton, Roma Knapman, Peggy Williams;* front: *Henry Brown, John Hext, Charlie Teague, ?, Doreen Pengelley, ? (possibly David Endacott), Phillip Goodall.*

(PETE WEBB COLLECTION)

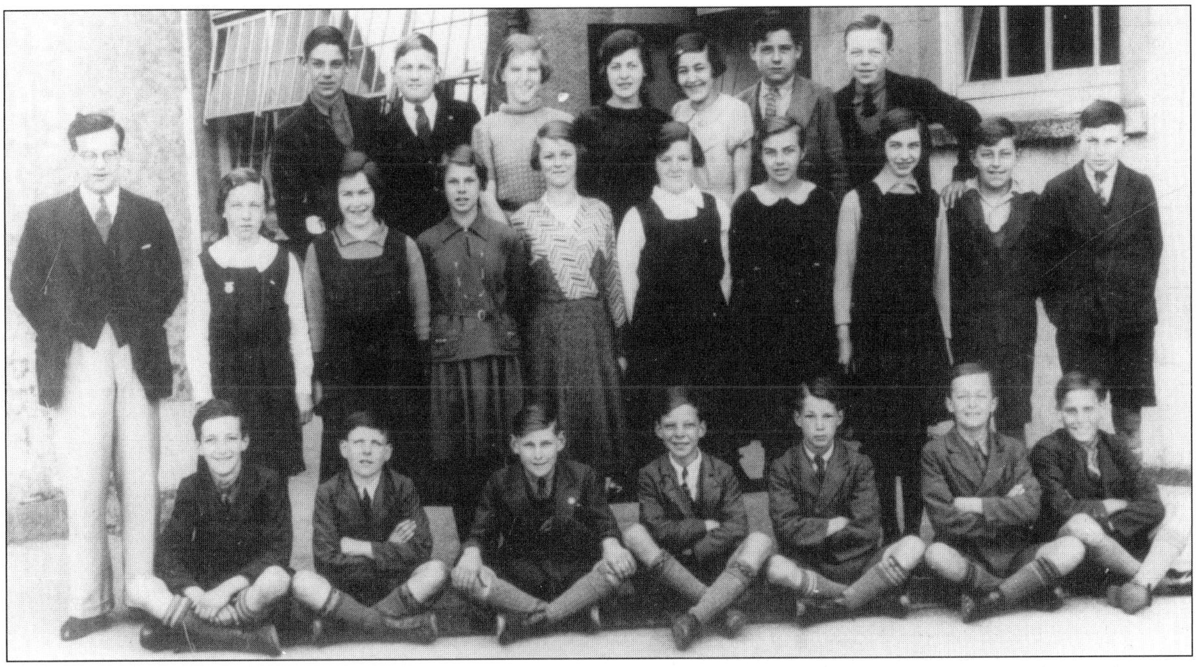

Ashburton County School, 1934/5. Left to right, back row: *Jim Easterbrook, Murray Bassett, Beryl Tall, Hilda Horton, Joan Parnell, Tom Eales, Alec Leaman;* centre: *Mr Evans, Eileen Boon, Jean Robertson, Stella Webber, Eileen Foot, Myrtle Endacott, Pearl Yolland, Edith Lang;* front: *Bill Hayman, Alf Goodwin, Alf Townsend, Stanley Birch, Ron Dennis, Gerald Beavis, Peter Wheeler.* (EILEEN EGBEARE COLLECTION)

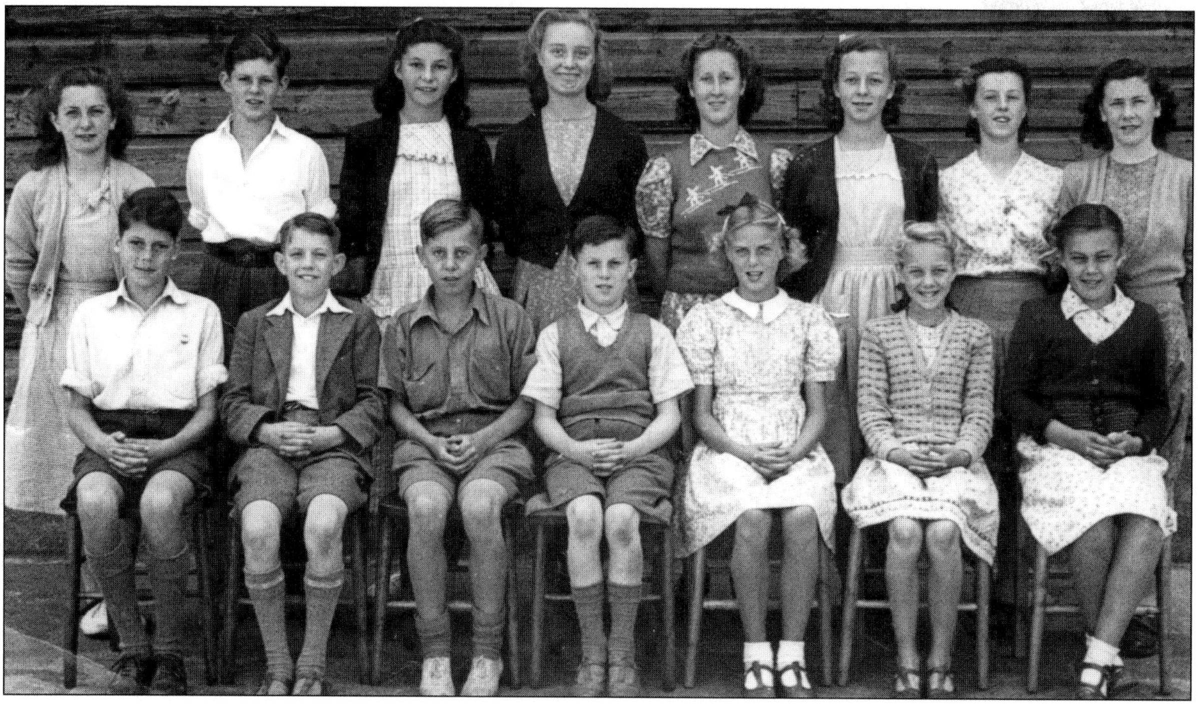

Ashburton school, 1948. Left to right, back row: *Josie (?) Townsend, Tommy Parker, Iris Waters, Daphne Peck, Marion Endacott, Gloria ?, Pauline Woodley, Betty Wellington;* front: *?, ?, Richard Schofield, David Woodley, Thelma Webber, Pat Webber, ?.* (WATERS COLLECTION)

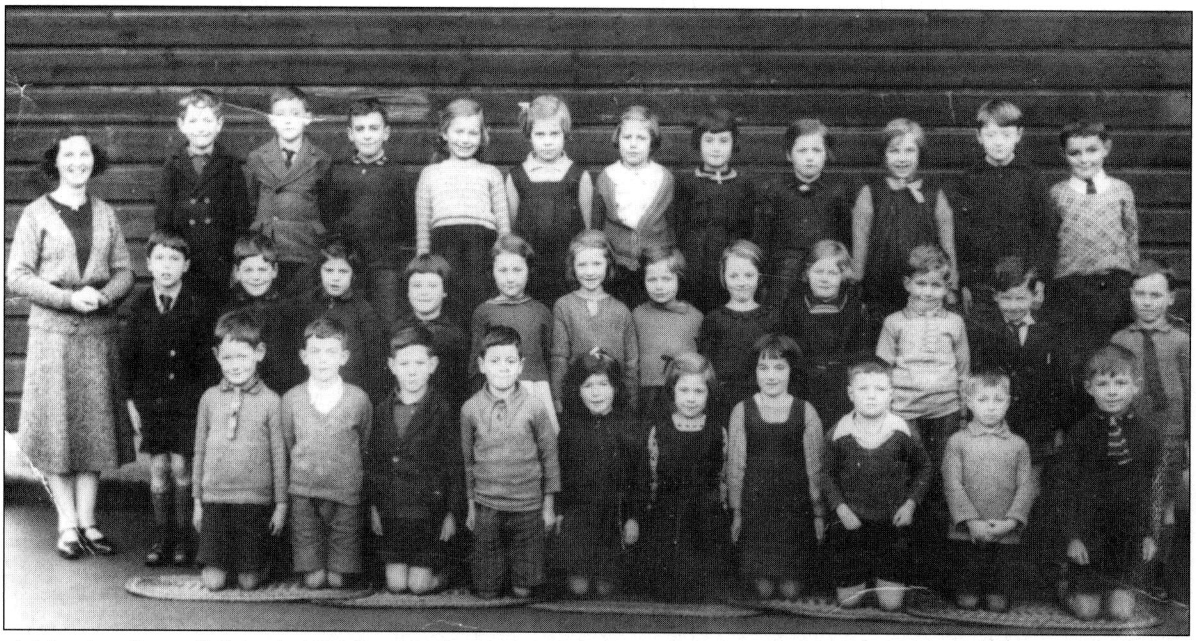

Ashburton Council School, 1938/9. Teacher, Miss Howell, with left to right, back row: *Charlie Yolland, Brian Germon, Terry Shorland, Margaret White, Edna Papworth, May Williams, Peggy Waters, Irene Wallace, Edith Webb, Tommy Easterbrook, Fernley Cock;* centre: *?, ?, Mary Germon, Beryl Brailey, Hazel Binmore, Ann Stevens, Joyce Lee, Jean Yeatman, Thelma ?, Gordon Wills, Desmond Grimes, Dennis Muggeridge;* front: *Billy Hext, Desmond Brinnicombe, Bill Yolland, John Lewis, Jean Davis, Betty Guest, ?, Carl Davis, ? Distin, Edgar ?.* (WATERS COLLECTION)

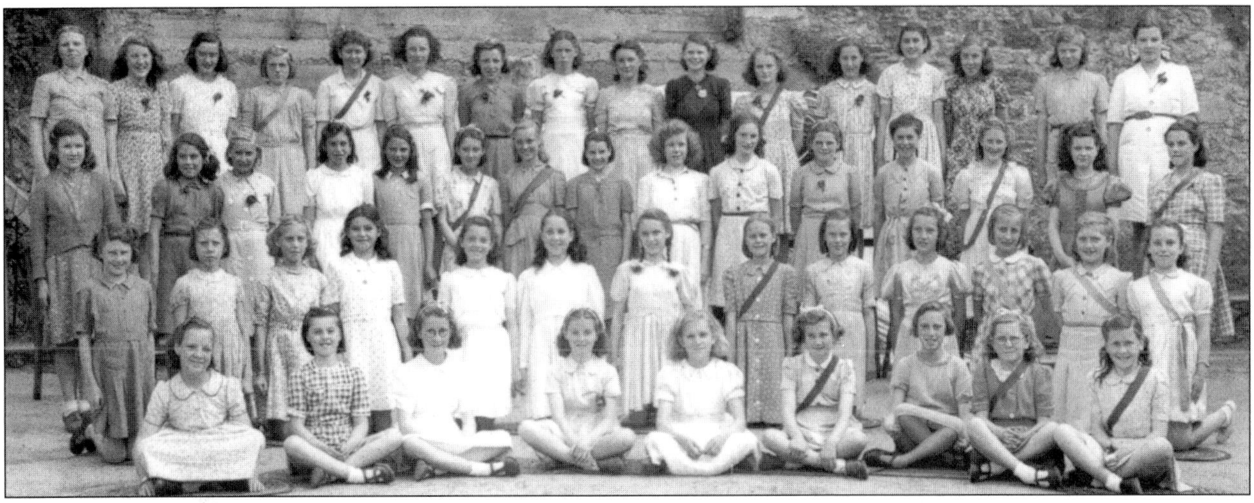

Ashburton School, 1943/44. Left to right, back row: *?, Dorothy Ellis, ?, Brenda Nosworthy, Margaret Hole, Margaret Bowen, Jean Curzon, ?, ?, Aubrey Beer, ?, ?, ?, ?, ?, Pauline Nichols;* third row: *?, ?, Joan Avery, Marion Routley, ?, ?, Daphne Peck, Carol Collins, June Horrell, Pat Tucker, ?, Jean Milton, ?, ?, Amy Lewis;* second row: *?, ?, Jean Eales, Iris Waters, Heather Smerdon, Martha Study, Margaret Ruth, Valerie Underhill, Agnes King, Sheila Poole, ?, ?, Sylvia King;* front: *Joyce Brailey, Pauline Woodley, Marion Endacott, May Whiddon, Marion Salter, Winnie Brailey, Mary Bartlet, Josie Townsend, Betty Wellington.*

English Heritage help from 1986. It is now a visitor centre and community letting rooms owned and run by the Guild of St Lawrence.

Bourne School/Board School

The next oldest school was the Bourne School, near the site of the present Primary School and funded by an 81-acre farm of the same name near Bickington. This was purchased for the sum of £500 given by two of Ashburton's MPs, Lord Middleton and John Harris, in 1754. Money was provided from the rent to teach Dr Bell's system to about 50 scholars in a free school. It was further supported by Mary Dunning, who left land in Staverton in 1805 for the teaching of ten poor girls. Buildings were erected around 1831 and William Honeywill was the master in 1850. In 1866 Samuel Husson was the master with Miss Mary Baker assisting and Miss Elizabeth Baker the infants' mistress. Husson was still there through the 1870s (later with his wife). In 1870 the infants moved to North Street under the guidance of Miss Ford and Miss French and later, in 1873, Misses Foote and Wotton. By the 1880s a school board had started which controlled both the Grammar School and the Bourne free school. It was later taken over and by 1883 was called the Board School, with 100 boys, 90 girls and 70 infants. Samuel Husson was still the master, with Miss Ellen Easterbrook teaching the girls and Miss Elizabeth Geaton the infants. In 1893 there was an average attendance of 123 boys, 109 girls and 102 infants. By this time Mr William

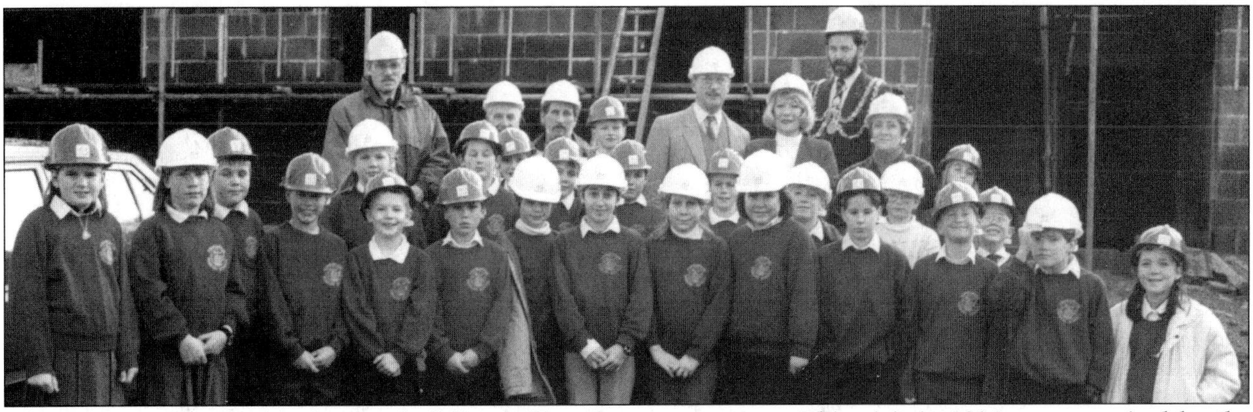

The Primary School with the new building still under construction. This visit in 1994 was organised by the contractors and coincided with the placing of the time capsule behind the school name. Portreeve Pete Webb and Bailiff Revd John Brown attended. Left to right, back row: *Keith Wills, Bailiff Revd John Brown, Foreman from Carkeek (builders), ?, Graham Gordon (headmaster), ?, Portreeve Pete Webb, ? (school secretary);* centre: *?, Mark Barber, ?, ?, Ashley (Joan Norwell's grandson), ?, ?, ?, Victoria Diamon, April Burt, Geoffrey Hicks;* front: *?, Sarah Bagnell, Ben Gardner, Clint Teague, Rob McNicol, ?, Holly Houlston, ?, Lindsey Cackett, ? Packham, Emily Veevers, Carl Oakenfold, Chris Lambell, Mark Lockward-Lee, Sarah Guest.* (JOHN MITCHELL)

Butchers was master, with Miss Ellen Easterbrook assisting and Miss Amy Hext teaching the infants and the school was supported by Devon County Council. By 1906 it was called the Elementary School, had been enlarged and had a growing average attendance. Amy was now Mrs Amy Butchers and by 1914 there was a Blundell scholarship attached to the school enabling a bright pupil to move to the Grammar School. In 1924 and 1925 further renovations and alterations were made costing £1,500. Average attendance continued to grow and at one time nearly 500 pupils attended, from infants to 14 and 15-year-olds. By the time the older children moved to 'the big school' in 1958, the age of leaving compulsory education had increased.

Ashburton Primary School, Whistley Hill

The original Primary School building was built in 1879 as the Elementary School. The school also used the site of the Grammar School when it closed in 1938 (St Lawrence Chapel was built in the fourteenth century and the side rooms were added in 1911, although the centre block of buildings was built during the Victorian era). Today pupils number about 215 boys and girls, aged from 5–11 years.

The Secondary School moved to the former boarding-house of the Grammar School in Balland Lane in 1958. The change from an all-age elementary school to a County Primary School took place under Mr C.J. Bawden, who was the original headmaster. Ken Watson came to the school as head in 1962 and

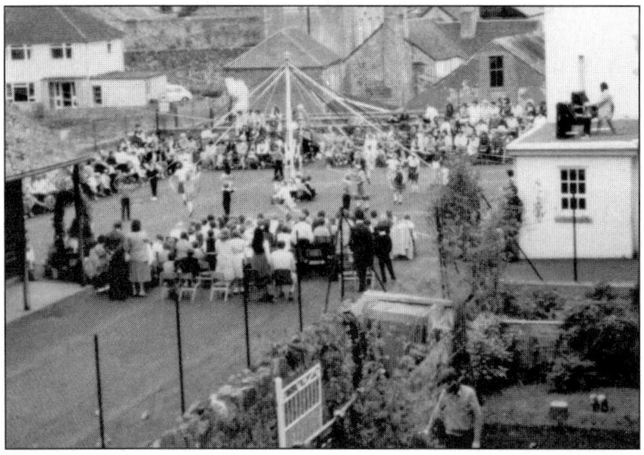

Maypole dancing at Ashburton Primary School in 1983. (PETE WEBB)

was there until 1971 (with a gap from 1966–7 when he was in Nigeria). He took up a post in South East Asia after leaving. He remembers that there were approximately 400 pupils with class sizes of around 40–45. There was a dedicated staff and discipline was quiet but effective. The school welfare system during this period worked well and helped problem pupils both in and out of school. School meals were cooked in the canteen on the St Lawrence site with an efficient ancillary staff ensuring first-class supervision and nutritious meals. Parental support was strong and the selection procedure (the 11-plus) was a significant part of school life.

He remembers a close working relationship with the Secondary School as well as co-operation with the Anglican, Methodist and Congregational churches. He also received a letter from Devon County Council about the future development and improvement of the buildings.

Major building works were eventually carried out in the mid-1990s at a cost of £1.3 million and the school ceased using the Grammar School site when the new classrooms were opened on the main site in Love Lane.

Other heads were Mr Norman Waterman (1971–1983) and Miss Marion Attrill (1984–1993). Miss Attrill, the first female head teacher the school had ever had, did most of the preparatory work for the reorganisation of the school on one site. Mr Graham Gordon was next and was there when the new school buildings opened. Mrs Ros Cooke came in whilst Mr Gordon was on sick-leave. She later became head teacher and is still there.

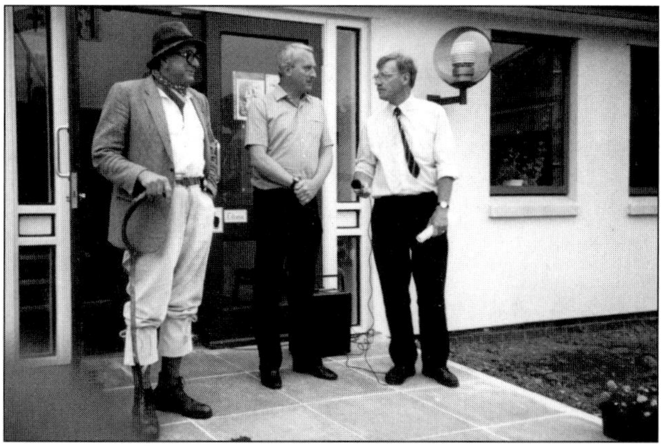

Primary school opening with Tony Beard, Graham Gordon and Mr Wills, 1995. (JOHN MITCHELL; PETE WEBB COLLECTION)

Greylands/Sands School

This stands half way down East Street on the east side. The school was founded in September 1930 as the Ashburton High School for Girls on the closure of the girls' side of the Grammar School. It had accommodation for 100 girls and five classrooms. Miss Thompson was headmistress in 1933 and 1935. By 1939 Miss Bowler and Mrs Wilson were the teachers. The school seems to have used Ireland House for a time with the Wilderness School as spare classrooms and a museum.

It was used as a summer language school by the nuns who ran it and a young German man called Klaus Hinst used to attend. He enjoyed his time there and used to tell the owners that if they ever wanted to sell, to let him know – and in the 1970s he

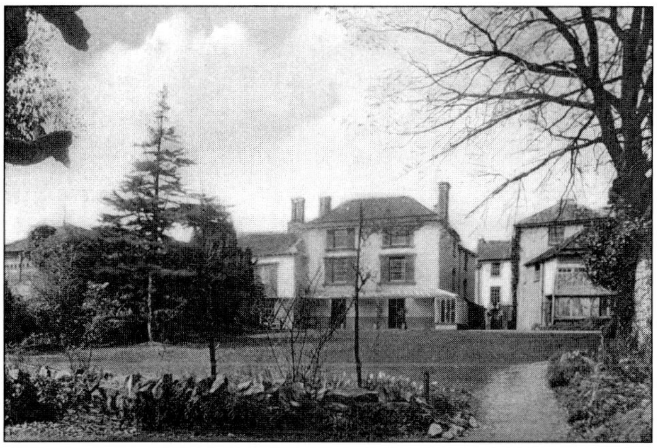

Greylands School, mid-1930s. (PETE WEBB COLLECTION)

bought it. It was used as a language school, called Greylands, with a playgroup in some of the rooms. It was also used by the Rudolf Steiner School from 1979 to 1981 until they moved to Sandwell Manor near Totnes and then to their present site, Hood Manor on the Buckfast to Totnes Road. In 1987 the Sands School started and was still there at the time of writing.

Wilderness School

This school was founded in 1933 on East Street near the War Memorial, as a boys' school and a breakaway from the Grammar School, under Henry Naylor. By 1939 it had been renamed Ashburton College for Boys. It later closed, although the exact date is not known.

Ashburton County School/Ashburton and Buckfastleigh County Secondary School/Ashburton School/ South Dartmoor School/South Dartmoor Community College

Ashburton and Buckfastleigh County Secondary School opened in 1958 on the site of the Ashburton Grammar School boarding-house. Built and opened in 1928 to provide improved accommodation for the Grammar School, which had been in St Lawrence Chapel for over 600 years, it was only used for ten years before the Grammar School closed. The main block was then used for a number of years as a remand home. In the 1950s it was decided to separate the County School on what is now the Primary School site and provide secondary education in this part of rural Devon. The catchment area was huge and covered most of South Dartmoor as well as the surrounding villages, along with Ashburton, Buckfastleigh, Holne, Widecombe, Moretonhampstead, Bovey Tracey, Liverton, Bickington, Woodland, Broadhempston and all points in between.

Mr Joe Reayer was headmaster here from 1958 until 1977. He inherited a 30-year-old main block with brand new classrooms and hall behind. He remembers the Ten Tors as always having been a great part of the school's activities; it first took part in 1960 and has continued to do so every year. Ten Tors was originally set up as a training exercise for the Junior Leaders regiment. Major John Joyner, who is well remembered by most people in Ashburton, was part of this development.

The year 1975 saw the start of a five-year comprehensive reorganisation programme and in April 1977 Mr Reayer left to be replaced by Mr Roger Burton in September of that year. Mr Burton remembers snow in February 1978 and the marks left by bulldozers from Glendinnings on the school drive.

Mr Burton left in April 1985 to be followed by Mrs Maureen Green. The name was changed soon afterwards from Ashburton School to South Dartmoor School. Mrs Green left in 1990 and was followed by Mr Ray Tarleton.

The Ashmoor Centre was built in 1992 giving a dual-use school and community sports centre which includes a fitness studio. Sixth-Form status was granted in 1992 and in 1994 the Sixth Form Centre was opened in Place House, a nearby eighteenth-century listed building. Owned by the local quarry, Glendinnings, it has been let for a nominal rent to the college on a 30-year lease.

Memorable in 1995 were both a new science block and the school's attempt to opt out, leave local authority control and become a grant-maintained school. After a parental ballot it stayed with the local authority. The college gained sports college status soon afterwards and is a recent winner of the Youth Sport Trust Innovation Award for Sports Colleges.

South Dartmoor Community College is an 11–18, co-educational comprehensive school, serving a wide rural catchment area of over 310 square miles of the south-eastern corner of the Dartmoor National Park. It includes the country towns of Ashburton, Bovey Tracey, Buckfastleigh and Moretonhampstead and many villages: Widecombe-in-the-Moor, Buckland-in-the-Moor, Liverton, Ilsington, Heathfield, Woodland, Scorriton, Manaton and North Bovey.

In 2000 and 2001 a new performing arts block with a dance studio, two drama studios, two music rooms with eight practice rooms, a recording studio and a general-purpose expressive arts room were built, while 2002 saw further improvements with new PE changing rooms, a new car park opposite the Sixth Form centre and another car park adjacent to the sports hall. The college reception area was extended to create meeting areas, improved office facilities and interview rooms.

A new three-storey classroom block containing English and mathematics rooms, a fourth ICT suite plus a huge new library and careers library were built in 2003. Classrooms in the original 1958 main block have been fully refurbished to provide teaching suites for geography and history. There are now some 110 teaching staff and 1,650 students at the

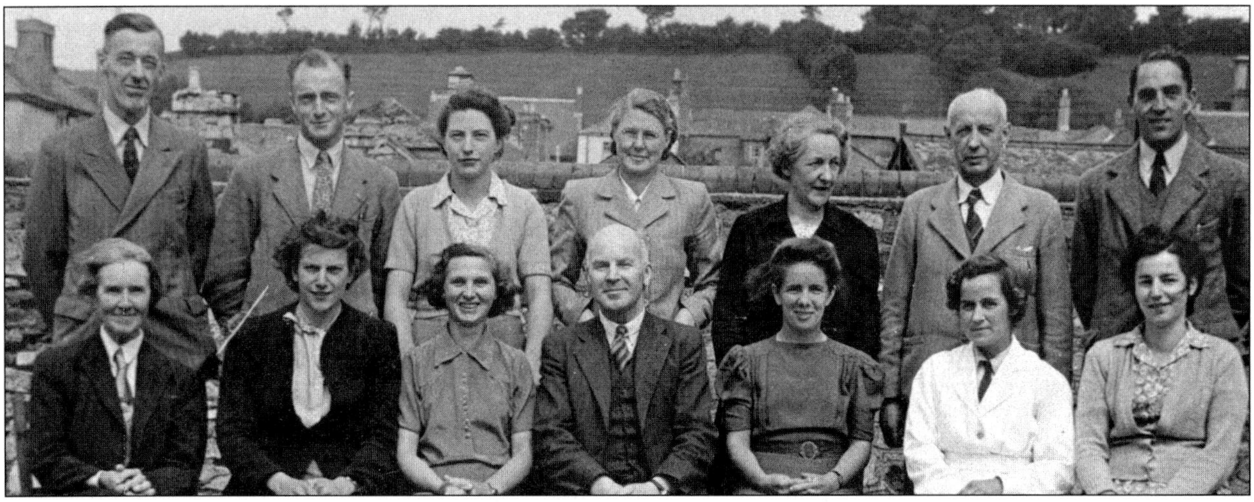

County School teachers, c.1945. Left to right, back row: *Mr Scragg, Lloyd Matthews, ?, Miss Lucy Luxton, Mrs Thorn, ?, Mr Shepherd;* front: *Miss Simpson, ?, Miss Holwell, Mr Bawden (head master), Mrs Blackler, ?, ?.*

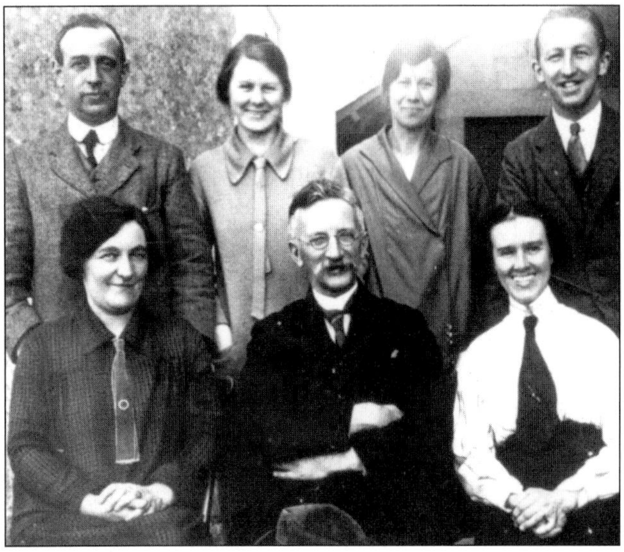

college, of whom over 250 are in the Sixth Form.

Other Schools

In 1823 and 1830 there were four academies apart from the Grammar School: J. Hannafords and William Honeywill, both specialising in mathematics, in East Street, John Herring with a boarding school in East Street and another mathematics academy with John Lopas in North Street. In the 1850s the Revd Dore, a Baptist minister, ran a classical school in East Street.

Left: *Teachers at Grammar School (pre 1938 closure).* Left to right, back row: *Mr Shepherd, Miss Luxton, Miss Hall (Tucker), Mr Colridge;* front: *Mrs Thorne, Mr Butcher (headmaster) and Miss Simpson.*

✥ CHAPTER 7 ✥

Utilities

Police

Up until the late-nineteenth century, the Court Leet and Baron Jury elected two and later four constables with powers to carry out such tasks as might be carried out by a modern police force. Their truncheons were originally their badge of office rather than a weapon. They were elected each year at Court and Law Day and were unpaid and unpopular, with no choice in the matter. The old lock-up was originally on Bowden Hill. Soon after the formation of the Devon Constabulary in 1856, the police station probably moved to Stapledon Lane. A police sergeant first appeared in trade directories in Stapledon Lane (or Back Lane as it was then known) in 1873. James Hobbs was the sergeant in the 1870s, followed by Abraham Knott (with one constable) around 1883 to 1893. A new police station was built around 1900 in St Lawrence Lane, which was sometimes called Station Road, with William Prew as sergeant with one constable. Later sergeants were Frederick Boughton (1910), William Frederick Luxton (1914, 1919), George Stabb (1923) and William George Hall (1926). They all appeared in trade directories with one constable.

Sergeant John Wills was based here from 1934 until 1941. Sadly he died, as a result of being caught in the blast from an unexploded device found on Dartmoor. His daughter, Joyce Coon, to whom we are grateful for the loan of his picture, remembers living in the police sergeant's house attached to the station. He was made a sergeant and moved to Bantham but Mrs Wills didn't like it there so they transferred to Ashburton. Sergeant Wills was well-known and highly respected and knew all the town's

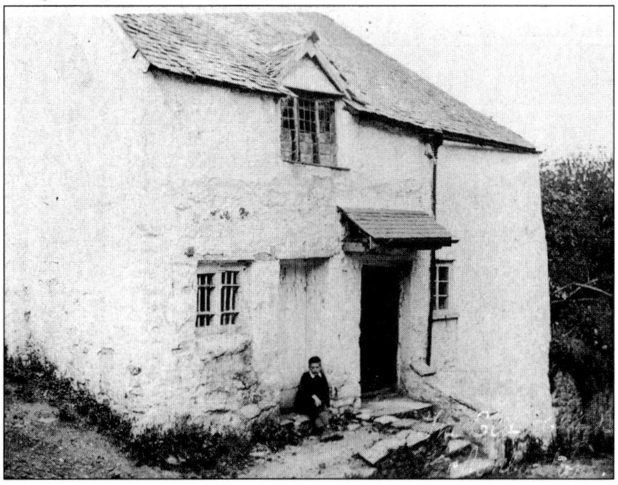

Above: *The Old Clink on Bowden Hill – from a postcard by Amy Hannaford from an earlier (Victorian) picture. It was used as the lock-up for the Court Leet constables before there was a police presence in town.* (PETE WEBB COLLECTION)

Below: *The semi-detached cottages built on the site of the Old Clink, 2001.* (PETE WEBB)

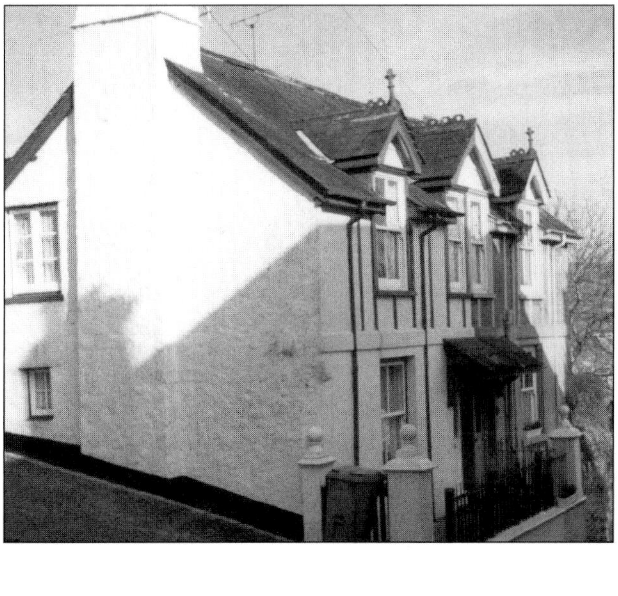

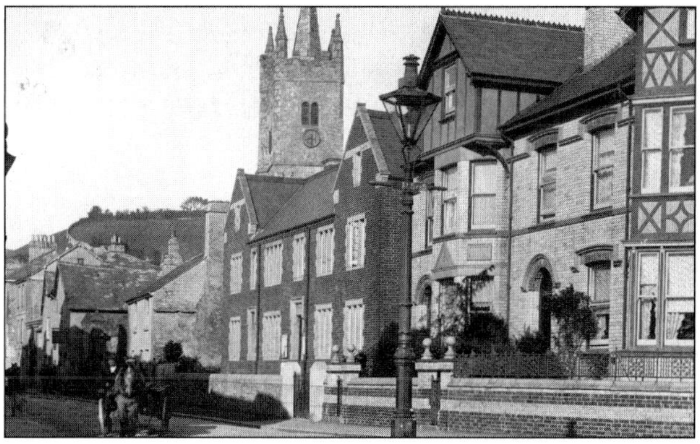

Above: *Ashburton police station in St Lawrence Lane, c.1915.* (PETE WEBB COLLECTION)

Below: *Sergeant Wills, 1938.* (JOYCE COON COLLECTION)

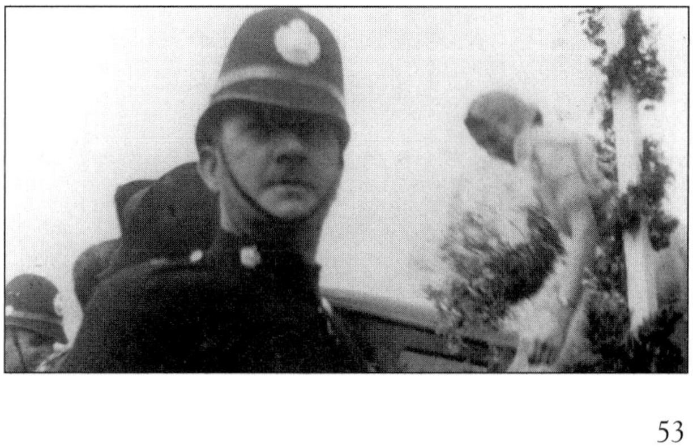

inhabitants. The Wills family lived at the police house in St Lawrence Lane. Other wartime serving police officers included Sergeant Mallet and Constables F. Beavers, Hawkins, Manley, H. Mugridge, Pope, Rice, Sedgemoor, F. Wearing and V. White. The police station moved in 1965 (as did other small stations at Buckfastleigh, Holne, Buckland and Bickington) to its present building in Eastern Road. All these parishes previously had a police house, where the constable would live within the area he worked. This was the same period that the Devon Constabulary amalgamated with the Cornwall force to become the Devon and Cornwall Constabulary of today. In the late 1990s the living accommodation at the present police station was turned into additional offices.

Ashburton Fire Brigade

Established in 1750, Ashburton is widely held to be the third oldest brigade in Britain. Originally a volunteer brigade and even today a retained force, Ashburton, up to the turn of century and beyond, had a horse-drawn pump. In those days, if a building was not insured by the company that employed them the firemen did not put out the fire.

In April 1885 a fire was reported in the congregational chapel schoolroom which was insured with Sun Fire Office. There was no mention of the firemen in the report, but Ashburton, like other small towns, ran a public brigade.

Exeter set up its first municipal brigade in March 1888 and Plymouth in 1891.

There were various fires reported and by November 1889 Captain Tucker was in charge. In 1891 he was mentioned, along with Messrs Clymo, Soper, Distin, Reddaway, Lear and Preston, all firemen at the station which was then in St Lawrence Lane. Captain Tucker was last listed in charge in 1893 but by 1902 George Foot was in charge with seven men.

In January 1907 there was a house fire in West End Terrace. By this time Captain Richard Soper was in

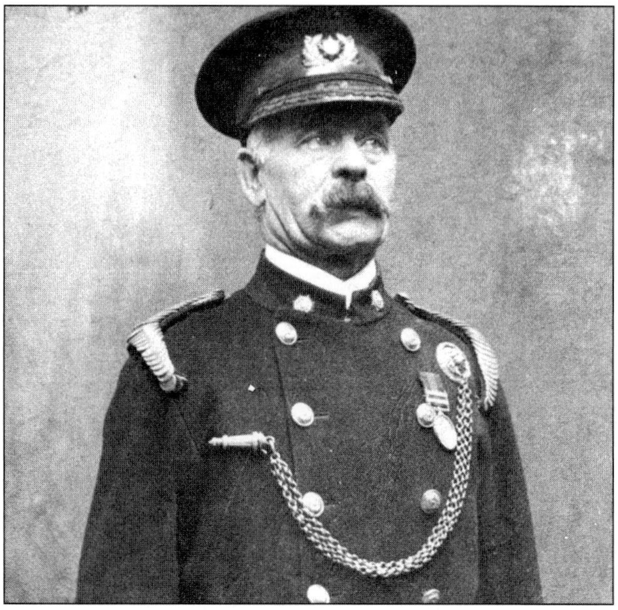

Captain French, 1928 – known as General French, he was also the blacksmith in St Lawrence Lane. The volunteer fire brigade was stationed across the road from the blacksmith's forge in the tall building between Nos.14 and 16 at the bottom of the garden. (ASHBURTON MUSEUM)

charge. There were regular fire drills in the Bull Ring under Captain Soper and in 1908 there was a complaint in a council meeting of the failure of an insurance company to pay the charge for the brigade attending a fire (in St Lawrence Lane near the Post Office). Captain Soper remained until March 1912 when the sub-captain J.D. Reddaway was elected captain by the brigade. A Mr E. Preston then became sub-captain in his place.

In the summer of 1914 new brass helmets were presented. There is a wonderful picture in the museum of James French, the blacksmith, in fireman's uniform. He was known as General French but there is no evidence to show he was ever the captain in charge. He was the blacksmith in St Lawrence Lane.

Captain J.D. Reddaway remained in charge of seven men in St Lawrence Lane until 1926. By 1933

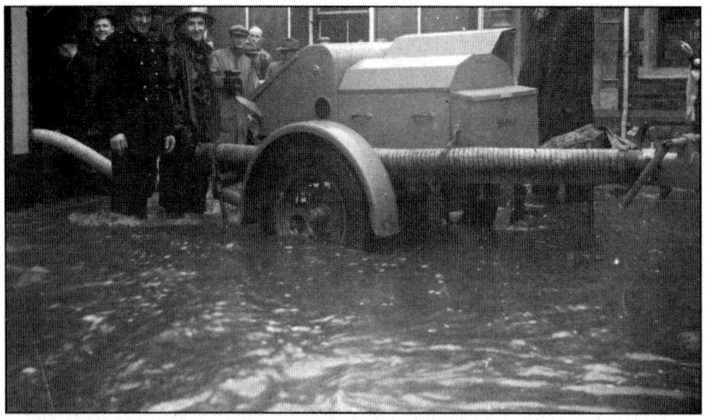

A flood in the Bull Ring, 21 November 1946, with firemen pumping out Bracewell's tobacconist. Pictured firemen, left to right: *George Mugridge, Eddie Cottle, Mr Pole (with flat hat).* (PETE WEBB COLLECTION)

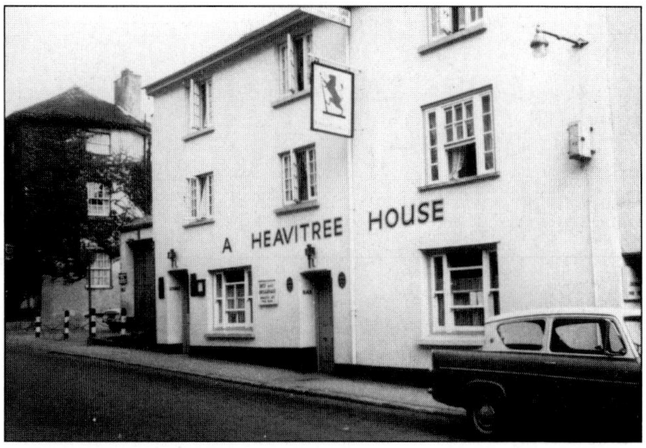

A mid-1960s view of the Red Lion with the fire station between it and the Golden Lion. (PETE WEBB COLLECTION)

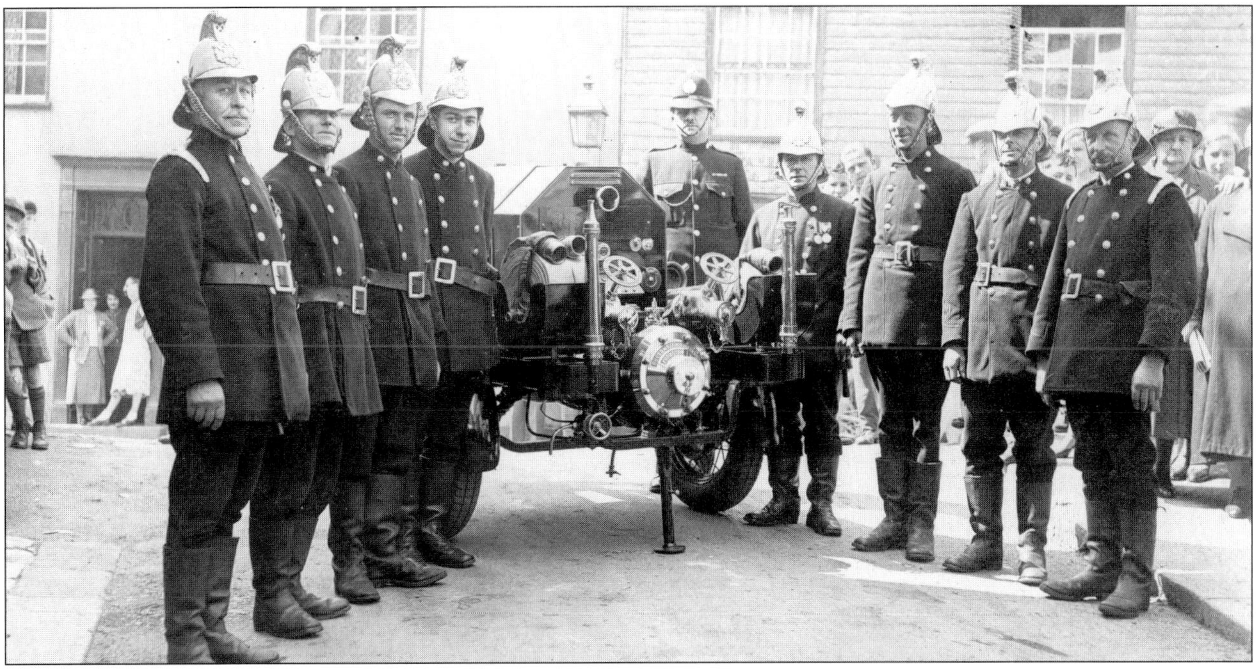

Ashburton Fire Brigade, 1930s. (Ashburton Museum)

their headquarters had moved to the Town Hall.

In 1935 the brigade was taken over by the local authority (though the men were still volunteers). They were still in the Town Hall with Captain William Edwin Knowling in charge.

In August 1937, at a fire in Linhay quarry, Chief Officer Bonstow was named in a newspaper article. The brigade merged with that of Newton Abbot the same year, along with Moretonhampstead, Bovey Tracey and Chudleigh. They were still using the Town Hall in 1939 and Ashburton was lucky not to have had the serious fires, caused by wartime bombing raids, suffered by Plymouth, Exeter and even Newton Abbot. The brigade moved to East Street after the war. The fire station in East Street was used in the film *Guilt is My Shadow* in 1950.

The present fire station opened in April 1965 in a new building along with the police station in Eastern Road. It has remained there ever since.

In 1973 Devon Fire Brigade was formed by the amalgamation of Exeter City Brigade, Plymouth City Brigade and Devon County Brigade. The Health and Safety at Work regulations of 1974 changed working conditions and in 1987 the brigade became Devon Fire and Rescue Service. In 1998 control of the fire service transferred from Devon County Council to

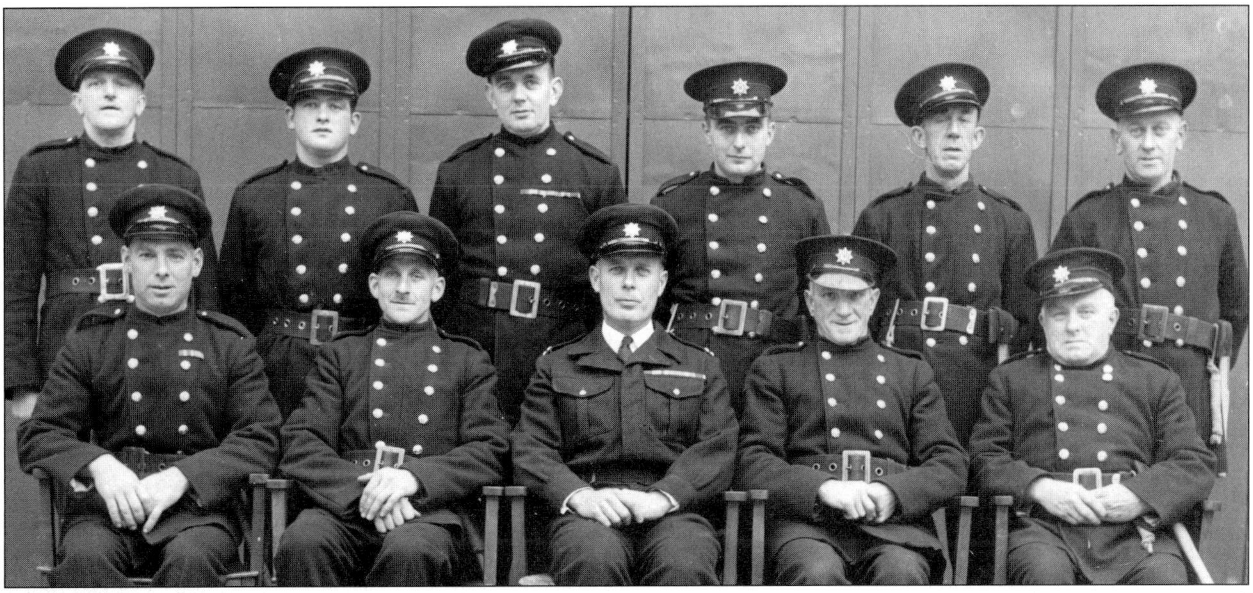

Ashburton firemen in 1954 – the fire station was in East Street at this time. Left to right, back row: *Fred Baker, John Baker, Dougie Williams, Bill Sergeant, George Endacott, Fred Egbeare;* front: *Bill Sergeant, George Mugridge, Vic Brooks, Jim Morrish, John Brixey.* (Photo from Eileen Egbeare)

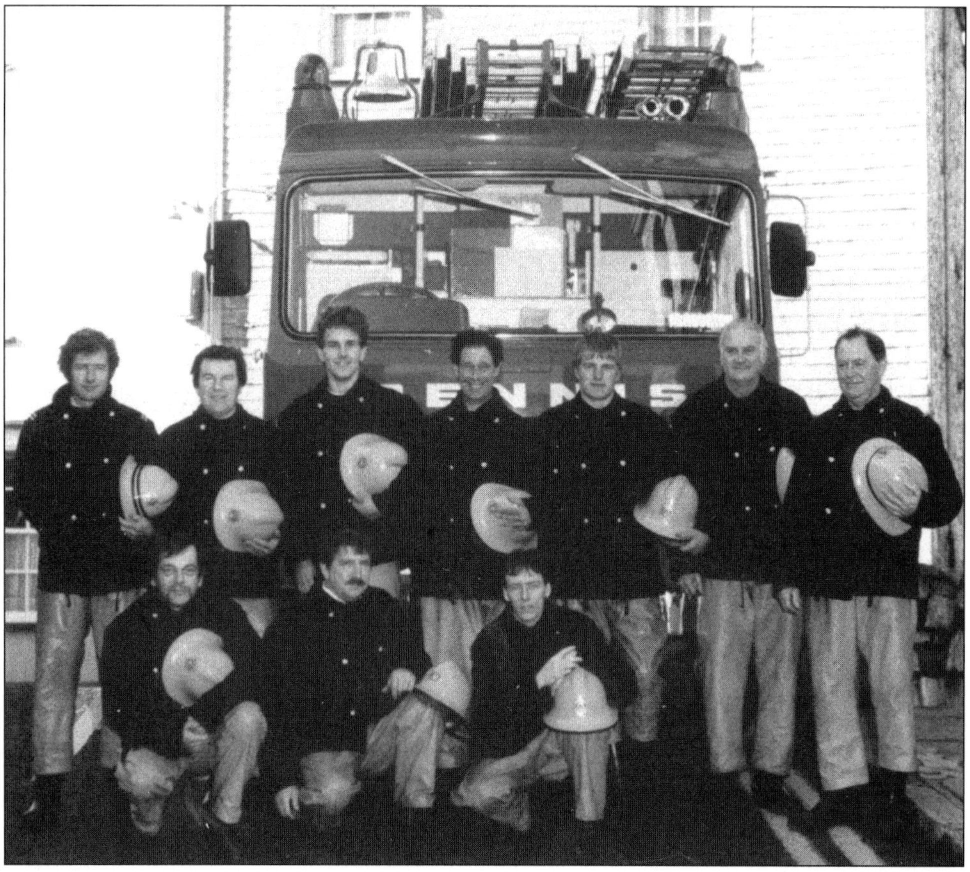

Ashburton fire engine, October 1985. The town's new Dennis engine pictured on King's Bridge next to the Town Hall. Back row, left to right: *Sub. Officer Bligh, Firemen Castle, Heywood, Underhill, Major, Wotton, Leading Fireman Bray;* front: *Firemen Torne, Bray and Parker.*
(ASHBURTON MUSEUM)

a Combined Fire Authority made up of representatives from the new Unitary Authority of Plymouth, Torbay and the remaining Devon County Council. Probably one of the worst incidents they had to deal with was a plane crash. A De Havilland Dash 7 crashed in a field just east of the town in 1999 and the firemen could not reach the plane. The all-terrain tender from Exeter Airport attended to put out the fire.

Devon has a total of 58 fire stations, ten being full time (crewed 24 hours a day). The remaining 47 stations, including Ashburton, are crewed by retained personnel. Ashburton has fared better than many similar towns with no serious fires during its history and most of the brigade's work consists of moorland fires and traffic accidents on the nearby A38.

Post Office

The postal service as we know it was for many years called the Royal Mail – originating in medieval times, when messages were carried by horse for the king. From the earliest times Ashburton was an important staging post with spare horses kept as it was mid-way between Exeter and Plymouth. As early as 1595 John Hext was the postmaster for Ashburton. By the seventeenth century the service had been expanded to include the carrying of private letters as a source of income to the Crown. In 1713, Ashburton had its first hand stamp. Richard Eales was postmaster in 1791 and William Lloyd in the 1820s. Originally in West Street (probably at the London Inn), by 1830 it had moved to East Street, first at the Golden Lion and then probably to the present site of the Ark (2004). The change to the penny post of 1840 had either William Barons or Sam Knowles in charge. In 1846 the railway came to Newton Abbot and Ashburton became a sub-Post Office with the mail arriving by train rather than stagecoach. William Barons was in charge, until Susan Lloyd Barons (his daughter or widow) took over around 1866. She remained until the late 1870s when William Edgecombe took over. William was named as the postmaster in July 1890 when the Portreeve arranged an impromptu meeting outside to celebrate the jubilee of the penny post. In March of that same year a new Post Office was being built in Station Road. The 1893 trade directory was the first to report the Post Office as being in St Lawrence Lane (or Station Road) with William Edgecombe still there until 1919. In the 1923 directory Frank Edgecombe first appears but no named postmaster is listed for the 1930s.

✦ CHAPTER 8 ✦

Agriculture and Markets

The land of Ashburton parish has been farmed for at least two millennia. The type of farming depends on many factors – some inherent, some changing.

The land which makes up the parish varies from the moorland of Dartmoor to the alluvial valley bottoms. The moorland has become less productive over time – the Bronze-Age folk would have found it more productive than it is today. The majority of the land off the moor is Grade 2 and 3 agricultural land, i.e. not of the highest quality. The soil nutrients depend to some degree on the underlying rock (and, as has already been seen, there are a variety of rock types to be found in Ashburton). This is quite apparent on the moor but less so elsewhere. The relief, too, will determine the type of farming possible and this to some extent influences the rainfall, as does aspect. Generally speaking the land is suited to stock grazing – this can include sheep, beef cattle and dairy cattle. Due to the relatively mild climate of South Devon grass is able to grow for many months of the year, thus enabling farmers to keep hardy stock out where ground conditions permit. The only snag is that the rain that keeps the grass growing is also likely to poach the ground.

Economic factors affect the type of farming adopted. Whilst not of the highest grade, cereals can be grown in the parish and have been grown in the past. For this to happen the demand for cereals has to be there. This reflects the price paid to the farmer.

Whilst the first people who farmed here were Neolithic people of over three millennia ago, it is not until the Bronze Age that we have any evidence of human presence. Dartmoor and its surroundings is one of the richest Bronze-Age landscapes in north-west Europe. The reave system and its culture on Dartmoor have been well studied and written about.

If you drive along the A38 toward Exeter and take the Newton Abbot turn-off at Goodstone you will notice on your left a number of small, oblong fields between the slip road and the road leading to Stormsdown. It has been suggested that the pattern of these strips of land was laid out in the Bronze Age, a relic of the Ripon Tor reave system. This is not to say that the field boundaries you see today were constructed then, but the original patterns have been 'fossilised'. Thus we have a direct link with the farmers of 3,000 years ago.

These farmers were largely self-sufficient, keeping all they required to live. The stock and cereal crops were primitive, not giving very high yields.

The Bronze Age gave way to the Iron Age (a change of culture rather than people). These were the people who built the hill forts. By and large they were pastoralists who produced animals for meat. However, unlike the previous culture, they not only produced food sufficient for themselves but also a surplus for sale, essential if they were to buy materials such as iron. In the neighbouring parish of Bickington Roman coins have been found. A trade of fat cattle is known to have existed with the citizens of Roman Exeter. The Roman road is traceable at least as far as Teigngrace so it is probable that the good Iron-Age farmers of Ashburton availed themselves of this opportunity. These were Celtic people who continued farming in this way until the arrival of the English (Saxons) in the eighth century. The changes the Saxon overlords brought were not in farming methods but in organisation. The majority of the population remained to do the work for their new overlords.

The next social change was the arrival of the Normans. Again the impact on the farming systems was not very marked. The development of the open field system of agriculture, which occurred in many parts of England, did not develop in this part of Devon. There were some common fields within the parish – in fact as you look around the parish what you see today is much the same as what the farmer of 1,000 years would have seen in terms of field patterns; a hedge or two removed but basically a Saxon, even Celtic, landscape. This also applies to the farm settlements. We have no direct evidence to demonstrate the type of crops grown during this period, but the value of the land suggests that they were oats, rather than the more profitable wheat and barley that were grown in the South Hams. In fact the type of farming was very varied and it is not wise to make sweeping statements. Life was difficult and culturally remote. In medieval times the main route west was north of Dartmoor, thus the 'up-country' influence was not felt. By the Tudor period stock was still the mainstay of farming, cattle being the most prominent. Draught oxen and dairy cows, although present, were outnumbered by beef cattle. Sheep, too, were important, not surprisingly bearing in mind Ashburton's woollen industry.

Devon's rural economy was, in the eighteenth century, studied by William Marshall, who remarked on the distinctiveness of agriculture in the South West. He was of the opinion that this distinctiveness arose from the practice of 'convertible husbandry'.

Today this would be known as ley farming. It was in essence ploughing grassland, taking two or three crops of cereals and then returning to grass for a number of years. The yield of cereals declined with each crop, the third yielding but 50 per cent of the first. The rotation of crops in this way was known as the 'old Devon course'. Cattle at this time were recognised as good quality. They were Devons – if perhaps not the sleek 'ruby red' seen today, nonetheless attracting attention from far and wide.

The crisis of the Napoleonic Wars precipitated a change in the system of agriculture adopted regionally and locally. Wheat and oats were the preferred cereals, although barley was grown and so too were turnips. The production of this root crop increased dramatically during the nineteenth century. The period until the 1870s was a prosperous time for agriculture. The 1841 tithe award lists all the landowners, tenants and their crops in the parish. Two particular points can be made from this survey. The first is the high proportion of arable in the parish (over 60 per cent). The second is the size of the farms. There were many small farms but by far the largest acreage was farmed in large units of over 50 acres. Perhaps this seems small by today's standards, but was not so then. A lasting heritage of these prosperous times is the number of new and added-to farmhouses and buildings built at this time.

Then by the mid-1870s came the slump. It was now possible, due to the emerging transport technology, to ship food around the country and across the world and accordingly prices fell. Arable in the parish declined as farmers turned to more traditional stock raising. Even this was not necessarily

List of farmers farming more than 40 acres in Ashburton, 1841

Holding (acres)	Tenant	Owner	Owner/ Farmer
Wellstore (261)	Hext and Scobel	Robert Abraham	
Auswell (111)	John Mugridge	Trustees	
Higher Auswell (49)	William Rowland	Trustees	
Rew Estate (73)	George Peters	Jane Bennett (Lord Clinton)	
Lower Hele (68)	John Berry	Jane Bennett (Lord Clinton)	
Pear Tree (53)	White	John Berry	
Headborough (51)	William Abbot	Lady Carew	
Higher Waye (48)	Geo. Mortimore	John Caunter	
Place Farm (70)	Thomas Maunder	Richard Caunter	
Whiddon (66)	Elias Easterbrook	Henry Caunter	
Furzley (212)	Richard and Will Underhill	Lord Cranstoun	
Pitley (62)	Stephen Yolland	Lady Freemantle	
Higher Mead (77)	Roger Hannaford	Samuel Hannaford	
Chuley (79)	Thos. Hext	Trustees	
Higher Hele (68)			Richard Hext
Alston (217)	William Helyer	John Huxham	
Lower Waye (47)	Thos. Huxham	John Huxham	
Rushlade (146)			William Kingwill
Coombe (43)	Jonas Skinner	Thos. King	
Horsehill (132)	John Hext, Bovey Hext and John Scobell	Revd Thos. Kitson	
Caton (110)	Will Skinner	Samuel Knowles	
Lower Bowdley (70)	Rob Palk junr	Rob Palk	
Goodstone (153)	Will Mann	Rich Savery	
Water (43)	Tom Oldrey	J. Savery	
Summer Hill (121)			William Sawdye
Owlicombe (75)	Jos. Skinner	Francis Shut	
Brownswell (70)			Thos. Smerdon
Whiddon (89)			Edward Smerdon
Brownswell (69)			Thos. Smerdon
Higher Bowdley (128)			William Smerdon
Goodstone (98)	Nicholas Tarr	Thos. White	
Hookes (73)			Thos. Widger
Goodstone (98)			Thos. Widger
Higher & Lower Lemonford (70)			Richard Wills
Druid (73)	Will Smerdon		Will Windeat
Halsanger (80)	Richard Mugridge	James Woodley	
Halsanger Down (399)	John Wills	James Woodley	

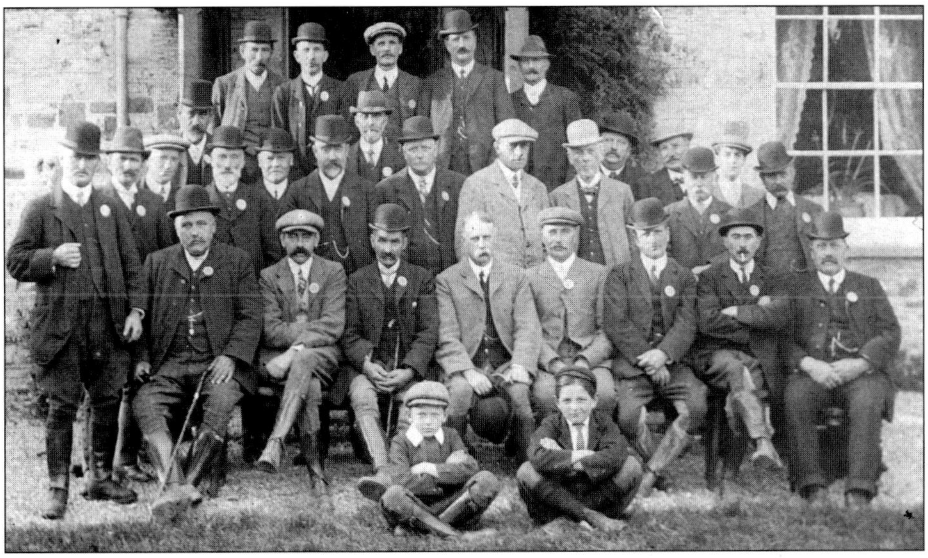

Beara ploughing match, 11 October 1911.
(GARTH GROSE COLLECTION)

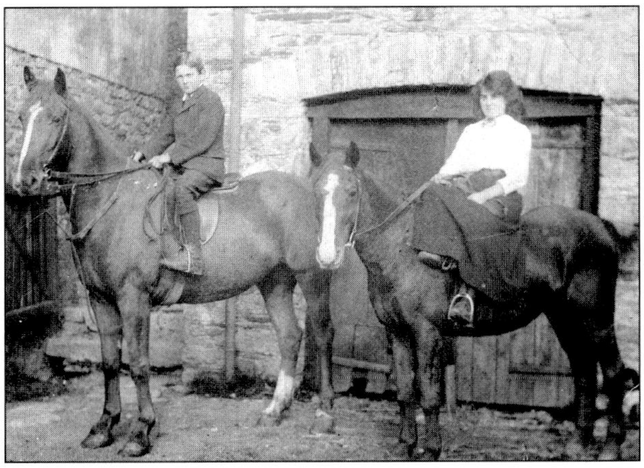

Pound House, 1912. (GARTH GROSE COLLECTION)

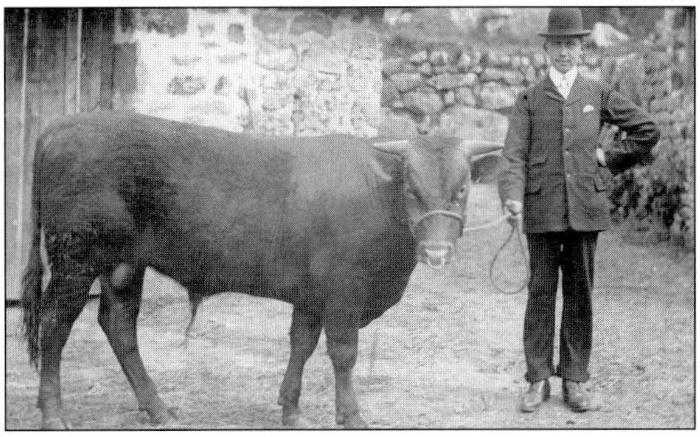

Robert Daw with bull, 1905. (PAT ORSMAN COLLECTION)

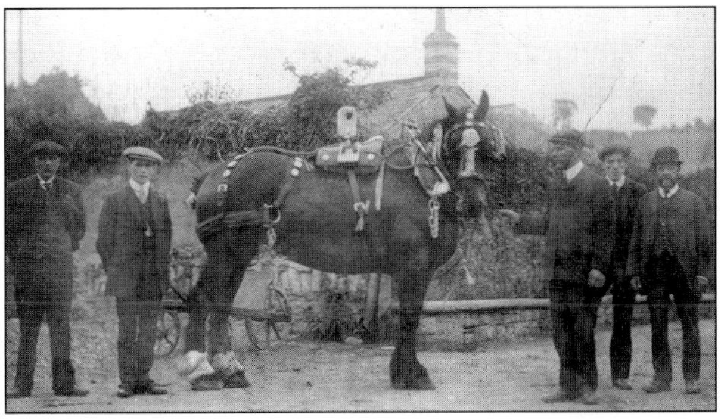

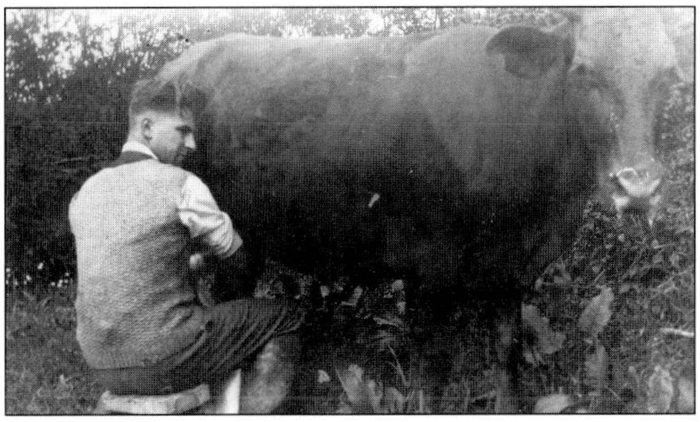

Jim Daw hand milking, 1940s. (PAT ORSMAN COLLECTION)

Above: *Shire horses at an unknown farm, c.1910. This picture was taken by Wilfred Evans. Possible names given are Hext and Roberts.*
(PETE WEBB COLLECTION)

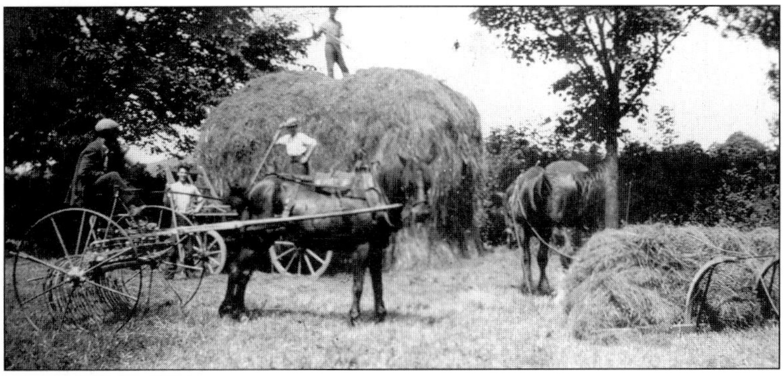

Right: *Haymaking at Druid in the 1940s.*
(PAT ORSMAN COLLECTION)

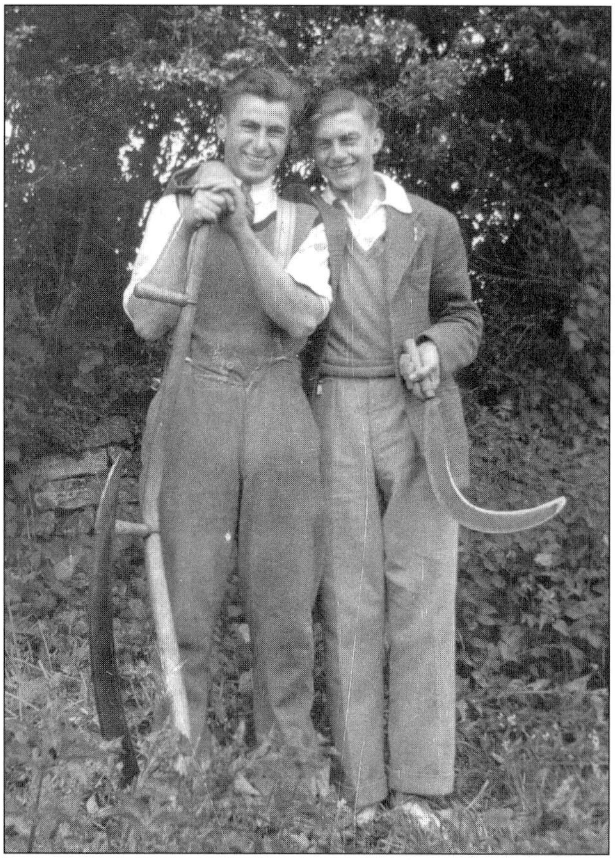

Scythers Jim Daw and Ken Burgoyne, 1940s.
(PAT ORSMAN COLLECTION)

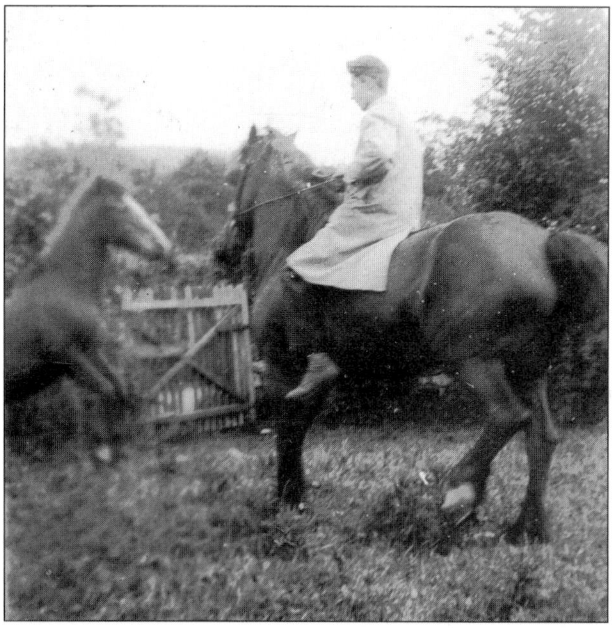

Wilfred (Robert) Daw breaking a horse in the late 1930s.
(PAT ORSMAN COLLECTION)

profitable. Wool prices, too, had slumped by the mid-1880s.

Sheep found in Ashburton at this time would have been of the Devon longwool, South Hams and Dartmoor breeds.

The period from the 1890s until the 1930s was one of decline in agriculture; cereals declined, grassland

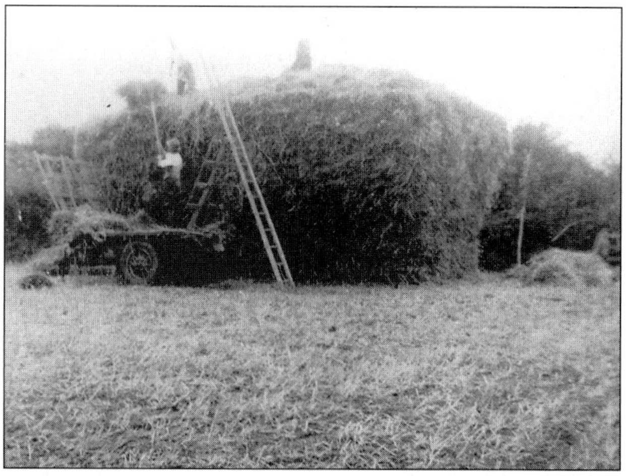

Rick building at Caton, 1940s. (GARTH GROSE COLLECTION)

was not replanted and poorer land went out of production; it was a depressing time for all.

In 1933 the Milk Marketing Board was created, guaranteeing for the first time a market for milk wherever it was produced – no longer would dairy farmers remote from larger areas of population be denied a market. Shortly afterwards the outbreak of the Second World War heralded a period of prosperity for agriculture. The MMB's guaranteed market for produce was further enhanced by the Agriculture Act of 1947.

The period 1950–80 was without doubt a halcyon era for British agriculture in general; Ashburton shared that prosperity. The dependency on local milk production was reflected by the percentage of grass – 80 per cent in 1964.

It could not and did not last. Since the mid-1980s farming has gone into decline. The abolition of the MMB signalled the start. Farmers locally have responded in a number of ways: turning to alternative enterprises, tourism for example, increasing size of dairy herds, returning to a more extensive system of production. The result has been the trimming down of agriculture, which it is hoped will prepare it for the challenges to come.

Markets

Markets appear as soon as surplus produce is available and it is has always been in the interests of those in authority to control them. Not only were unauthorised markets curtailed, but legitimate markets were controlled by taxes of one sort or another. The granting of a market was important to the local community, who were able to buy food, freeing them from the trouble of producing it, although most townsfolk had allotments on which they grew some produce. The market also provided an outlet and therefore a source of produce to other areas. Fat cattle and sheep were usually the mainstay of Ashburton's agriculture and sales of these commodities attracted buyers from far and

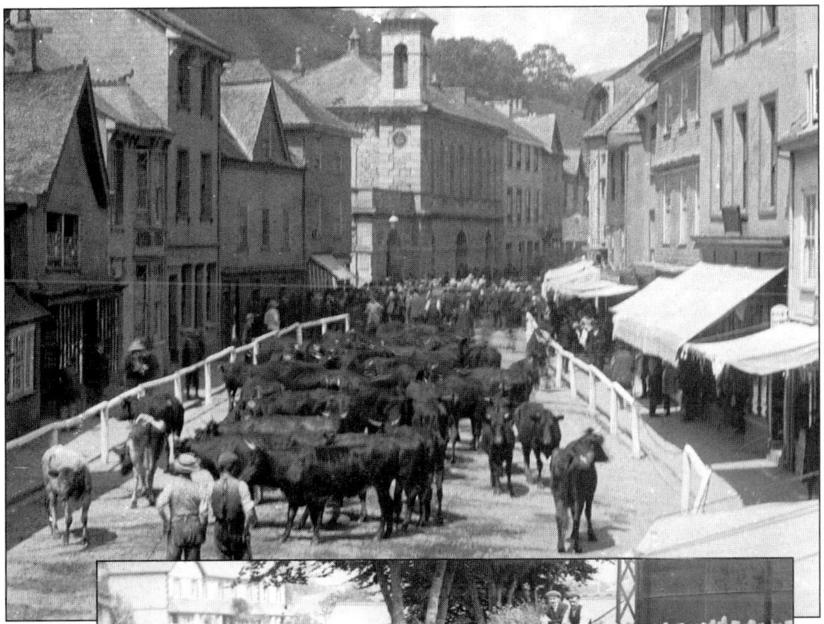

Market in North Street. Until the Cattle Market at the bottom of St Lawrence Lane opened in 1909 livestock sales were held in North Street. The cattle were driven down off the moor, sold in North Street and then loaded up into cattle trucks at the railway station. Sheep and pigs were sold further up North Street. Note the white fences, erected to protect the shops and pedestrians. The metal inserts still visible in the kerbstones today were not for the rails, as commonly thought, but for the uprights of the shop blinds.

(PETE WEBB COLLECTION)

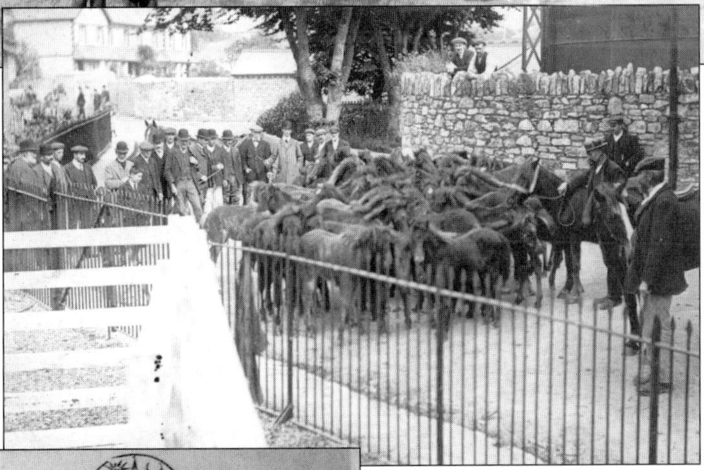

Pony sales, Parish (Chuley) Road. The ponies were driven down off Dartmoor and after they were sold put into the white pens on the left to be loaded into railway trucks for distribution.

(PETE WEBB COLLECTION)

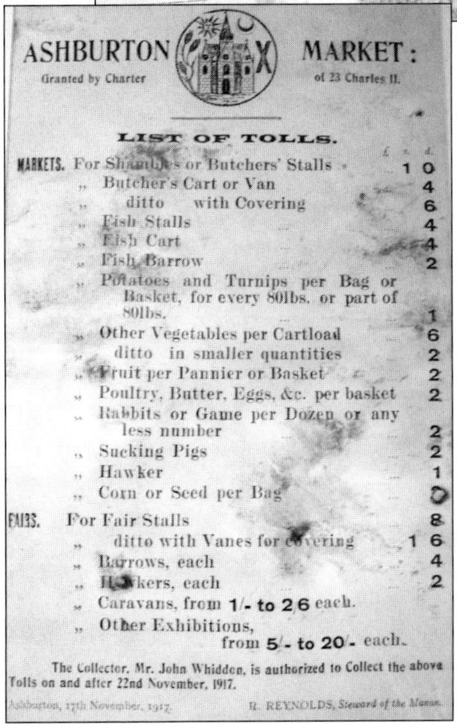

ASHBURTON MARKET:

Granted by Charter of 23 Charles II.

LIST OF TOLLS.

		£	s.	d.
MARKETS.	For Shambles or Butchers' Stalls		1	0
,,	Butcher's Cart or Van			4
,,	ditto with Covering			6
,,	Fish Stalls			4
,,	Fish Cart			4
,,	Fish Barrow			2
,,	Potatoes and Turnips per Bag or Basket, for every 80lbs. or part of 80lbs.			1
,,	Other Vegetables per Cartload			6
,,	ditto in smaller quantities			2
,,	Fruit per Pannier or Basket			2
,,	Poultry, Butter, Eggs, &c. per basket			2
,,	Rabbits or Game per Dozen or any less number			2
,,	Sucking Pigs			2
,,	Hawker			1
,,	Corn or Seed per Bag			0
FAIRS.	For Fair Stalls			8
,,	ditto with Vanes for covering		1	6
,,	Barrows, each			4
,,	Hawkers, each			2
,,	Caravans, from 1/- to 2/6 each.			
,,	Other Exhibitions, from 5/- to 20/- each.			

The Collector, Mr. John Whidden, is authorized to Collect the above Tolls on and after 22nd November, 1917.

Ashburton, 17th November, 1917. R. REYNOLDS, *Steward of the Manor.*

List of tolls for the market.

(ASHBURTON MUSEUM)

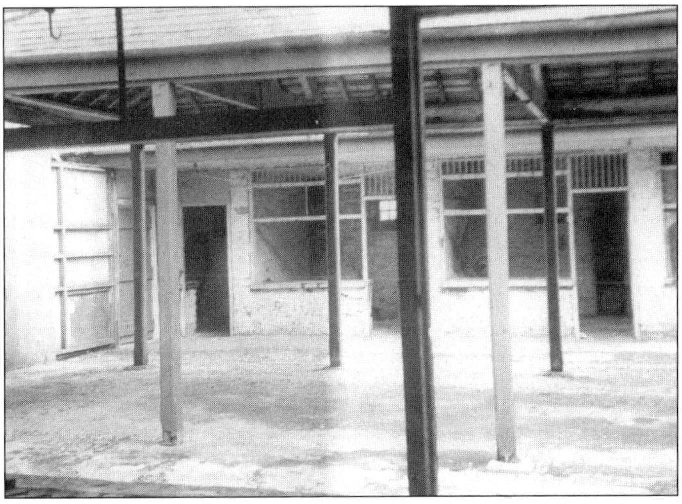

Inside the pannier market, c.1950. The enclosed stalls were lock-ups and on three sides around the outdoor area. Note the granite gutters taken from the old market demolished in 1850. Before the First World War, 'gentry' provided a soup kitchen in one of these stalls for the poor people. A basin cost a penny and could feed a family of four.

(PETE WEBB COLLECTION)

near. This also benefited the town as visitors usually spent money on other items as well – not least the alehouses on market days.

It was therefore of some importance when, in the eleventh or twelfth century, Ashburton was granted a licence to hold a market. Further grants were made to Bishop Stapledon in 1313 by Edward II. This granted a weekly market to be held on Saturdays and two three-day fairs once a year either side of the feast of St Lawrence and either side of the feast of St Martin. The market tolls, which were considerable, were the property of the Borough of Ashburton, as opposed to the manor.

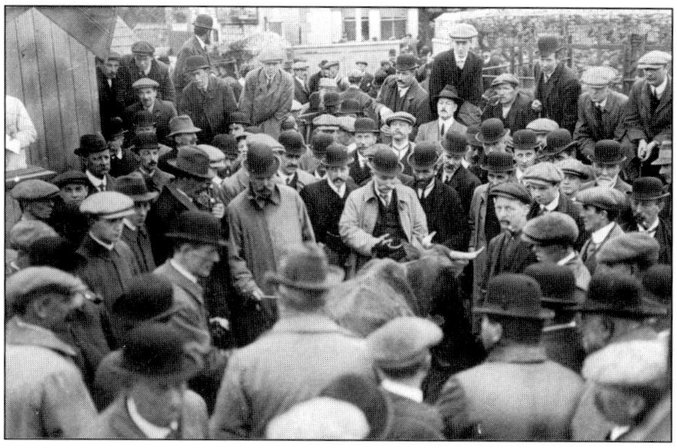

Sawdye cattle auction. (ASHBURTON MUSEUM)

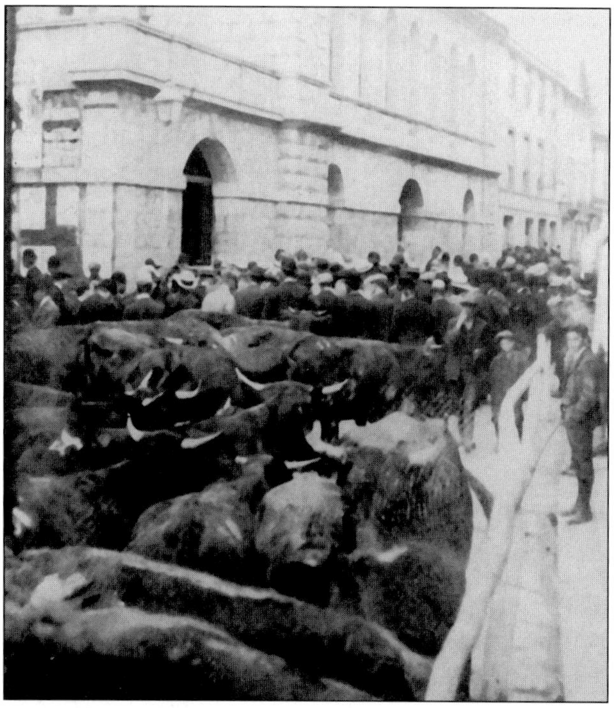

The last fair, 1909. (GARTH GROSE COLLECTION)

However, with the failure of the borough to become incorporated the dues were collected by the Guild of St Lawrence. As previously explained, the Guild of St Lawrence fell foul of the Chantries Acts (see p.10).

The market became the property of the Prideaux family, who let it to the Fords of Ilsington for £300. In the seventeenth century there followed a dispute between Thomas Prideaux senr and Thomas Ford senr, the first of many involving these families about the value of tolls, both wishing to get their share of the cake.

In 1670 John Ford set up a weekly market in Ashburton on Tuesdays without the authority of either Crown or Parliament. This was disputed by Yard, the owner of Newton Market, who maintained his market lost revenue, mainly in wool, as the wool from Dartmoor, formerly going to Newton, went to Ashburton instead. Ford lost his case. Notwithstanding this defeat he applied for the grant of a weekly Tuesday market, which he obtained. This yarn market proved its worth. An example of the courts' attempt to stamp out unauthorised trading is found in the case between the owners of the market tolls of Ashburton and one Robert Badcock. Perhaps it is fair to say that it was the interested parties who gained much from tolls and who used the courts to stamp out unauthorised trading.

Evidently Badcock was allowing trading of yarn between producers and clothiers to take place at the Traveller's Rest (then in Ashburton Parish). Most of the evidence came from those who supported Badcock. Presumably the case was not proven.

Lyson's writing in 1822 refers to markets being held on the first Thursday in March, June, August and November.

The Market Hall stood at the junction of North, East and West Streets and was pulled down in 1849. By this time the yarn trade had dwindled but the livestock trade continued to be held in North Street until the opening of the new market in 1909 near to the railway station – a convenient site for rail transport of livestock. The pannier market closed in the 1960s and was pulled down. Cattle markets were held between the First and Second World Wars and various occasional seasonal sales were held, such as the sheep sales. Some of these continued until recently (2000/2001). Then, in 2002, came foot and mouth which was the death knell to over 800 years of recorded history of markets in Ashburton.

CHAPTER 9

Transport

Roads

Whilst today we consider the A38 trunk road to be the main road it is, by comparison with the other roads of the parish, a newcomer. A glance at a map of the area reveals that many of the roads lead up to Dartmoor. If we take the lane from Goodstone as an example, we note that the lane crosses over the A38 and meanders all the way to the open moor at Cold East Cross. There are no farms on this lane. Stormsdown is a Victorian development. We know from documents that Goodstone was certainly in existence by the fifteenth century, but the site as a farm is much older. The Bishop of Exeter retained the Herebere Estate, now just over the border in Bickington parish, to gain access to the grazing rights that this estate had on Dartmoor. The track which was used to move stock to and from the moor for summer grazing was the lane in question. Evidence from Herebere indicates that these settlements are at least 2,000 years old and could even be prehistoric. Other lanes in the parish, however, converge on the town, suggesting that they developed as the town grew. Again they lead to the moor, used in all probability to move stock to the markets and manufactories of the town. The road past Druid was an important route for pack animals bringing goods from further afield. One of the roads leading out of Chagford is called Ashburton Road – today only a tourist would use that way to get from Chagford to Ashburton, but it does indicate the importance of the route.

As movement of people and goods increased in distance, routes developed not on greenfield sites as today's motorways tend to do, but rather by developing pre-existing roads and tracks. One impression of roads is given by Celia Fiennes in 1695. As she left Ashburton she wrote:

> *Thence I went for Plymouth... and here the roads contract and the lanes are exceedingly narrow and so covered up you can see little about, an army might be marching undiscovered by anybody, for when you are on the heights that shew a vast country about, you cannot see one road.*

The development of coach traffic sped up the process. The coach route to Newton Abbot followed the route via Goodstone, Gale and Herebere before joining the present route at Mill Cross. The Plymouth to Exeter road came through Buckfastleigh into the town centre and out through Bickington village past the Traveller's Rest. The eighteenth century saw the development of turnpikes. The Chudleigh to South Brent turnpike was formed in 1755 but developed in the early-nineteenth century. The toll-houses at Goodstone and Dart Bridge (Buckfast) in Ashburton parish are witnesses to this 1820s development. As traffic volume grew it became clear that Ashburton would need a bypass. A single-carriageway road was opened in 1933. This road was constructed as part of the unemployment relief schemes, referred to as the '£2 million schemes'. This was upgraded to a dual carriageway in the late 1960s and early 1970s as part of the Plymouth to Exeter dualling.

What type of transport used these roads? At first the packhorse was universally used, being the only form of transport able to use the tracks then in existence. Carts were used locally to move materials around. The advent of the stagecoach in the seventeenth century enabled people to move from place to

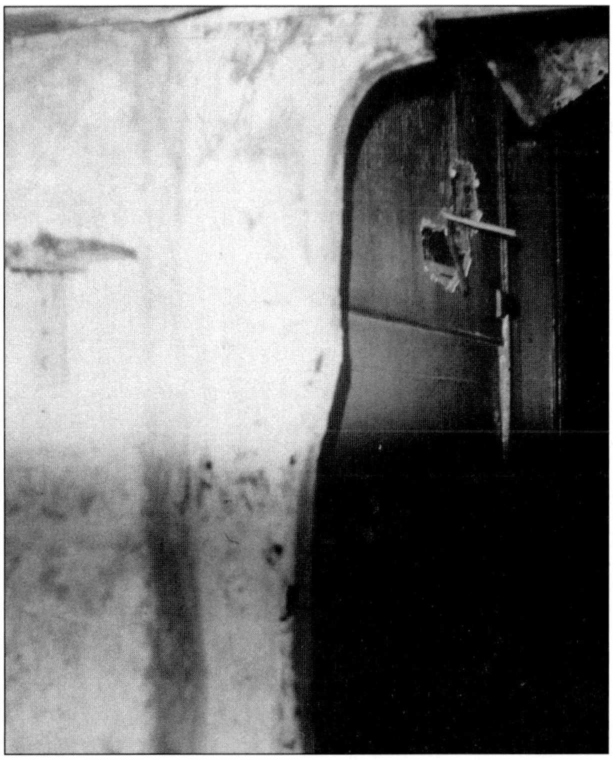

Medieval doorway, North Street. This photograph was taken by the Amenities Society immediately before the houses were demolished in 1971. The unusual shape was to allow packhorses to pass through without unloading.

(PETE WEBB COLLECTION)

Right: *The end of the original bypass looking towards Pear Tree. This is where the original 1935 bypass ended. When the road became a dual carriageway in the early 1970s this became the Exeter-bound slip-road.* (PETE WEBB COLLECTION)

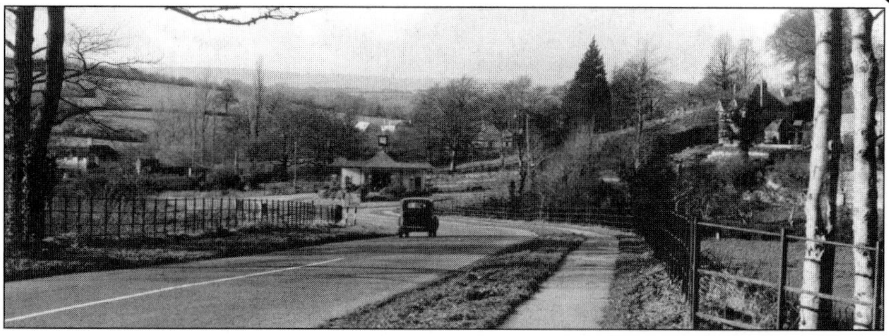

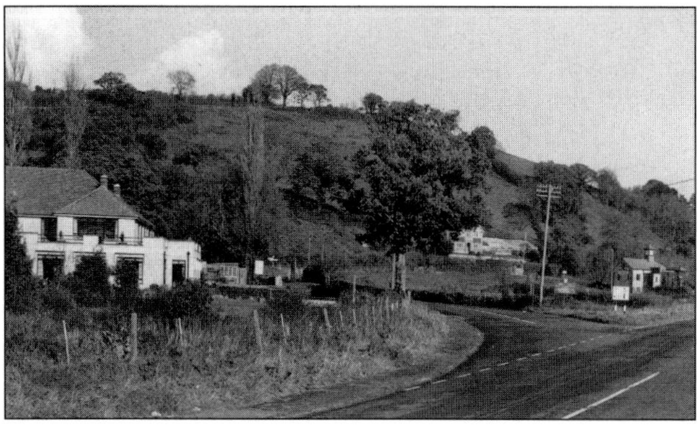

Pear Tree motel and garage, c.1950. Newly built Dropping Wells is in the background.
(PETE WEBB COLLECTION)

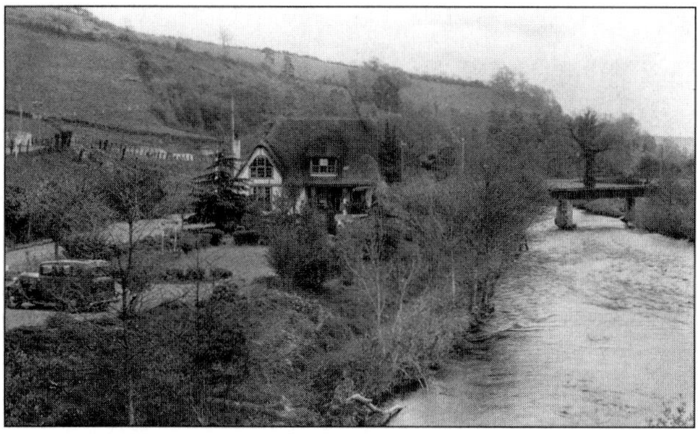

Salmon Leap Café with the railway bridge over the Dart to the right, c.1930. This has now been replaced by the A38 bridge and the Little Chef café. (PETE WEBB COLLECTION)

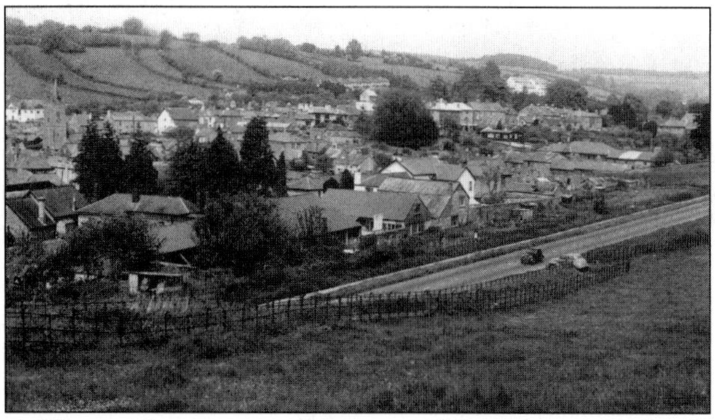

Ashburton bypass near the centre of the town soon after it was opened in 1933. The sheds immediately in front are now part of Outdoor Experience (formerly Ashburn Caravans). (PETE WEBB COLLECTION)

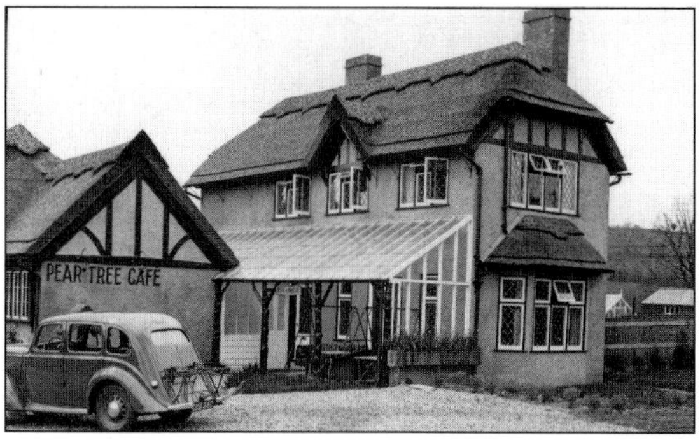

Pear Tree Café in the 1940s. (PETE WEBB COLLECTION)

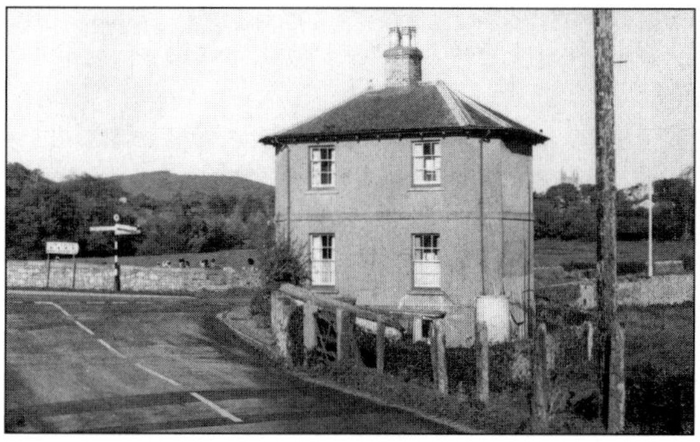

Toll house in the early 1970s, just prior to being demolished, looking from the South (Totnes). Ashburton is to the right and Buckfast to the left.
(PETE WEBB COLLECTION)

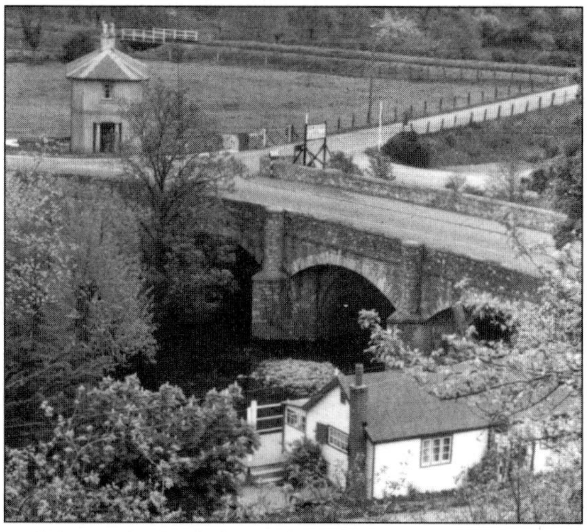

Toll house looking down from the hill. A good view of the bridge over the Dart and the road to Totnes around the 1960s. (PETE WEBB COLLECTION)

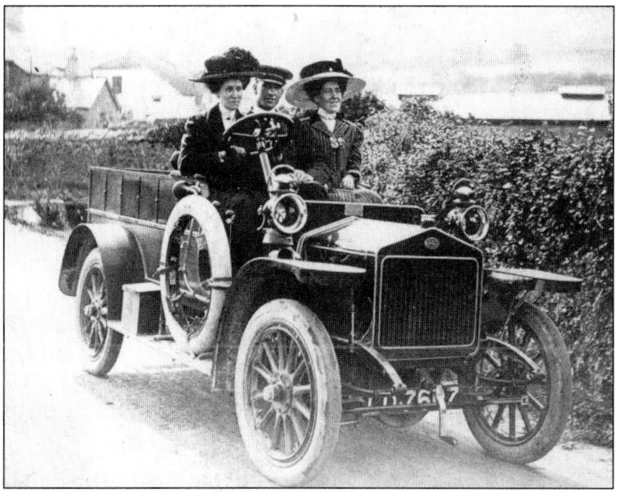

This car in Balland Lane is a 1906 or 1907 15hp Siddeley, sold by the Wolseley Tool & Motor Car Company.

(PETE WEBB COLLECTION)

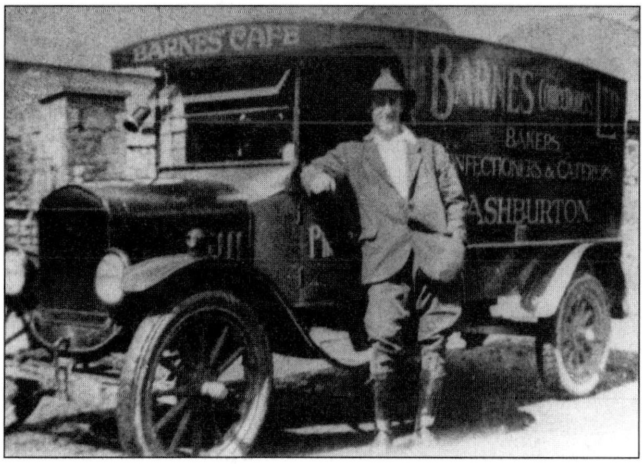

Bill Endacott with one of the first vans in Ashburton – Barnes the baker's delivery van, 1930s.

(PETE WEBB COLLECTION)

place in a more convenient fashion – convenience being a relative term because, by today's standards, stagecoach travel was slow and uncomfortable. The turnpike made things a little easier. The Royal Mail used the turnpike road. Of the various coaches which went through Ashburton the most famous, because it was the fastest, was the Devonport Mail. It made the journey from London to Devonport in 21¼ hours, covering 219 miles at just over ten miles per hour. Only 23 changes of horses were needed! In 1830 it left Chudleigh at 4.10p.m., arriving at Ashburton at 5.05 and Plymouth at 7.48. One of the most famous coachmen on this route was a burly, powerful man named Harvey, who was very conscious of his prowess in driving the coach, named Defiance. He was always anxious to better the time taken for the coach, which went via Newton Abbot on its journey from Devonport to Exeter and rarely took longer than 3½ hours – never longer than four, to undertake the trip. Until the turnpike was built the preferred route west was via Newton Abbot. The next development in transport to and from the town was the railway.

By the early-twentieth century the motor bus began to be developed and it was not long before it began to seriously compete with the railway – before the First World War was the only period when the railway had a virtual monopoly.

One of the earliest businesses in the motor trade in Ashburton was that of Ernest Oscar Babbington, who was trading as a car hirer by 1916. Following the First World War he moved his premises to East Street. He went into the motor bus business in 1922. A feature of these early vehicles was their registration mark – EB for Ernest Babington! Devon General also ran a bus service to the town to enable people to visit the Wednesday Newton Abbot market. Babington followed suit. Competition for trade had begun.

In 1922 the routes were extended to Torquay. Babington adopted the name 'Blue Cars' and his vehicles were generally considered to be more comfortable than Devon General's buses. Not to be outdone, the latter company introduced buses with pneumatic tyres. By 1930 Devon General had had enough of this wasteful competition and opened negotiations for the purchase of Blue Cars. In 1927 an agreement was reached whereby, except for the Buckland school contract, the Motor Bus Company passed into Devon General ownership. Babington kept the garage in West Street opposite the church.

The other motor bus company at this time was Gayton's Coaches, of East Street. Like Babington, Gayton started business as a motor engineer, moving into the bus business in 1920. He ran a service to Newton Abbot which he later extended to Torquay. However, with the introduction of licensing by local authorities, by 1924, when permission was refused for the Torquay route, buses terminated at Newton Abbot. With the growth of Blue Cars and their takeover by Devon General, Gayton withdrew from the motor bus business in 1927.

In 1930 only one motor bus remained in Ashburton, and Gayton saw the opportunity to re-enter the bus business. School contracts and tours were the mainstay of the business during the period up to the Second World War. The war saw the buses used mainly for war work – troop movement in particular. Once peace came the business thrived again, opportunity being taken to purchase new and more comfortable buses. In 1951 the last of the Gayton family died and the business was taken over by Mr Percy White, who continued to run the business unchanged. The schools contract business, however, after the initial impetus provided by the opening of the new Ashburton and Buckfastleigh Secondary School (South Dartmoor Community College), became more difficult and in 1964 Mr Nock, who then ran the business, ceased trading.

Transport, however, is not just about public transport. Just as pack-horses were important in the early days of Ashburton, transport of goods today is still as important, if not more so. In 1925 W.F. Miners

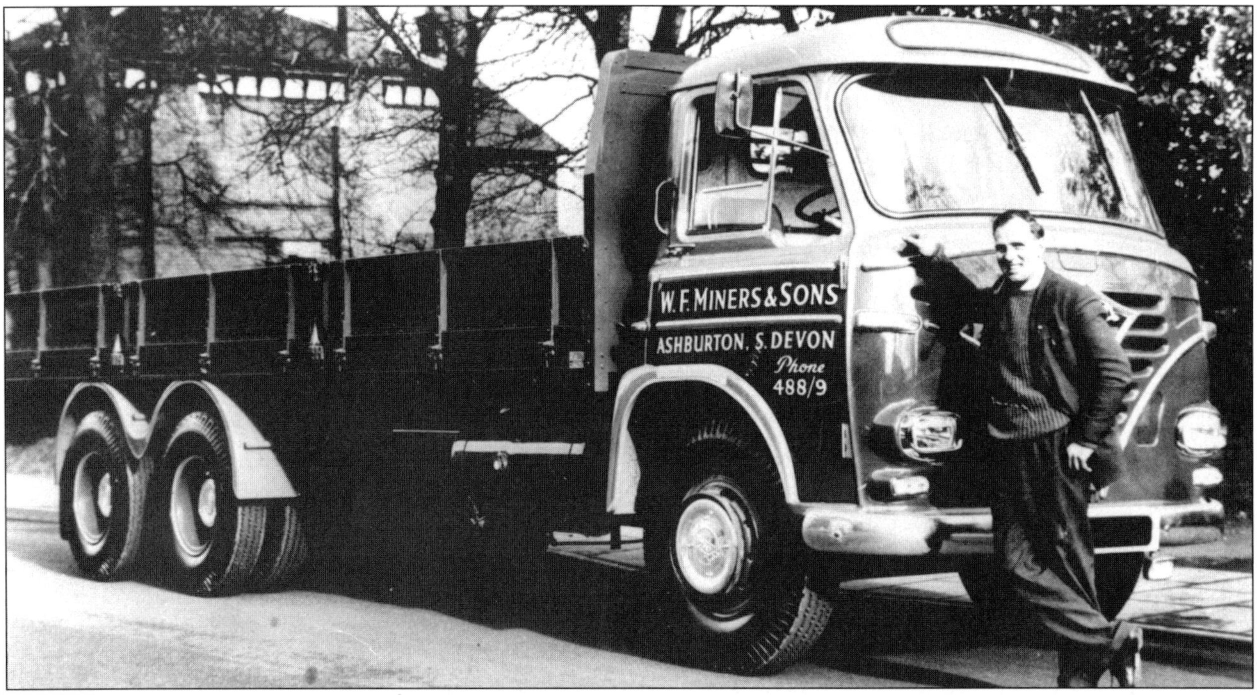

Fred Miners with W.F. Miners' lorry, early 1960s. (PETE WEBB COLLECTION)

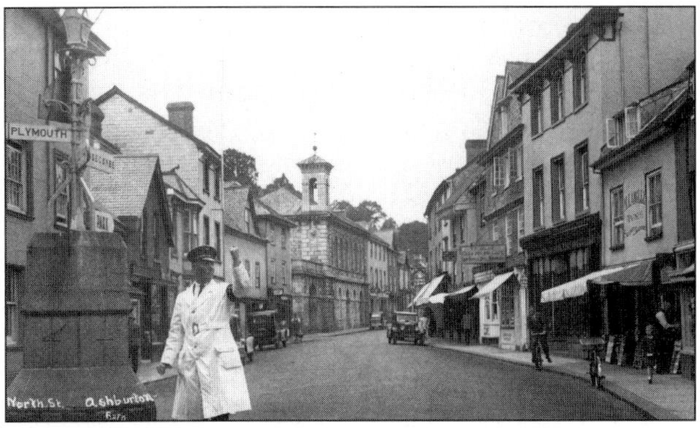

Bill 'Wizzbang' Hatch, traffic warden, directing traffic during the 1950s. (RUTH BROTHERS; PETE WEBB COLLECTION)

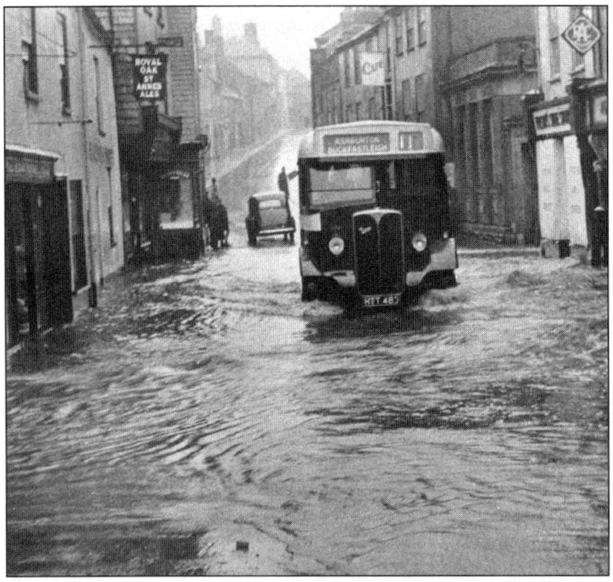

Bus in the 1946 flood, Newton to Buckfastleigh Route 11. (PETE WEBB COLLECTION)

founded the first motorised haulage company in Widecombe, which he moved to Ashburton in 1963, although in the early days horse-drawn vehicles predominated. The firm continued to develop and in 1968 the new office block was opened by Mr R.F. Harris, the Portreeve. This was on the site of the old umber mine. As trading with continental Europe increased, especially after 1973 when the UK joined the European Community, W.F. Miners and Sons were not slow to take advantage of the opportunities this presented. The company, however, was broken up in the early 1990s and the site became houses, but is still called Miners Close after the family who used it for so many years.

Ashburton Railway

By the early 1840s the age of the train had arrived, with engineers such as Isambard Kingdom Brunel bringing the Great Western Line from London to Exeter. It was always expected that the line would extend to Plymouth and beyond but the route was originally uncertain. In 1845 two Acts of Parliament were passed, one sending the route through the centre of Ashburton and the other through Newton Abbot. Promoters of the Ashburton choice even went to the expense of hiring carriages and pedestrians to walk before the inspectors to try and make the town seem busier than Newton. Thankfully for the architecture and buildings of Ashburton, Newton was chosen.

The next hurdle was to link Ashburton to the railway and a meeting held at St Lawrence Chapel in June 1845 agreed that a link should be made between Ashburton and Newton. At the same time a rival

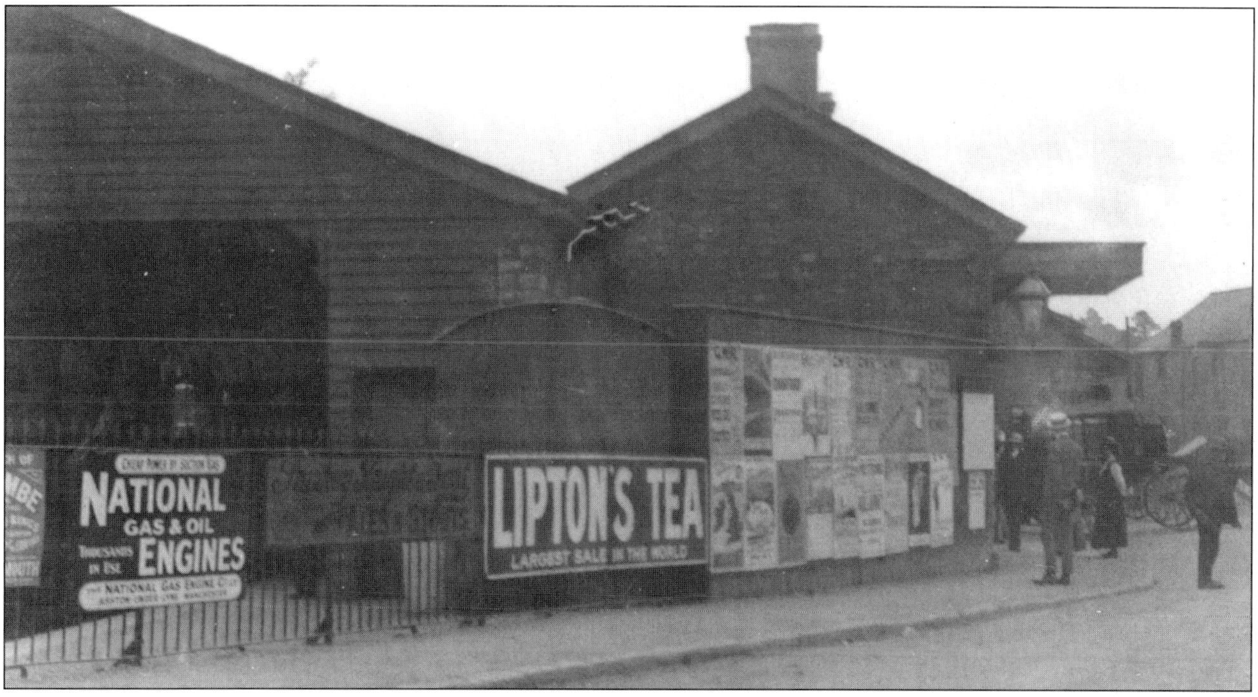

The railway station, c.1905. Note the large domed chimney on the engine under the canopy. (PETE WEBB COLLECTION)

group decided the link should be between Totnes and Ashburton. The South Devon Railway had arrived at Totnes from Exeter on 20 July 1847 and was extended on to Plymouth in May 1848. The route to Totnes was chosen.

Unfortunately the loss of Ashburton's MP and the demise of the woollen industry brought about a decline in the town's prosperity. This was followed by 20 years of the population moving away, the loss of the coaching trade due to the railway reaching Plymouth and a general downturn in the town's wealth and energy. The town's connection to the railway foundered.

A further Act of Parliament was passed in May 1863 to construct a branch to Buckfastleigh, after much meeting and pressure by the local communities, with a second Act required and the extension on to Ashburton approved two years later, on 26 May 1865. Construction came to a standstill in 1867 and only a further Act of Parliament granting an extension of time saw building work restarted in 1868 with another contractor.

The branch was originally constructed in broad gauge and opened to traffic on 1 May 1882, with major celebrations in Ashburton. The church bells rang out, bands paraded the streets throughout the day, flags and bunting decorated the town's shops and houses and the day of celebration culminated in

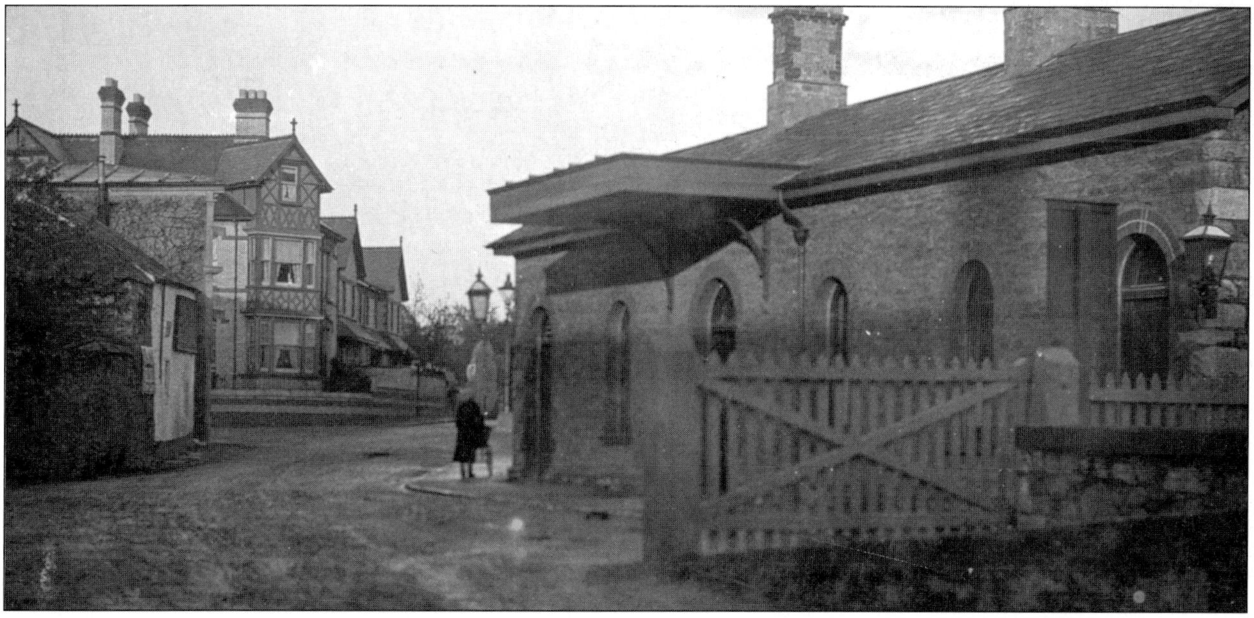

The railway station looking back towards Clithero House, c.1915. (PETE WEBB COLLECTION)

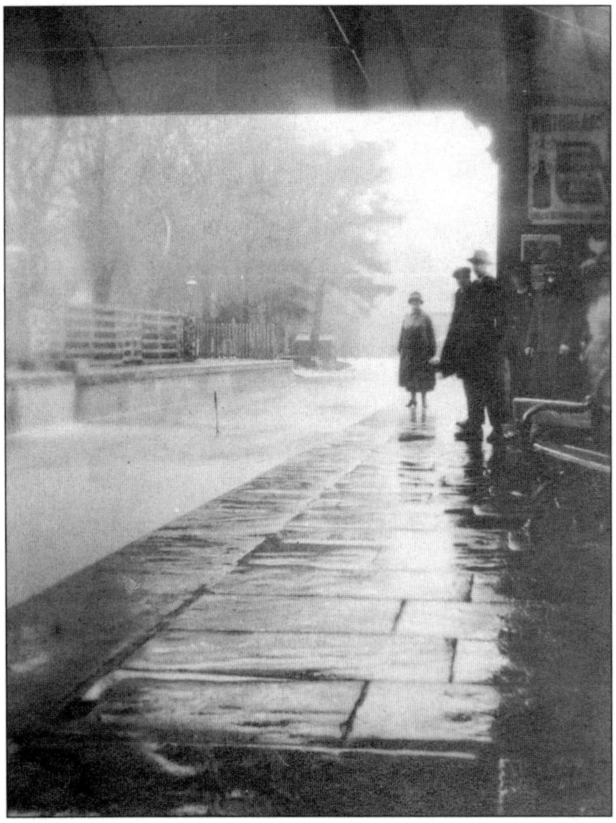

Ashburton railway station flooded, January 1925.
(PORTREEVE'S JOURNAL)

a party well into the night.

Originally operated by the South Devon Railway, it was taken over by the Great Western Railway in 1875 and the line worked by the Buckfastleigh, Totnes and South Devon Railway as their agents. The line was converted to standard gauge, along with the rest of the region, on 21–22 May 1892. This was a major feat of engineering work, with the whole country converted over a single weekend.

The year 1896 saw the demise of the company and it went into liquidation to be taken over by the GWR in 1897. Other railways were proposed and some constructed over the next few years, including links to the main line at South Brent and also through to the Teign Valley line.

The line never really made much profit, although the freight from the weekly cattle market, umber and other goods, both in and out, remained good. The passenger service, though, even with publicity, never really took off, with most passengers preferring to travel via Newton Abbot rather than Totnes and on to Ashburton.

By the late 1930s, the car was here to stay and the line closed to passengers in 1958, ten years after being taken over by British Railways. Freight traffic, now mainly consisting of cattle, continued at the rate of five trains a day for a while. The slow decline continued until 1962, when the line was finally closed. The last goods train ran on Friday, 7 September 1962.

Negotiations by the Dart Valley Railway Company and the Great Western Society were immediately started to acquire the line. Ashburton was originally planned as the headquarters station and to house a museum. Negotiations and objections dragged on from 1962 to 1967 until the DVR finally agreed to relinquish the Buckfastleigh to Ashburton section. The Dart Valley Railway Association was inaugurated on 22 October 1966 with a special train,

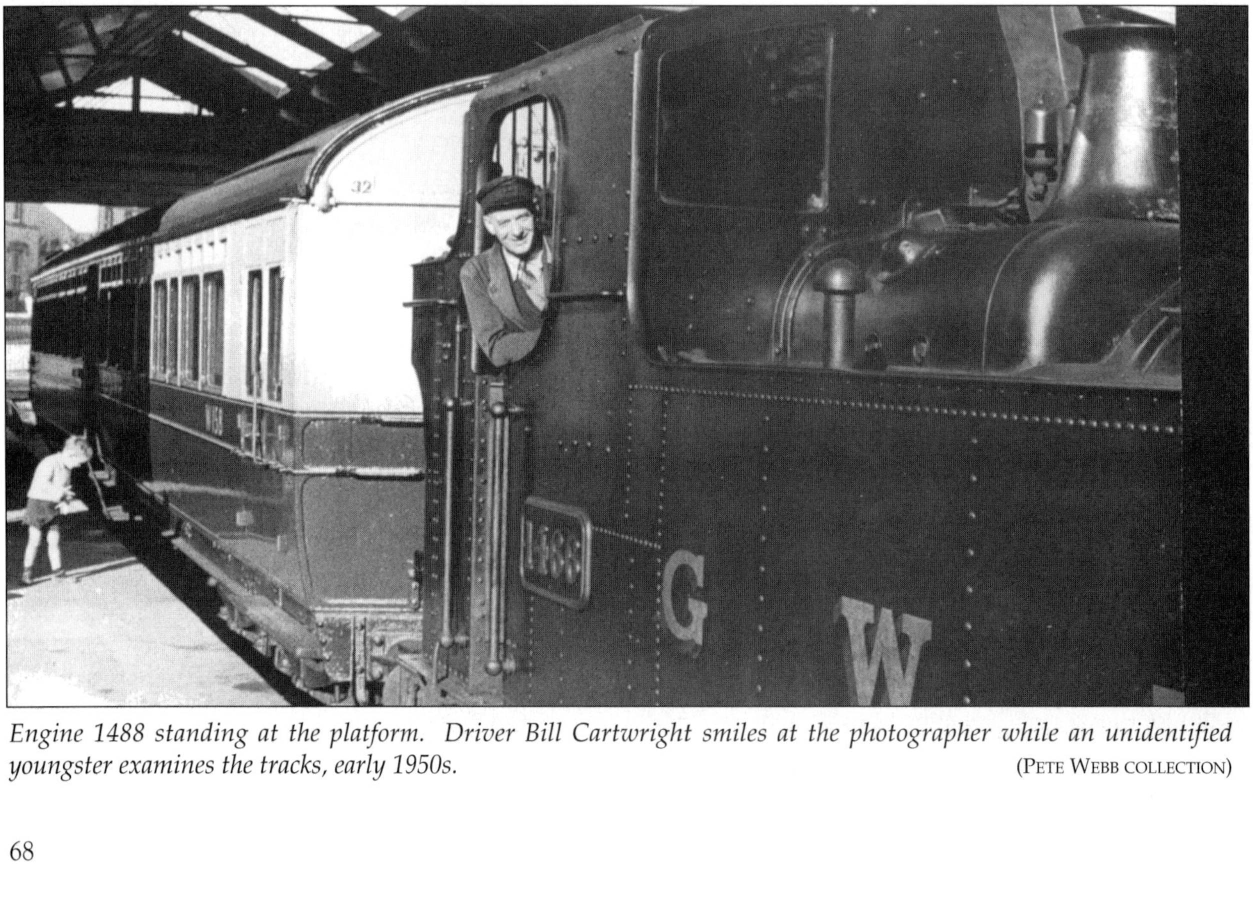

Engine 1488 standing at the platform. Driver Bill Cartwright smiles at the photographer while an unidentified youngster examines the tracks, early 1950s.
(PETE WEBB COLLECTION)

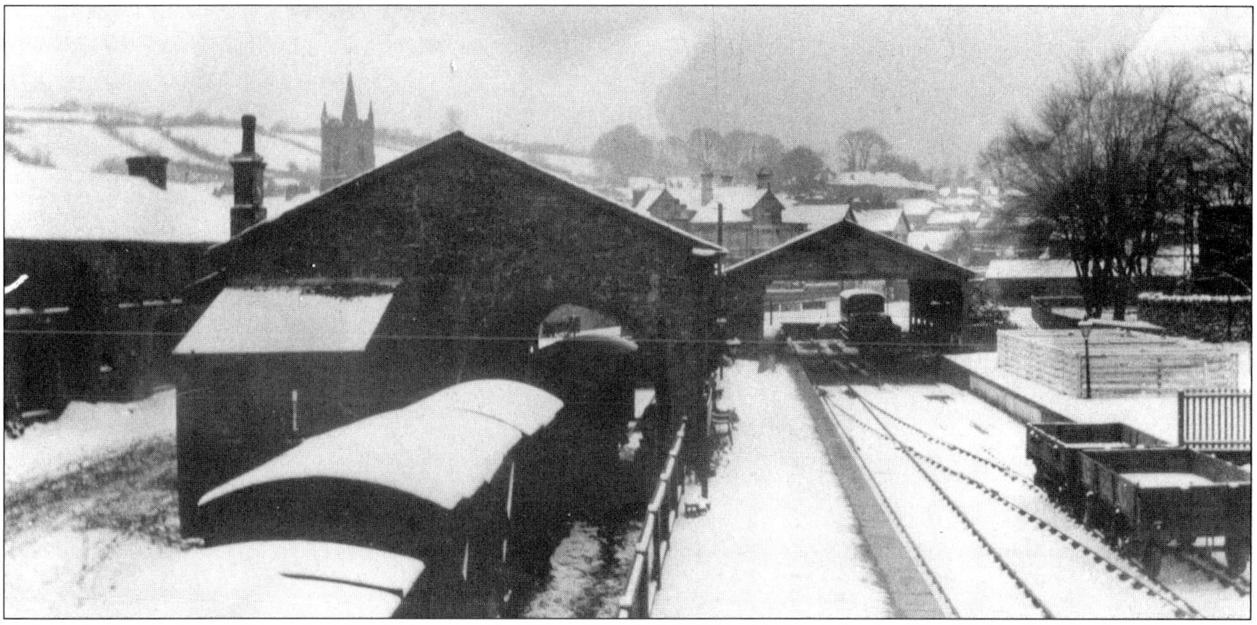

Railway in snow, 1934. (ASHBURTON MUSEUM)

the first to carry passengers since 1958, travelling the line from Totnes to Ashburton.

The line finally reopened on 5 April 1969 and on 21 May Lord Beeching performed the official opening ceremony. The occasion was marked by his comment, 'If I had not closed this branch I could not now be opening it', and by the Portreeve, Michael Webster, riding in the engine in a brand new Portreeve's robe, which he managed to get dirty.

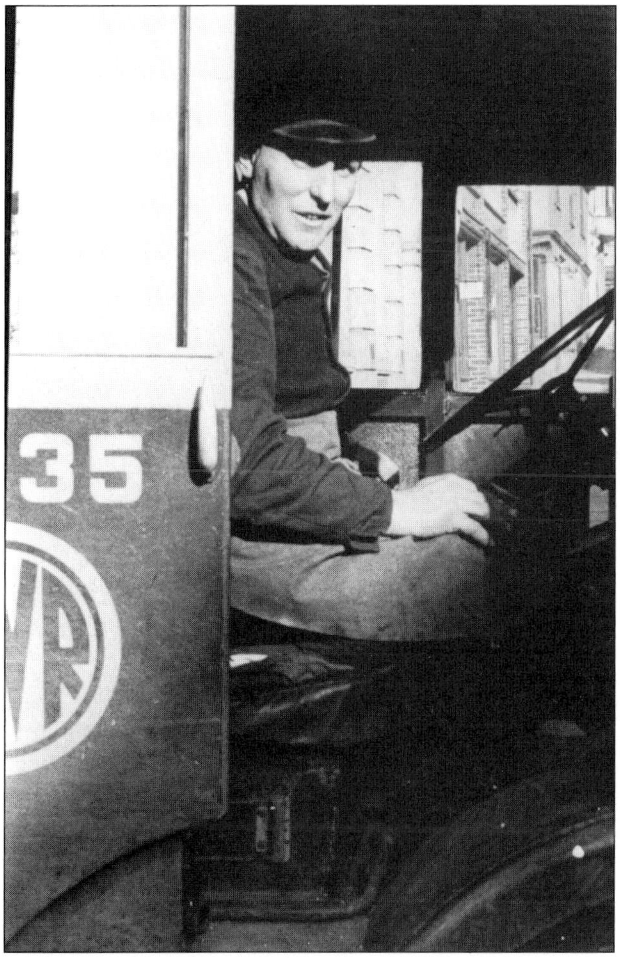

GWR lorry with driver, late 1940s. (PETE WEBB COLLECTION)

The section from Ashburton to Buckfastleigh was only leased by the DVR, as the Ministry of Transport had already acquired that section for road improvements. Special trains for the carnival and steam galas still used this section, but it was mainly used for storage and repairs. The last trains ran on 2 October 1971 after another hard-fought battle to retain this section. It was finally down to the cost of a bridge over the slip-road at Pear Tree, as the Ministry of Transport had made alternative plans if the town was willing to pay for this bridge. With three 12 or 14-coach trains coming into Ashburton from Totnes, Bristol and London on that last day, the town traders regretted that they had not fought harder and raised the money needed. The DVLR (Dart Valley Light Railway) took over the Paignton to Kingswear line the following year and eventually closed the Buckfastleigh to Totnes section in October 1990. The following year a new company, the South Devon Railway Trust, took over the line with a 25-year lease and ran it as the Primrose Line, using mainly volunteers.

A recent (2004) feasibility study by Exeter University looked into rejoining this section and it could be done, but not along the exact route, which is now covered by the A38 Expressway, and it would not be likely to come right into the town centre. The first stage of ensuring a future for the line and the SDRT was to recently purchase the lease and line from the DVLR (Dart Valley Light Railway).

A pleasant country walk called Bulliver's Way covers the section from near the engine shed to Pear Tree. It was named after the engine that used the line and was opened in April 1979. Owned by

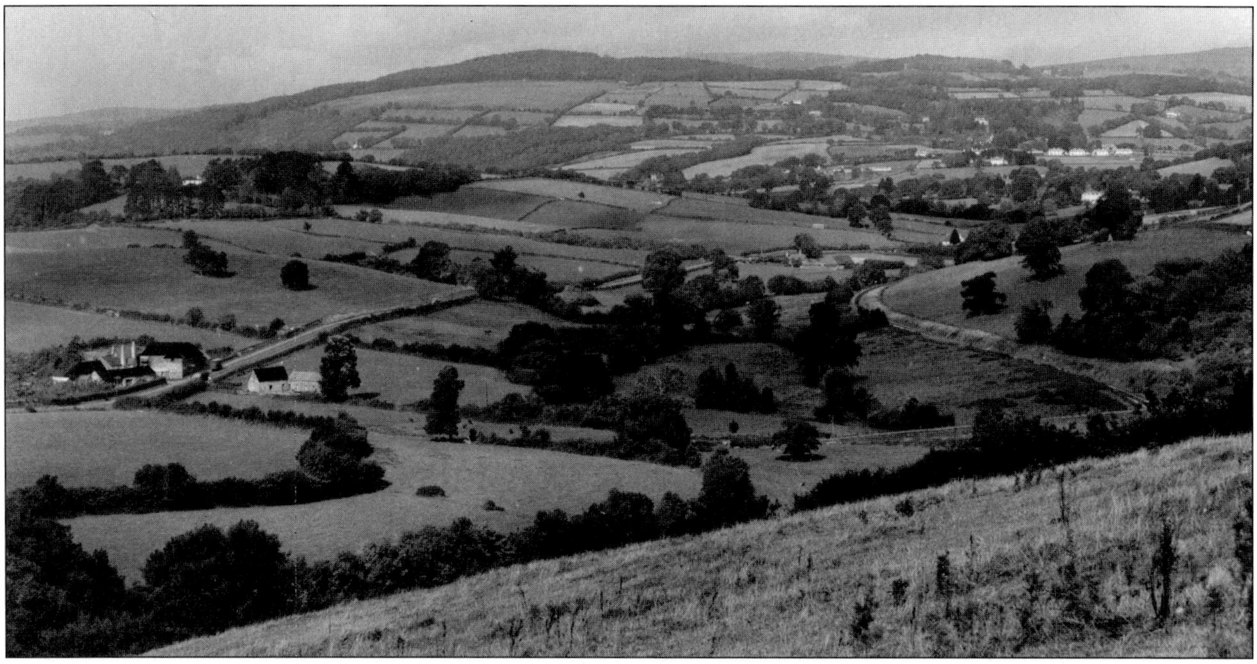

Pridhamsleigh looking up the Ashburn Valley, circa 1950. The then A38 is on the left and the new dual carriageway follows the line of the railway on the right. (PETE WEBB COLLECTION)

Dartmoor National Park Authority, it was given to the Town Council in 2003.

Local Memories

Eileen Egbeare remembers travelling on the train as a child. She especially remembers the annual Sunday school outing on the second Wednesday in July. The group usually went to Teignmouth, leaving the town on special trains at 9a.m. Accompanied by mums, the two Miss Butlers and often Sunday schools from other churches in the town, five or six coaches filled with excited kids would arrive at the seaside for a day on the beach. A tired but happy group would arrive back after what was, for most families, the only time they saw the sea, with buckets of shells and some seaweed to hang by the back door to tell if it was going to rain.

Others remember the train missing a passenger and the driver, on seeing them in his mirror, stopping and backing up to pick them up. Gordon Dumble remembers this happening as he travelled by train to work in Plymouth in the 1950s. Barry Fezzey's mother remembers the same thing happening to her if she missed the train on her way to work at Totnes during the Second World War.

Gordon told of another occasion when the same driver, Bill Cartwright, again had occasion to back up when a group of hikers were left behind. They had been on the platform for a couple of hours and had been unable to open the carriage doors. When the guard was told of this he proceeded to push the carriage door open, to the amazement of the hikers who had been attempting to pull the doors open. The guard further informed them that the next time they travelled the Great Western Railway would arrange a carriage with outward-opening doors for their convenience!

Ashburton being prone to winter flooding often meant that the station became unusable due to the line being flooded up to the platform. Some remember ponies from the annual fair being loaded in their hundreds and the November fair having as many as 90 wagons laden with cattle. Others remember their school days, coming into Ashburton for its Grammar School in the 1920s and 1930s until it closed in 1938 and afterwards, in the 1940s and 1950s, going the other way to Totnes.

CHAPTER 10

Industries

Ashburton's Tin and Copper Mining Industry

The first sure references that exist to indicate Ashburton's involvement with the Devon tin industry come following the stannary charter granted by King John in 1201. This charter was to form the structure for the development of the stannaries in the counties of both Devon and Cornwall, and granted certain liberties to those searching for tin, namely:

> *to mine for tin and dig turves for smelting tin everywhere in our lands, moors and wastes and in those of all persons whatsoever in the said county... as has formerly been done.*

The history of the stannary institutions begins in the eleventh century or early-twelfth century with the requirement to pay tax (coinage) to the king. Ashburton's role as centre for the administration of the collection of duty payable to the king on all tin produced enabled it to become one of three towns designed as stannary towns in the county of Devon, the others being Chagford and Tavistock. At a later point Plympton became the fourth stannary town in the county as a result of the volumes of tin being brought by tinners from Dartmoor to be weighed and sampled for the assessment of duty, and to be marked before it could be sold. With the formation of the stannaries came the development of stannary law under which all the tinners were governed.

As part of the structure of the stannaries there was the need to enact the legislation under which the tin industry would be governed. Between the years 1474 and 1786 there were at least 13 meetings of the Great Courts or Parliaments. These parliaments were held at Crockerntor in the centre of Dartmoor, some 396m above sea level close to Two Bridges, unless otherwise adjourned to another location. These parliaments called for each of the four stannary towns to send 24 representatives, or stannators as they were called. However, by the final meeting of what was by then termed the General Stannary Court, held in Moretonhampstead in 1786, Ashburton would send five representatives, while Chagford would send the largest number (seven), and Plympton and Tavistock would send one and four representatives respectively.

During the early years of Ashburton being a stannary town, the tin came from the many stream workings which were recovering alluvial tin from the rivers flowing off Dartmoor. However, by the end of the fifteenth century there are records referring to tin working within the actual parish of Ashburton. Certainly by the year 1492/3 there were already major workings at Owlacombe, then known as

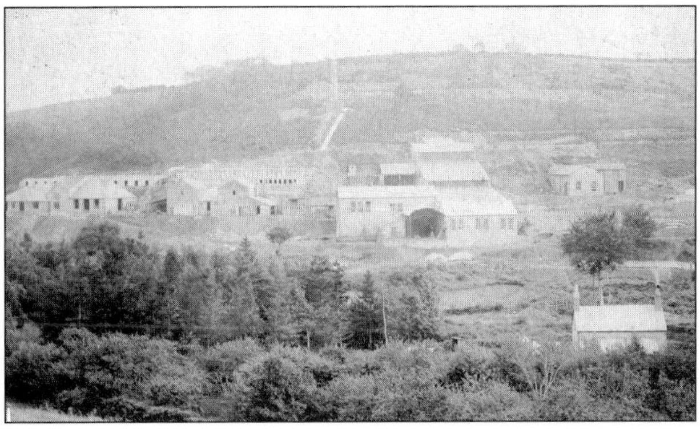

Owlacombe Mine, c.1908. Still a working mine at this time, it had just reopened. It finally closed in 1912, although it was reworked for a short period in the early 1930s. (PETE WEBB COLLECTION)

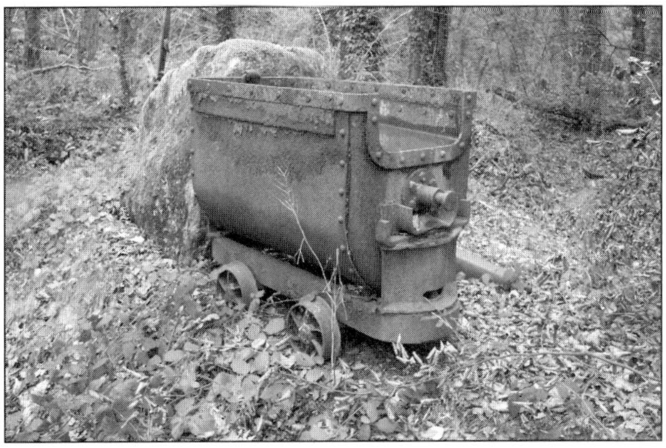

A trolley from Owlacombe Mine. (STUART HANDS)

'Owlecombe Worke'. The documentary evidence also points towards opencast workings at Whiddon woods. The Ministers' Accounts of Henry VII in 1504 refer to an increase in rent on the tin works above 'Wheddowne' (Whiddon), which were leased to Nicholas Southcot and John Berd for the term of 60 years, that being the 19th year of the same term. The height of tin production during this period was in the years between 1500 and 1550. However, following this there was a steady decline as reserves were exhausted, and new reserves became far more difficult to find. The English Civil War also had an impact on the industry, and resulted in production coming to a halt as men were called up for military service. Over the coming years there would develop a cycle of intense activity followed by many years of inactivity.

By the start of the nineteenth century there was renewed activity which would, over the next 100 years, lead to the opening of a number of mines within the vicinity of the town of Ashburton. Today, the only visible signs of this activity are the overgrown remains of the engine house of Druid Mine which, over the period of its operation, was promoted under a number of different names including 'The Arundell United Copper Mine' and the 'New Victoria South Devon Mining Company Limited'. The mine reached a depth of 96 fathoms below the surface, but in all respects the operation, like many others, was dogged by financial failure. The failure, in 1855, of Strahan, Paul & Co., who were the company's bankers and also large shareholders at the time, resulted in a suspension of operations. The production figures available for the period between the years 1845 and 1913 show that the total revenues generated from sales amounted to just over £75. A footnote to the operations by the Arundell Mining Company is the fact that it was one of only two companies who failed to settle their accounts with the Buckland in the Moor estate for the purchase of timber.

The most secluded of all the mining operations within the parish was the short-lived but fittingly named Queen of the Dart Mine, close to the River Dart, whose output during the years between 1854 and 1857 amounted to 579 tons, which were sold for £2,127. Also close to the River Dart were opencast workings in Ausewell (Awsewell) Woods, whose origins are obscure but which date back to the sixteenth century.

However, the most significant mining activity within the locality of Ashburton were the workings at Stormsdown and Owlacombe Mine (previously known as West Beam Mine these operations would later come to be known as Ashburton United). They were worked in the nineteenth century, again between 1914 and 1920 and finally in 1925. The dumps from these workings would also be reworked to recover tin in about 1937, and finally in 1958 by Roskudda. These workings would finally bring to an end Ashburton's association with the Dartmoor tin industry.

The Woollen Industry

From the early Middle Ages and through most of its recorded history, England has been famous for its wool. The best wool in the world was produced in England, and Ashburton's proximity to Buckfast's Cistercian Abbey as well as the support of Bishop Stapledon, ensured a thriving woollen industry in the town. Bishop Stapledon founded the Guild of St Lawrence, in around 1314, to look after the Chantry Chapel and his seal, which is now used as the town crest, includes the teasel plant – the badge of the fullers. He procured a weekly market as early as 1310, as well as fairs on the festivals of St Lawrence and St Martin.

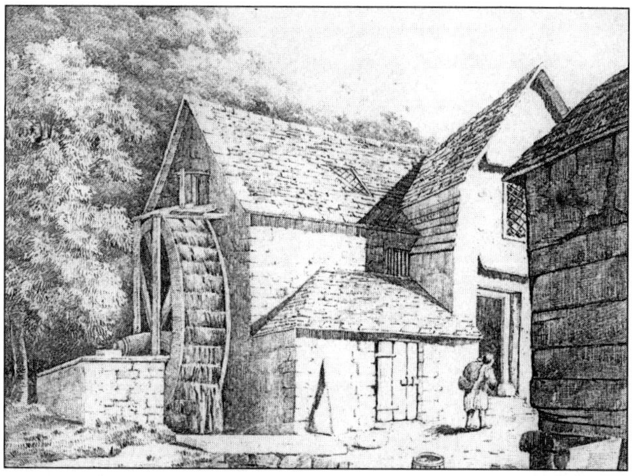

A drawing of the water mill, North Street, c.1850.
(PETE WEBB COLLECTION)

The thirteenth century saw England producing the finest-quality wool in Europe and by the fourteenth century large quantities of broadcloth were being exported.

Devon had only a moderate share in this trade, which was mainly concentrated in areas near the abundant swiftly-flowing rivers.

A petition from Ashburton's inhabitants to Richard II (king from 1377–99) to grant them exemption from market tolls (Ashburton being a royal manor) showed, however, that the trade had not died out, even though the Hundred Years' War with France brought about a slump in Devon's cloth exports.

A map prepared in 1605 shows seven mills along the course of the Ashburn, which is just above the town. From the top these were Belford Mill (locally called the Coffin Mill because of its shape), Lurgecombe Mill, Rew (Tucking or Rewe) Mill, North Mill (opposite Mill Lane), Daws (flour) Mill, and Town Mill (still working in the 1950s and now part of a sheltered-housing complex). Gages Mill and Furzleigh Mill, now both establishments providing accommodation and food, can be seen on the old main road to Buckfast, the latter just before the Ashburn joins the Dart.

The Fabyan family, who first appeared in Ashburton around the middle of the sixteenth century, were important serge makers right up to 1815. The Reformation brought an influx of foreign manufacturers and by the early-seventeenth century Devon had a thriving cloth industry once again. A weekly market in Exeter, from 1538, brought London merchants to Devon. They purchased large quantities of Devon 'kersies' and 'dozens' from the surrounding areas and small towns including

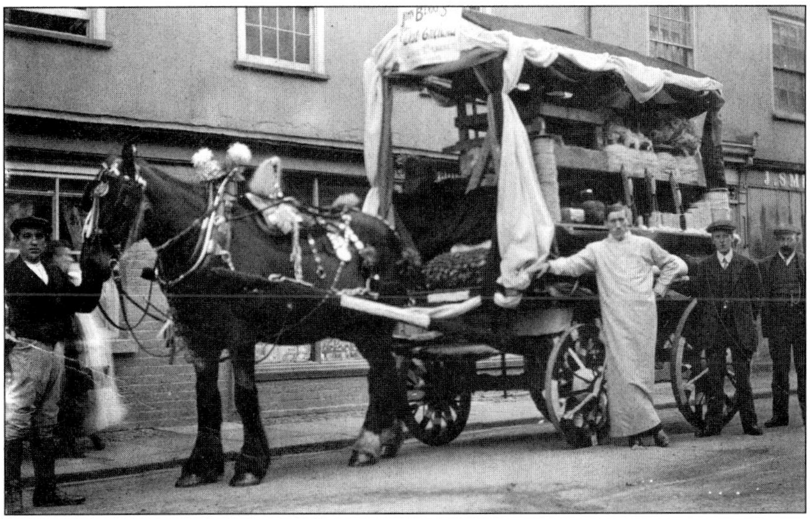

Mr Berry's carnival float with Jack 'Buckie' James, Alf Townsend and Charlie Steer on the right and an unknown chap holding the reins. The original card was given to Pete Webb by Jack Barnett, who was Buckie's nephew, c.1920. Soon after this picture was taken the firm started to use Ford lorries.
(PETE WEBB COLLECTION)

Berry & Sons, Woolsorters and Wagoners – these nine gentlemen were obviously in Berry's employ and, according to Jack Barnett, are left to right, back row: *Frank Royal, Jack 'Buckie' James, Charlie Steer, Wal Lear, ?, Sam Howis;* front: *Tom Hamm, ? Steer, Bill Adams.*
(PETE WEBB COLLECTION)

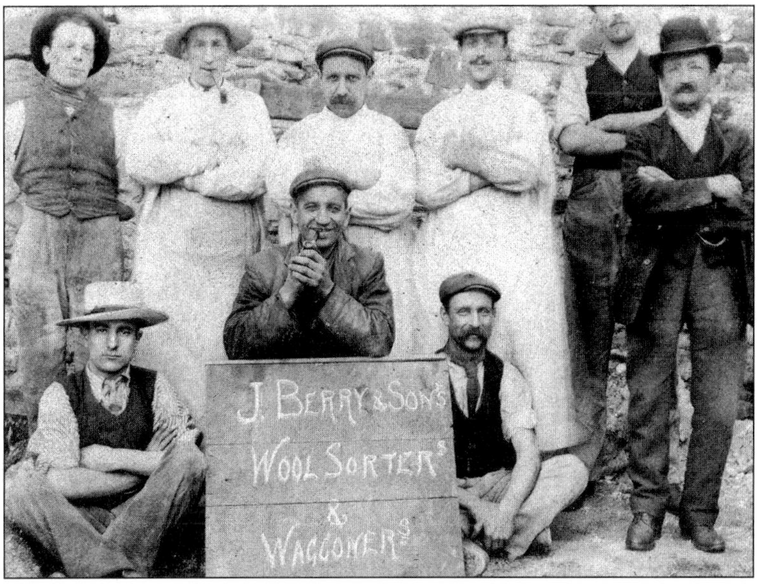

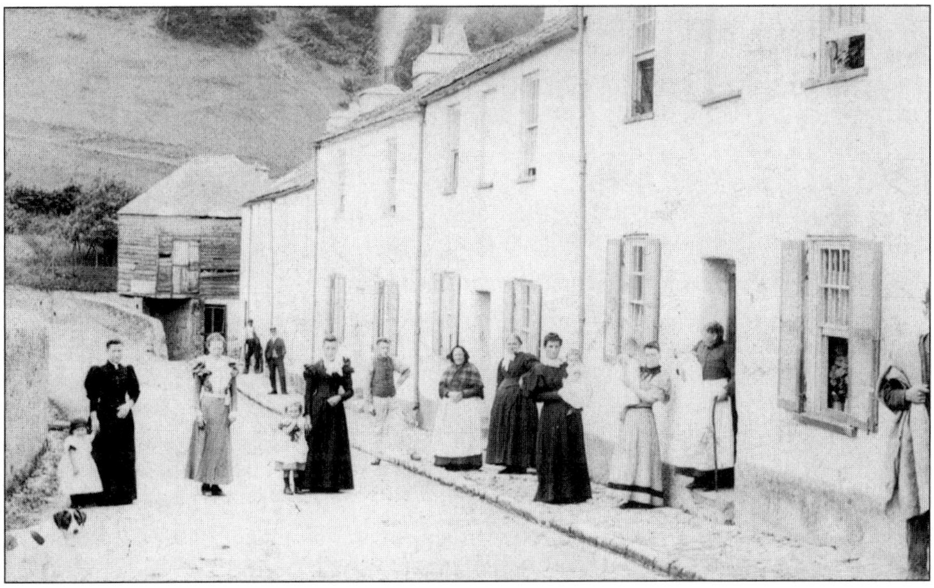

Headborough cottages, c.1910. This row of two-up, two-down woolworkers' cottages still has a single entrance for each pair. A woollen loft can be seen above the shed at the bottom.
(PETE WEBB COLLECTION)

Ashburton. Sir Walter Raleigh obtained licences from Elizabeth I allowing the export of unfinished cloth and Ashburton must have felt the benefits of the trade that came about from this.

Serges increased as the main product of the area in the seventeenth century. This was mainly a cottage industry carried out in the homes of poor local people. Combers, who were often poor spinsters, bought the wool from the farmers at the market. The next week they took the yarn back to market to be bought by the weaver. The serge maker met the weavers weekly and collected the products of their hired looms. Others who owned their looms were able to get a better price from local merchants. The serge was then sent to the Exeter market as unfinished cloth or sold on to the local fulling mill.

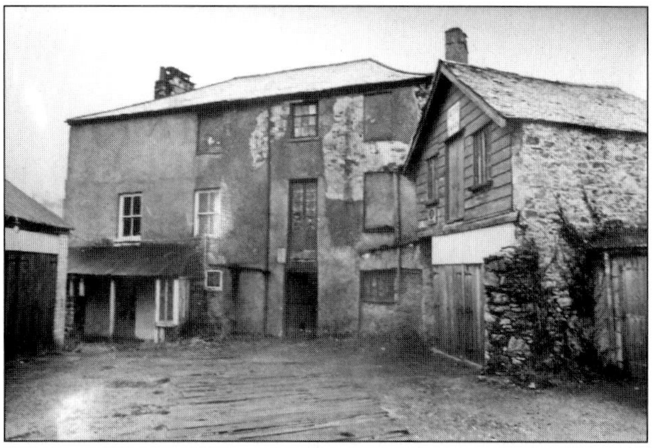

Town Mill outside. Note the wooden planks in the foreground which cover the leat, 1950s.

(ASHBURTON MUSEUM)

In this final part of the process the cloth was cleaned and shrunk in soapy water. Last in this chain was the clothier, often a man of means with a large house in the town. He either bought the cloth at the market or employed the weavers himself, giving out the yarn with the proper proportions of abb and worsted together with glue to size the 'chain' before tying it to the loom. It was then woven to be returned the following week when they were paid.

The clothier was mainly a man of leisure and he spent much of his time using his wealth to improve his land and house. With money to spare he could employ men to work for him. Most of the 'improvements' to waste land in the parish can be attributed to clothiers, who would attend the weekly markets at Exeter and meet the city merchants, who in turn travelled widely and met traders from all over Europe. This gave the opportunity of gathering news from abroad, and overseas gossip, thus ensuring a ready audience back in the town's pubs and inns.

The invention in 1767 of the Spinning Jenny had a great impact on the manufacture of yarns, with the first machinery arriving around the end of the eighteenth century. The ample supply of water both to supply power and to wash the wool was utilised to the full. Wool was purchased direct from the farmer and stored in newly erected buildings after sorting. It was then washed and dried in the lofts, of which there are a few left (the best example is the long building between the two sections of the town's car park). Mills were erected and kept busy with work from the whole area. Usually brought in by donkey or packhorse, some was collected by the mill's master or his agent from some central point. This also had the effect of making those unwilling to devote more time and capital outlay to their business to fall behind and leave their trade. The loss of some cottage industry jobs was compensated for by the large numbers of employees needed in the mills and sorting sheds. At the time there was no retirement age and older people had no option but the workhouse when they were unable to work. Mr Berry and others saved many from this fate by giving the old and infirm easy work for a small wage.

Mr Caunter started his first worsted mills in Ashburton in 1817 with the other well-known names in the industry being Hamlyn, Churchward and Berry. In the 1890s, due to unfavourable working conditions in the mills, a union representative from Plymouth tried to persuade some of the workers to join the union. Messrs Berry would not recognise the men's right to join a union and a strike started in December 1891. The strike dragged on with meetings, protests and lockouts and the workers were eventually given an ultimatum – either leave the union or lose your job.

Many of the workers at the time lived in Buckfastleigh, and those from Ashburton felt they owed their employers (the Berry brothers lived in

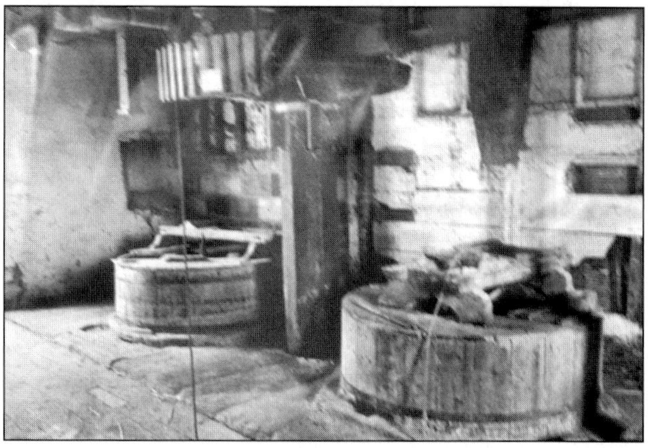

Town Mill inside, late 1960s, showing equipment just before removal. The mill now forms the meeting rooms of St Andrew's Close complex. (ASHBURTON MUSEUM)

Ashburton at Waverly and Kenwyn Halls) a greater allegiance and carried on working. This was seen as strike breaking by the others and ever since there has been a certain animosity between the two towns. Mr Simeon Berry, the head of the firm, died in March 1908 at they age of 79, still leading an active working life.

The industry was already in decline by this time

with the change of policy by the East India Company in 1830 and the large, powerful coal-driven mills in the North of England producing cheaper and better cloth.

The industry struggled along and still produced some goods locally at the time of writing. The CWS mill in Buckfastleigh only closed in the last ten years and the mills at Buckfast still produced carpets and other woven goods. Yet in Ashburton, all that remained of this major source of the town's former wealth was a small number of buildings along with other evidence, such as leats to power the mill.

Ashburton Marble and Glendinning

Most people probably miss the very large limestone quarry to the east of Ashburton as they drive past on the A38 or leave Ashburton going towards Exeter.

Since the late 1950s the Glendinning family has gradually acquired more and more of it. The story goes that two brothers, Ernie and Jack Glendinning, stopped on the outskirts of town to buy petrol. They had been on the lookout for a limestone quarry in the South West and, noticing a cloud of dust, went to investigate. The result was that they purchased the first of two quarries in the vicinity. This was the small 14-acre Linhay Hill Quarry, purchased in the late 1950s from Mr Frank Jackson Badcock, a local builder and landowner.

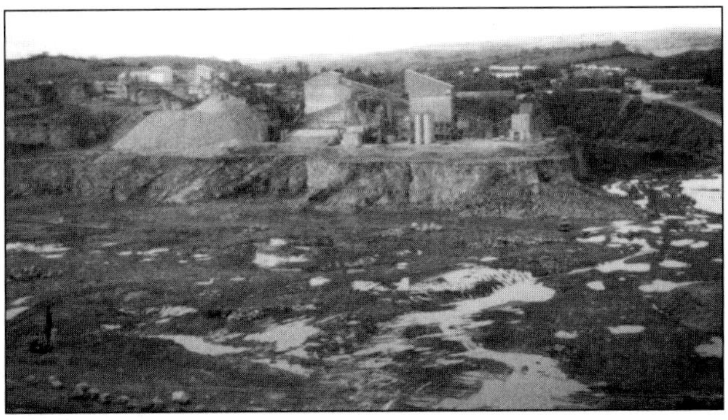

Glendinning Quarry, 2001. (PETE WEBB)

The second and best known of these was Jenkins Quarry whose product was the famous Ashburton Marble (which is actually a form of limestone). This was purchased in 1971 by the Glendinning family. At one time this was the only quarry in England producing marble, examples of which can still be seen in many places today even though it is no longer quarried in any great quantity. It is mainly black with a fine tracery of uneven pink and cream lines running through it. Used extensively for grander public buildings such as town halls, banks and churches around the world, some of the famous buildings that have used Ashburton marble are the United Nations Building in New York, the Baptismal Bath in Melbourne Cathedral and the Royal Bank of Canada in Port of Spain, Trinidad. The United States was probably the biggest market in the 1960s. In London the Post Office Tower, the Geological Museum, the Millbank Development, Torino Restaurant in Oxford Street, the Londonderry House Hotel and the Hilton Hotel have all used it. Closer to home it can be found in Exeter Cathedral, County Hall in Exeter, the Britannia Royal Naval College in Dartmouth, Ashburton's own Parish Church of St Andrew's and also Buckfast Abbey. The monks at the Abbey sometimes refer to the marble as coming from a small quarry on the outskirts of Buckfast but the magnificent black marble examples in the Holy Sacrament Chapel are definitely from Ashburton.

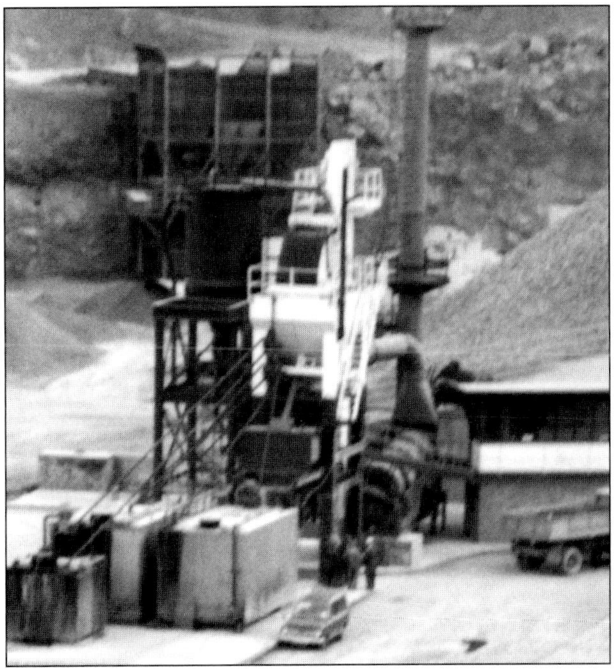

Glendinning Quarry, circa 1960. (ASHBURTON MUSEUM)

Because of its delicate nature it could not be blasted out and was originally cut by hand. Some early examples of this are seen in church tombs from the sixteenth century but later it was cut with a system of wires. One Robert Foulton, who invented the steam ship, in the eighteenth century developed a method of polishing the marble for which he was awarded a gold medal. Later it was taken for polishing in large blocks to the Jenkins works in Torquay. In a *Mid Devon Advertiser* article of December 1961 the owners were named as Building Specialists (Overseas) Ltd, who ceased trading as late as the 1990s, but the production of the marble had already ceased in 1970. Most of the kerbstones around the Bull Ring in the centre of town are a pink example of the product and look their best when wet.

The original quarries were called Strawberrybushes or Jenkins Quarry (the marble quarry), Linhay Hill and Lower Waye. From those small beginnings the quarry has grown even more with the acquisition of surrounding land and it now (2004) covers over 100 acres and employs over 200 people. The family still owns the works, with Ernest's son, Ian Glendinning, the operations director and Jack's son, Clifford Glendinning, the transport manager. The company still occasionally sells large blocks of the limestone which is then taken away to be cut and polished. Their main products are aggregates, ready- mixed concrete and coated aggregates (bitumen macadam) but they also supply larger stones for everything from sea defenses, walling stone and concrete products right down to sand and particularly agricultural lime for the local farmers – previously produced by the many lime kilns so common in this area and the rest of Devon.

Umber Mines

Ashburton's umber mines were the principal ones not only in Devon but in the whole country. In the mid to late-nineteenth century very little umber was mined anywhere else in the country. The umber was an impure form of iron oxide, which was mined in two principal areas of Ashburton. The two principal mines were in Cock Orchard, near the bottom of Bowden Hill off West Street, and behind the cottage hospital off Eastern Road.

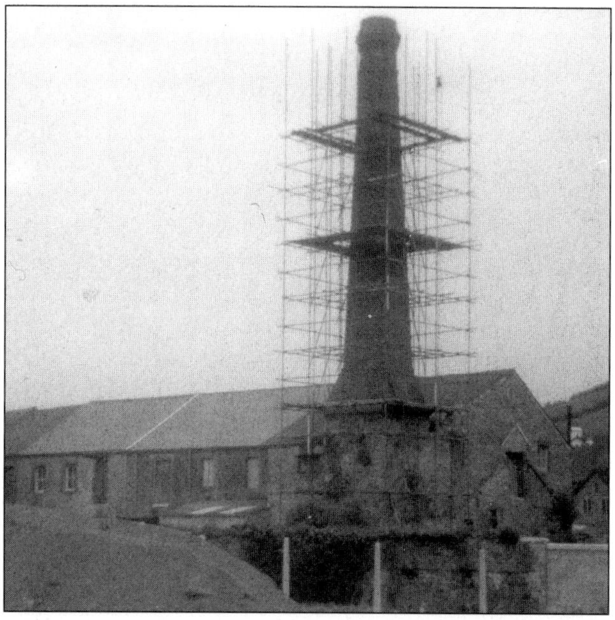

Umber chimney being demolished in the summer of 1980. At the end of what was Tuckers seed store there are now (2004) offices for Greymatter and other computer firms.

(PETE WEBB)

The umber was mined in a clay-like form from pockets rather than seams, leaving shallow, open quarry-like areas from the 'opencast' method of extraction. The main use was for paint, brown paper making and as a colouring agent in the local woollen industry. The last umber mine was off Dolbeare Road and during the late 1870s and early 1880s was known as The Roborough Umber Co. It was owned by Beer, Musgrove & Co., with Nicholas Pascoe as mine captain and J.C. Musgrove of Torquay as manager. By the late 1880s it had a John Chegwiddon as mine captain and no longer appeared in trade directories. The mine known as the Ashburton Umber Mine Co., which appears from 1889 to 1939, was in East Street and seems likely to be the same one, especially as Nicholas Pascoe appears as the mine captain for both. Nicholas lived in Rose Cottage in Balland Lane and was joint proprietor in 1902 with William Henry Hoskins. From 1906, W.H. Hoskins appears on his own and Nicholas died in 1908. The industry had died out by 1910, apart from a brief revival during the Second World War when it was used for camouflage. The Truro Colour Company were the last to mine the umber, with a Mr Weaver as the manager when it closed around 1946.

The bed, or pocket, of umber was some 30ft thick and extracted by sinking large rectangular pits. These were infilled before the next pit was dug. It is not certain when they finally closed but it seems likely it was soon after the Second World War. The Roborough Works, as they were known, were immediately beside the haulage yard and under what is now (2004) the Emmets Park estate and the telephone exchange in front, although the area of umber probably overlaps.

W.F. Miners & Sons moved from Widecombe, where their business was established in 1925, to green fields farmed by the Horrell family. The yard was excavated from these fields and expanded with the business until Miners Brothers broke it up in the early 1990s. It is now a close of houses called Miners Close.

✥ CHAPTER 11 ✥

Nineteenth-Century Ashburton

The nineteenth century was one of great change for Ashburton, as it was throughout Britain. Electoral reform took place in this century. Scientific and technological innovation resulted in traditional industries giving way to the factory system. Agriculture, too, benefited from these changes, although the agricultural labourer did not.

A useful source of information about the early part of the century, where there are few other sources, are the trade directories. What they have to say about the town is often copied from other sources, but the names and trades they list are most useful. It is not until the decennial census that we have fuller details. Piggot, in 1823, describes Ashburton as 'one of the neatest towns in Devonshire'.

White, in his directory, says of the town that there are 'three good streets with many neat houses and well stocked shops.' He also refers to the decline in coach traffic since the opening of the railway and notes the decrease in population due to the decline in the manufacturing of serges and blankets. John Berry in North Street and Richard Caunter in West Street are the only two manufacturers mentioned. In 1823, in addition to these, were Peter Sparke of Kingsbridge Lane and Solomon Tozer of East Street. There were tin mines at Whiddon and Waye.

Millers who receive a mention are William Underhill at Furzleigh, Richard Willing at Lurgecombe and Stephen Yolland at Towns Mills. All these mills still survive today, although not as they would have been in 1850. This is particularly true of Town Mill.

It is of interest to note that there were two Baptist ministers in the town at this time – the Revd Samuel Hebditch and the Revd Charles Tippet. As mentioned in Chapter 3, very little is known of this community of Baptists.

Population of Ashburton from 1785–1921

Year	Population
1785	2500
1801	3080
1831	4165
1841	3841
1851	3432
1861	3062
1871	2952
1881	2891
1891	2762
1901	2678
1921	2362

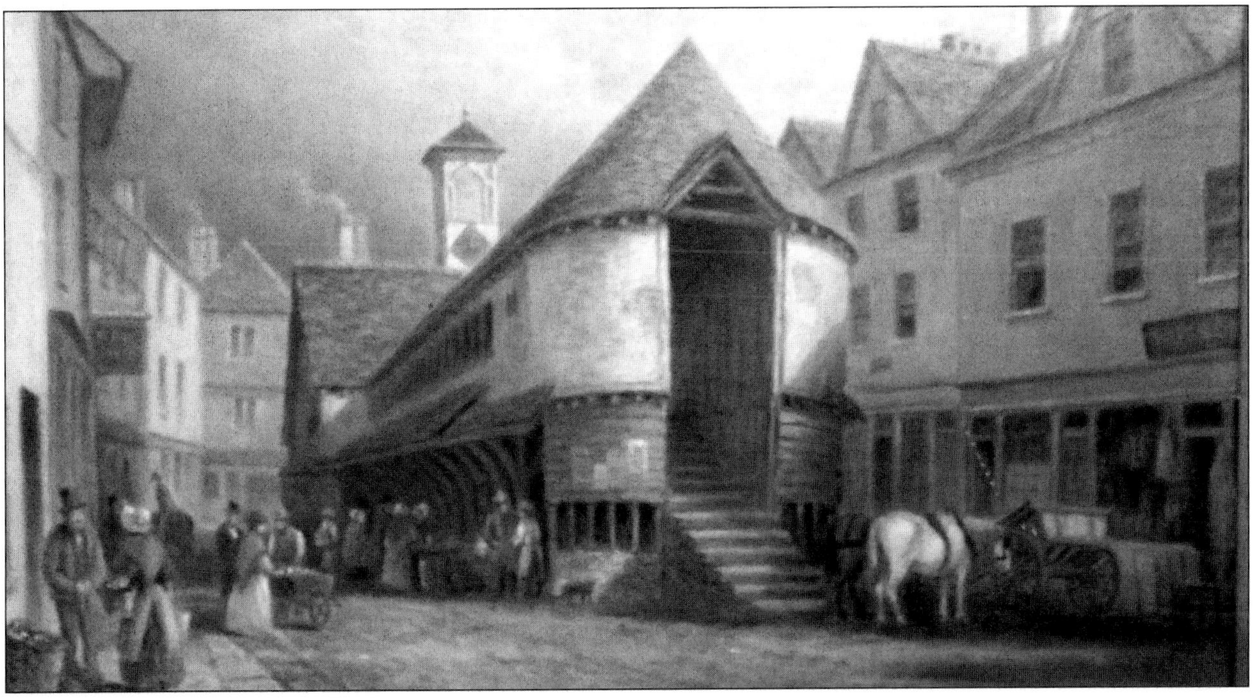

Painting by Frederick Foot of Ashburton's old market, presented by Mrs Sawdye to the Guild of St Lawrence to be displayed in the town. (STUART HANDS; ST LAWRENCE CHAPEL)

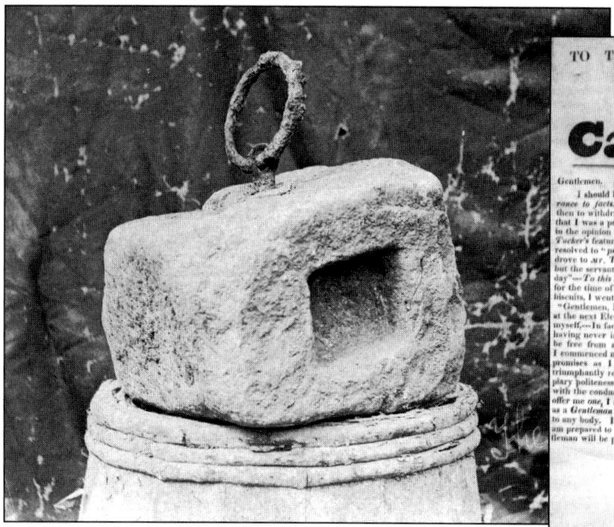

Ashburton 'bull ring', c.1890, from an old picture postcard so probably a replica (but you never know!). Another stone reputed to be the bull ring is at the base of St Lawrence Chapel tower. (PETE WEBB COLLECTION)

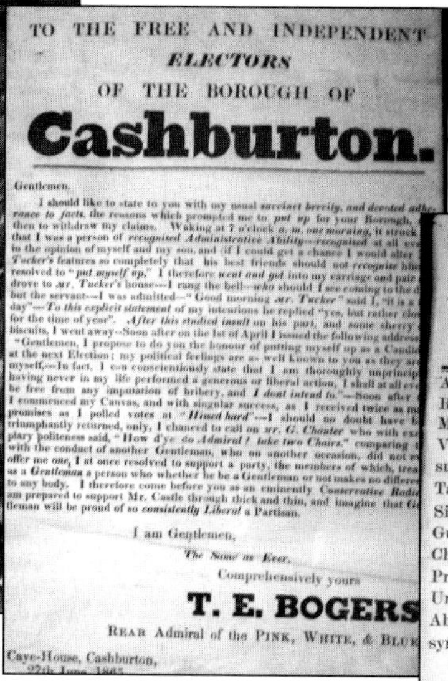

TO THE FREE AND INDEPENDENT
ELECTORS
OF THE BOROUGH OF
Cashburton.

Gentlemen,

I should like to state to you with my usual *succinct brevity, and devoted adhe-rance to facts*, the reasons which prompted me to *put up* for your Borough, then to withdraw my claims. Waking at 7 o'clock *a. m. one morning*, it struck that I was a person of *recognised Administrative Ability—recognised* at all eve to the opinion of myself and my son, and (if I could get a chance I would alter *Tucker's* features so completely that his best friends should not *recognise* him resolved to "*put myself up*." I therefore *went and got* into my carriage and pair drove to *Mr. Tucker's* house—I rang the bell—*who should I see coming to the d* but the servant—I was admitted—"Good morning *Mr. Tucker*" said I, "it is a day"—*To this explicit statement* of my intentions he replied "yes, but rather clo for the time of year". *After this studied insult* on his part, and some sherry biscuits, I went away—Soon after on the 1st of April I issued the following addres "Gentlemen, I propose to do you the honour of putting myself up as a Candi at the next Election; my political feelings are as well known to you as they are myself,—In fact, I can conscientiously state that I am thoroughly unprincip having never in my life performed a generous or liberal action, I shall at all eve be free from any imputation of bribery, and *I dont intend to*."—Soon after I commenced my Canvas, and with singular success, as I received twice as m promises as I polled votes at "*Hived hard*"—I should no doubt have b triumphantly returned, only, I chanced to call on *Mr. G. Chaster* who with exe plary politeness said, "*How d'ye do Admiral! take two Chairs*," comparing with the conduct of another Gentleman, who on another occasion, did not ev *offer me one*, I at once resolved to support a party, the members of which, trea as a *Gentleman* a person who whether he be a Gentleman or not makes no differe to any body. I therefore come before you as an eminently *Conservative Radi* am prepared to support Mr. Castle through thick and thin, and imagine that Ge tleman will be proud of so *consistently Liberal* a Partisan.

I am Gentlemen,

The Same as Ever,

Comprehensively yours

T. E. BOGERS

REAR Admiral of the PINK, WHITE, & BLUE

Caye-House, Cashburton,

Victorian election poster. (ASHBURTON MUSEUM)

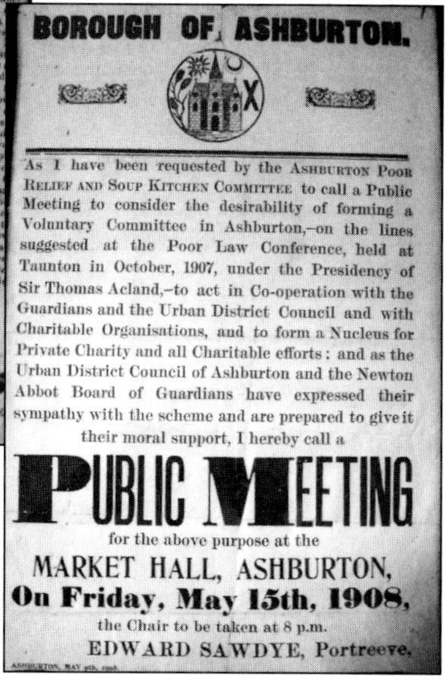

BOROUGH OF ASHBURTON.

As I have been requested by the ASHBURTON POOR RELIEF AND SOUP KITCHEN COMMITTEE to call a Public Meeting to consider the desirability of forming a Voluntary Committee in Ashburton,–on the lines suggested at the Poor Law Conference, held at Taunton in October, 1907, under the Presidency of Sir Thomas Acland,–to act in Co-operation with the Guardians and the Urban District Council and with Charitable Organisations, and to form a Nucleus for Private Charity and all Charitable efforts: and as the Urban District Council of Ashburton and the Newton Abbot Board of Guardians have expressed their sympathy with the scheme and are prepared to give it their moral support, I hereby call a

PUBLIC MEETING

for the above purpose at the

MARKET HALL, ASHBURTON,

On Friday, May 15th, 1908,

the Chair to be taken at 8 p.m.

EDWARD SAWDYE, Portreeve.

Notice about a soup kitchen. (ASHBURTON MUSEUM)

The nineteenth century was one of continued decline in population, along with the decline of traditional industries, particularly woollen manufacturing. The loss of passing trade was never recovered in Victorian times. Coupled with the decline in industry was that of the rural labour force, particularly as agriculture went into a slump. The figures for 1921 show that the decline continued well into the twentieth century. Things did not really start to improve until the late 1960s.

Where the people of Ashburton were born, as listed in the 1851 census

52.9 per cent in the parish
17.9 per cent within 5 miles of Ashburton parish
17.4 per cent within 25 miles
9.5 per cent within 125 miles
2.3 per cent over 125 miles away from Ashburton
(The percentage figures for the neighbouring parish of Bickington are similar: 49, 28, 16, 5, 1.)

The following shopkeepers are listed in the 1851 census:

- 9 butchers
- 4 chemists and druggists
- 4 earthenware dealers
- 29 grocers
- 2 hairdressers
- 4 ironmongers
- 6 drapers
- 7 milliners
- 6 tailors
- 3 watchmakers

How different from today! They must all have made some sort of living.

By 1857 Billings notes in his directory that this 'once flourishing town' might return to 'something like its former bustle and activity' should the proposed railway from Newton Abbot materialise.

Having lost one of its MPs in the Reform Bill of 1832, the sole remaining Member was from Lockerbie in Scotland, one Robert Jardine.

How had things changed by 1870? The *Morris directory* lists the various inhabitants who subscribed to the directory. The numbers of retail trades listed are as follows:

- 7 bakers
- 1 bookseller
- 8 shoemakers
- 15 shopkeepers (presumably grocers of some kind)
- 1 hairdresser
- 3 ironmongers
- 4 drapers
- 2 milliners
- 7 tailors
- 1 watchmaker

Some of the more unusual trades were: marine store dealer, of which there were two in Ashburton (although the town is so far from the sea) and cider retailer (most farms of the time made their own). In Victorian times cider was far more popular as an alcoholic beverage than beer. There was also a drill instructor and a veterinary surgeon. The only manufacturer listed is John Berry. It is known that Richard Caunter's mill in Bickington went out of business as a serge manufactory some time in the 1860s. His

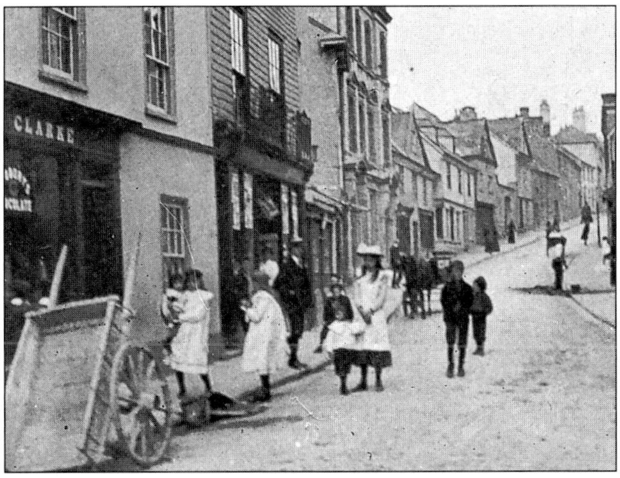

Shops and tradesmen at the bottom of East Street, c.1890. (PETE WEBB COLLECTION)

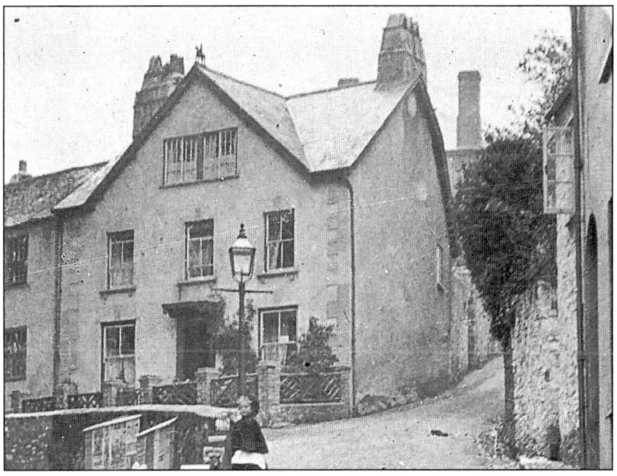

Mayflower House at the bottom of Bowden Hill, c.1890. During the Civil War the horseman on the roof denoted a safe house for Cavaliers – this original figure was stolen in the mid-1990s and replaced with a copy. (PETE WEBB COLLECTION)

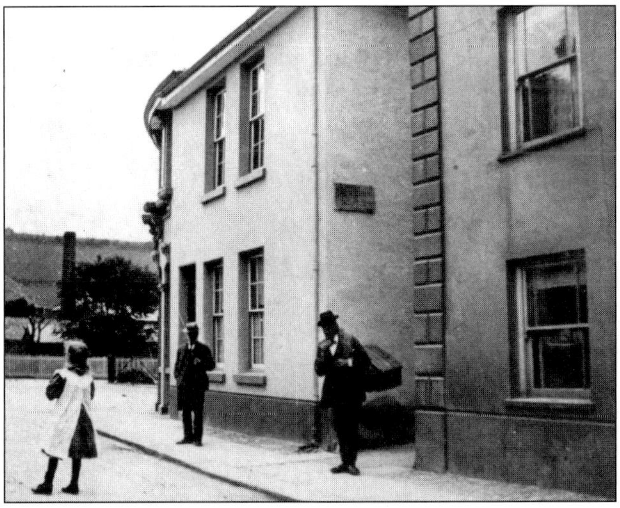

Pedlar, St Lawrence Lane. (PETE WEBB COLLECTION)

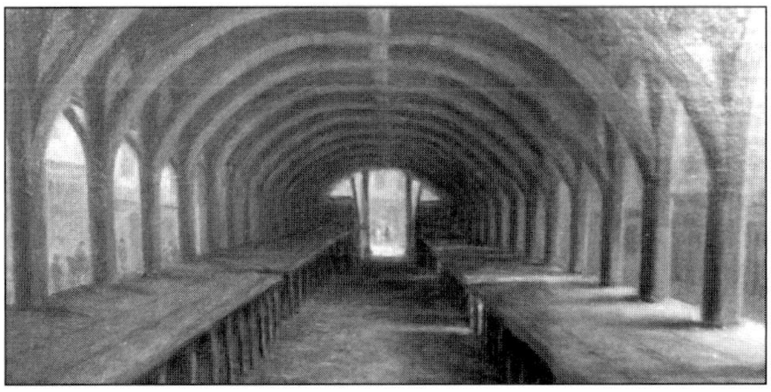

Interior of Ashburton's market. (STUART HANDS; ST LAWRENCE CHAPEL)

Ashburton plant may have gone the same way. Besides the Grammar School – headmaster at the time the Revd George Flood – there were Lord Middleton and Mrs Harris' Charity School in Bowling Green with Samuel Husson (master) and Miss Mary Baker (mistress), and an Infant School on North Street with Miss Ford and Miss French (mistresses).

The public establishments were gasworks, Inland Revenue, library, market house and Stamp Office. Among the places of worship were the Bretheren, who get their first mention in *Kelly's Directory* of 1873. The arrival of the railway did not bring the long-hoped-for upturn in prosperity.

In 1879 John Satterley was born in North Street. John later became an academic in Canada (see p.91). Thus far in our look at Ashburton in the nineteenth century we have relied on written sources. In 1952 John Satterley presented a paper to the Devonshire Association called 'Memories of Victorian Ashburton in late Victorian Days.' This is a fascinating document and we make no apologies for making much use of it in looking at Ashburton in the last 20 years

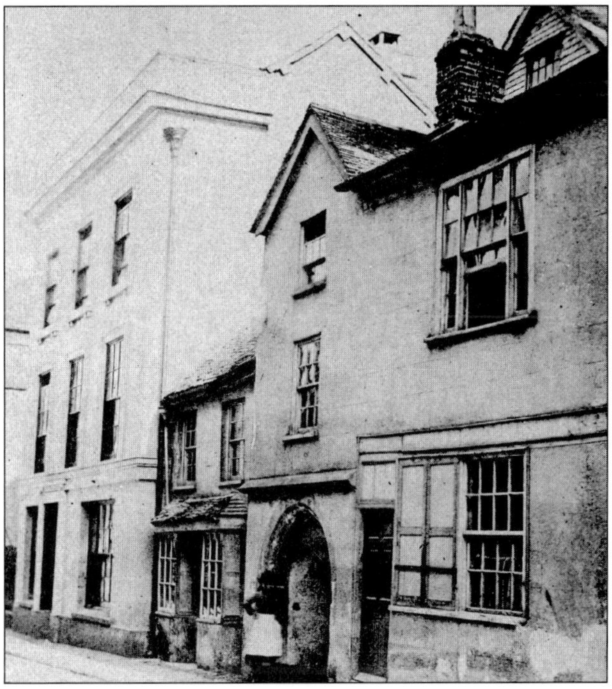

Medieval arch in West Street (c.1890) from a postcard by Amy Hannaford. On the left is the original St Andrew's House, demolished in the 1960s. Behind this building was the Dolbeare Pewter Works. (PETE WEBB COLLECTION)

of the nineteenth century. It is not often we have an eye-witness account, particularly one by an eminent scientist such as Satterley. As John Satterley left Ashburton in 1898 and rarely returned to the town, his thoughts on the period were fossilised and not polluted by later events.

He describes himself as poor, his father being a journeyman carpenter earning 24s. (£1.20) a week. He is not mentioned in *Kelly's Directory* for the period, the only mention of a Satterley being a shopkeeper in Station Road, while John's family lived in North Street. He was one of seven and rarely saw the better-off folk of the town but was just grateful for their charity. He lived in and among his local contemporaries, mixing only at school and chapel with other working-class children from other parts of the town.

Satterley describes the town as having a certain graciousness. The lesser gentry lived in well-kept houses in East and West Streets with good gardens behind. He mentions the few trees to be found in the centre of town – the laburnums at the Congregational Chapel; a horse chestnut just by the Post Office and another laburnum along St Lawrence Lane. An orchard extended from the Grammar School to Heavyhead Lane (Woodland Road). Where Vealenia Cottages now stand there was a box hedge. South of this was Ladwell orchard, where the now redundant cattle market stands. The Great Western Railway planted sycamores along the line, between the line and Parish Road.

This was a pleasant walk but more popular with the townsfolk was the Terrace Walk, which provided good views of the town and neighbouring hills (and still does for those prepared to leave their cars at home).

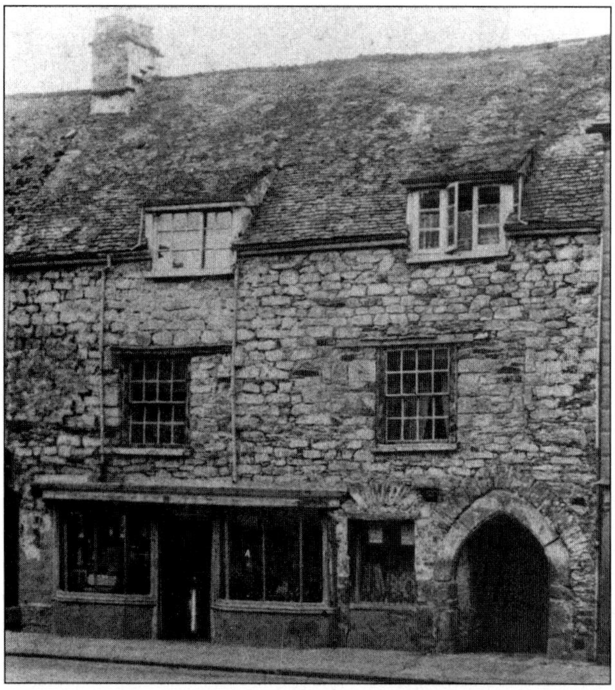

The former Mermaid Inn, c.1900. This picture was lent to Pete Webb by Mrs Parker, a descendant of the Boon family who owned it at this time (no relatives of the current owners Alan and Anne Boon).

(PETE WEBB COLLECTION)

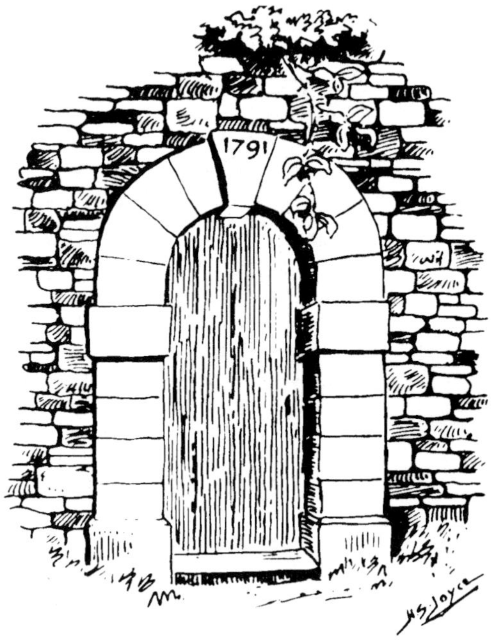

The old reservoir in Roborough Lane. These doors are the entry to a huge cavern made of brick which was part of the town's water-supply. The supply was brought to Ashburton in 1791. Water was piped to this reservoir from the hillside behind. In 1867, Sir Robert Jardine, Ashburton's last MP, donated Chuley Reservoir.

(H.S. JOYCE; PAT ORSMAN COLLECTION)

Public Utilities

In 1867 Sir Robert Jardine MP installed the Chuley supply by building the reservoir which piped water to the conduit in the Bull Ring. This conduit was deemed a 'traffic hazard' and removed during Mr Underhill's tenure as Chairman of the UDC. The conduit was adjacent to his tobacconist's shop. In Roborough Lane there was another reservoir or cistern which had wooden doors. When the boys used to throw stones at this a reverberating sound was emitted – thus every boy thought it his duty to throw a stone! Over the conduit was a bay tree from which it was young John's job to collect a few leaves each time the family had baked mackerel. Sewage at the time was dispersed through pipes onto the lush meadows at Gages ('Gaggs' to the boys).

A gasworks was installed by the railway station in 1840. A total of 36 public lamps were fed with gas from these works. Soft coal, possibly from Bovey, was used by the poor whilst the rich bought hard coal at £1 a ton.

A volunteer fire brigade was formed when John was very young. He recalls a fire at Furzley (sic) Mill.

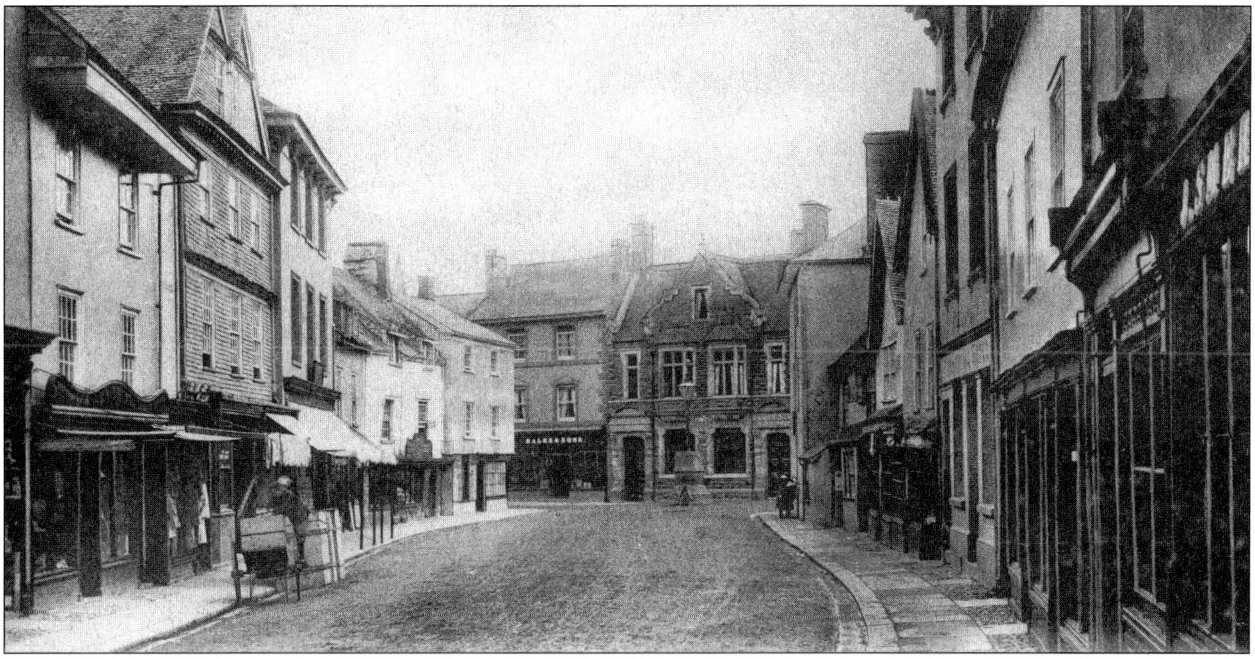

North Street, c.1900. (PETE WEBB COLLECTION)

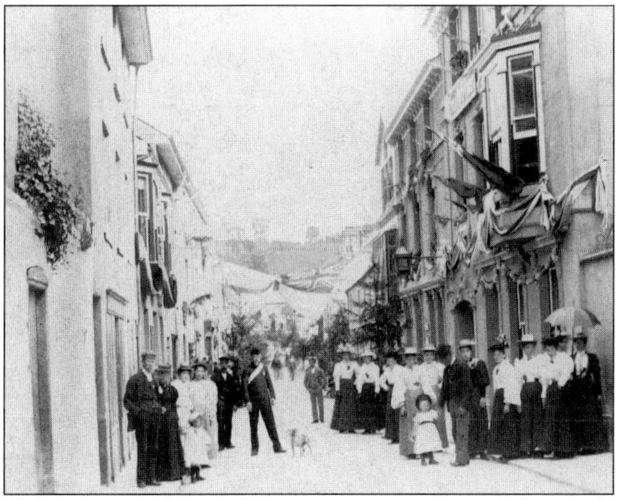

Station Road, 1887. (ASHBURTON MUSEUM)

The Buckfastleigh Brigade tackled the blaze on the south side and Ashburton on the north. However, one brigade lifted its hose and soaked the other, thus precipitating a water fight between the two brigades! History doesn't record who started it; according to Buckfastleigh it was Ashburton, and vice versa! The rivalry between the two towns has always been intense.

For milk there were dairies but poorer families collected it, in cans before breakfast, direct from the farm – either Hele or Westerbrook. Scald and tea milk were available, the latter richer and usually containing a few lumps of clotted cream.

Satterley recalls two breweries in the town. Travelling, except for long distances, was done on foot or perhaps by hitching a lift on a farmer's cart – not much faster but easier on the feet. Roads were dusty in summer and muddy in winter – in either case to be avoided if possible. The distance the postman had to walk in all weathers is also described. Postman Mr F. White went to Holne Park and the Chase and then on to Holne village, back to Holne Cot and Newbridge, delivered to Hannaford, then up Newbridge Hill to the Poundsgate sub-Post Office and its local delivery. Here he had a little room where he mended shoes and boots during his resting period before returning to Ashburton for the evening post. He was usually offered a cup of tea at Holne Chase. The bare bones of the directories give none of this fascinating detail of Victorian daily life!

Satterley goes on to describe the religious life of the time. His family were chapel – Congregationalists to be precise. Chapel folk in those days learned little of what was going on in the town's other religious establishments. The Berrys, manufacturers mentioned earlier, were chapel people, at least until the Revd Oliphant had special afternoon service for Berry's workers who were out on strike for better wages. This angered the Berry family, who then forsook the chapel for church.

The occasion all the youngsters looked forward to was their annual treat for the 'Band of Hope' given by the Amery brothers at Druid, near the old mine. Following a meal provided by the brothers, a bonfire was made and Mr Fabyan Amery told some of his inimitable stories around the flickering fire.

John Satterley's education began at a dame-school kept by his grandmother Satterley, who lived at the East Street end of Heavyhead Lane (Woodland Road). From here he went to the Board School and then to the Grammar School and on to a university education in London and Cambridge. He was always grateful for the education he received at Ashburton Grammar School, particularly the encouragement of the head, Mr Mortimore, and the Amery

Golden Jubilee Celebrations, 1887

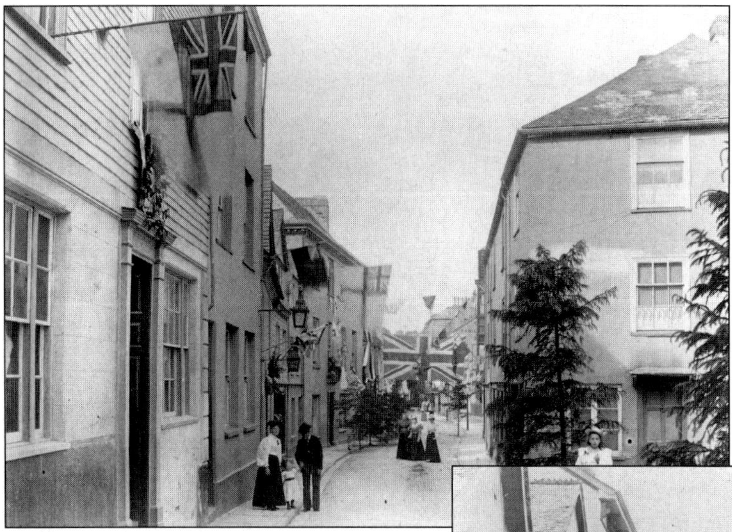

West Street, 1887.
(ASHBURTON MUSEUM)

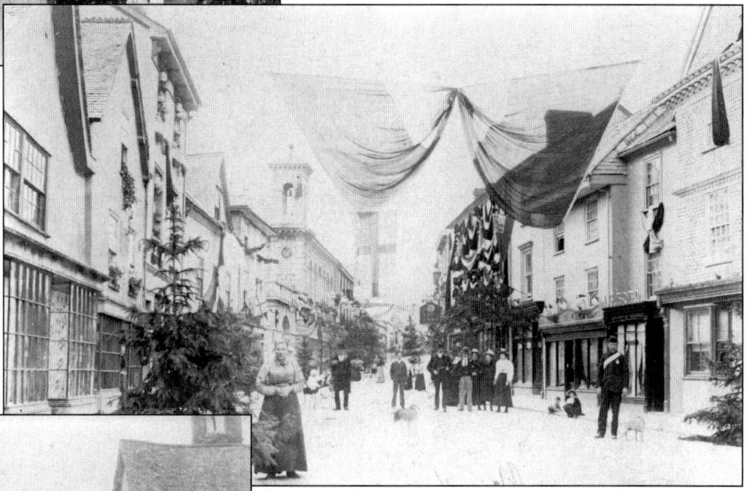

North Street, 1887.
(ASHBURTON MUSEUM)

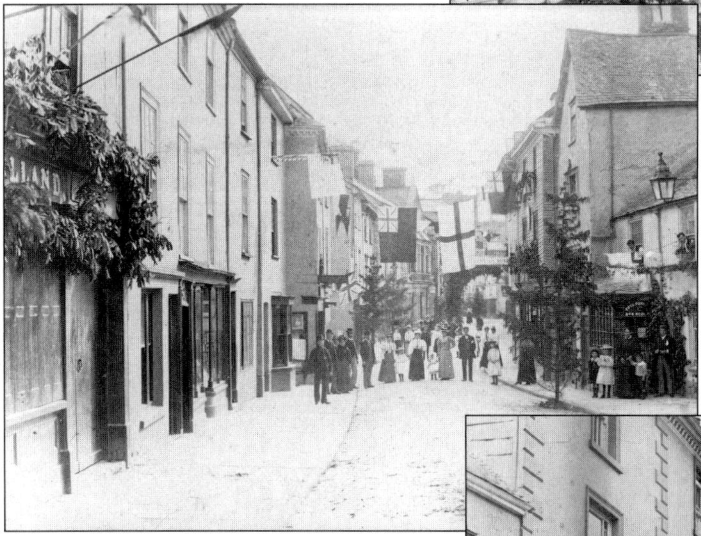

East Street, 1887.
(ASHBURTON MUSEUM)

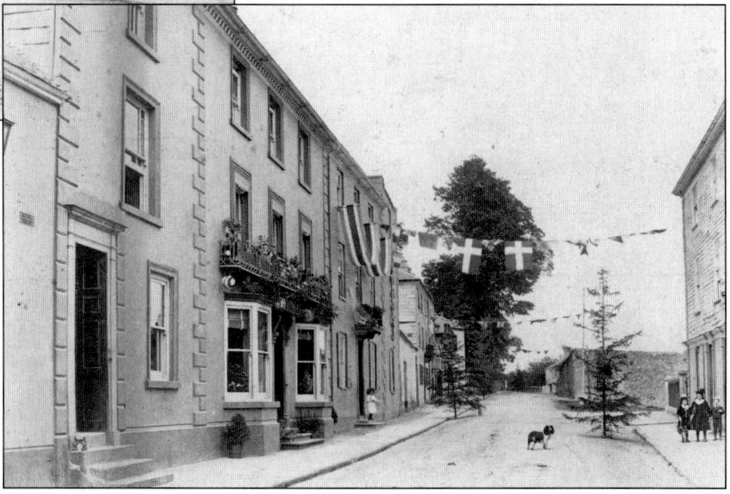

Looking the other way in East Street.
(ASHBURTON MUSEUM)

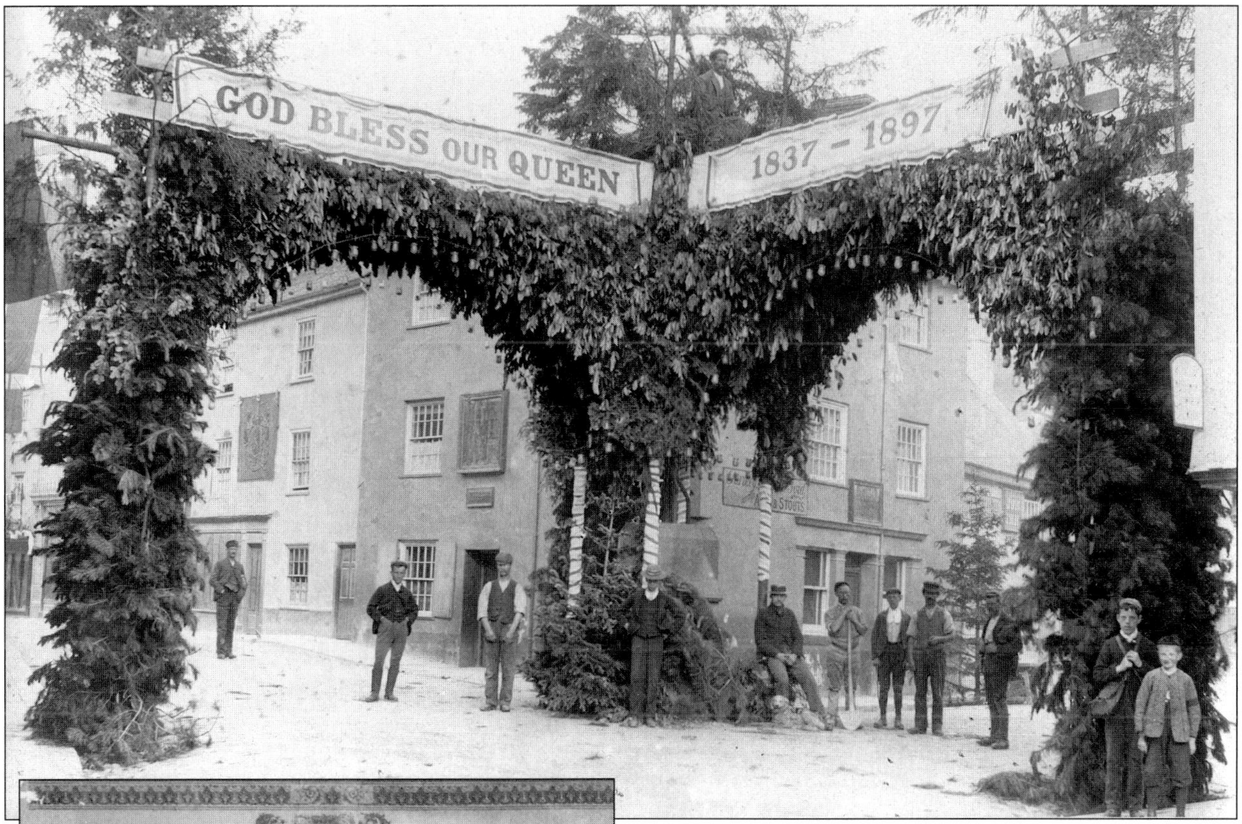

Above: *Decorations for Queen Victoria's Diamond Jubilee, 1897.* (ASHBURTON MUSEUM)

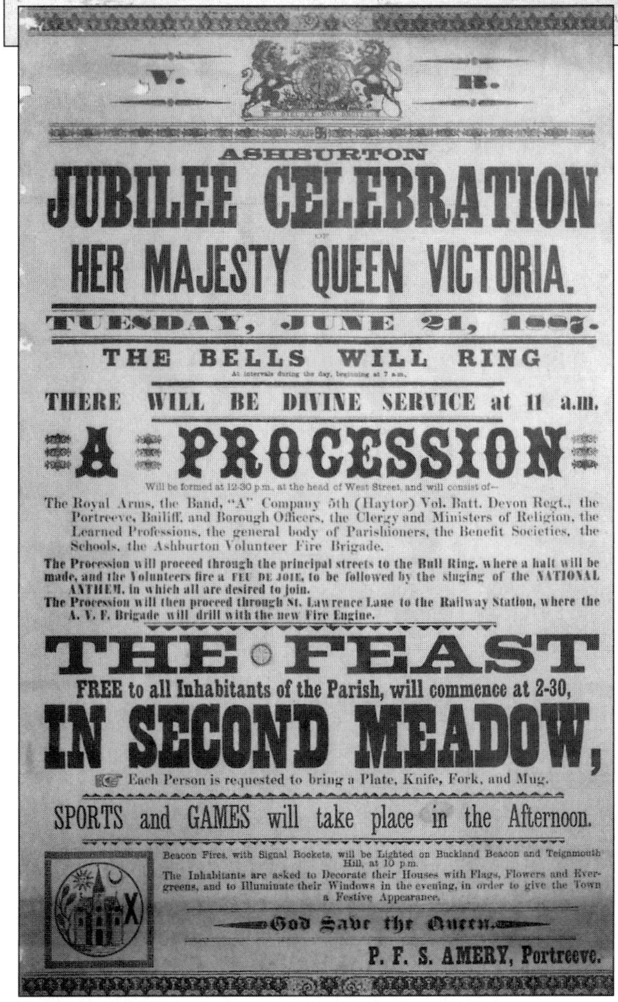

V. R.

ASHBURTON

JUBILEE CELEBRATION

OF

HER MAJESTY QUEEN VICTORIA.

TUESDAY, JUNE 21, 1887.

THE BELLS WILL RING

At intervals during the day, beginning at 7 a.m.

THERE WILL BE DIVINE SERVICE at 11 a.m.

A PROCESSION

Will be formed at 12-30 p.m., at the head of West Street, and will consist of—

The Royal Arms, the Band, "A" Company 5th (Haytor) Vol. Batt. Devon Regt., the Portreeve, Bailiff, and Borough Officers, the Clergy and Ministers of Religion, the Learned Professions, the general body of Parishioners, the Benefit Societies, the Schools, the Ashburton Volunteer Fire Brigade.

The Procession will proceed through the principal streets to the Bull Ring, where a halt will be made, and the Volunteers fire a FEU DE JOIE, to be followed by the singing of the NATIONAL ANTHEM, in which all are desired to join.

The Procession will then proceed through St. Lawrence Lane to the Railway Station, where the A. V. F. Brigade will drill with the new Fire Engine.

THE FEAST

FREE to all Inhabitants of the Parish, will commence at 2-30,

IN SECOND MEADOW,

Each Person is requested to bring a Plate, Knife, Fork, and Mug.

SPORTS and GAMES will take place in the Afternoon.

Beacon Fires, with Signal Rockets, will be Lighted on Buckland Beacon and Teignmouth Hill, at 10 p.m.

The Inhabitants are asked to Decorate their Houses with Flags, Flowers and Evergreens, and to Illuminate their Windows in the evening, in order to give the Town a Festive Appearance.

God Save the Queen.

P. F. S. AMERY, Portreeve.

A poster announcing Ashburton's celebrations for Queen Victoria's Golden Jubilee in 1887.

(ST LAWRENCE CHAPEL)

brothers. During the school holidays John and his brother had an agreement with the Amery brothers to deliver the newspaper to Druid and learned a great deal by reading it on the way. They usually spent the morning with the brothers, either in the tree nursery, in Boro Wood, at the old mine or walking the Buckland Drives. The young lads learned a great deal from this informal education. The Board School boys always called the Grammar School boys 'ducks' and hailed them with 'quack, quack'. If a fight was likely the cry was 'best man or blow'. If the boy being assailed said 'blow' then a fight ensued; however, if 'best man' was said the one assailed acknowledged the superiority of the assailant and was let off with a half-hearted blow.

At this time virtually all the shops were privately owned, the owner living over the shop. The Co-op was the first store to open with a manager. The *Kelly's Directory* for 1893 lists Veale as the manager. Other stores included:

10 bakers
1 beer retailer
7 butchers
1 dairy
3 dressmakers
4 drapers
1 glass and china shops
5 grocers
5 greengrocers (not mentioned before)
2 hairdressers

2 ironmongers
1 milliner
6 shoemakers
9 shopkeepers (trade not given)
7 tailors
2 watchmakers

There was still a marine store dealer. The directory also records the presence of the cottage hospital.

The wooden shutters of the shops were removed at 8.30a.m. and replaced by 7p.m. There was no lunch break but there was a half day on Wednesday. The town's appearance changed little during these formative years. The two banks, Lloyds and Natwest, were built at this time. The Post Office moved from East Street to St Lawrence Lane and Vealenia Terrace was built. Cattle markets were held on the third Saturday of the month – on the Friday evening a Mr Coleman would fence in the bottom of North Street, leaving just the pavements for pedestrians. Four times a year Ashburton became a hive of activity when the fair came to town.

Satterley also describes the industries of the town (see Chapter 10). His mother used to clean and retrim ladies' straw hats. This was done using oxalic acid. His father made blocks of various sizes on which the hats could be pressed and kept until returned to their owners. Workers kept long hours – 7a.m. to 5p.m. in summer and an hour less in winter. On Saturdays they would finish at 3.30pm. There were no holidays except the statutory ones. One occupation in which the children of the town were engaged was whortleberry (bilberry) picking – 'urts' to the locals. It was hard work but got the children into the open where they were able to observe nature close at hand. At the end of the day they bought the urts home, perhaps 2–3 pints per boy being average. These were sold to a Mrs Walker for 3d.–4d. a quart (1.5p. per litre). This picking was done first in Awsewell Wood, then on Holne Moor as the urts ripened there. It was a heavy load to bring home so boys rarely went picking more than two days in a row. Oak ripping was another occupation in which children were engaged. The purpose of this was to provide bark for the tanneries. The oaks were 'cropped' on a 20-year cycle. Boro Wood and Whiddon Scrubbs were cropped like this. The work was popular and earned 6d. per day (2.5p).

Professor Satterley then goes on to describe what life was like in the home. Food was cheap but wages were low so all the poorer families lived a frugal life. A baker called Peachey baked doughcakes. The dough was fetched in a tin by a housewife who re-kneaded it and then returned it to be baked. The speciality of another Baker, Mr Battishill, was Ashburton splits (plain until cream or jam was added). On Sundays the large family used to enjoy a joint, often baked in Mr Peachey's oven. No dessert was the order of the day. During the week tripe, liver and skirt sufficed. A Mr Lang used to hawk foreign meat around the town – 'never makes proper gravy' was the wisdom of the time. Fish was brought up from Brixam – herring, mackerel, dabs and whiting – all alive! Vegetables were produced in the allotments. Potato cakes were very popular and there were always sweets, of course. As well as the usual offering, each sweet boiler had their own speciality, like Mrs Hayman's 'Stingo' caramel. And there was also Mr Whiddon's ginger beer. Children were kept occupied doing domestic chores, such as blacking the grate, cleaning the cutlery and taking out the ashes and sifting them. The highlight of the year was bonfire night.

Thus was life in late-Victorian Ashburton – a town in which traditional industries were declining or had ceased altogether. It was to be at least another 60 years before fortunes changed.

✥ CHAPTER 12 ✥

Worthies of Ashburton

It will come as no surprise to most readers that during its long history Ashburton has produced sons and daughters who have made a significant contribution to society, either nationally or locally.

Whilst not everyone in this selection of worthies was born in the town, those who weren't were educated here or made a contribution to its life. The selection is inevitably one personal to the authors.

Bishop Walter de Stapeldon (now spelt Stapledon) 1261–1326

A Devonian probably born in Monkleigh or Annery, he went up to Oxford, a university he later richly endowed with a college which was to become Exeter College. He was elected to Bishop in 1307 and became a Professor of Canon Law. He sped up the rebuilding of Exeter Cathedral and was in great favour with Edward II, who made him his treasurer. In 1310 Edward granted the bishop a fair to be held in Ashburton and in 1314 the bishop granted to Ashburton the Chantry Chapel of St Lawrence on condition that after his death a priest be appointed to pray for his soul. The priest's stipend was £4.13s.0d. (£4.65). Stapeldon's favour with the king caused him to be absent from his diocese – he attempted to mediate between Edward and his consort, Isabella, who, through her favourite Mortimer, encouraged the French to effect a landing on the Suffolk coast. The king took refuge in the Tower and left London in the bishop's charge. In 1326 Stapledon was attacked, stripped and beheaded by the London mob, who threw in their lot with Isabella; a sad end for a man to whom Ashburton and Devon owe a great deal.

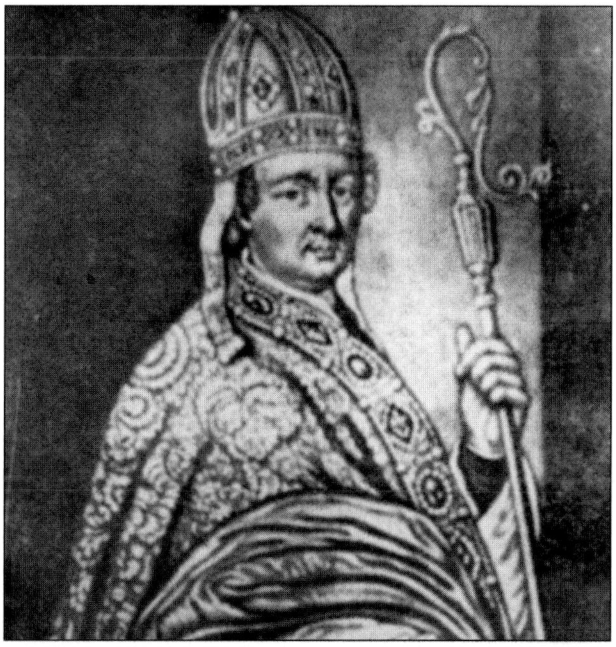

Bishop Stapledon (original in Exeter College, Oxford).

John Ford, 1586–1640

His ancestors held leading positions in the town and one of his family made a bold attempt to establish a woollen market in 1670, much to the annoyance of Newton Abbot traders.

The second son of one Thomas Ford, he was baptised at Ilsington. Educated at Ashburton Grammar School, when only 16 or 17 years of age he was admitted to the Middle Temple in London, which had a noble roll of past members.

Ford was soon at work writing and one of his first attempts, at only 20 years old, was a tract entitled *Honor Triumphant or the Peeres Challenge.* 'Master John Ford of the Middle Temple', as he was known, wrote about 18 plays, some of which are lost. Those surviving include *'Tis Pity She's a Whore* (performed in about 1626, printed in 1633), a study of incestuous passion between brother and sister. His other plays include *The Lover's Melancholy* (1629), *The Broken Heart* (1633), *Love's Sacrifice* (1633), in which Bianca is one of Ford's finest psychological studies of women, *The Lady's Trial* (1639) and *The Chronicle History of Perkin Warbeck* (1634). Dwelling on themes of pathos and frustration, the plays were popular with audiences of the day.

Little is known of his domestic life and where he died other than that it was far from his beloved Devon, somewhere in London.

Lord Ashburton – John Dunning, 1731–83

John Dunning was born just outside Ashburton parish at Gulwell, in the parish of Staverton and near the Pear Tree end of town. Gulwell Farm was demolished to make way for the A38 dual carriageway.

The family originally came from Walkhampton, and John's father, also named John, married Agnes Jutsham (daughter of Henry Jutsham of Modbury) and moved to Gulwell. John senr, an attorney-at-law,

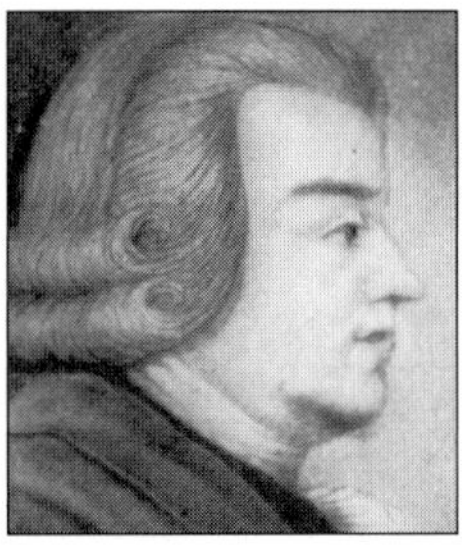

John Dunning.

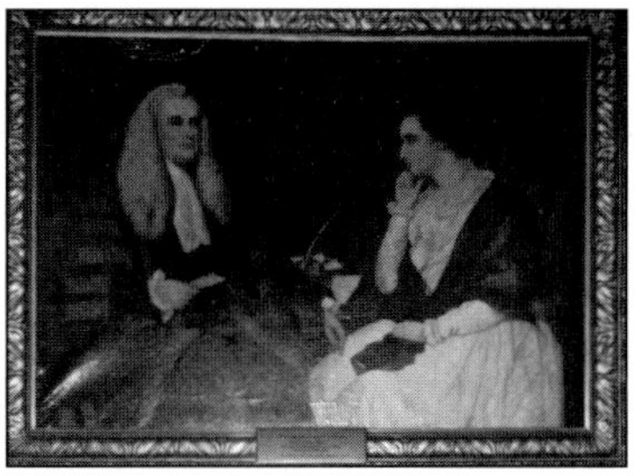

A painting in the Town Hall of Lord Ashburton and his sister Mary. (PETER HOWDEN)

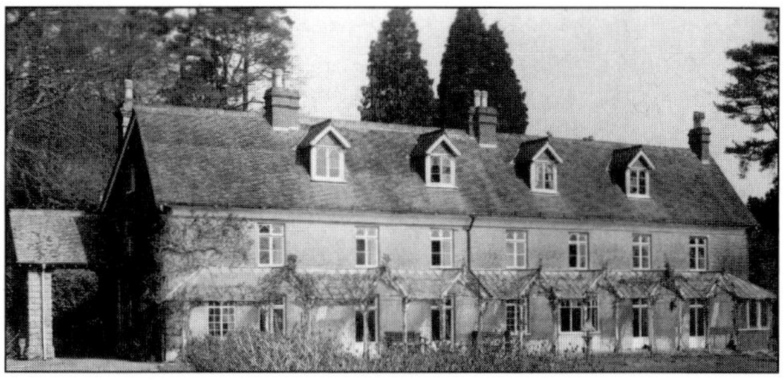

Spitchwick House (pictured here in the 1920s), home of Lord Ashburton, later his widow and now (2004) home of Mr Simpson. (PETE WEBB COLLECTION)

moved into Ashburton. John junr was born on 18 October 1731, went to Ashburton Grammar School (St Lawrence Chapel) until the age of 13, and for five years was an articled clerk for his father. One of his father's clients, Sir Thomas Clark, became his patron and in May 1752 he was entered as a student at the Middle Temple. Dunning was called to the bar in 1756 but his ungainly appearance hindered his progress.

He gained estates in Ashburton, Widecombe, Staverton and Holne by foreclosing on outstanding loans and his skill in the courtroom eventually gained him the position of Solicitor General. In the mid-1760s he met many men of letters as a fellow member of the Literary Club, including Goldsmith, Sir William Jones, Joshua Reynolds, Gibbon and Burke as well as Boswell. Around the same time he purchased the manors of Spitchwick and Widecombe.

Later, in March 1780 at the age of 50, he married Elizabeth, the daughter of John Baring of Exeter who founded the Baring Bank. Two years later, in April 1782, he became a baronet, Lord Ashburton. Failing health made him move to the coast but he died at Exmouth on 18 August 1783. He is buried in St Andrew's Church, Ashburton.

He was succeeded by his son Richard, the second Lord Ashburton of the first line, who died without issue. The title of Lord Ashburton was revived in 1835 by Alexander Baring, the son of Elizabeth's brother, Francis.

His widow Elizabeth lived on for many years at Spitchwick.

William Gifford, 1756–1826

William was born in Ashburton of a seafaring family and attended Bourne School from the age of eight. He was left an orphan in 1867 and sent to sea by his guardian. He was unhappy, and Brixham fishwives used to gossip about him on their trips to Ashburton selling fish. Ashburton's tight-knit community made such a fuss that his godfather brought him ashore and apprenticed him to a tailor. His misery continued, as his new employer was a tyrant. William

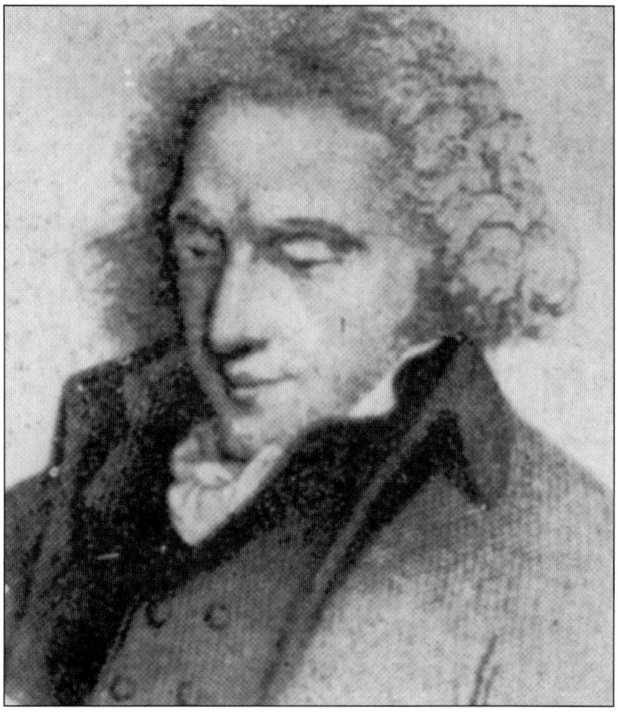

William Gifford.

Cooksey, a surgeon of the town, heard of his plight and with other benefactors raised a fund to buy off his apprenticeship and pay for a place at the Grammar School. There he thrived and went on to be educated at Oxford and became a man of letters as editor of the *Anti-Jacobin Review* in 1798 and later, for 15 years, of the *Quarterly Review*. He never forgot the people of Ashburton and when he died in 1826 he left the then magnificent sum of £2,000 to help the poor of the parish. This charity gave gifts to the town's poor until it was combined in 1985 with 20 other charities to become Ashburton's Relief in Need, which still helps the needy today.

John Ireland, 1761–1842

John, a butcher's son, was born five years after Gifford. They both went to Ashburton Grammar School. Ireland went on to Oxford, where he was Bible clerk at Oriel and completed his degree.

Having taken Holy Orders he was a curate at Kingsteignton for a short time before moving as vicar to Croydon in Surrey. He married a Devon lass, Miss Short, and while still a young man was made prebendary of Westminster Abbey. On the death of Dr Vincent 14 years later he became Dean of Westminster Abbey and officiated at the coronations of William IV, George IV and Queen Victoria, the only Dean in history to crown three monarchs, having held the post for a total of 26 years.

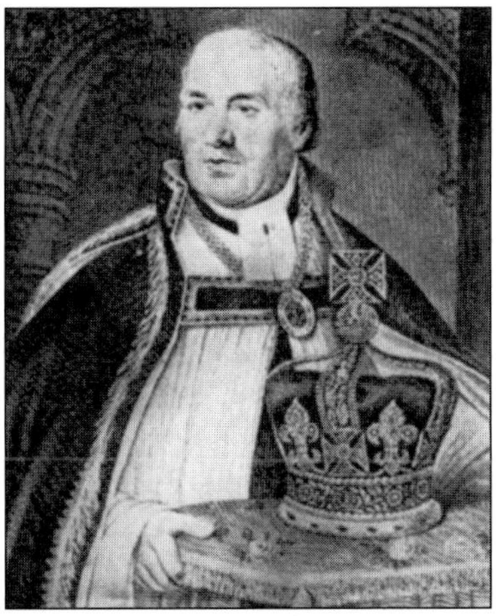
John Ireland, Dean of Westminster.

He founded the Ireland Scholorship in 1825 and gave £10,000 to establish a Professorship of Scriptures at Oxford. In 1841 he bought a large house in East Street as a residence for the headmaster. It cost £1,000 and he gave a further £1,000 to form a fund by which the house could be maintained. A trust was set up to look after it and the house was passed to the governors in 1923. It is now a block of flats, still called Ireland House, belonging to the local authority, Teignbridge District Council.

Miriam Adams, 1781–1858

Miriam was the letter carrier to the Post Office for over 40 years. She travelled the area on a donkey accompanied by a dog called Traveller. In 1815, she was thought to have brought the news of Waterloo to the people of Ashburton. When she died in October 1858, a tombstone was erected in her memory in Ashburton's churchyard and mentions the 'uniform cheerfulness and strict fideity' with which she carried out her duties.

Richard Carlile, 1790–1843

Carlile is arguably the Ashburtonian who should rank at the very highest level of the sons of Ashburton, but one who has no memorial in his native town. He was a controversial character; were it not for him we would not have achieved the freedom of the press we so value today. Perhaps it is because of his implacable enmity of all things related to the establishment that he has no memorial. When Ashburton School had school houses named after various worthies from the town it did not see fit to have a house named after Carlile. Who was he and why did he cause so much discomfort to the establishment?

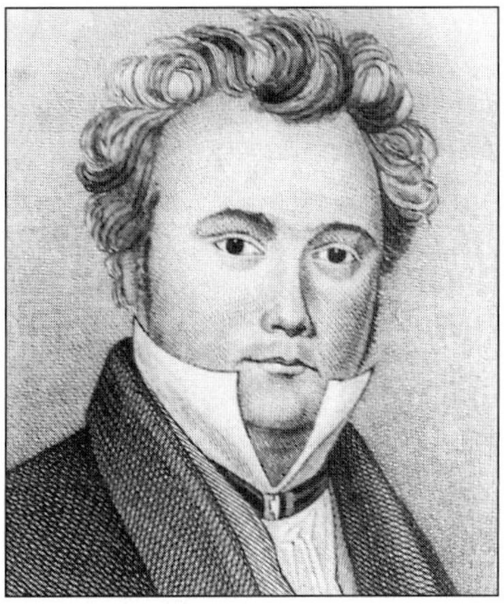
Richard Carlile.
(ST LAWRENCE CHAPEL)

Born in Heavyhead Lane (Woodland Road), Ashburton, in 1790, he attended the Grammar School. At 12 he had to leave the town to find work. After various jobs he ended up in London. Between 1815 (Waterloo) and the Reform Bill of 1832 Britain was ripe for revolution. The Government of the day was only too aware of what had happened across the Channel and did all in its power to stifle the freedom of the press. In 1817, having borrowed 20 shillings, Carlile bought 100 copies of a radical weekly, *The Black Dwarf.* This introduced him to Mr Sherwin who enabled Carlile to set up business as a printer, a condition being that he published *Sherwin's Weekly Political Register,* another 'subversive' publication. He also republished Hone's parodies of the prayer book (reading these publications helps one to understand the controversial nature of Carlile's work). Another publication of 1817, *The Order for the administration of the loaves and fishes or Communion of Corruption's Host commanded to be read at the treasury the day preceding all cabinet dinners,* follows the pattern of the prayer book until we find:

> *Then shall follow the Collect for the ministry belonging to the House of Lords*
> *Let us pray*
> *'Mighty Prince whose kingdom may not be lasting; whose power is finite; have mercy on the whole host: and be so ruled by thy chosen servants, Liverpool Sidmouth etc and their associates that they may above all things aggrandize themselves and dependents and that we may faithfully serve, honour and humbly obey them in view of and hoping for further benefits according to thy word and ordinance; through Castlereagh our Chief. Amen.'*

For doing this Carlile spent 18 weeks in prison. This short sentence made him defiant. The Peterloo Massacre, the slaughter of protesters in Manchester in 1819, provided him with the opportunity to show to the nation (or those who could read his articles) how corrupt the government of the day was. The result – three years' imprisonment and a £1,500 fine. His printing shop closed, however his wife promptly reopened it. From prison he directed the publication of his paper *The Republican.* His wife Jane was arrested, and his sister took over – some family, the

Carliles! Jane was arrested too and all three Carliles ended up together in Dorchester Gaol. Volunteers took over until they in turn were arrested only to be replaced by others. In the face of what seemed an unlimited supply of those willing to fight for the freedom of the press the authorities gave up.

Many of Carlile's writings may seem distasteful, even to twenty-first-century eyes, yet he was single minded in pursuing what he considered to be right. He believed that free expression of opinion was essential for political progress. For his efforts he spent nine years and three months in jail. When he died in 1843 the battle was nearly won. G.M. Trevelyan, the social historian, wrote:

> *For this* [freedom of expression] *Carlile suffered more and achieved more than any other Englishman of the nineteenth century, a son of whom Ashburton should feel justifiably proud.*

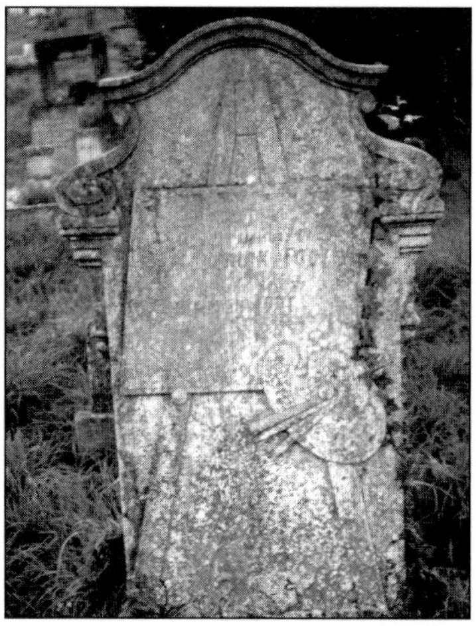

Grave of Frederick Foot, artist.

(PETE WEBB)

Frederick Foot, 1831–80

Born in Ashburton in 1831, Foot was a prolific painter and sketcher of Dartmoor, and the Torquay Natural History Museum contains many of his fine drawings of buildings and mine workings around the moor. His work mainly dates from the 1850s and 1860s. He was a self-taught artist and his work is considered to be a remarkable record of the period. M.R. Hansford Worth collected many of his drawings and bequeathed them to the museum. Foot's sister was a court dressmaker and married Mr Lomax, the tax inspector living in East Street.

Foot died at Lustleigh, where he had a studio in 1880, and is buried in Ashburton. His tombstone is carved in the shape of an artist's easel.

Rt Hon. Charles Seale-Hayne, 1833–1903

Charles Seale-Hayne was the Member of Parliament for Ashburton (mid-Devon) from 1885 to 1903. He was a member of the Liberal Party and Paymaster General in the fourth Gladstone Government from 1892–95. He was a descendant of a well-known family of Devonshire landowners living near Dartmouth. It was said the the Haynes bought respectability into the family and the Seales brought the money! He died a bachelor in 1903 and, by a will made 20 years earlier, directed that the bulk of his wealth of over £90,000 should form

> *a trust to establish and endow a college to be erected in the neighbourhood of Newton Abbot, for the technical education of artisans and others, without distinction of creed and for the special encouragement of the industries, manufactures and products for the county of Devon.*

His intention was perhaps a college with a wider portfolio of courses, but in October 1902 the foundation stone was laid for the Newton Abbot Science, Art and Technical school. The agricultural college was built for the first students to attend in 1914 but the First World War interrupted and it was 1919 before the college began business in that capacity.

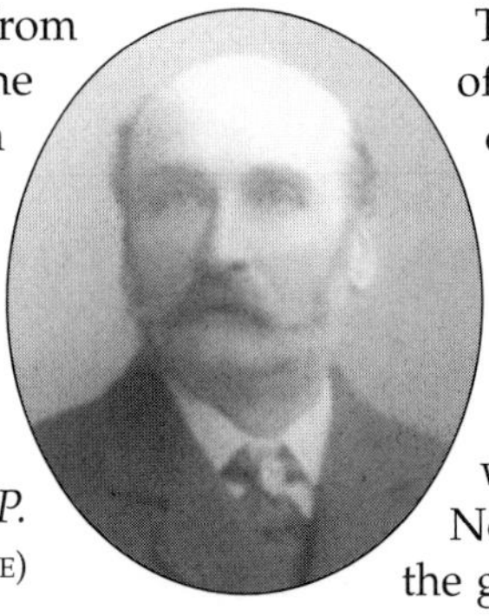

Rt Honourable Charles Seale-Hayne MP.

(SEALE HAYNE)

William John Wills, 1834–61

Wills was a native of Totnes who attended the Grammar School in Ashburton and was a boarder in Ireland House. He was not a brilliant scholar, but one who showed interest in science. His family moved to Ipplepen and, after leaving school in 1850, William went to Guy's Hospital in London where he studied chemistry, obtaining his certificate in 1852. In the same year he sailed, with his brother, for Australia. In 1854, in the gold town of Balarat, he demonstrated his scientific bent by inventing a device for the accurate weighing of gold. He undertook a number of jobs, one of which enabled him to learn the science of surveying. By 1857 he had his own surveying party working for the district surveying department.

In 1859 the Royal Society of Victoria was considering an expedition to cross Australia from Melbourne in the south to the Gulf of Carpentaria in the north.

A team was chosen, with Burke as the leader and Wills as surveyor. They left Melbourne on 20 August 1860 in a long procession of 27 camels, with horses and wagons laden with stores.

There were soon problems with the weight of the supplies and a decision was made to dump some when they reached Balranald by the Murray River – supplies which would be sorely missed later. By September tensions were causing a split in the party. In October they reached the Darling and, due to a resignation, Wills was appointed second in command. In November they reached Coopers Creek and the group split again. Burke, Wills, King and

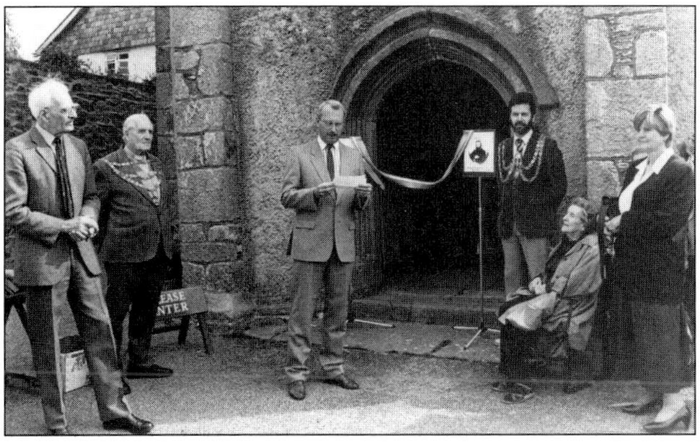

The opening of St Lawrence Chapel in May 1994 at the Guild of St Lawrence coffee morning and start-of-season exhibition on Burke and Wills – first across Australia (William Wills was a pupil at the Grammar School). From left: *John Joyner (chair of Guild), Revd John Brown (Bailiff), Graham Gordon (then headmaster of Primary School), Portreeve Pete Webb (the author), Mrs Childs, Wills' great niece* (seated), *Mrs Cocks (Mrs Child's daughter).* (JOHN MITCHELL)

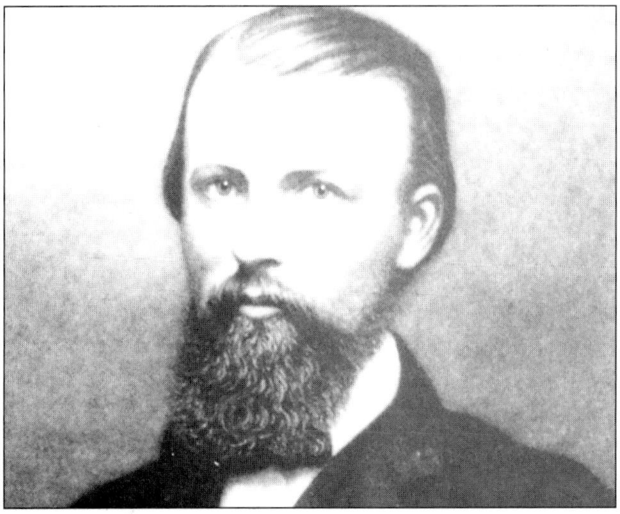

William Wills. (ST LAWRENCE CHAPEL)

Grey made for the Gulf of Carpentaria, leaving on 16 December. The next stage of their journey was through a variety of terrain – desert, stony desert, lush land and jungle. They arrived at Cloncurry, about 170 miles from the sea. After 30 miles of being bogged down in swamp, on 30 January 1861, they abandoned the camels there.

That we know all this is due to Wills, as he was the only one to keep a field book. On 11 February they found themselves again in swamps and Burke and Wills pressed on alone until they reached a point where there was an 8in. tide and the water was brackish – they had reached their goal. The mangrove swamp prevented their reaching the coast itself and supplies were running low so they were forced to return the 700 miles to Cooper's Creek where there were good supplies of food. Getting weak and now missing the supplies they had left in Balranald, on 21 April Burke and Wills made it to Cooper's Creek only to find that Brahe, who had waited months for their return, had departed just nine hours before. By 28 April both groups were in a bad way. After an abortive attempt to try a different route Burke and Wills were forced back to Coopers Creek, again missing a search party. By now food had run out and they survived on Nardoo seed, a native plant. William Wills died on about 28 June and Burke shortly afterward on about 1 July. Their bodies were recovered and buried with honours. Memorials to these pioneers exist in Melbourne and Totnes.

Amery Family of Druid

P.F.S. and J.S. Amery were the sons of John Sparke Amery of 'Druid' and his wife Frances (she was the daughter of the Revd T.W. Windeatt of Totnes). John Sparke Amery (the elder) was born at Narrowmore, Lustleigh. He was adopted by his uncle, P.S. Sparke, an Ashburton woollen manufacturer, and succeeded to his business. He retired with the decline of the woollen industry and devoted himself to farming at Druid. Peter Fabyan Spark Amery (1839–1907), born in Ashburton on 2 September 1839, was educated at Ashburton Grammar School and Canstadt in Germany. He succeeded to the Druid estate on the death of his father in 1878.

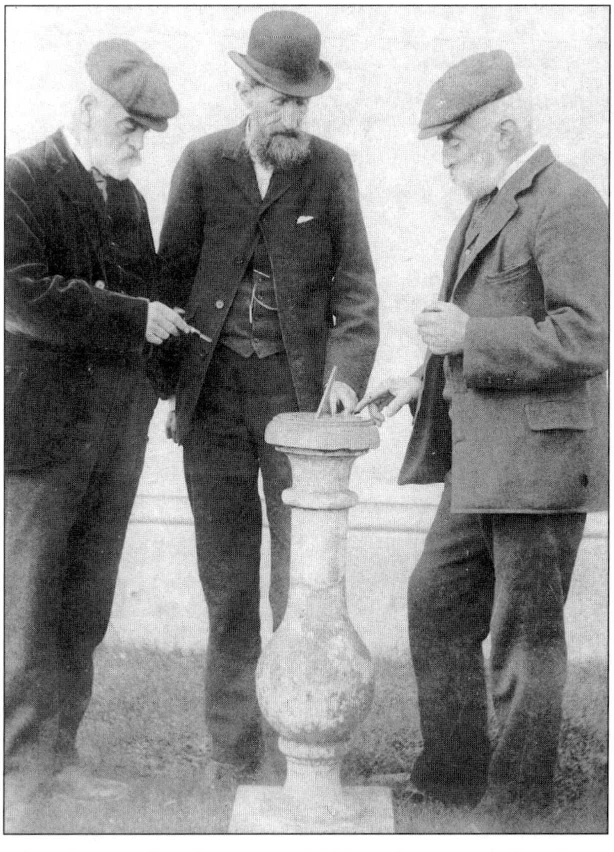

The Amery brothers – a 1920s picture of the three brothers Fabyan Amery, John Amery and Jasper Amery of Druid House. (PETE WEBB COLLECTION)

He served as Portreeve over several years, was a member of Ashburton School board, a County Councillor from 1901 until his death in 1907, a governor of the Grammar School and much more besides. He also served on many local charities. The Congregational Chapel (Great Meeting) owed much to him and his ancestors (the Fabyans and Sparkes). He was a member of the Devonshire Association, Teign Naturalists' Field Club and editor of *Devon Notes and Queries.* He was also author of books such as *Ashburton in ye good old times (recollections of Robert Prideaux 1510–1525),* published in 1882. Other publications are listed as *County Fairs & Revels 1878* and *The Haytor Volunteers 1888.* He also wrote articles such as 'Hill Forts near Ashburton', TDA 1873 and a TDA presidential address in 1924 on Old Ashburton. He is listed as owning property in North Street in 1897 but not as owning Druid, yet is listed again with John in 1901 as owning Druid (possibly a joint ownership).

He was also involved with the Ashburton and Haytor Volunteers from 1859 as a private, then as a sergeant in 1860, an ensign in 1861, a lieutenant in 1862, a major in 1879 and hon. lieutenant-colonel in 1886. He retired in 1899. The volunteers had a rifle range at Rippon Tor (still in use by the Army in the 1970s) and sharpshooters of such a good quality were produced by the company that up to the First World War they were sought after as snipers. P.F.S. Amery died after a short illness on 26 July 1907 and is buried in Ashburton churchyard.

John Sparke Amery (the younger) was born 27 September 1845 and educated at the Grammar School and at Dr Holmes' School in Plymouth. He first appears in 1850 trade directories as being at Druid. By 1856 there was also a Mrs Amery in East Street. He was named as a JP and magistrate in 1866, 1893, 1902, 1906, 1910, 1914, 1919, 1923 and 1926 (also in 1870, 1873 and up to 1883 when he is listed without JP), but is not in the 1933 listing. He was as active as his brother in many charities, associations and bodies. He was also a member and president of the Devonshire Association and an editor of *Devon Notes & Queries.* He was taken ill in 1923 with four or five years of slow recovery until again falling ill in 1928. He died on 13 April 1929

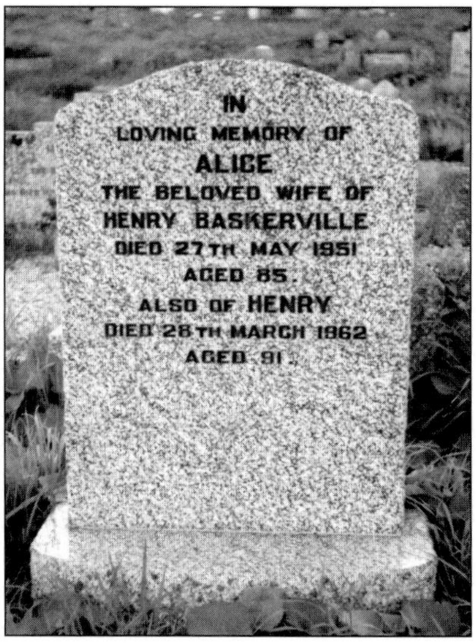

Henry Baskerville's grave.
(PETE WEBB)

In 1897 he was listed as owning property in Berry's Meadow near Great Bridge but not as owning Druid which, according to the Register of Electors, he had acquired by 1901.

He was connected with Ashburton Congregational Church (for history see 1915 publication by Edward Windeatt – who took over Druid as a benefactor of Amery's will on his death). In 1934 the Rt Hon. L.S. Amery presented the 1610 Flemish stained-glass window in memory of his two cousins, Fabyan and John Amery. The Amerys were also great scholars and travellers and would give lantern shows of their pictures. Both brothers were great benefactors. They were friends in the true sense to both rich and poor, to the famous, such as the scholar R.H. Worth, and to the unknown, such as their aged housekeeper, Mrs Rowlands, who started in service to their mother aged 13 and died at Druid after continuous service aged 78.

Joseph Henry Blampey 1889–1910

Blampey was a photographer around the turn of the century, mainly taking portraits. Many Victorian views and portraits of town figures are from Mr Blampey's studio.

Henry Mathews Baskerville, 1871–1962

Henry Mathews Baskerville, known to all as Harry, was born in 1871 at Ipplepen. He left school at the age of 11 and started work for only 4 shillings a week (about 20p), living-in with his employers. At the age of 15 he obtained a better position with the Robinson family of Park Hill, Ipplepen. He worked for the Robinsons for 20 years, his main duties being in the stables looking after their two horses and driving one of their three carriages.

Fletcher Robinson was a student at Oxford and would tell his friend, Arthur Conan Doyle, the story of 'the wicked squire' – supposedly based on the Cabel family of Holne and Buckfast. The two friends would come down to the family home in Ipplepen and travel to Dartmoor in a carriage driven by Harry. On one of these trips, Doyle asked for permission to use his name and *The Hound of the Baskervilles* was named.

In 1907, after Mr Robinson's death, Harry obtained work with Mr John Sawdye, auctioneer and proprietor of first the London Inn and later the Golden Lion. Harry was well known in Ashburton and was an active member of the community – the family had an inscribed first edition of Conan Doyle's book, acknowledging his part in it. Harry died on 28 March 1962 and is buried in Ashburton churchyard.

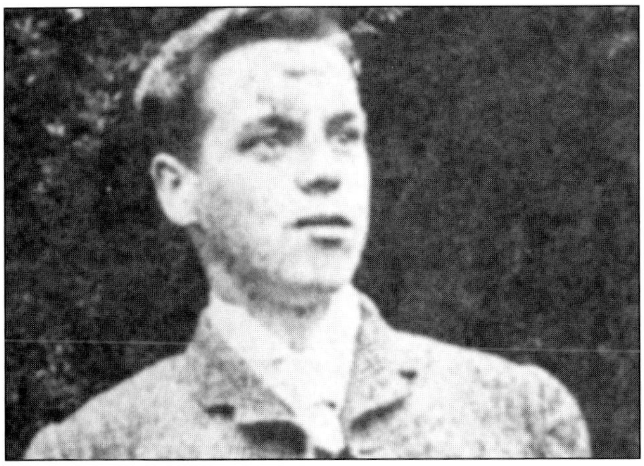

Sydney Endacott. (JOAN HUMPHRIES)

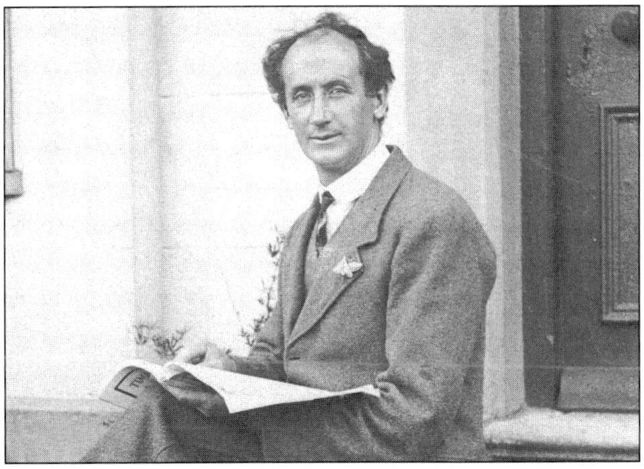

Professor John (Jack) Satterley. (PETE WEBB COLLECTION)

Sydney Endacott, Devon artist, 1873–1918

Endacott was born 14 June 1873 near the church in West Street, Ashburton and in 1893 went to the USA for about a year before returning. He worked as a sculptor, woodcarver and possibly a stained-glass painter for J. Wippell Co. of Exeter. Sydney married Bertha Lillie Haydon in 1903 and their only son, Bernard, was born in 1910 at about which time Sydney was serving as an art instructor at Exeter Art School. He later went freelance and produced paintings for Worth's Gallery (Moll's Coffee House) until his death in 1918. His wife, Lily, carried on for some years producing paintings for the postcard market and died in 1952.

The Ruth Brothers

Alan Leonard Ruth and Kenneth Ruth were brothers who took photographs and produced postcards of Dartmoor and South Devon. They moved to Ashburton in the 1930s from Aveton Gifford, where their father, Jasper, had been a photographer and postcard publisher.

From 1939 they appear in trade directories as being in North Street. In the 1950s they went their separate ways, with Alan moving to Newton Abbot and Kenneth to West Street. Many of the 1940s and 1950s views in this book are from their camera lenses. Kenneth moved in the late 1960s, initially to Dartmeet and later to Newbridge. His shop was used by the Boston family, who produced commemorative photographic plates and china until closing in the late 1970s.

Dr John Satterley, 1879–1963

(brother of Amy, below – see also Chapter 11)

Born in Ashburton, John Satterley was a pupil of Ashburton Grammar School and gained a scholarship to the Royal College of Science in London from 1898 to 1901. He also attended St Johns College, Cambridge, and from 1903 to 1912 worked under Sir John Thompson at the Cavendish Laboratory in Cambridge. He married May (née Randall) in 1905 and they had two children.

They emigrated to Canada in 1912 and he worked for over 38 years at Toronto University. He worked on helium balloons during the First World War and his lectures at the university on liquid air were renowned.

He had a long connection with the Devonshire Association and was made a life member in 1919. He gave the Presidential Address at Sidmouth in 1935 and wrote many articles on physics as well as local history. He retired from the university in 1950 and continued to live in Toronto where he died in 1963.

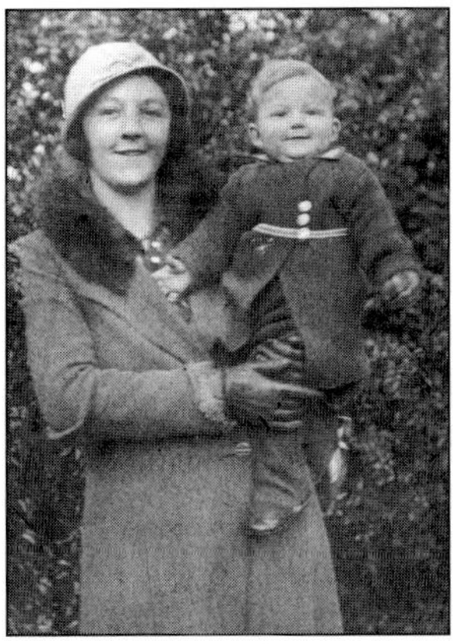

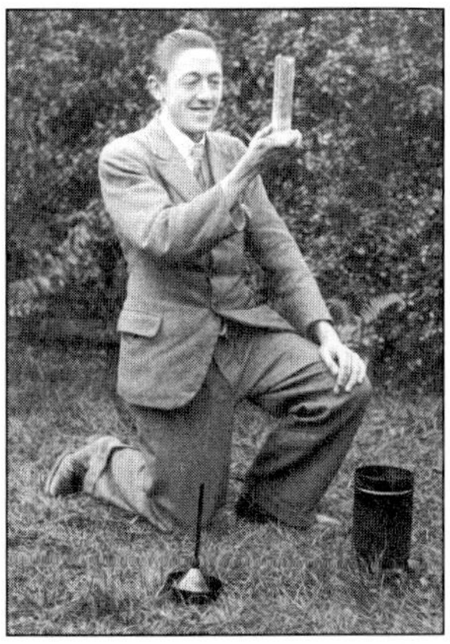

Left: *Amy Hannaford with daughter Ruby.* Right: *Bill Hannaford, Amy's son. Not only was Bill an amateur weatherman, he was also the town's barber. They lived in what is now the museum.* (PETE WEBB COLLECTION)

Amy Satterley, 1881–1965

Born in Ashburton, Amy Satterley was taught photography by J.P.S. Amery at Druid House. Most of the Victorian and early 1900s photos in this book are from her camera lens. She married William Hannaford, a local baker, and they moved to

Kingsbridge. She gave up her photography until he died of pneumonia in 1912, and without family support moved back to Ashburton, lived with her parents in Vealenia Terrace and took up photography again. She helped keep house when her mother died and travelled all over the area with a large tripod camera taking pictures. She remarried again in 1923 and became Mrs White but still carried on with her photography. Her pictures were of an excellent quality. Moreover, it was unusual for a woman to earn a living from photography at that time. She moved to Mapledon House in West Street and had a tea room there. She gave up photography around 1937 when her husband died and moved to 1 West Street, now the home of Ashburton's museum. Her son Bill, who lived with her, was an amateur weatherman and the town's barber. His barber's chair was in the little room at the back above the river. Amy died in 1965 aged 84.

Wilfred (Taffy) Evans, 1888–1917

Born around 1888, chemist's assistant Taffy, or Dewi as he was also known, learnt about photography and produced postcards in a very small way at the family chemists at 7 West Street. Trade directory entries for the family appear from 1881 to 1919.

In 1916, at the age of 28, he appealed against his call-up to fight in the First World War. His father was in his 70s and Taffy carried out most of the work, but because he was not a qualified chemist, his appeal failed. He must have had a strong premonition of what was to happen as he was killed in Flanders in July 1917. The chemist's shop remained in West Street (see p.27) until the early 1980s when Holman and Ham, as it had become, moved to its present position in North Street. It is now (2004) Lloyd's the Chemist.

Amy Francis Jones MBE, 1889–1983

Amy Jones was born in 1889 and lived with her parents (Michelmore) in the Railway Inn (now the Silent Whistle). She married in 1913 and moved to Stonepark. She was variously a teacher at the Primary School, a school governor, a Town Councillor, chair and president of the local Conservative Association and active in St Andrew's Church. She became Ashburton's first female Portreeve (No. 1,144) in November 1964 and was awarded an OBE in 1976. She was also chairman of Ashburton UDC and died in 1983, aged 96.

Alan Hope

Alan followed a long line of eccentric landlords at the Golden Lion. He first came to Ashburton with his wife, Norma, in 1978 after a long career in the music business under the name of Kerry Rapide. In 1990 the Golden Lion became the headquarters of the Monster Raving Loony Party, which was formed by Alan's musical colleague, Screaming Lord Sutch, in the 1960s. The party's presence in Ashburton for their annual conference brought a lot of colour to the town for a week or so, as well as representatives of the world's press and a lot of people. Alan was a one-man tourist attraction in his own right. He took over as the party's leader in 1999 after Sutch's death. Alan's politics did not go down well with everyone but he served the town well not only as a town councillor and briefly as Mayor, but also as the tourism representative of the Town Council. He helped get the original tourist information caravan in the town's car park over ten years ago and was still involved as a member of the council when the present information centre was opened in 1998. Alan sold the pub in the summer of 2000, and it has since been turned into two large houses with another eight on the land behind. Alan is now (2004) the landlord of the Dog and Partridge at Yately in Hampshire and still leads the party.

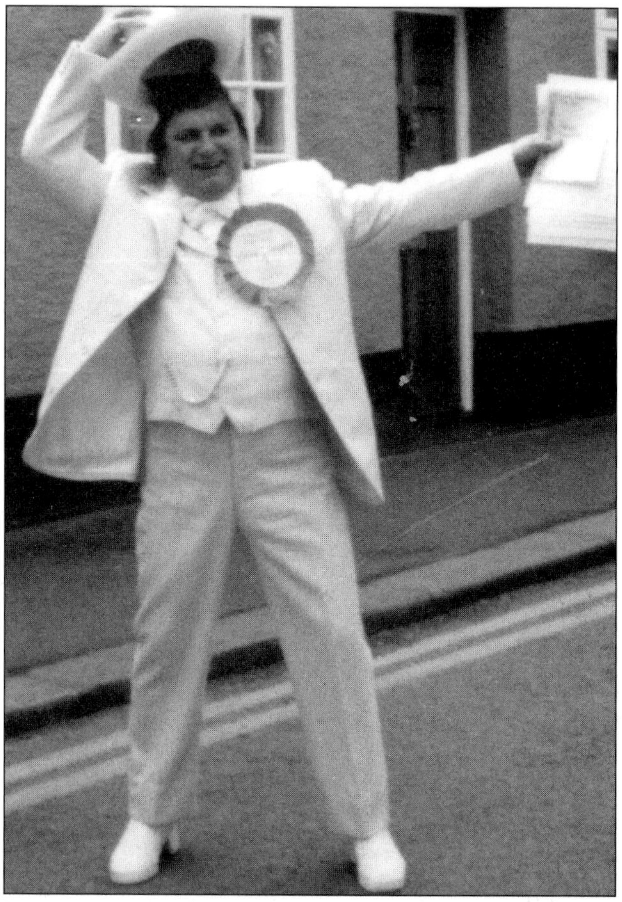

Alan Hope returning along St Lawrence Lane having just met Sir Geoffrey Howe (the then Chancellor of the Exchequer) at the cattle market in June 1983. (PETE WEBB)

✣ CHAPTER 13 ✣

Leisure

Ashburton Theatre

During the 1950s Ashburton had a successful theatre company in an old barn in West Street. Moyra Babbington, who had attended a theatre school in London, persuaded her mother Audrey to let her use the old barn, which lay empty next to her father's bus garage. Formerly, their fellow Buckfast Players, a group formed in 1940 to entertain the troops, had used the Old Mill Theatre in Buckfast but had to vacate their building.

Partitions were erected and a stage built over the old inspection pit. Some 70-odd seats were purchased from Torquay Pavilion, lighting installed and a former beach hut converted into a box office. The dressing rooms were still used by the Babbington family buses except when there was a performance. These were then converted into professional dressing rooms with all the mirrors and lights necessary for a full-time theatre.

For many years plays and pantomimes were put on, often to packed houses, to entertain the local population. In 1950 *Jack and the Beanstalk* played to a full house of 110–115 for ten days. Right through the 1950s some well-known plays of the day had their first showings at the theatre, including *White Doves of Bardon* by Phöebe Rees, *Golden Harvest* and *Crescent Moon* by Christian Michell, *Adelaise* by James Forsyth and the world premier of *Joy in the Morning* by P.G. Wodehouse.

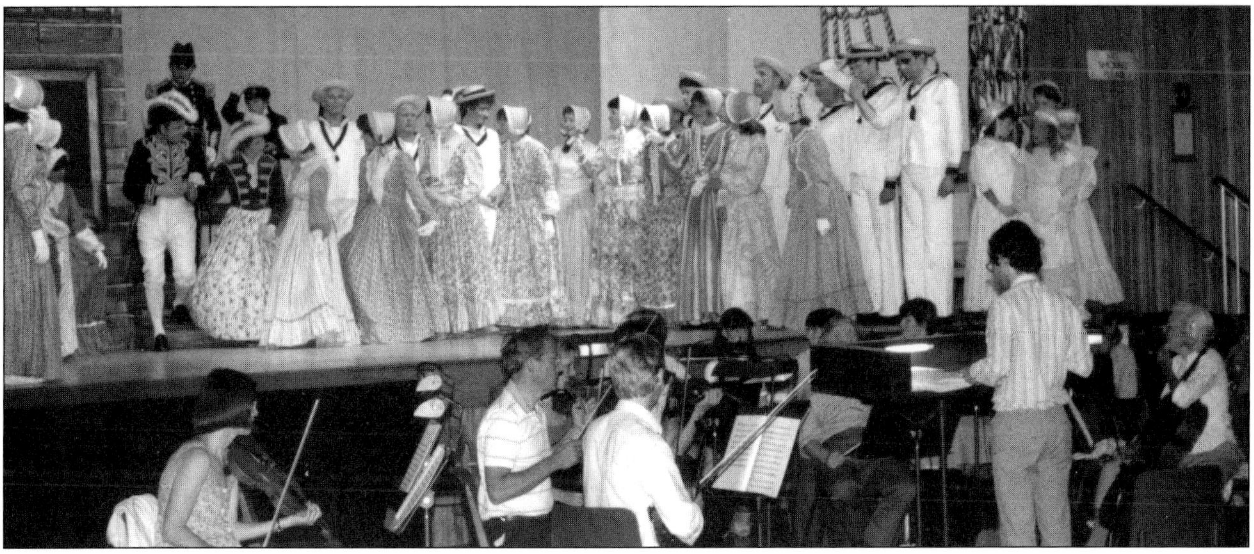

HMS Pinafore, *Ashburton Festival, 1984.* Cast includes: *Steve Coleman, Roger Burton, Terry Palminter, Jonathan Watts, Dave Garrard, Bill Harman (Admiral), Gail and Paula Harman, Sue Latimer, Annette Osbourne, Catherine Casey, Betty Gilbert, Pat Shaw, Jeanne Allen.* Orchestra includes: *Janet Wellingham and Pauline Ballard.*

(JEANNE ALLEN COLLECTION)

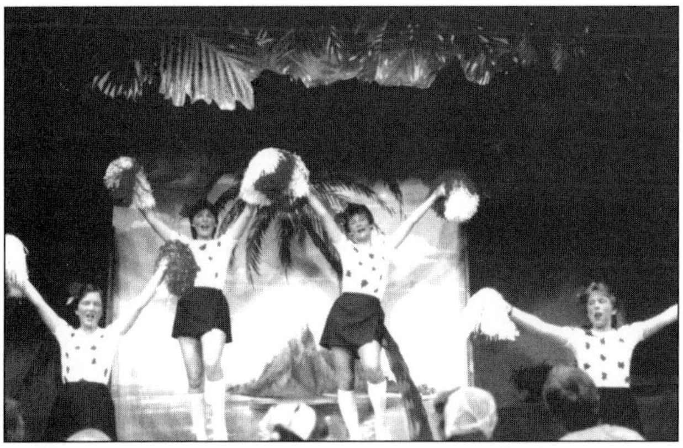

South Pacific *with* left to right: *Stella Allen, ?, Ester Gilbert, Sarah Billing. Teignbridge Theatre Company, 1987.* (JEANNE ALLEN COLLECTION)

The first new Wodehouse since the Second World War the script was given to the company by Mr Thompson of Teignmouth. Needing £200 for a new roof in the summer of 1954, the players were pleased to have such a 'scoop'. Mr Thompson had written to the author in New York some years previously when his own operatic company was in difficulties and had been given the manuscript as a gift. Hearing of the Barn Theatre's difficulties he had in turn given them the play.

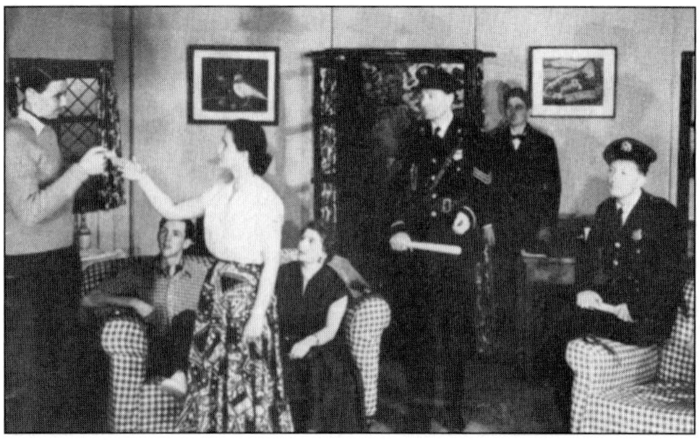

The cast of Joy in the Morning, *a Barn Theatre Production which starred Kendrick Bishop, Alan McQuillin, Doreen Thurley, Michael Edwards, Hazel Inglis, Tony Armstrong, A.E. Sproston, David Weaver and Michael Rich.* (PETE WEBB COLLECTION)

Other plays such as *Arms and the Man* by Bernard Shaw, Shakespeare's *Henry VIII* and *The Peacemakers* by Christian Michell, to name but a few, were also performed there. Other groups such as the Dartington Players, Newton Abbot Repertory Co., Plymouth Shakespeare Company and Liverpool Strolling Players used the theatre, but it was mainly the local players themselves who put on regular performances.

Plymouth Theatre Company thought the town a cultural blackspot and mention is made in *Great Disasters of the Stage* by William Donaldson of a performance of *The Golden Pathway Annual.* Six actors had learned 20 parts between them and the stage-hands took ten hours to erect the set. Posters and free tickets had been distributed around the town but when the curtain went up only one man was sitting in the audience. The play went on and he duly applauded and left when they had finished.

Films were also shown (including the film premier of *All Along, Down Along* in 1951) and the theatre was still going in 1956 but it is not certain when it finally closed.

Audrey Babington died in 1962 aged 75 and was sorely missed by both family and fellow members of the Buckfast Players. Other prominent members who will be well remembered in the town were Doreen (Dee) Thurley and Queenie Hawkins (Dumble).

Guiding

Guiding started in Ashburton in October 1923 with Miss Heath as acting captain and the Misses Luxton

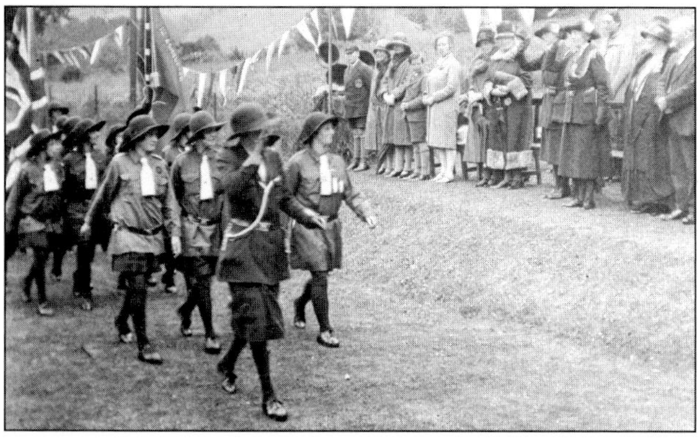

In St Andrew's vicarage garden, 1925. Lady Clinton, County Commissioner, is taking the salute. By her side is the Portreeve, Revd Arthur H. Thompson, with Mrs Thompson at his side.

(RUTH WESTALL AND LORNA HARVEY COLLECTIONS)

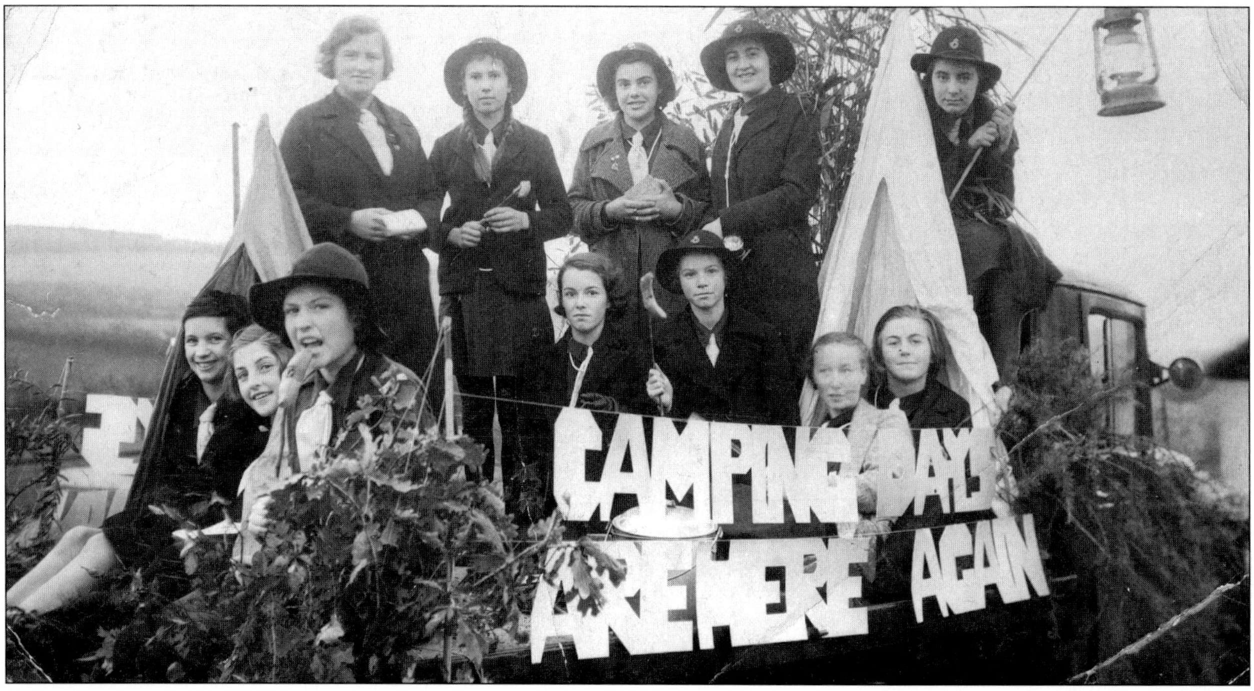

Guides, 1941. Photo includes: *Pearl Yolland, Joan Parnell, Betty Butler, Hazel White, Joyce Grose, Beatrice Barnett, Joyce and Madge Dewlands, May Bales.* (GARTH GROSE COLLECTION)

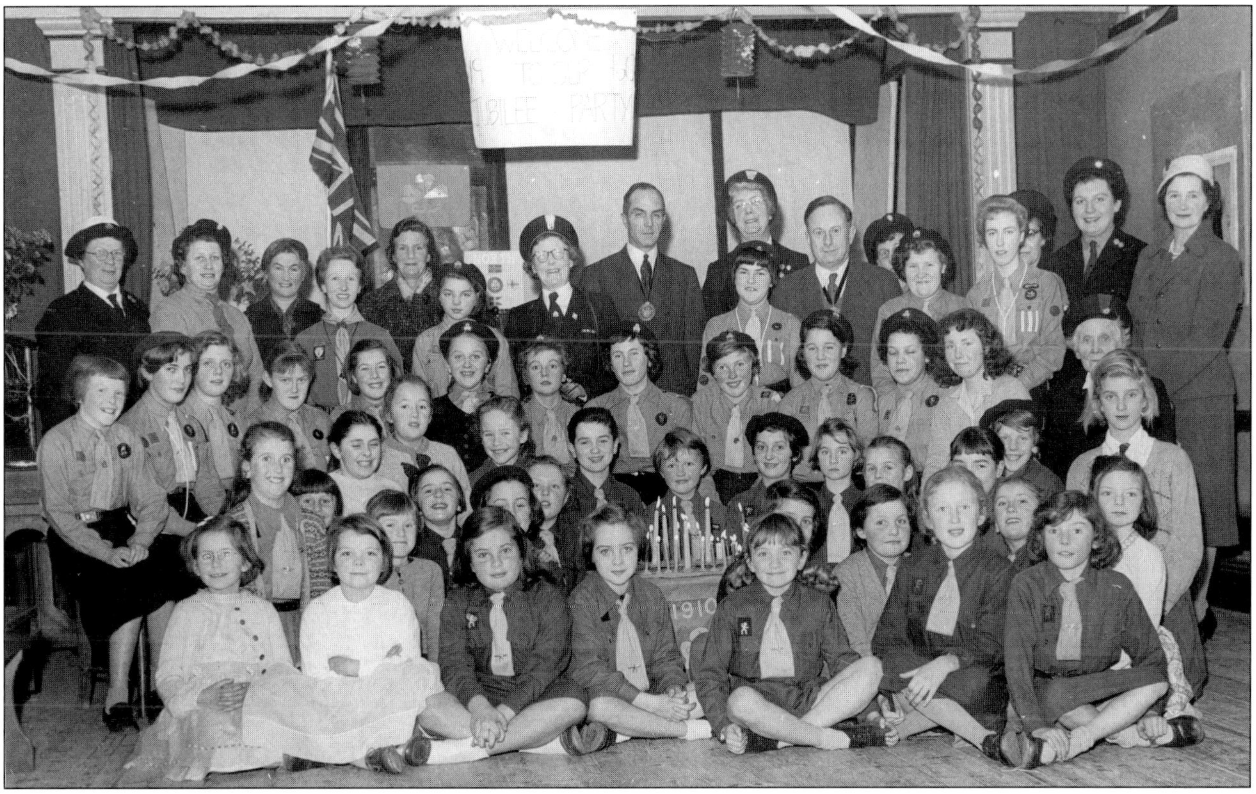

Guiding's Golden Jubilee celebrations in Ashburton in 1961. Photo includes: *Ruth Windeat, Doris Turner, Mrs Jones (vicar's wife), Olga Churchward, Betty Bindloss (County Commissioner), Portreeve Christopher Gamble, Mrs Mellor (District Commissioner), Lionel Gambel, Lorna Harvey, Julia Whidborne, Wendy Gill, Elaine Whidborne, Mary Stanbury, Mrs Webb.* (RUTH WESTALL AND LORNA HARVEY COLLECTIONS)

and Pengilley as her assistants. After initial training, six Guides made their promise on 15 December in St Lawrence Chapel. At the same time, Mrs Thompson, wife of St Andrews' vicar, appealed to adults to form a Local Association, now known as The Friends of Guiding, with the sole purpose of raising funds to put towards guiding expenses. About 40 people came forward. By January 1924 there were 30 Guides (aged 12+) with Brownies (7–11 years) and Land Rangers (14+ years). There was also a Sea Ranger unit and a Cadet unit, formed to train 14-year-olds to become adult helpers. There was great excitement on 12 April 1924 when Lady Clinton, County Commissioner, came to enrol the new company and members of the Local Association. Guiding in England has its headquarters in London, with regions around the country (the South West HQ is in Salisbury), divided into county, division and district, each with its own commissioner. Each district is made up of units from the surrounding towns and villages – Ashburton, Buckfastleigh and Ilsington are in Ashburton District. They are all part of Teignbridge Division which includes the districts of Ashburton, Bovey Tracey, Newton Abbot, Teignmouth, Chudleigh and Dawlish.

Over the years Guiding has played a large part in the life of the town, the girls participating in most carnivals, the ale tasting and medieval fayres, pantomimes, church parades, helping at hospital fêtes, etc. St Andrew's church hall has been used for meetings of Brownies, Guides and Trefoil Guides (recycled Guides!) for the past 80 years. However, for a period in the 1960s they had their own headquarters in what had been the Golden Fleece Public House, St Lawrence Lane (now Nos.17 and 17a) when it became vacant.

Camping for Guides and pack holidays for Brownies have played a big part in the girls' training for independence, usually in individual units but sometimes the girls joined larger division camps to mark special occasions, such as at Prince Hall in 1984 for the 75th celebrations. Division swimming galas, camp competitions and camp-fires have all been enjoyed and many good turns done for people at home and abroad. In 1987 the Rangers and Venture Scouts held a gang show and raised £500 for the Portreeve's Fund to help talented youngsters to achieve their ambitions.

In 1984 Ashburton District Guides planted trees on ground behind Pear Tree garage to mark 75 years of Guiding. A light was lit in London and carried around the country in many different ways, arriving in Ashburton by car then going on to Totnes by steam railway. In 1935 trees were planted on the old A38 road to commemorate the Silver Jubilee of King George V and a stone placed to mark the occasion. In 1996 the stone was cleaned and a wooden seat, donated by the Brownies, was put in place.

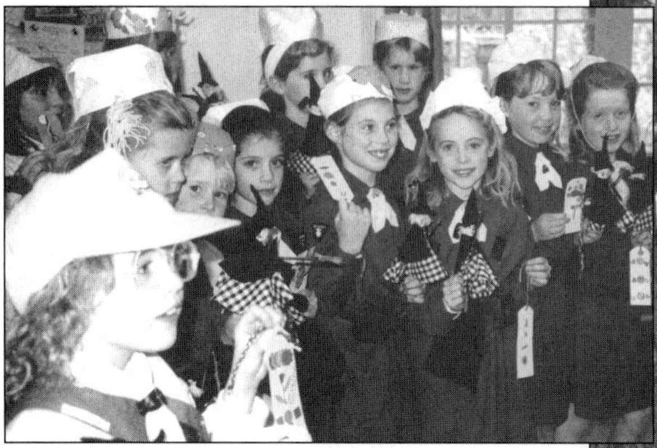

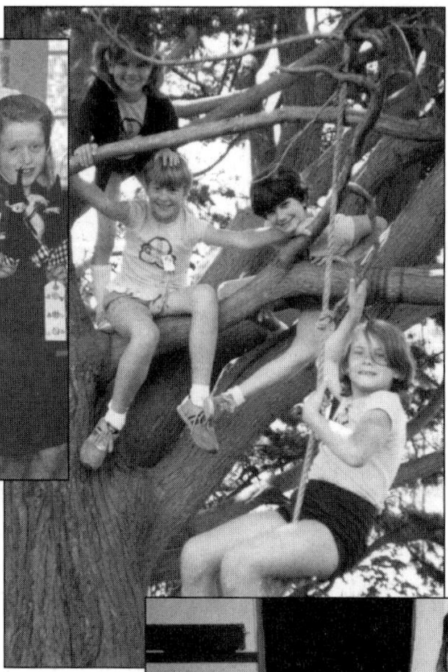

Ashburton Brownies (1st Pack) enjoying a pack holiday in 1985 at Noss Mayo. In descending order: *Ellysia Graymore, Kate Hamlyn, Sarah Shaw, Corinne Webb. This photograph appeared in colour on the back cover of the 1987 Brownie Annual.* (MARION WALE; RUTH WESTALL COLLECTION)

Above: *Lorna Harvey gave a shield which is competed for each year by the Brownies in the district. Here they show off some of their craft work.* (RUTH WESTALL COLLECTION)

Right: *Guide Thinking Day is an international event, held as near to 22 February as possible, celebrating Guiding worldwide. Here, on 18 February 1987, 2nd Ashburton Guides display items from other countries.* Left to right: *Sarah Priddle, Ellysia Graymore, Corinne Webb, Shona Major.* (RUTH WESTALL COLLECTION)

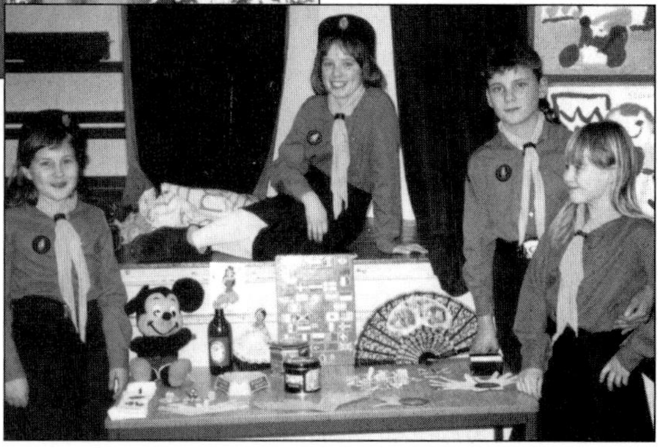

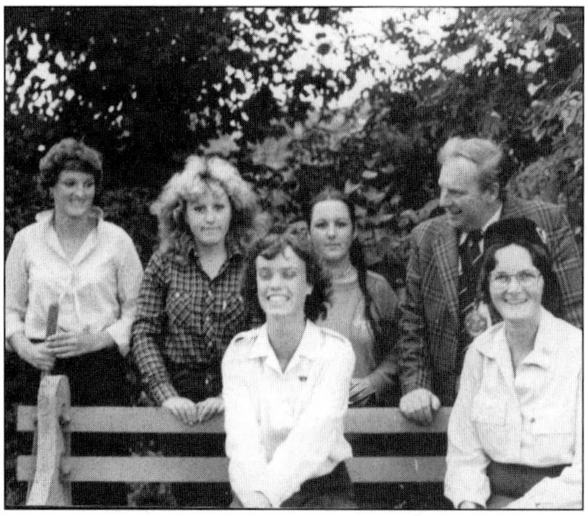

Left: *Rangers at St Gudula's Well, 1981.* Left to right, back row: *Ione Woodger, Tina Randels, Kay Randels, Portreeve Ron Southcombe;* seated: *Wendy Downie, Jeanne Allen (leader).* (JEANNE ALLEN COLLECTION)

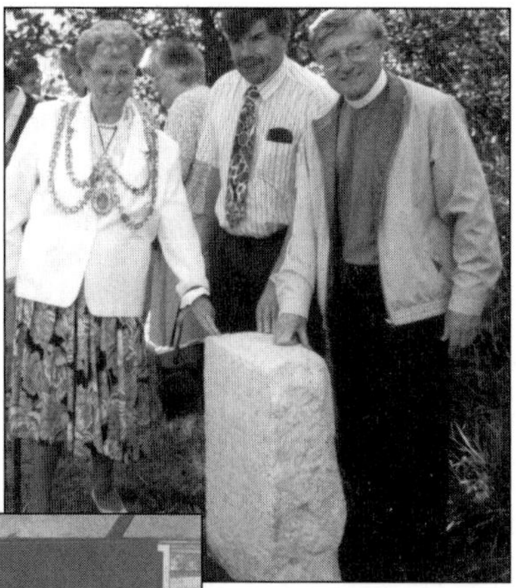

Left: *Dedication of stone on 16 July 1996, with Portreeve Mrs Eileen Egbeare, Mr Brian Miller and Revd Peter Gregson.* (RUTH WESTALL AND LORNA HARVEY COLLECTIONS)

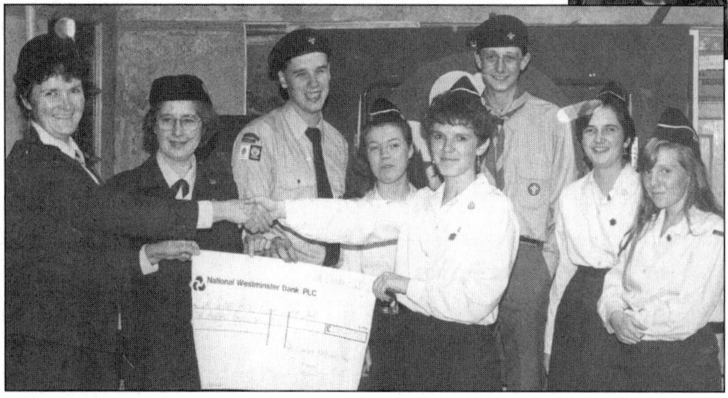

Left: *In 1987, members of the Ranger unit and the Venture Scouts put on a gang show and raised £500 for the Portreeve's Fund to support talented youngsters in the town.* Left to right: *Jeanne Allen, Ruth Westall, Christopher Hall, Gail Hallett, Elaine Starkey* (holding cheque*), Michael Hall, Stella Allen, Sarah Johns.* (RUTH WESTALL COLLECTION)

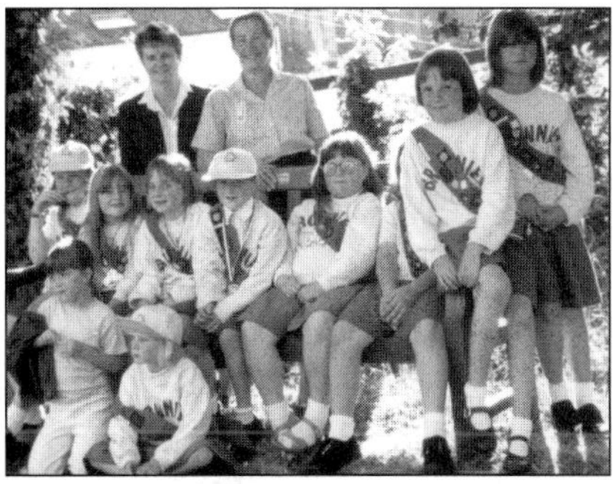

Left: *This picture shows the dedication of a Brownie seat at the top of Whistley Hill, to mark both the closure of the 2nd Ashburton Brownie Pack and the cleaning of the neglected Guide stone which had been erected to commemorate the planting of trees on the A38 in celebration of the Silver Jubilee of King George V in 1935.* Photo includes: *Pat Crook, Betty Gilbert, Emma Horrell, Aimee Foot, Kelly Stater, Avril Smerdon, Keelie ?, Pia ?.*

(RUTH WESTALL AND LORNA HARVEY COLLECTIONS)

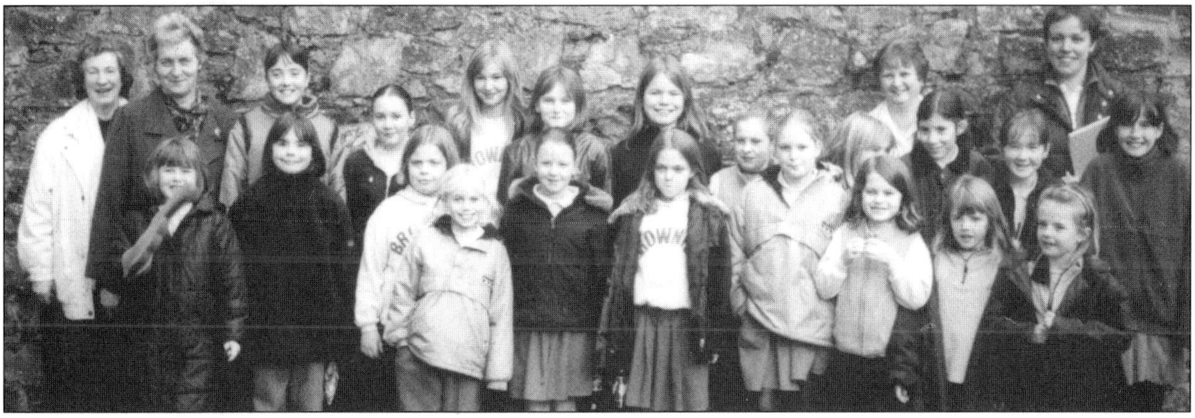

The 2nd Ashburton Brownies on a theatre outing, 2001. Pictured are: *Betty Gilbert, June Wills, Katherine Parker, Heather Exley, Carmen Tyler, Bethan Lee, Pat Crooke, Sally Lang, Sian Pugh, Megan Lee, Amber Millen, Olivia Lang, Eleanor Cramner, Hannah Thompson, Molly Andrew, Katie Murray, Emma Setherton, Natasha Whale, Sarah Thompson, Georgie Chew, Holly Cutts, Rosie Cramner, Sadie Andrew, Ruth Andrew.*

(STUART HANDS)

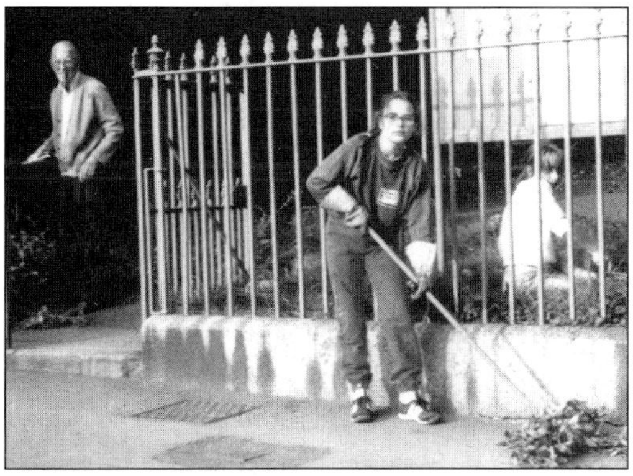

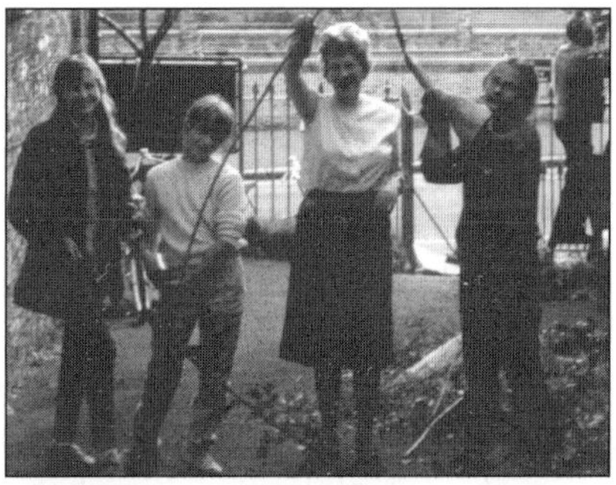

Guides' good turn. Left to right: *Becky Williams, Jacqui Chamberlain, Ruth Westall, Samantha Dennis.*

(RUTH WESTALL COLLECTION)

Above: *Guides doing a good turn tidying the grounds of the United Reformed Church (Great Meeting) in return for being allowed to store their equipment there, September, 1985.* Left to right: *Revd H.M. Westall, Samantha Dennis, Jacqui Chamberlain.*

(RUTH WESTALL COLLECTION)

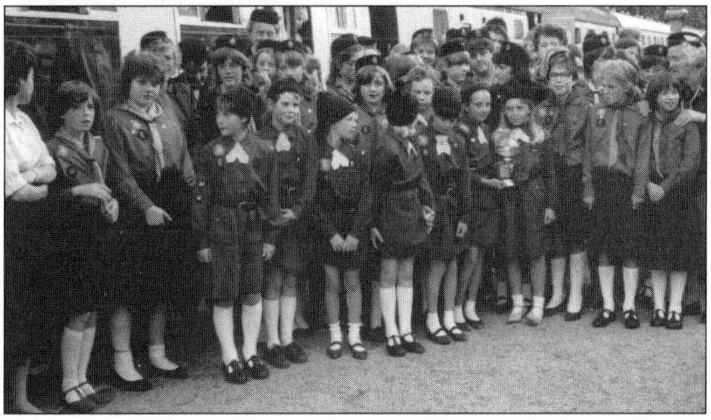

Right: *As part of the 75th Anniversary celebrations a 'Guiding Light' started from Buckingham Palace (the Queen was a Guide and Sea Ranger) and was carried round the country using various forms of transport. Here it is about to be taken on the Dart Valley Railway steam train at Buckfastleigh en route to Totnes, July 1985.* Photo includes: *Mary Hands* (with glasses) *and Catherine Jefferies.*

(RUTH WESTALL AND LORNA HARVEY COLLECTIONS)

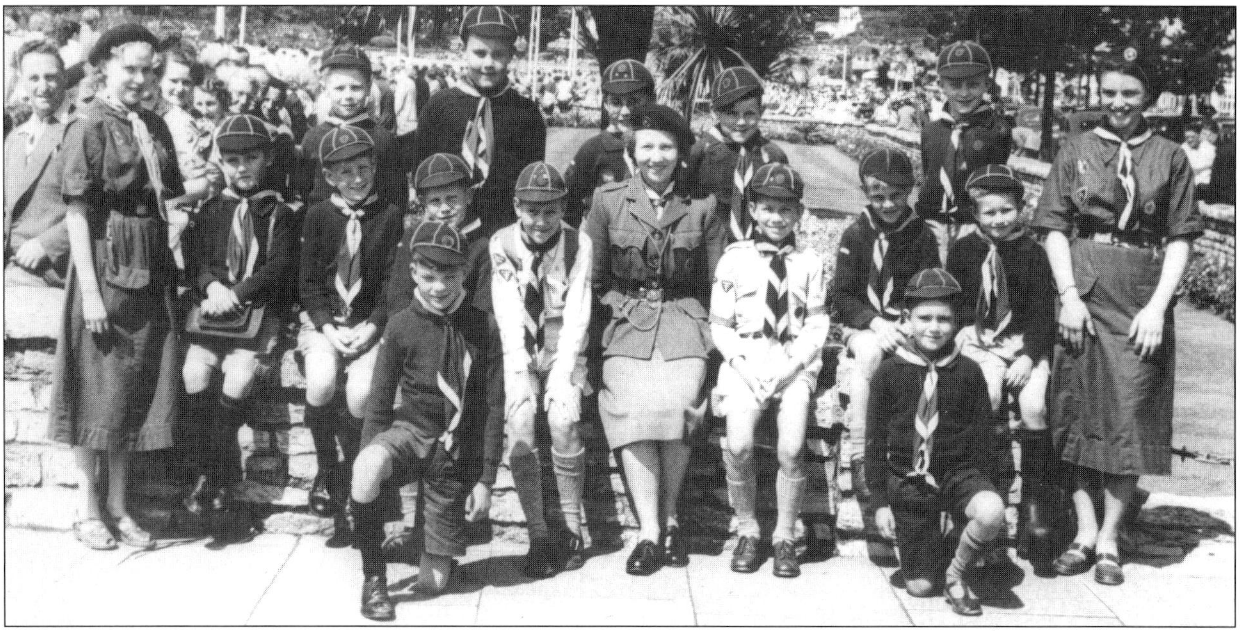

The 1st Ashburton pack, 1954, at Torquay. Left to right, back row: *Richard Smith, Derek Roberts, Lennie Combes, Peter Farley, Richard Willis;* centre: *Pat Daw, Michael Morgan, Graham Monnington, Les Vickery, overseas visitor, Olga Churchward, overseas visitor, David Tubby, Robin Bly, Margaret Downing;* kneeling in front: *Peter Cubit, ?.* (PAT ORSMAN COLLECTION)

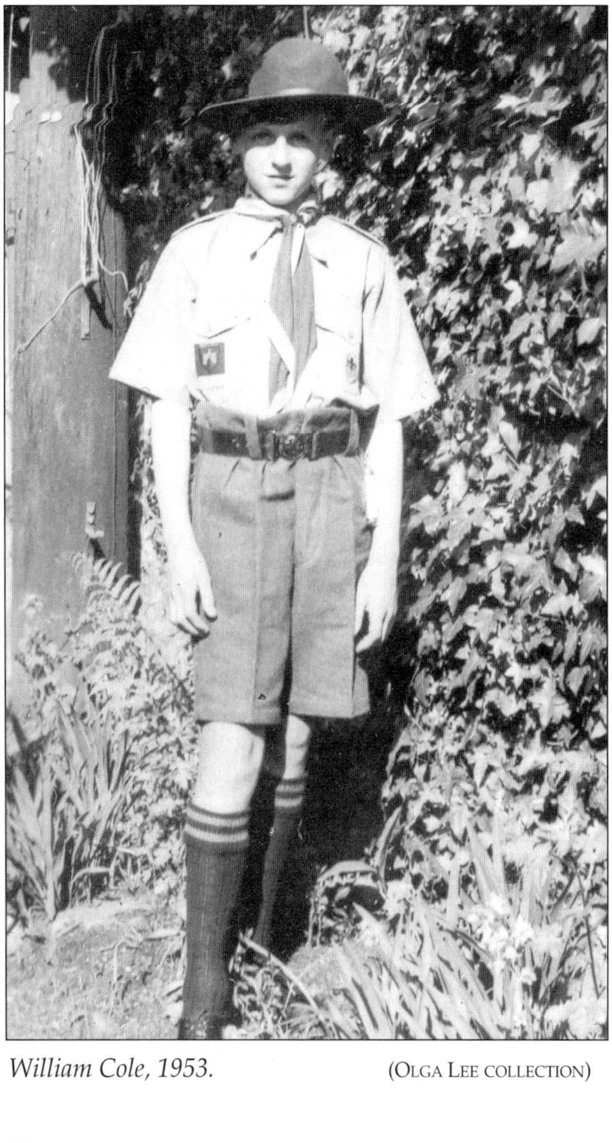

William Cole, 1953. (OLGA LEE COLLECTION)

Ashburton also had its own Rangers Unit for a number of years. The Guiders were Jeanne Allen and Elaine Cory.

Scouting

The origins of scouting in Ashburton are not known. In 1945 Olga Churchward became the youngest Akela (Cub leader) in Devon. Olga kept a log which runs from 26 February 1945 until her resignation on 11 February 1966 – 21 years as Akela of the 1st Ashburton Cub Pack. Through my contribution to this book I have become aware of just how much the town of Ashburton owes to people like Olga. Many of the clubs which help to give Ashburton its sense of community would have folded long ago without

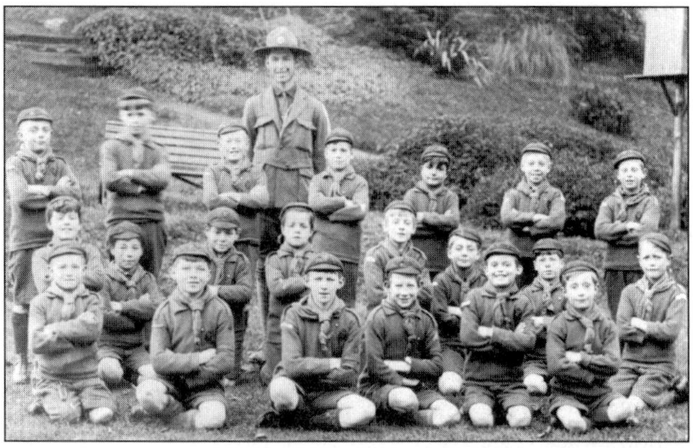

Ashburton Cub Scouts in the 1920s. Photo includes: *B. Callard, H. Yolland, C. Bray, K. Lear, F. Woodgates, L. Northcott, J. (Skinny) Leaman, J. Nosworthy, J. Milton, D. Brooking, B. Brooks, A. French and master Sergeant.* (ASHBURTON OF YESTERYEAR)

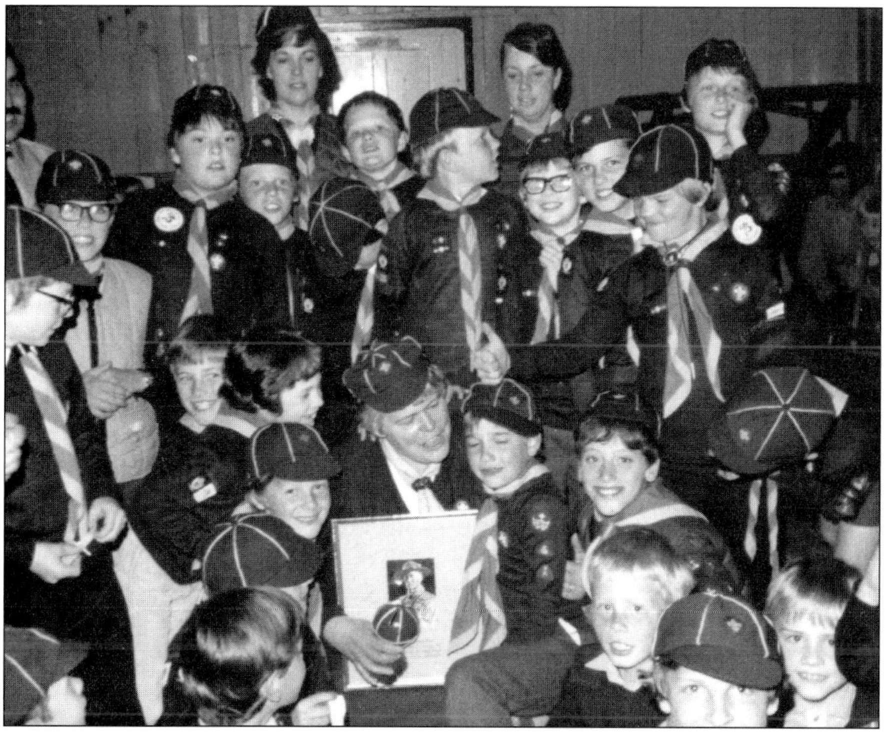

Mavis Head's last night as Akela (Cub leader), 1982. Photo includes: *Derek King, Margaret Stott, Wendy Trewin, Dean Hartland, Richard Radcliffe, John Hoare, Michael Beale, Andrew Plum, Michael Easton, Simon Garrard, Stephen Donald, James Dean, Ross Hallett, Mavis Head, Malcolm Sheldon, Martin Snarey, Gary Mounce, James Arnold.*

(MAVIS HEAD COLLECTION)

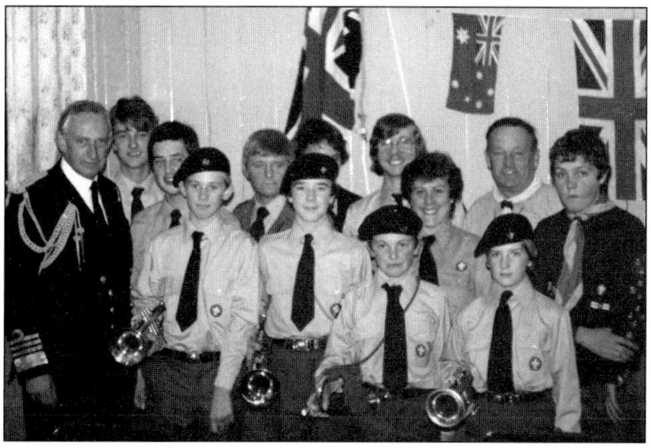

Ashburton Scouts Band, early 1980s. Photo includes: *Admiral Eberley, Garry Olden, Simon Durrant, John Gale, Tony Pugh, John Hilson, Ian Ritson* (with glasses), *Graham Hill, Pam Giles, Peter Head, Alan Norman, Trevor Head.* (MAVIS HEAD COLLECTION)

such dedicated service. The log records the names of all the Cubs who, at one stage or another, were members of the pack. As an example, let us take the year of the Queen's coronation – 1953.

There were three sixes: Red Six – Michael Braund, Gordon Pearle, David Brooks, Michael Bennett, Michael Stone, Brian Roberts, David Owen; White Six – Peter Hamlyn, John Cole, Leonard Boyce, John Neale, Peter Farley; Blue Six – Adrian Daw, Stuart Pearle, Brian Blair, Lennard Coombes, Douglas Mixted, Richard Smith. Pat Daw (Kim to give her pack name) was assistant Cub leader at the time. Besides doing the usual activities in the hut, the pack went out on trips whenever possible, such as a visit to Paignton Zoo, or a hike up to the top of Buckland Beacon where they admired the marvellous view.

On 6 August 1956 a Devon Scout pageant was in Torquay and the pack visited the Ashburton Scouts, who were taking part in the jamboree. It was a

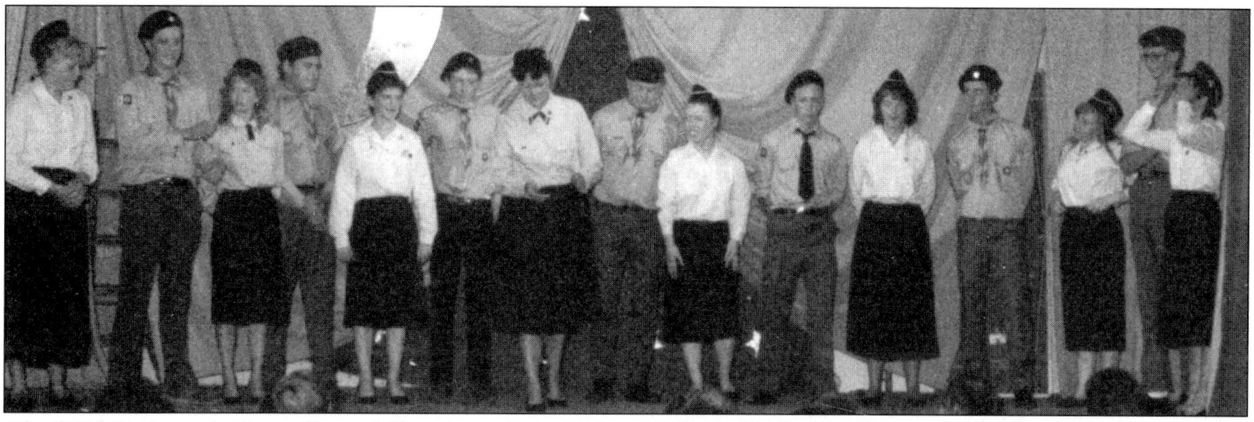

The 1987 Portreeve's Gang Show, full cast on stage. Left to right: *Julia Smith, Christopher Hall, Elaine Corey, Jonny Hoare, Janet Starkey, Andrew Plumb, Jeanne Allen (Guider), Peter Head (Scout Leader), Gail Hallett, John White, Angela Whale, Mark Chamberlain, Sarah Johns, Michael Hall, Stella Allen.* (JEAN ALLEN COLLECTION)

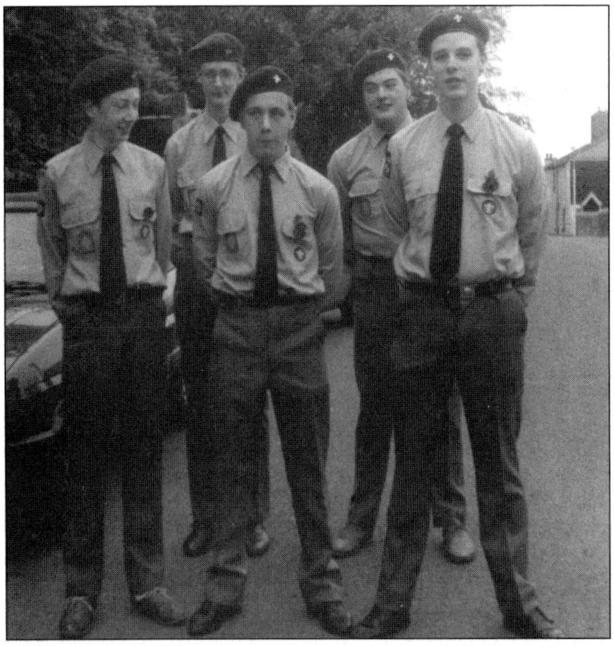

1st Ashburton Venture Scouts. Left to right: *Andrew Plumb, Michael Hall, Jon White, John Hoare, Christopher Hall.* (MAVIS HEAD COLLECTION)

glorious summer's day and the pageant was attended by the Chief Scout, Lord Rowallan. It was not long before a replacement was found for Olga, who by this time was Mrs Lee. Mrs Mavis Head, who had moved from Ipplepen with her husband Peter, took the reins. The pack continued in good heart until she resigned as Akela (leader) in 1982, continuing as group Scout leader until September 1995. Peter's arrival in Ashburton was opportune as he too was able to assist the Scout troop; he was appointed assistant district commissioner. During his tenure of office Venture Scouts were started in Ashburton. One of the highlights was the gang show staged in 1987. This was known as the Portreeve's Gang Show and was held to raise money for the Portreeve's Appeal – the Portreeve at the time being Mr Neil Room-Doubleday. This was a joint venture with the 1st Ashburton Rangers, whose leader was Jeanne Allen. Another success story was the formation of the Scout band. An achievement of which the troop was rightly very proud was the raising of funds, £460 by public subscription, to build the Scout headquarters in 1962. It was achieved through the hard work of boys, parents and friends. Sadly there is no Scout troop in Ashburton today; boys show little interest and red tape discourages people from volunteering their time and effort.

Ashburton Carnival

Ashburton's rich and varied history is closely connected with the ancient Saxon office of Portreeve. The Portreeve of the day has always been connected with fund-raising activities in the town and the present-day carnival, as well as providing entertainment, is primarily a fund-raising event.

One of the earliest written references to the carnival is a description in an article from November 1891 referring to 'Mr Fawkes' Carnival in Ashburton'. At this time it was held to raise funds for Ashburton hospital. As the town was predominantly a farming community and the summer months far too busy, it was held after the harvest was brought in and concluded with a bonfire in the Bull Ring – in those days, of course, there was no tarmac to consider.

The 1891 event was organised by the town's youth and commenced with a rousing salute of canons at dawn. Nothing happened for the rest of the day until dusk when flaming tar barrels were carried through the streets, with balls of fire and numerous squibs and crackers ignited. A procession of floats led by the Liberal band proceeded from the top of East Street through the town, finishing at the Bull Ring. Music was played, numerous fireworks let off and the bonfire ignited.

The visiting firemen from Totnes had to leave early because of the times of trains, but Ashburton's brigade managed to extinguish it themselves. There was no report of any other fires which, with the amount of burning material in the town during the evening, seems surprising.

The November carnival carried on for many years with the money divided between the hospital, St John Ambulance and local midwives. Some time after the First World War it became a summer event.

The modern-day carnival starts with a fête on the last Saturday in June and finishes with the procession on the first Saturday in July. For many years famous

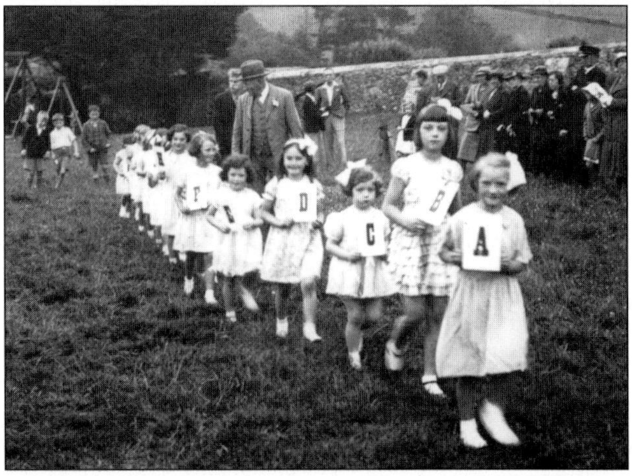

Prospective carnival princesses. The onlookers include: *Georgina Webb, Mrs Davis, Dolly Parsons, Winnie Muggeridge, Amy Jones, Mrs Hext, Florrie Hamlyn.* (WATERS COLLECTION)

artists appearing in the Paignton's Pavilion Theatre opened the fête, among them Dickie Henderson (1969), Sid James (1971), Kenneth Connor (*Carry On* films – 1972), and Billy Burden (1976). Singers such as The Bachelors (1973) and Dana (1986) also opened

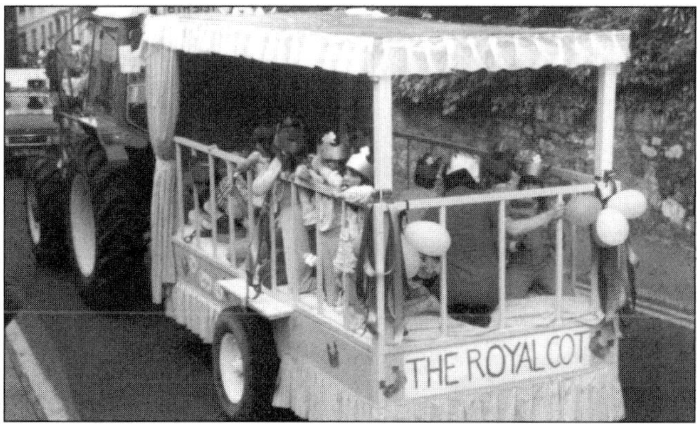

Above: *The Brownies' float at the carnival, 1980s.* (PETE WEBB)

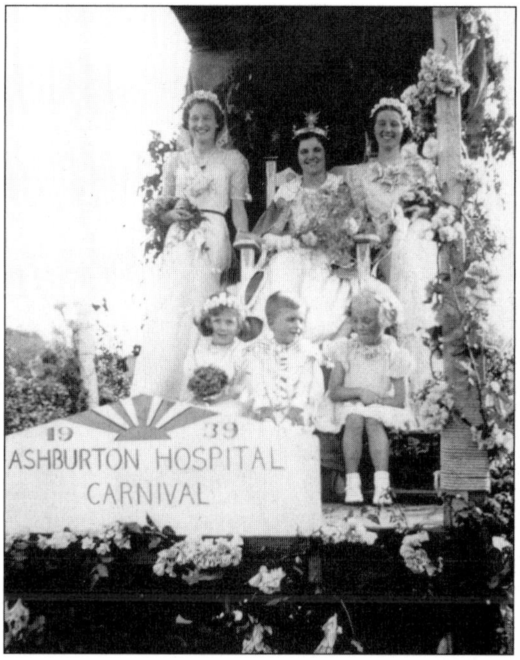

Right: *Ashburton hospital carnival queen's float in 1939. Queen, Margaret Stone; attendants, Winnie Brooks and Phyllis Nightingale.* (JOYCE COON COLLECTION)

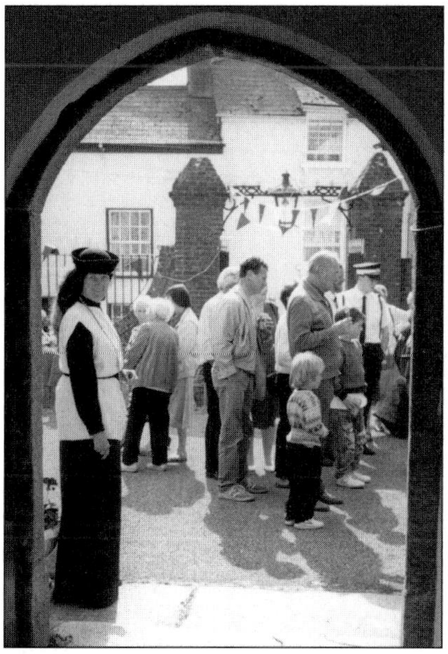

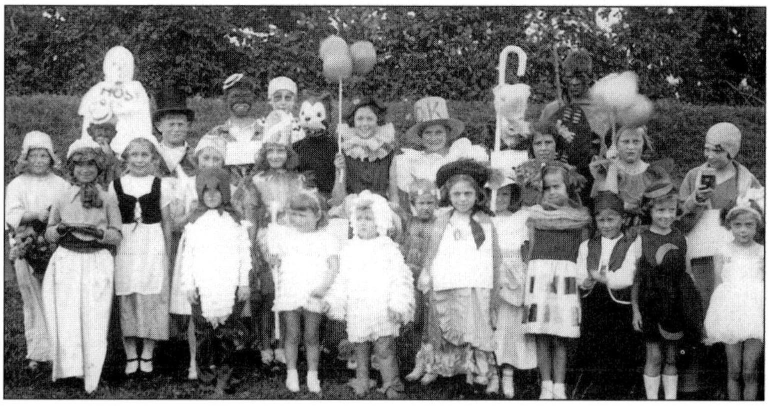

Above: *Picture of pedestrians in Ashburton carnival, taken in a field in Balland Lane, c.1935.* Photo includes: *Nancy Finch, Francis Davies, Joan Palmer, Mary Baker, Beatrice Barnett (*with bathing cap*), Mary Endacott (Joe's sister), Brayley and Margaret Wotton, Cecil Palmer (*with top hat*), Mary Townsend, Christine Dickens, David Endacott (Joe's brother), Pat New, Betty Hamlyn, Jean Baker.* (CHRISTINE DICKENS)

Archway looking out of St Lawrence Chapel, Ashburton ale tasting, 1989. Jeanne Allen is in medieval costume in the doorway. (JEANNE ALLEN COLLECTION)

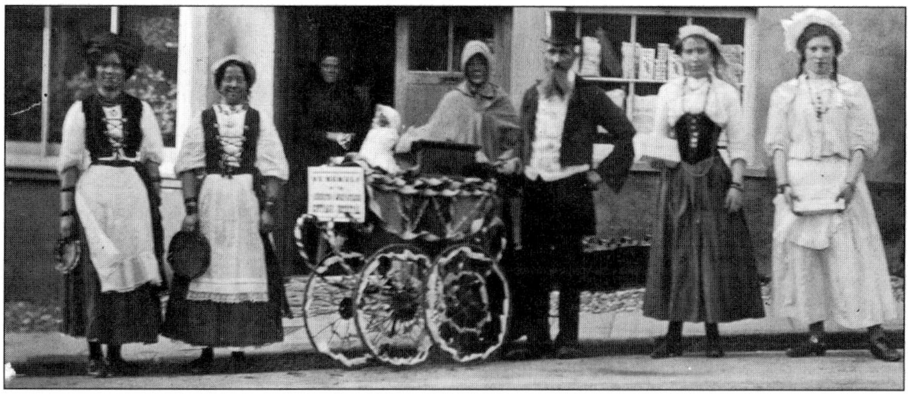

Carnival pedestrians group from a 1920s carnival in East Street outside Mr Mapp's shop (No. 33), now a private house recently renovated. (PETE WEBB COLLECTION)

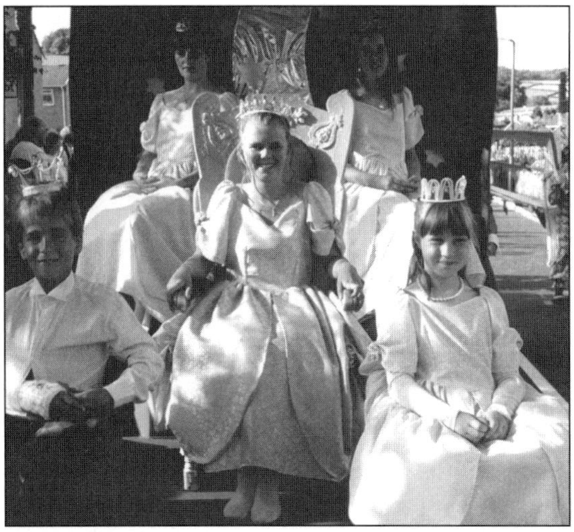

Carnival queen, 1994. At back: *Sherie Thorn, Sarah Viney, Ruth Aggett (queen);* front: *Luke Webb (prince) and Emma Larard (princess).*
(JOHN MITCHELL; PETE WEBB COLLECTION)

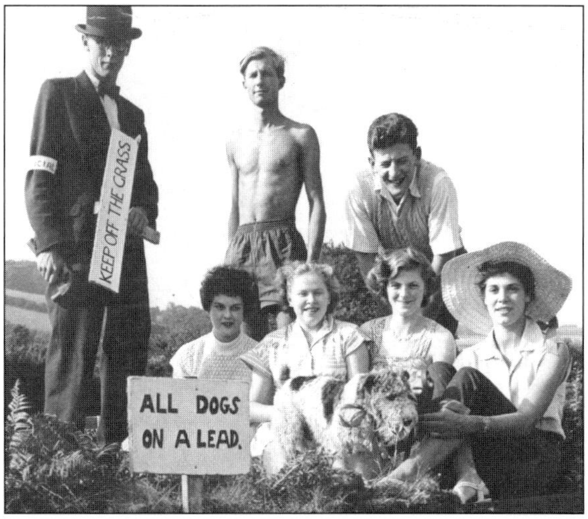

Carnival float for Young Conservatives, 1950s. Standing: *Michael Armstrong, David Moore, Henry Lang;* sitting: *Pat Blamey, Pat Daw, Daphne Tuckett, Shirley Masters.* (PAT ORSMAN COLLECTION)

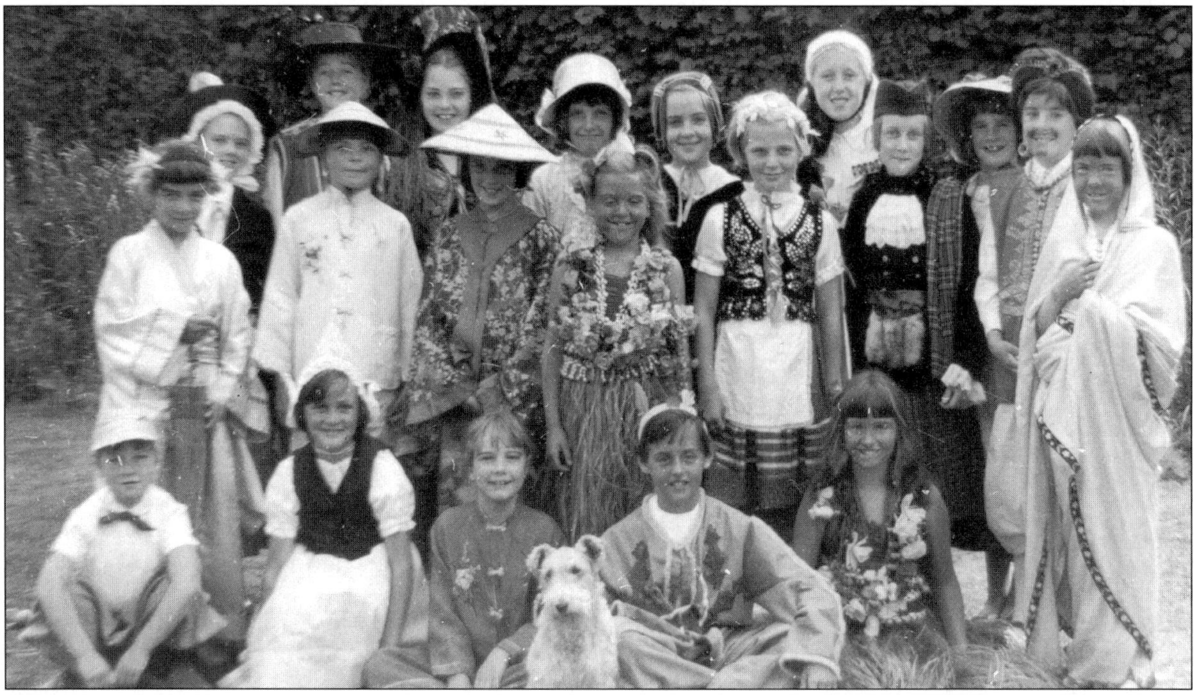

Brownies took part in most carnivals. Here, in 1961, is their entry, 'Guiding Round the World'. Second from right, back row is Christine (Cross) and on the right in the front row is Jeannette Taylor.
(RUTH WESTALL AND LORNA HARVEY COLLECTIONS)

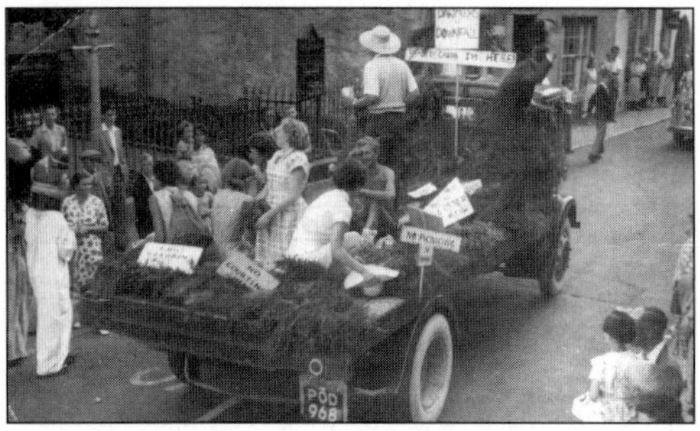

Young Conservatives' float at Ashburton carnival, 1955. (PAT ORSMAN COLLECTION)

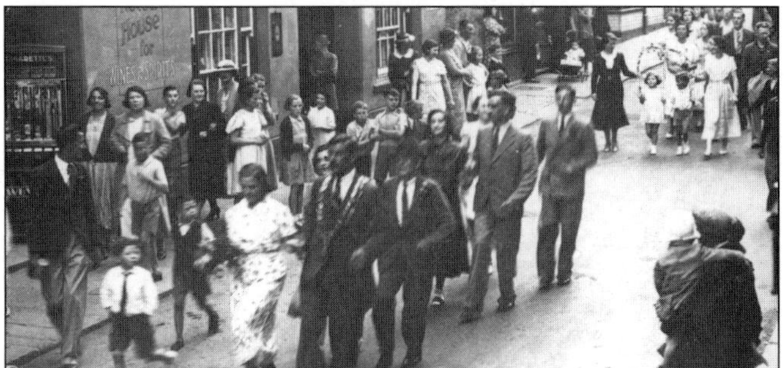

Carnival furry dance, 1950s. (WATERS COLLECTION)

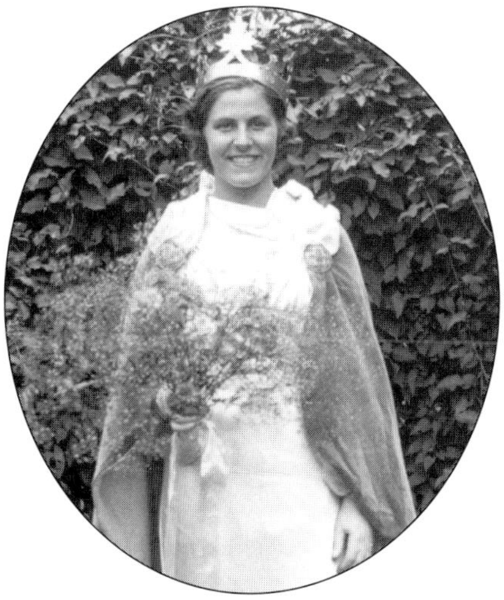

Above: *Carnival queen, 1938, Eileen Martin.* (WATERS COLLECTION)

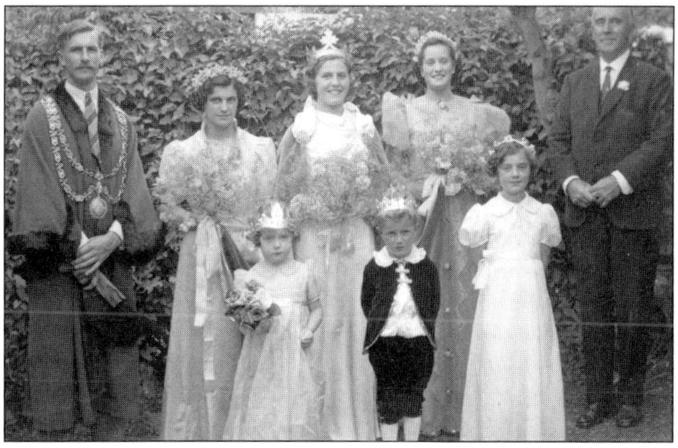

Above: *Carnival queen Eileen Martin, attendants Margaret Stone and Margery Basset, princess June Horrell, prince Paddy Harding, attendant Betty Peck with Portreeve Peter Whitley, 1938.* (WATERS COLLECTION)

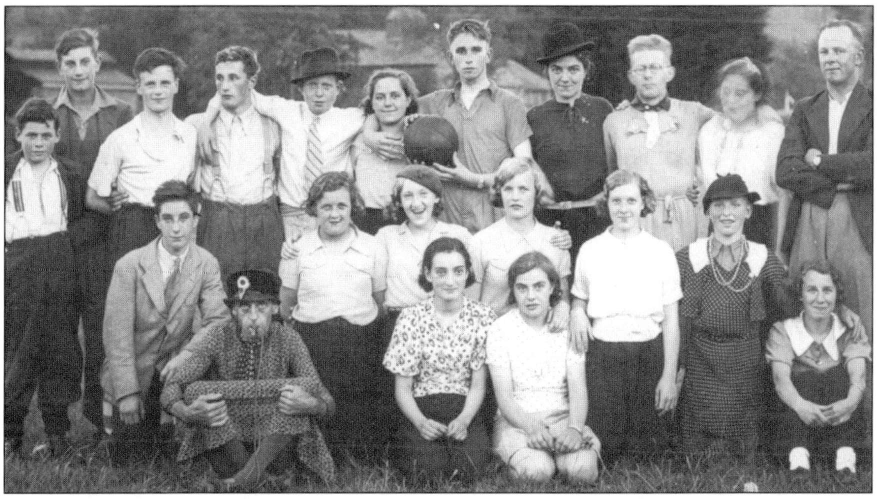

Left: *Ashburton carnival in the 1930s.* Fancy dress football match includes: *Masters Gilbert and Bickford, B. Heslake, E. Royal, S. Denham, F. Pomeroy, C. Harding, F. Bernett, L. Hext, I. Bishop, B. Clarke, M. Bishop, B. Northcott, C. Cross, P. Yolland and F. Knowles.* (ASHBURTON OF YESTERYEAR)

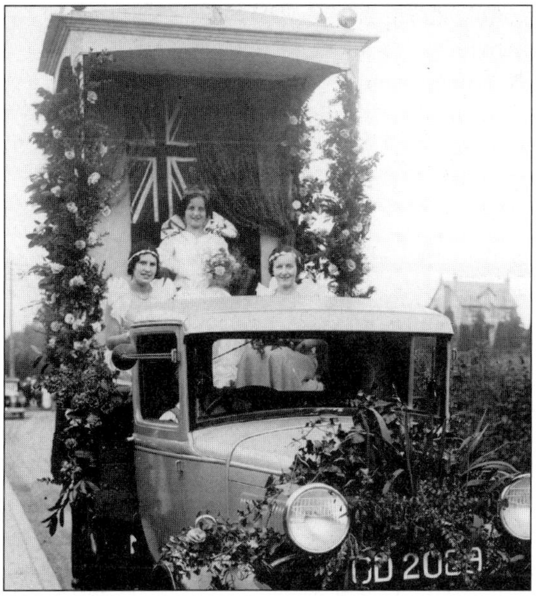

Above: *Carnival queen.* (PAT ORSMAN COLLECTION)

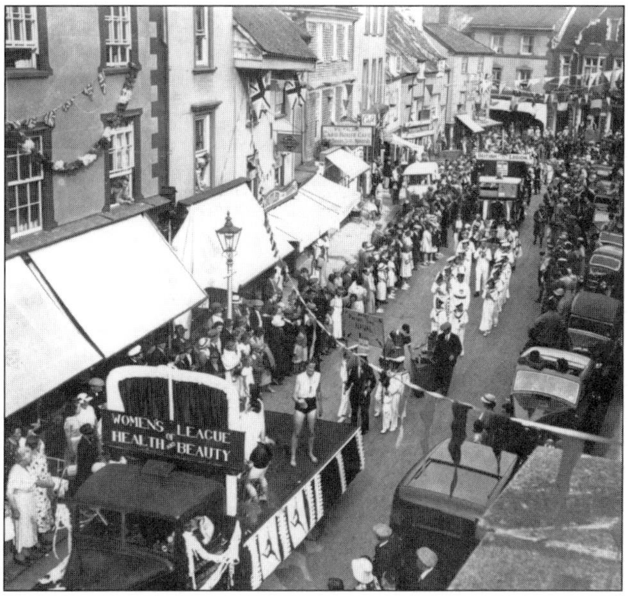

Above: *The carnival procession in North Street, c.1950.* (CARNIVAL COLLECTION)

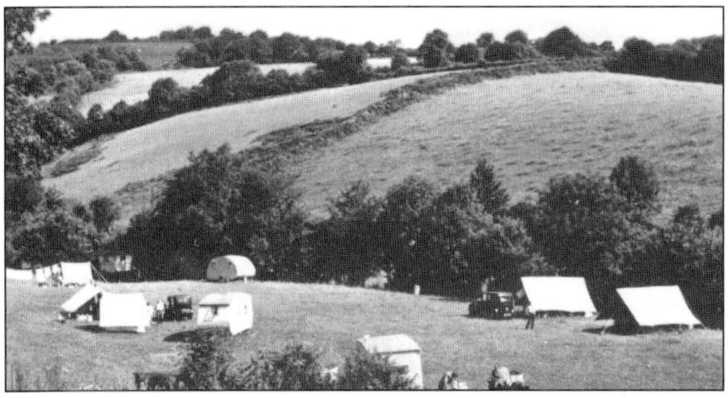

Above: *Waterleat caravan site, looking east, c.1950.* (PETE WEBB COLLECTION)

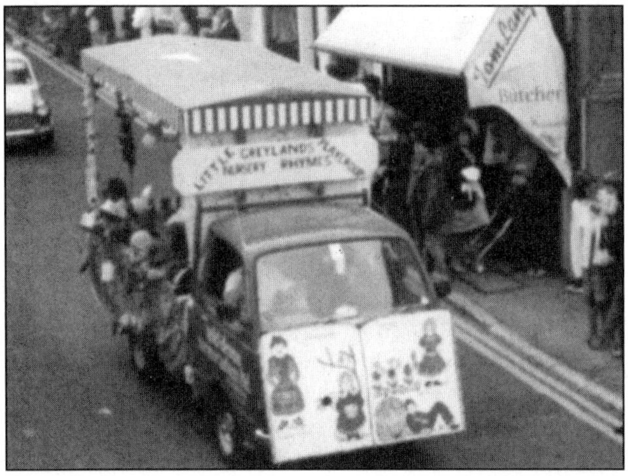

Above: *Carnival float, 1980s, Greylands School play group.* (PETE WEBB)

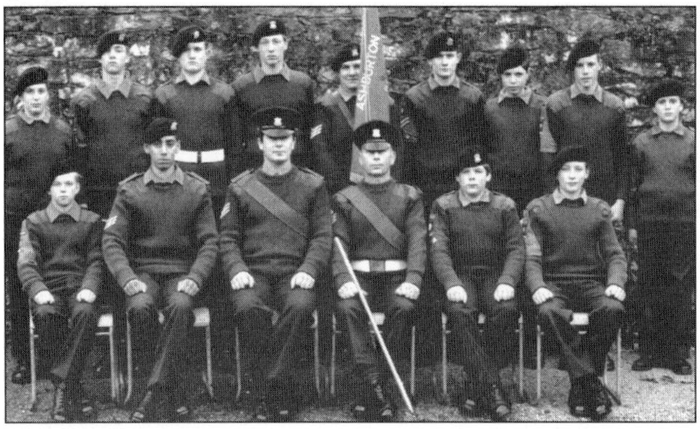

Above: *Ashburton Army Cadets, summer 1993. Sgt Cook and a group of cadets including Andrew Webber, Simon Gregson, Daniel Ravenscroft, Leon Cook, Darren and Michael Penfold, Charlotte ?, Westley Cliff, Tina Newton, Kerry Flood.* (JOHN MITCHELL)

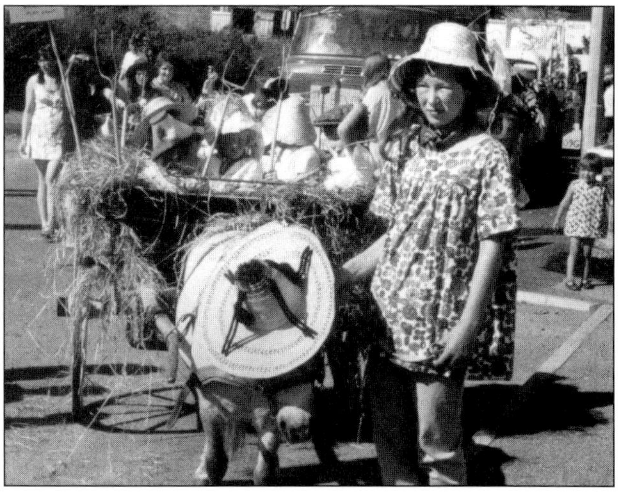

Above: *Goodstone playgroup. Sally Armstrong leading trap. Boy in cap with hand on head John Hands, 12 July 1969.* (STUART HANDS)

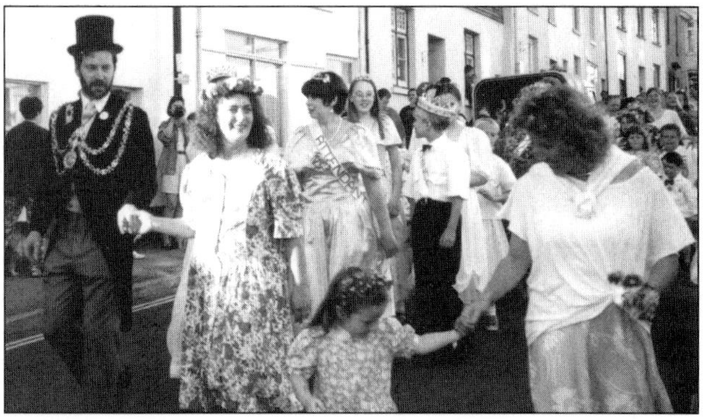

Above: *Pete and Viv Webb leading the furry dance at the 1994 carnival.* (PETE WEBB COLLECTION)

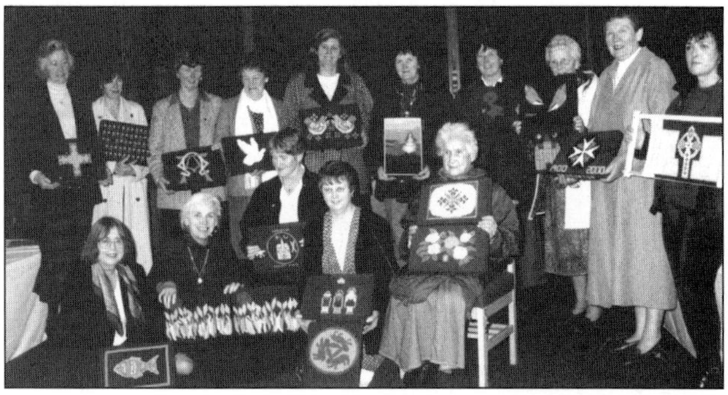

Above: *Millennium cushions. Ladies proudly show needlework they undertook to celebrate the millennium.* (WENDY MAJOR)

the fête, with many local TV and radio personalities playing their part – Sally Jones and Fern Britten in 1980 and 1981 (Westward TV), Craig Rich (BBC), David Rogers and Ian Sterling (TSW). These days it is likely to be a more local character willing to take part without a fee.

A busy week of events followed such as children's fancy dress, fun runs (in the last 20 years), ale tasting (now a separate event) and the earlier floral dance (or furry dance), finishing in the recreation ground with a barbecue on Thursdays, concerts, pub games and quizzes.

Thought to be one of Devon's oldest surviving carnivals, over recent years the November event has been revived in addition to the week of summer activities. Large amounts are still raised annually for local charities and many townspeople who have moved away choose that week above all others to 'come home'.

CHAPTER 14

Ashburton and Buckfastleigh Cottage Hospital and St John Ambulance

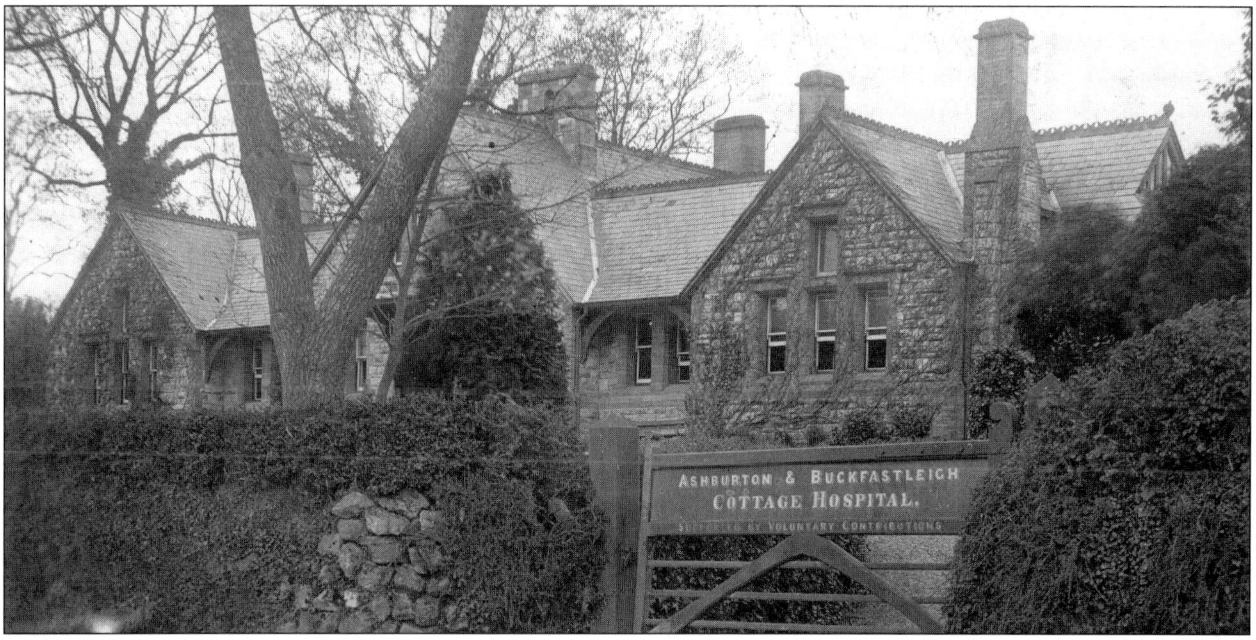

An early view, c.1905. (PETE WEBB COLLECTION)

Ashburton's cottage hospital was first proposed in August 1875 at a public meeting under the chairmanship of Baldwin John Bastard of Buckland Court. £300 had been raised by November of the same year and in February 1876 the hospital had opened in Blogishay Lane near the railway station.

By 1886 it had already been decided that a new building was needed and in 1887 Willow Mead, in Western Road, was donated by Mr Abraham. The cost of construction was £1,240 with work carried out by Hurrel & Roberts of Plymouth. The building was completed in 1888 but allowed to dry out before being used.

The hospital was officially opened the following August by the Lord Lieutenant of Devon, Lord Clinton, who was also the newly appointed chairman of the newly formed Devon County Council.

The original building consisted of a central two-storey entrance with two single-storey wings, each having a four-bed ward and one single-bed ward. Behind the entrance were the kitchens, operating theatre and other rooms. Various additions were made to the original building including a new day room to commemorate Queen Victoria's Diamond Jubilee. In 1910 and 1920 further additions and improvements were made thanks to the Hamlyn family. In 1928 central heating was added at a cost of £74.10s. (£74.50).

The nurses lived in the hospital in those days and worked a 12-hour day, starting at 6a.m. and finishing at 8p.m., with two hours off. They were on duty seven days a week with just one half day and one Sunday a month off. Their wages were about 8s.6d (about 40p) a week.

Throughout its life the hospital has been very well supported by the town – from raising funds to build it, support through carnivals and dances right up to the present-day League of Friends which, formed in 1973, has provided thousands of pounds for equipment and additions. Ashburton's carnival is thought to be one of the oldest in Devon and was first set up to fund the hospital in 1875. In its early years it was called the Hospital Carnival and was held in November.

The end of the Second World War left many small cottage hospitals struggling to survive and Ashburton's was no exception. Indeed, high costs and shortages of staff were a threat to the very existence of cottage hospitals right through the 1950s. It was not until 1972 that the worth of community hospitals and the way they adapted to local needs was recognised. In the 1990s major improvements were carried out at Ashburton hospital in further recognition of its worth. This work was opened by Lord Tebbit in December 1992.

Community hospitals provide local care where it might not otherwise exist and take patients from larger hospitals to recuperate after serious illnesses,

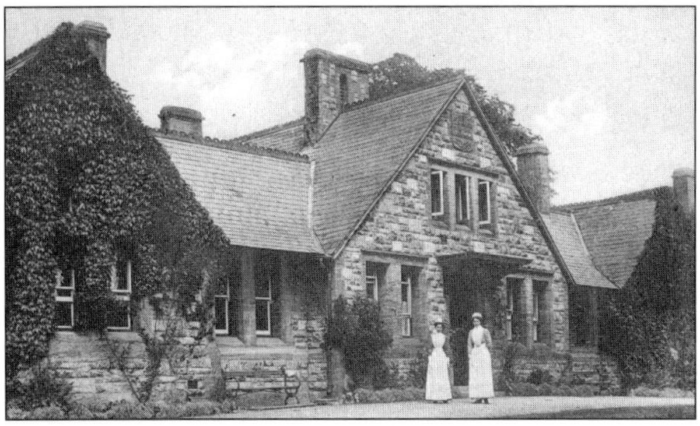

View of Ashburton hospital, opened in 1889, with nurses outside, c.1910. (PETE WEBB COLLECTION)

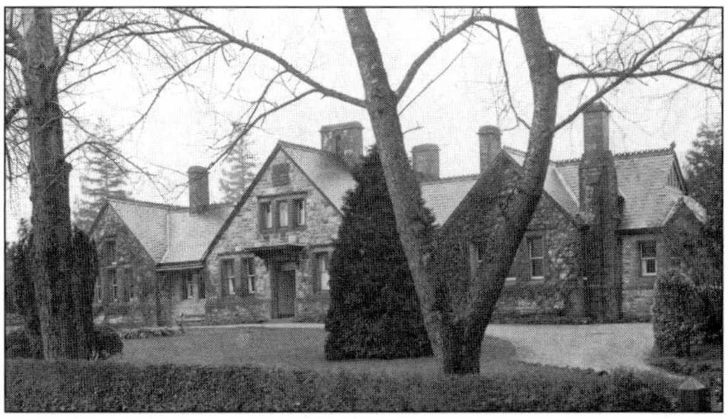

Another early view of the hospital taken by 'Dewi' Evans before the First World War – this time without ivy. ('DEWI' EVANS; PETE WEBB COLLECTION)

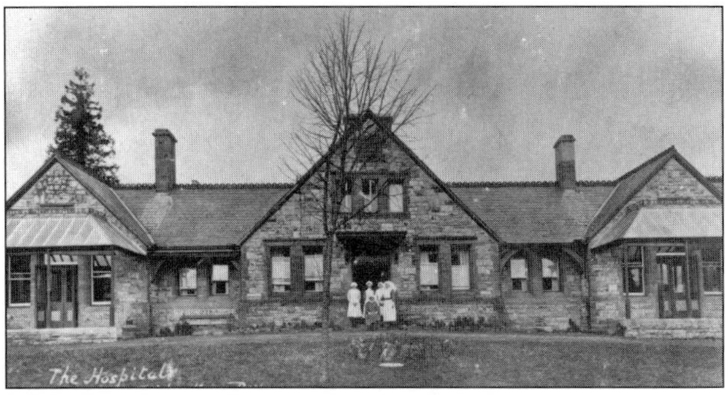

Above: *Late 1920s view soon after the verandahs were added and ivy removed in 1925.* (PETE WEBB COLLECTION)

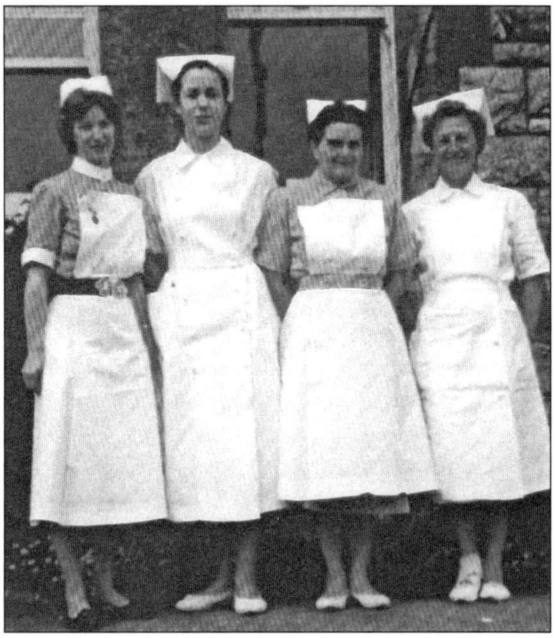

Right: *A group of four nurses in the late 1950s.* Left to right: *Sister Elizabeth Mathews with Nurses Sylvia Allen, Ellen Bligh and Eva Rowe. Picture lent by Ellen Bligh (née Wheatley) and used in* Ashburton Cottage Hospital. (PETE WEBB COLLECTION)

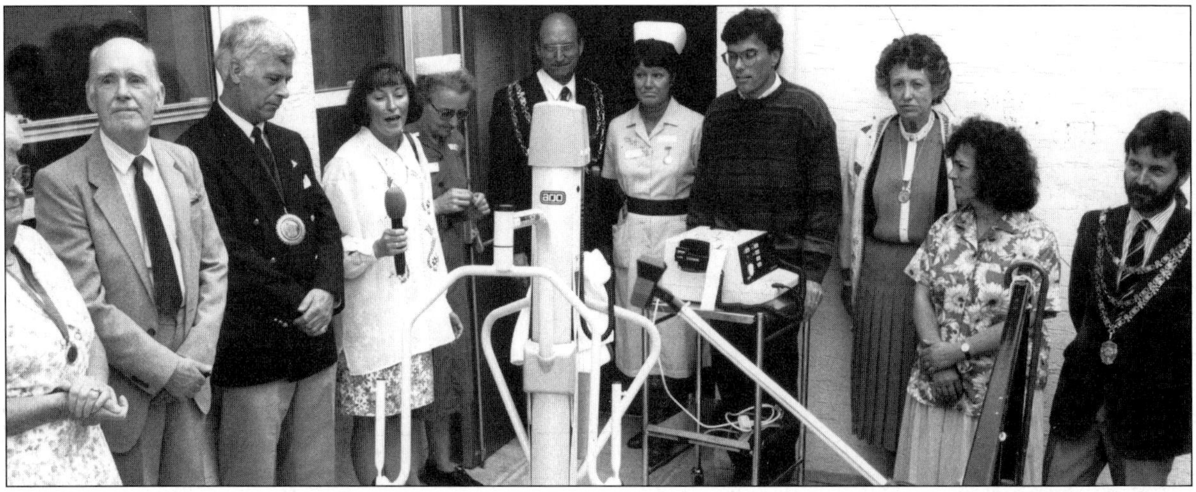

Hospital fête, August 1993, with the Hospital League of Friends presenting the hoist and defibrillator. Left to right: *Mrs Alice Russel (chair of LoF), Henry Bradford (founder in 1973), Mike Murray (Mayor), Julie Smith (locality manager), Sister Wendy Gibson (matron), Portreeve Bill Ward, Nurse Pam Castle, Dr Paul Thomas, Joan Ward, Viv Webb, Pete Webb (Bailiff).* (JOHN MITCHELL)

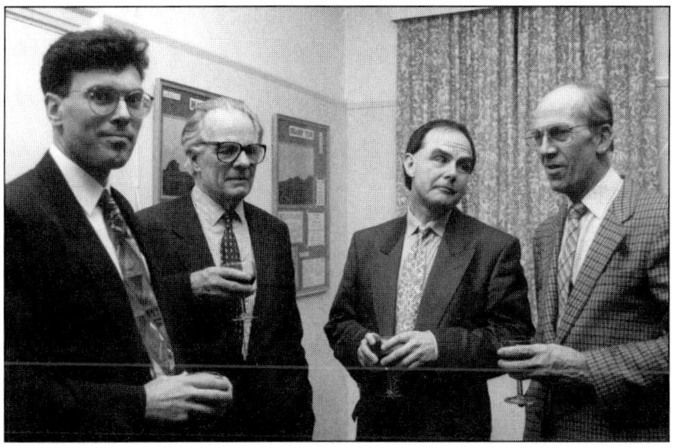

Any Questions team. Left to right: *Dr Paul Thomas, Sir Anthony Parsons, Mr Ray Tarleton (headmaster), and Norman Tebbit MP, 1994.* (JOHN MITCHELL)

making beds available for more urgent cases. Their happy and homely atmosphere, often with personal care from the patient's own GP, as well as being within easy reach of friends and family, are all factors in their favour.

The St John Ambulance Brigade – Ashburton Division

The present Brigade headquarters were opened in April 1939, some 39 years after the division was formed with just 16 members and a superintendent.

The early history is a bit scanty but First Officer Butchers was there from the start, became the divisional superintendent in 1909 and remained until his death in October 1927. In its early days the brigade met in the Grammar School and later the Council School became their headquarters. Mr Lambshead was secretary until 1911 and other stalwarts of the early years included John Endacott, Sergeant Loveridge, Corporal Wills and especially James Mortimore (the headmaster of the school).

In the early years there was no uniform and the members just wore an armband and a cap with the now accustomed uniform first used in 1904. Each year the members had two events it was essential to attend: the annual re-examination and the annual inspection. Originally carried out by their own divisional surgeon, the annual re-examination, due to a change in regulations, was later carried out by Dr Williams of Buckfastleigh.

A special feature of Ashburton is that it remained an independent division. Pressure came from Newton Abbot for Ashburton to join them but it never happened. Even today it is still independent. The brigade's ranks were depleted during the Second World War due to members being on active service but numbers remained sufficient to carry out their public duties and picked up again after the war.

The present ambulance hall was constructed from four self-contained cottages, each with three or four rooms. They were derelict and about to be demolished when the brigade bought them and spent many months, almost entirely by their own hands, removing all the internal structure and leaving just the roof and outside stone wall. From the superintendent to the youngest cadet of the time they all mucked in and helped, but by far the bulk of the work was carried out by Stan Gill (see Chapter 20). He gave all his spare time, evenings and weekends, for over six months.

The main structural work was carried out by Brooks of Buckfastleigh and the wooden block floor laid by Gibbonds of Exeter. Made of Colombian pine, as is most of the other wooden panelling, it has stood the test of time and remains to this day.

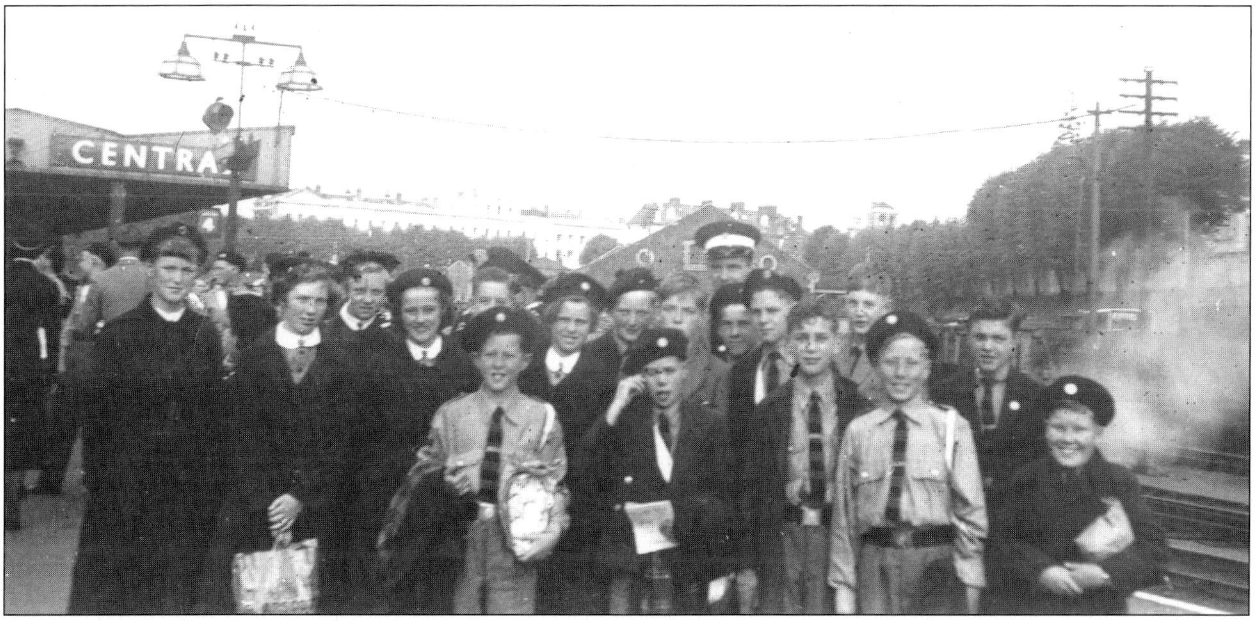

St John Ambulance cadets outing at Exeter, mid-1950s. Left to right: *Shirley Russell, Maureen Morgan, Nancy Taylor, Valerie Cole, ?, Paddy Dobell, ?, Martin Daw, Adrian Daw, ?, ?, ?, ?, ?, Douglas McRea, John Smith, ?, Brian French.* (PAT ORSMAN COLLECTION)

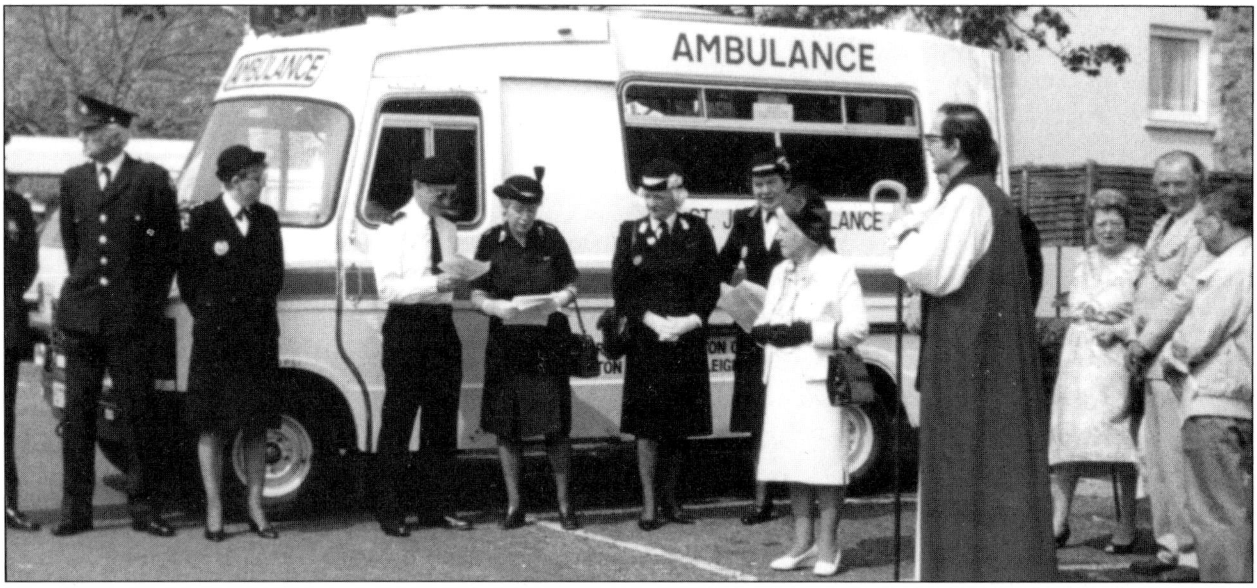

St John Ambulance Brigade's new ambulance being blessed by the Bishop of Exeter in 1988. Left to right: *John Caunter (Div. Supt), Anne Kemp (now Bovey, County Director), Mo Glossup (South Devon Area Commissioner), June Pierce (Area President), Mrs Joan Williams, Mary Woollacott, Mrs Gracey* (white dress*), Very Revd Hewlett Thompson (Bishop of Exeter), Eileen Egbeare (Mayor), Portreeve Phil Poole and Revd Ivor Halliwell (vicar of Ashburton's St Andrew's Church).*

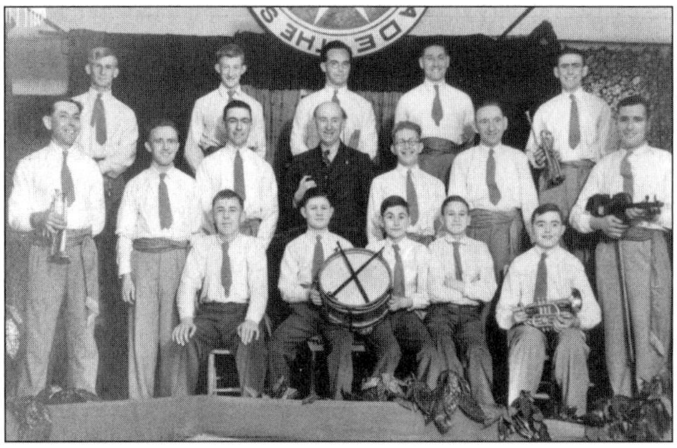

Concert party formed to raise funds. Left to right, back row: *Whittey, Nicholls, Langler, Bonstow, Stan Gill;* centre: *W. Gill, Boon, Ivor Gill, Royce, Harding, Stanbury, Rooke;* front: *Tucker, Gilbert, Parnell, Tall, Yolland.*

During the Second World War, the first women joined the Brigade and formed the nursing division.

A major achievement soon after the completion of the hall was the purchase in 1948 of the Brigade's first motor ambulance. Prior to this the hand litter, which is still on display in the hall, had been used. The cry often went out, 'Lend us a hand, lads!' to watching boys as the litter was pushed up East Street, complete with casualty, on the way to the hospital.

Much of the fund-raising for the Brigade in the early years was tied in with that for the hospital and the midwives, these being the three recipients of funds from the Ashburton carnival.

The Brigade was out in all weathers and conditions until 1970, when much of the work was taken over by the Area Health Authority.

Today the division acts as a mobile first-aid unit at public events around the county. Anywhere there are large numbers of the public, you will see their distinctive uniforms. Continuous training, both for members and for the public, is also an important part of their work. Equipment is loaned out when needed and they also run a club for the less active elderly residents of the town.

Ashburton's St John's is also a quadrilateral division with adults and youngsters of both sexes working and training together. This gives the younger members a good grounding for adult life and many go on to become fully trained nurses, ambulance drivers, teachers and services personnel. Three former members have even recently served in the Iraq War.

CHAPTER 15

Events

This chapter comprises photographs illustrating the various events, serious and not so serious, which have taken place in Ashburton over the years. Fire, flood, film making and visits from royalty have all taken place in Ashburton, as these photos illustrate.

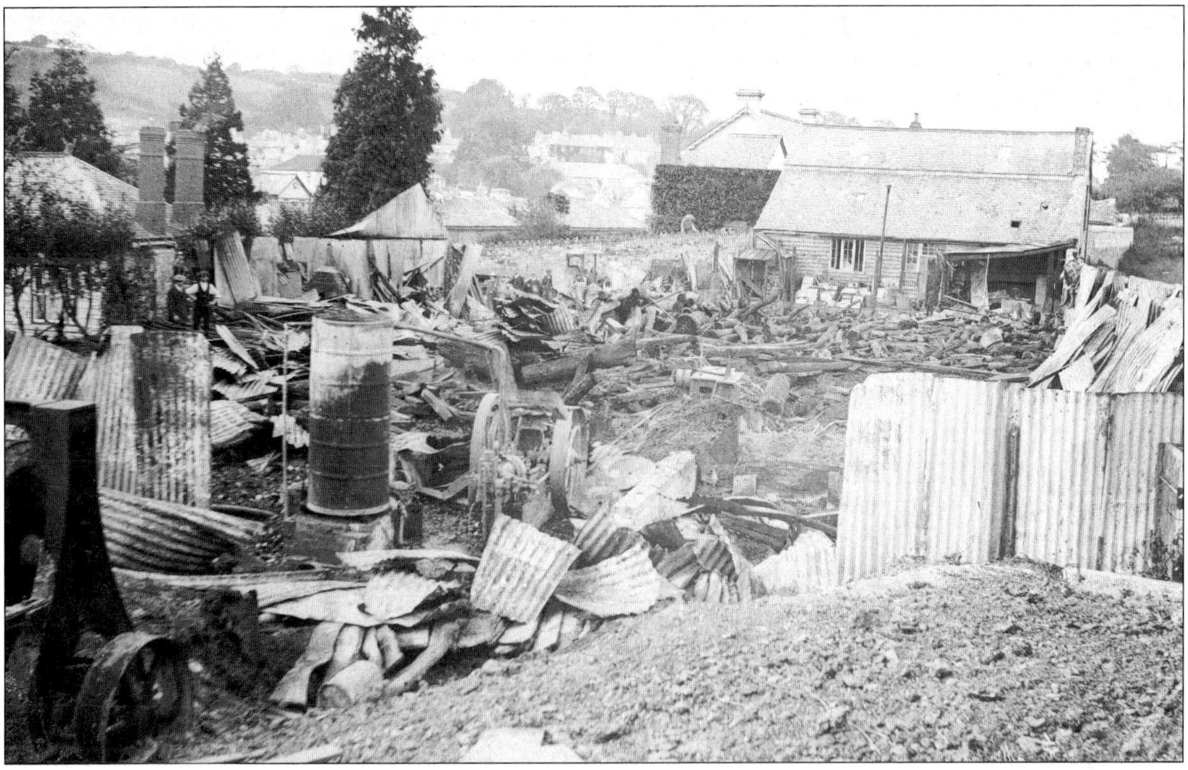

Fire in Badcock's builder's yard in Chuley Road, in 2004 the premises of Outdoor Experience (formerly Ashburn Caravans). This was in May 1918 and the picture was taken by Amy Hannaford. (PETE WEBB COLLECTION)

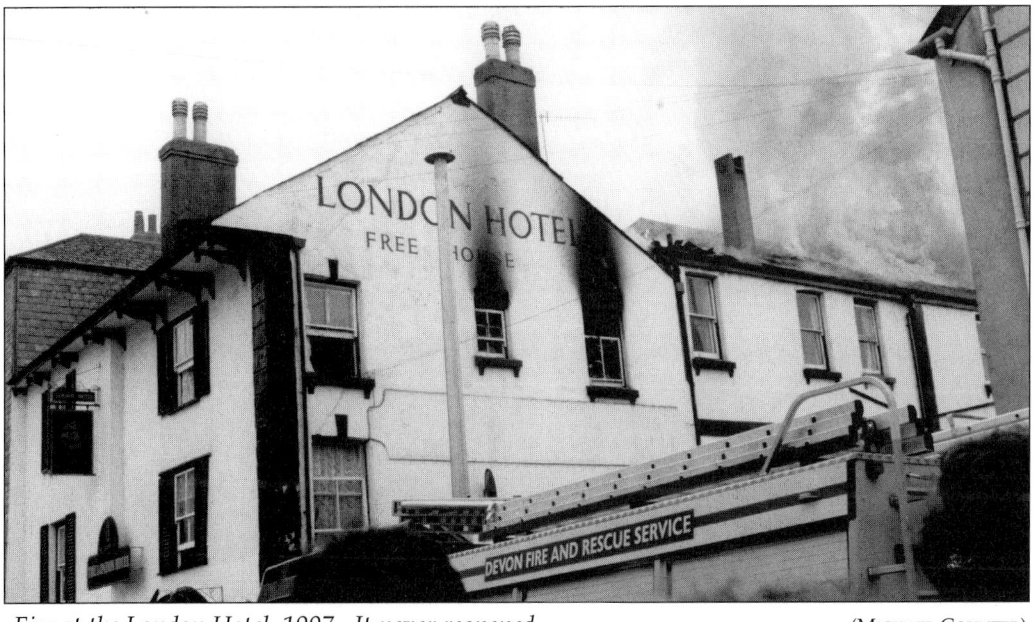

Fire at the London Hotel, 1997. It never reopened. (MICHAEL COUNTER)

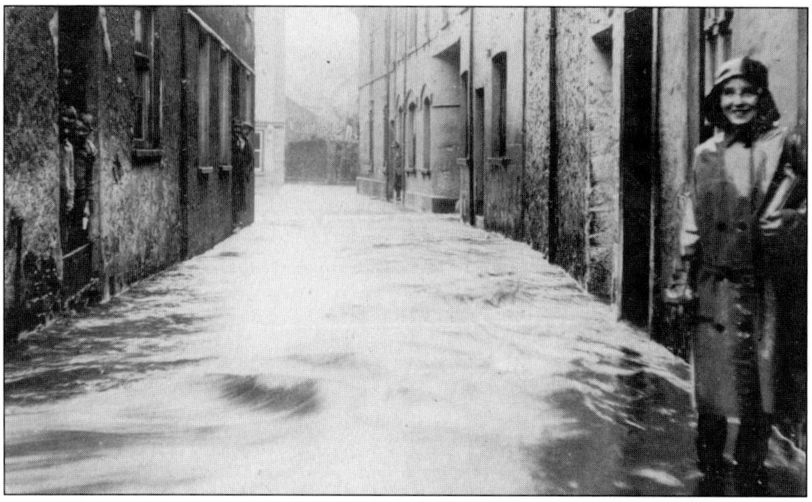

Floods in Kingsbridge Lane in 1929. Note the buildings behind the youngster, now demolished, and the wooden boards to try and keep the water out on the left.
(PETE WEBB COLLECTION)

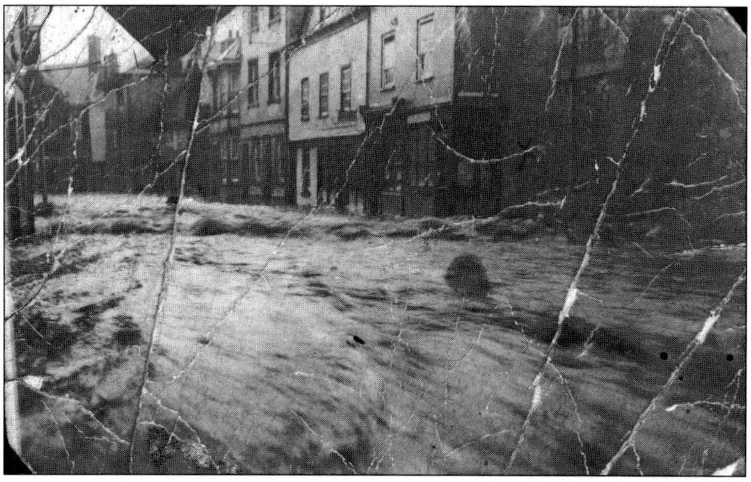

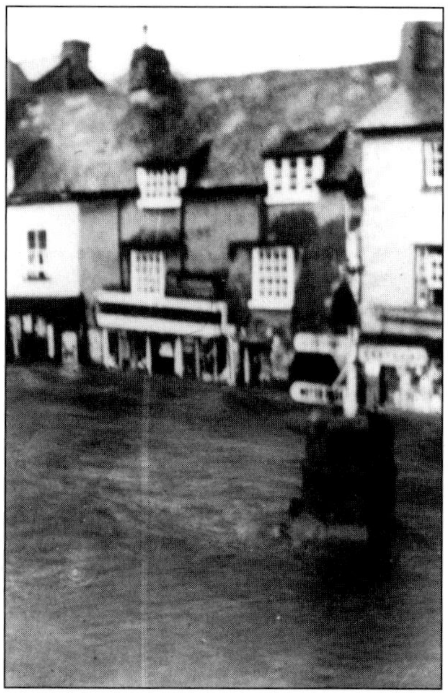

Above and right: *North Street in August 1938, flooded to a depth of nearly six feet.* (PAT ORSMAN COLLECTION)

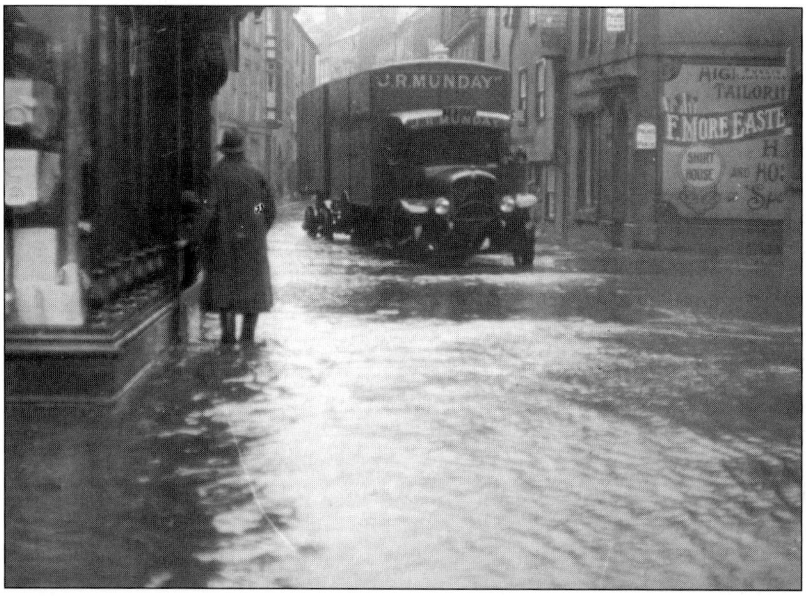

Left: *Another view of the November 1929 flood, this time in West Street with a furniture lorry with trailer struggling though the water. Note the wooden planks on the right. In those days this was the main road between Exeter and Plymouth.*
(PETE WEBB COLLECTION)

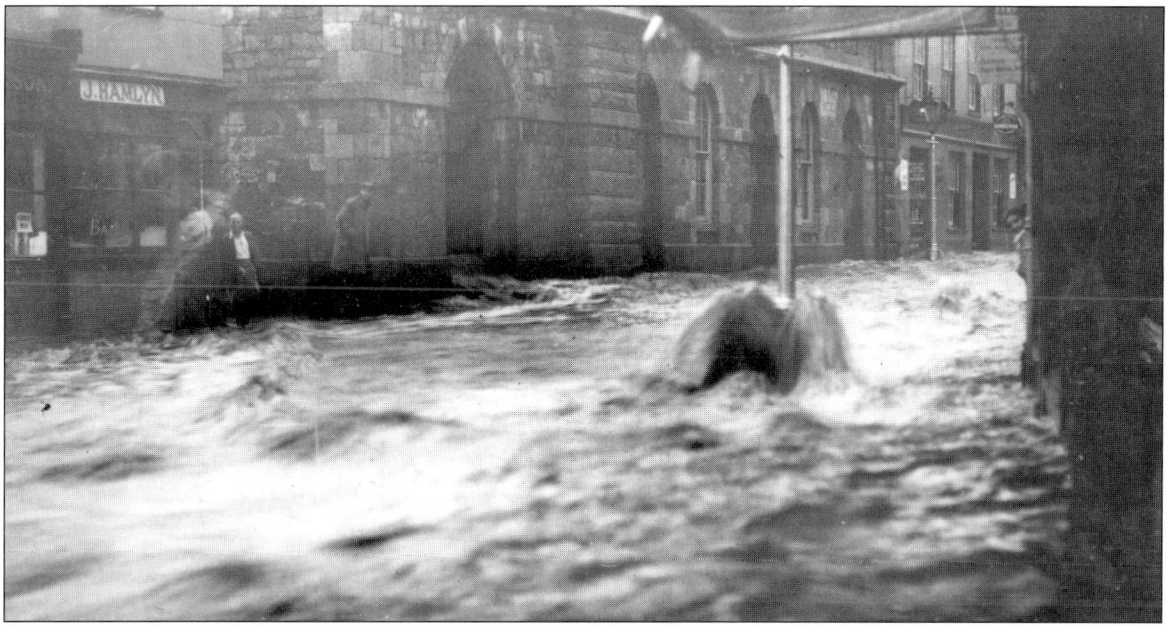

Above: *Another view of North Street in the flood of August 1938. Mr Hamlyn can be seen in the door of his butcher's shop and note the water coming out of the Town Hall door. This end has now been altered and King's Bridge is just behind.*
(PETE WEBB COLLECTION)

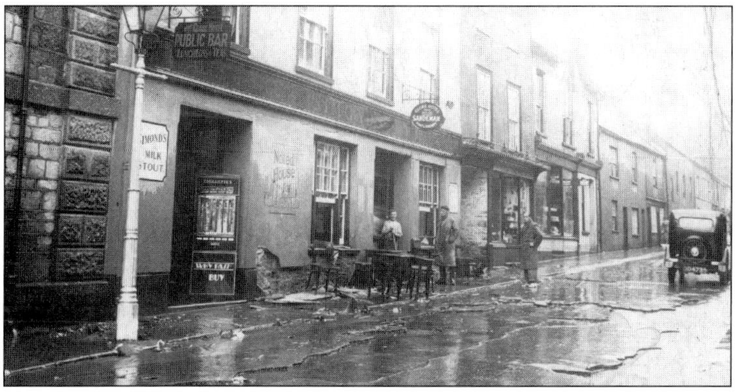

Left: *The 1938 flood aftermath – looking up North Street outside the Globe. Note the damaged tarmac.*
(PETE WEBB COLLECTION)

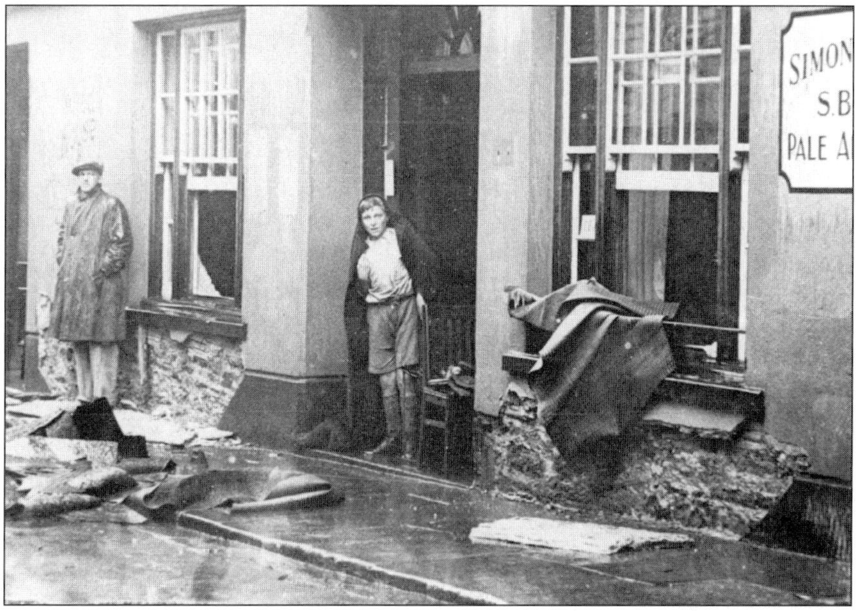

Right: *The 1938 flood aftermath – clearing out the Globe Inn.*
(PETE WEBB COLLECTION)

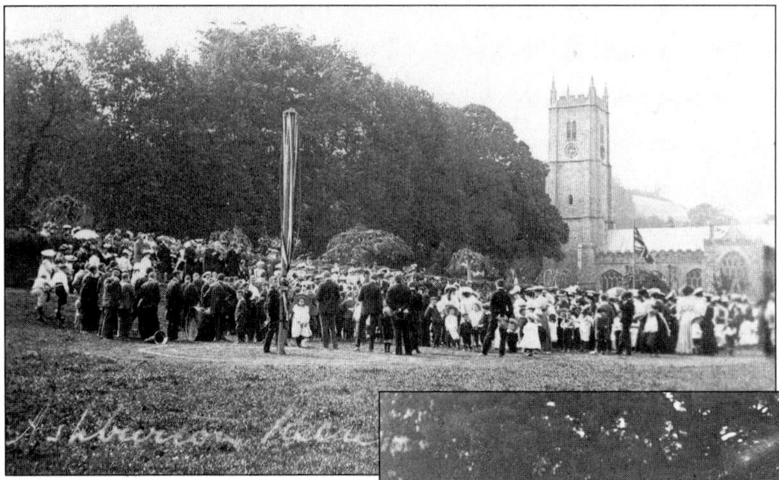

Left: *Opened in 1904, the new recreation ground is here being used for maypole dancing on 29 May 1907. Note the lack of visible trees next to St Andrew's Church.*
(Amy Satterley; Pete Webb collection)

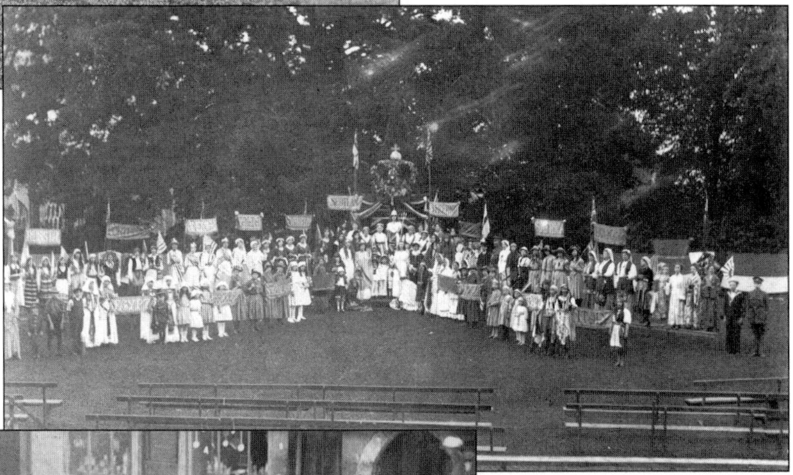

Right: *Empire Day in the vicarage garden, year unknown.*
(Pete Webb collection)

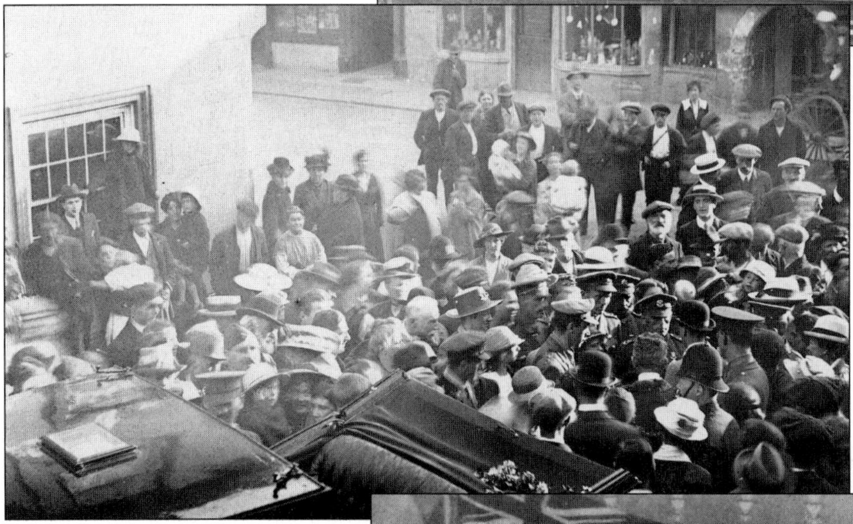

Left: *The visit to Ashburton by the Prince of Wales in June 1919 – here being presented to the Portreeve (to the left of the policeman front right and the chap in the bowler – probably the chairman of the Urban District Council). Note also the posies of flowers on his open-topped car.*
(Pete Webb collection)

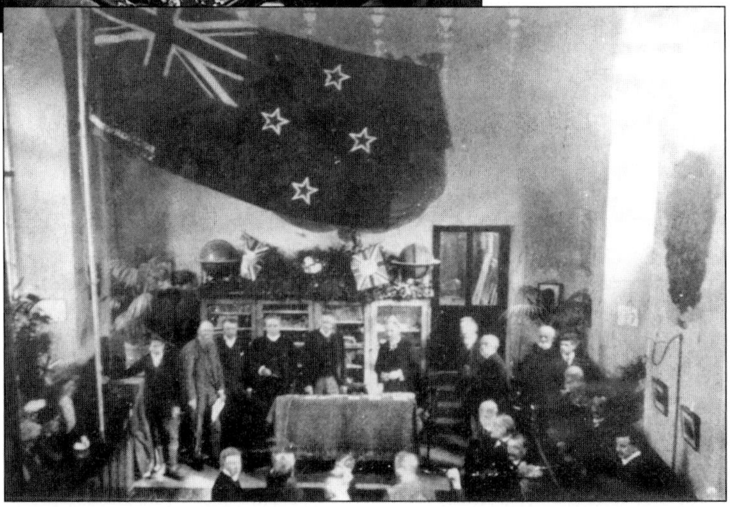

Right: *Presentation of the New Zealand flag to Ashburton Grammar School from the town of Ashburton, New Zealand, c.1910. Note the incorrect union flag.*
(St Lawrence Chapel)

Right: *Hero worship – three young Ashburton lasses wait patiently for Peter Reynolds to sign autographs during a break in filming. The 1950 film* Guilt is My Shadow *was filmed in and around the town and included Patrick Holt, Elizabeth Sellers, Lana Morris, Avice Landone, as well as Peter.* Left to right: *Margaret Pitts (now Dodd), Christine Pitts (now Gibbons) and Susan Daw. Margaret and Christine lived in East Street and lost contact with Susan when the family moved to London.*

(MARGARET DODD COLLECTION)

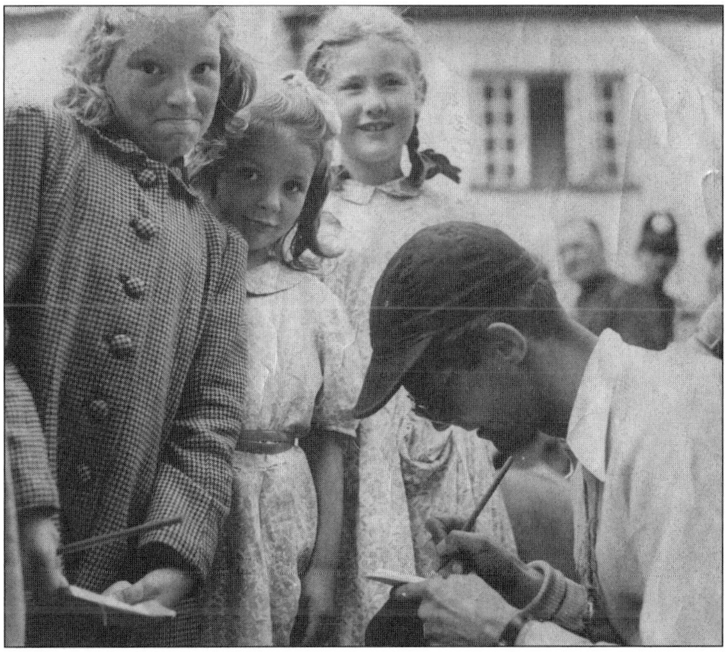

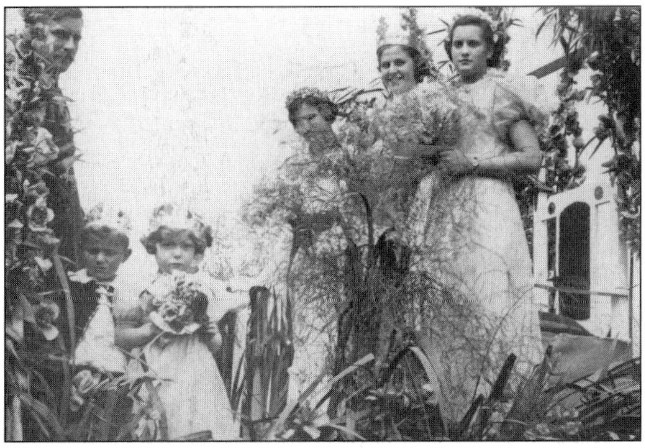

Above: *Prince Paddy Harding, princess June Horrell, attendant on queen's left Margaret Stone and right Margery Bassett, queen Eileen Martin, 1938.*

(WATERS COLLECTION)

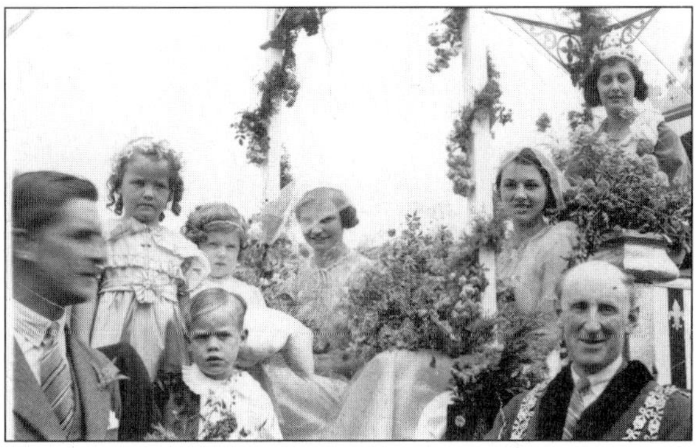

Above: *Carnival, 1937, with Peter Whitley (Bailiff), Sheila Bligh (princess) and Leslie Townsend (prince). The small girl is June Horrell. The attendants are Edith Stone and Myra Brown, and the queen Eileen Martin.* (ST LAWRENCE CHAPEL)

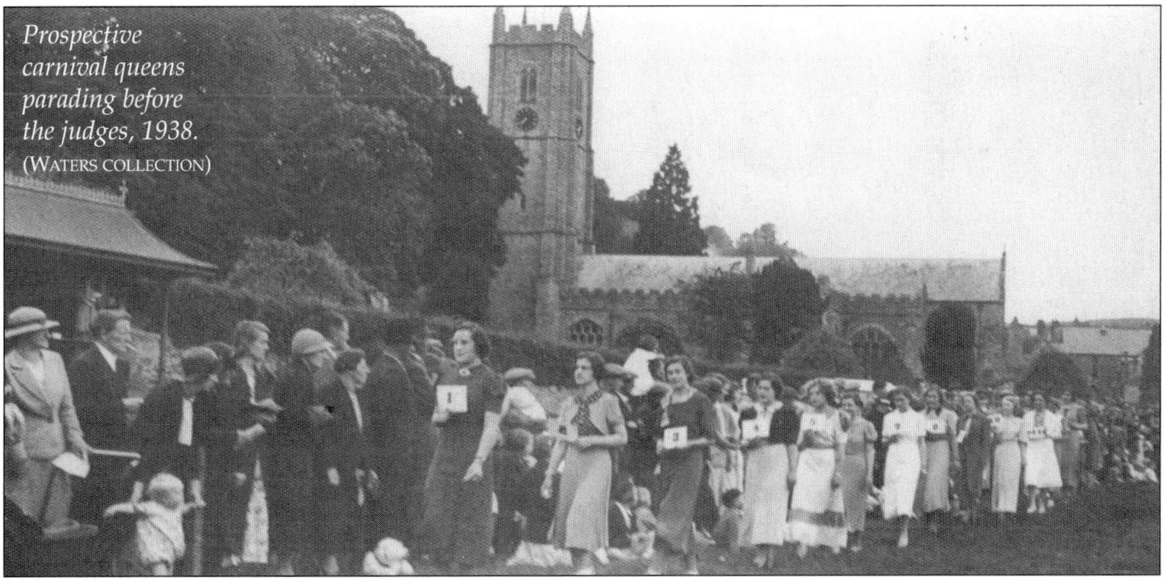

Prospective carnival queens parading before the judges, 1938.
(WATERS COLLECTION)

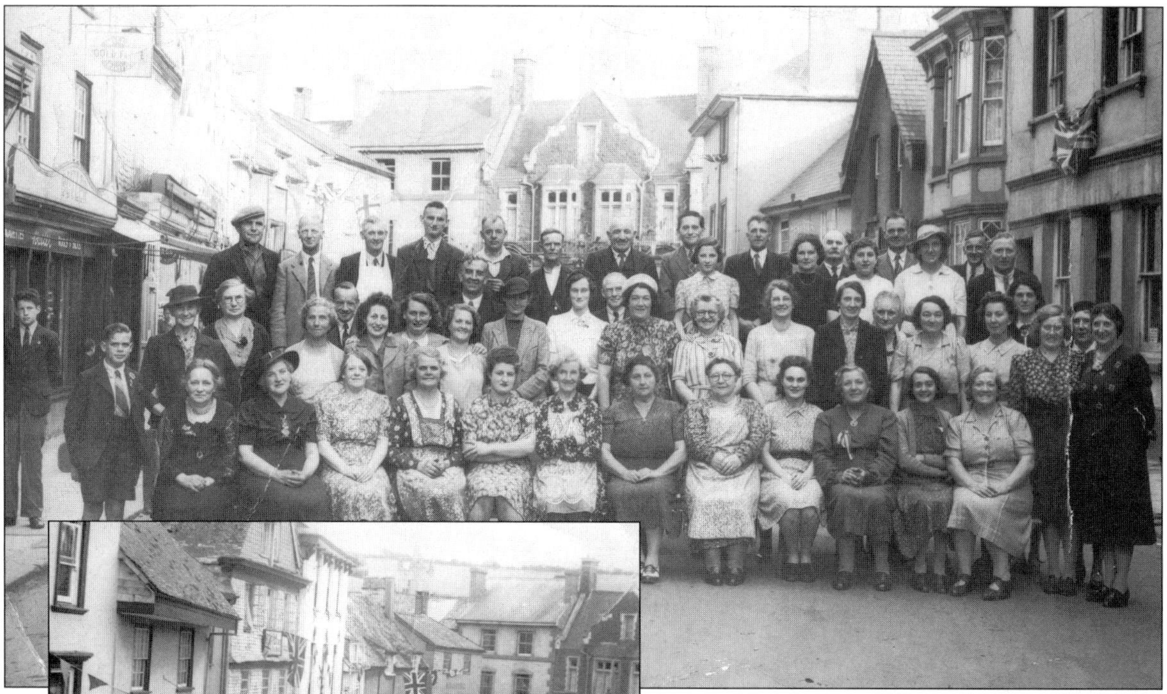

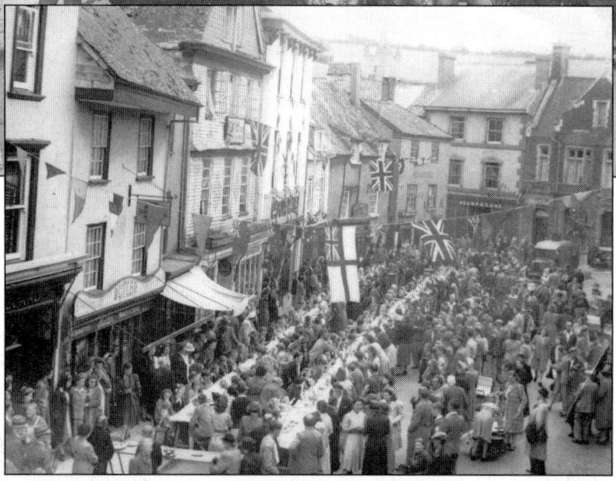

Above: *Ladies in North Street (who probably cooked and prepared the food for the street party).*

Left: *Victory street party celebrations in North Street, 1945.*

(Henry Lang collection)

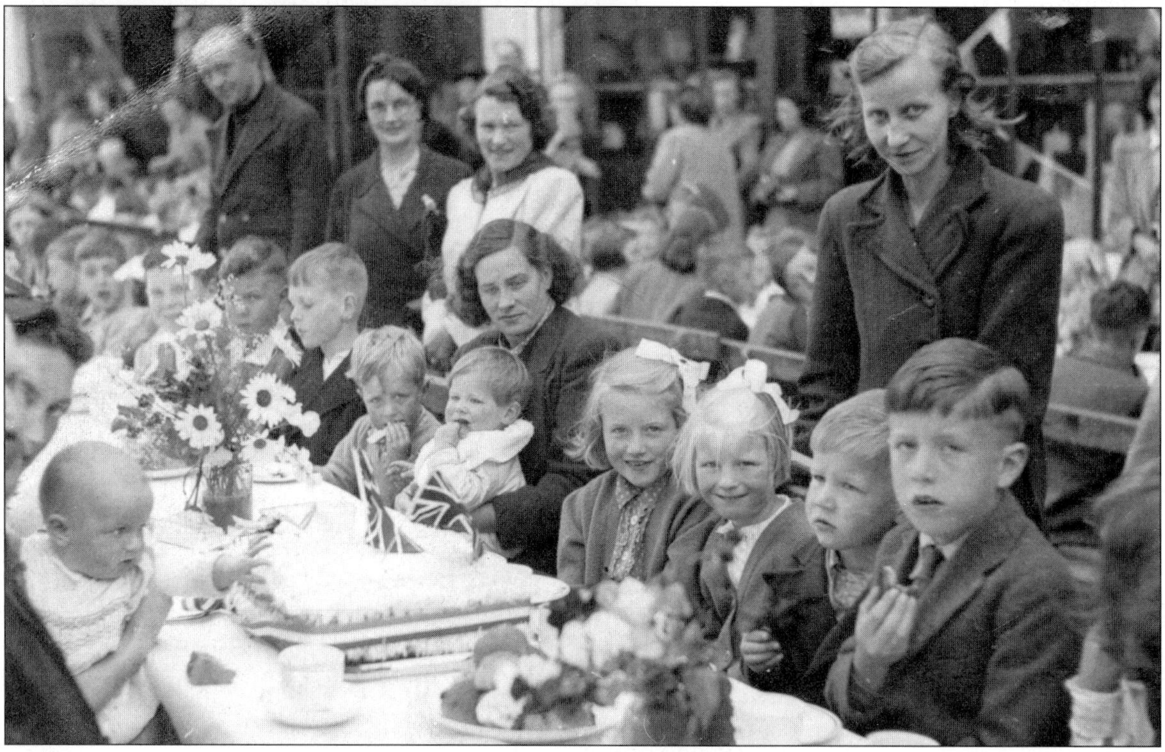

Victory party, 1945. The ladies at the back are Kath Northway and Nell Northway. The lady sitting down is 'Tiny' Daw, with her sons Adrian and Martin (Pat Orsman's mother and brothers). (Pat Orsman collection)

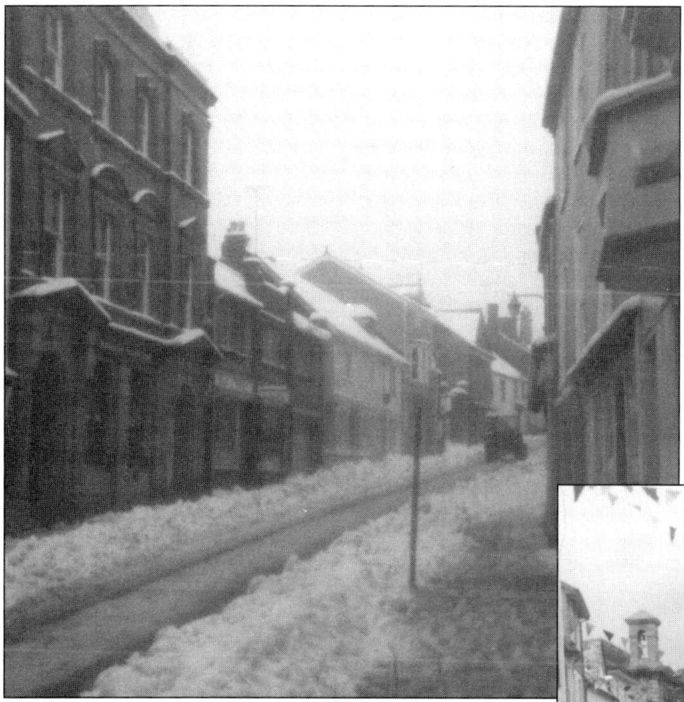

Left: *Snow in East Street, February 1978. The only vehicles capable of movement were Glendinning's diggers, which spent almost a week clearing the snow.* (PETE WEBB)

Below: *Ashburton Festival, 1980. Folk dancing in the Bull Ring.* (PETE WEBB)

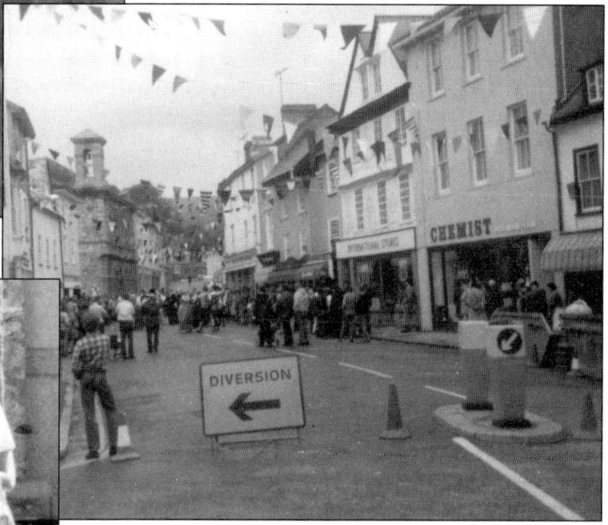

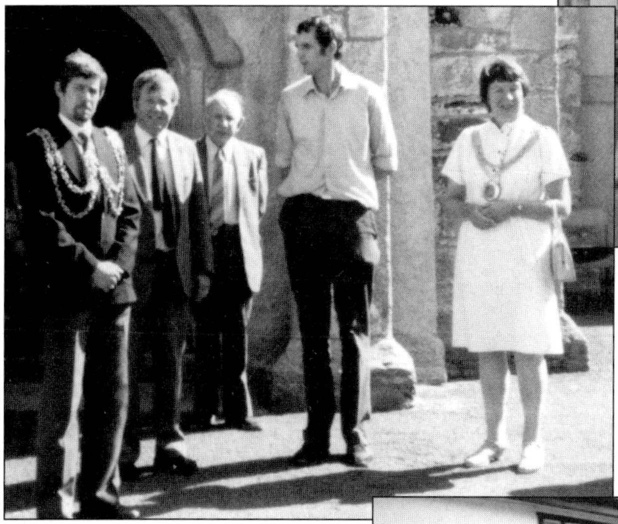

Left: *St Lawrence Fair, 1983.* Left to right: *Portreeve Adrian Daw, Eric Blatchford, Stan Gill, Fred Christophers, Mary Woollacott.* (PETE WEBB)

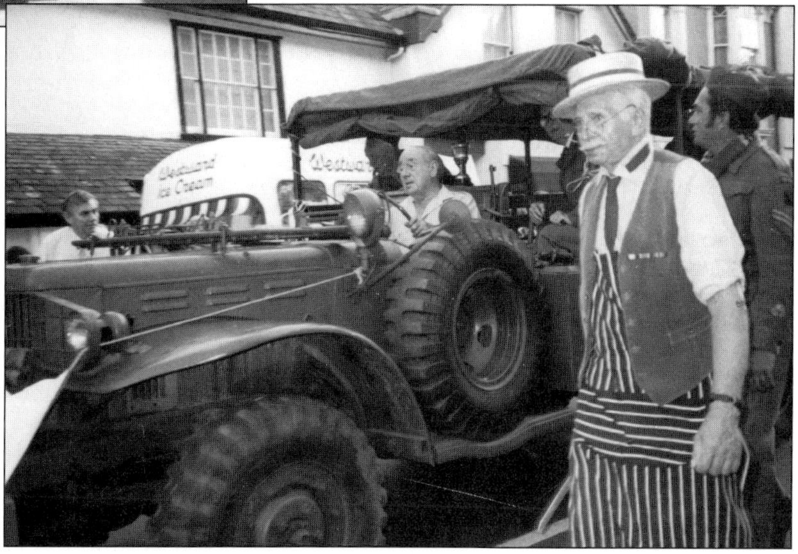

The 1997 carnival. Dad's Army on Parade –The Royal British Legion with Bill Freeman as butcher Mr Jones. (PETE WEBB COLLECTION)

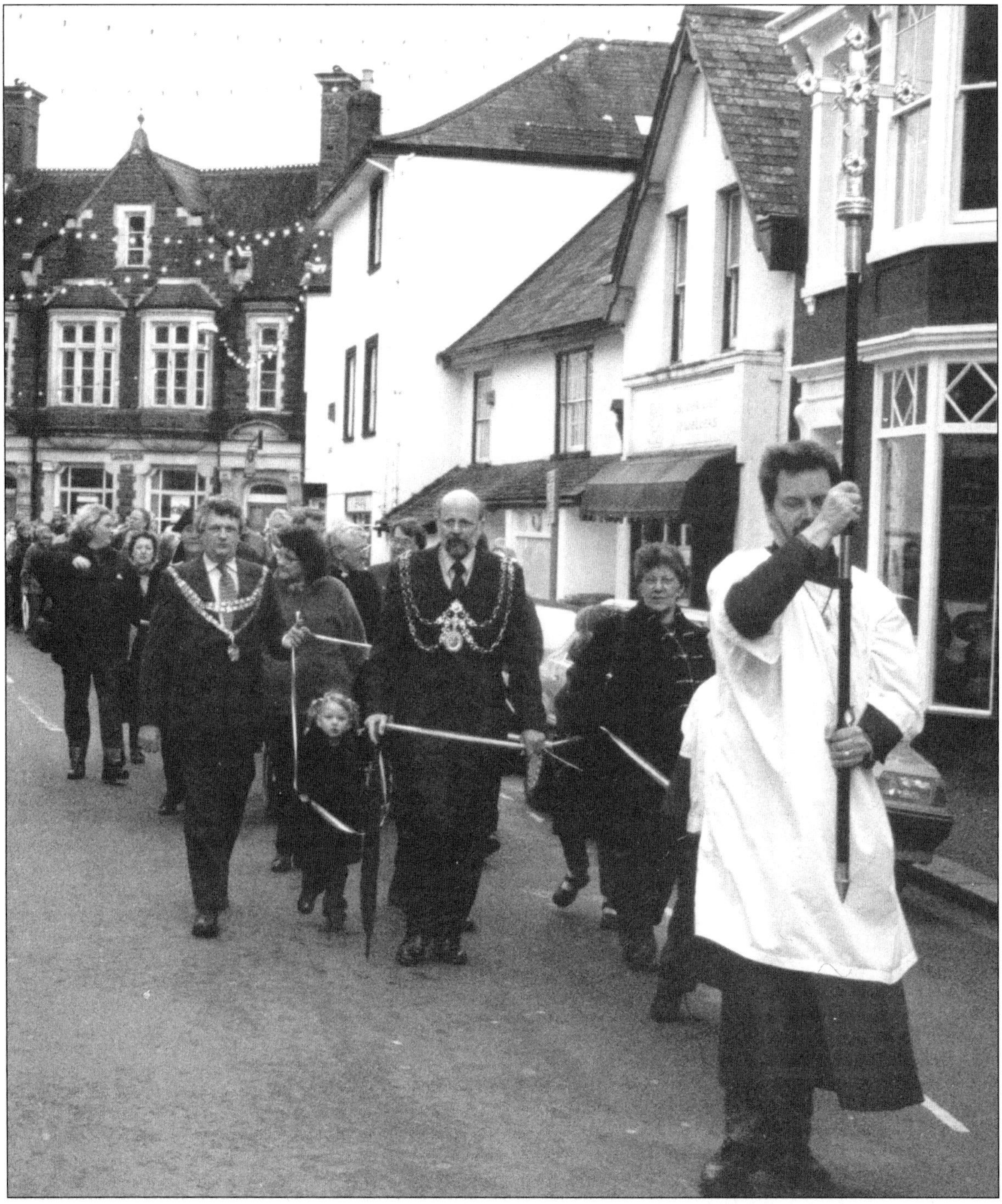

Millennium parade, New Year's Day, 2001. Pete Webb (with church cross), Portreeve Chris Monington and wife Linda and Bailiff Paul Knowles and wife Noreen lead the town. (KAREN KNOWLES; PETE WEBB COLLECTION)

CHAPTER 16

The Office of Portreeve, Bailiff and Other Officers of the Court Leet and Baron Jury

Tradition has it that the first Portreeve of the Borough of Ashburton was appointed in the year AD820 around the time of the first Saxon King of England, Egbert. After the Norman Conquest many boroughs got permission for their Court Leet to elect a Portreeve and other towns revived the title in the fourteenth century.

The word 'Portreeve' is derived from the Saxon words 'Port' for market or market town and 'Gerefa' meaning official. The term was used to describe the person appointed by the crown to oversee the market and the town. The chief duty of the Portreeve was to be a witness and recorder for the sale of property and livestock. He was often the only person able to read and write in Latin and draw up a legal document. He was the overseer of coinage, the returning officer for Ashburton's MPs, responsible for Church taxes, fixing fines, keeping a register of suspicious characters and many other duties. It would be a mistake to think of the Portreeve as a modern-day local government officer or a judge, nor did the office hold the power of life or death. He presided over the Court Leet and the jurors of the jury would have been the judges. The Court Leet elected the Portreeve and ensured the smooth running of the town.

Both courts are now Borough Courts. The Manor Courts have not met in Ashburton since 1908. As Borough Courts, their deliberations were only valid if they met within the borough. Both St Lawrence Chapel, the present meeting place, and the former Golden Lion where they used to meet are within the borough. The Town Hall and the Exeter Inn, where they were reputed to have once met, were within the manor.

After the Norman conquest, many small borough towns like Ashburton were given the right to elect a Portreeve and Ashburton is thought to be one of the first to be granted such a charter, around AD1190. Ashburton's list of Portreeves is almost continuous, with names such as John Ad in 1300, John Toukes in 1325, Robert Lichel in 1335, Will Taylor in 1372, Will Halgewell in 1392, Robert Corbet in 1394 and John Dobbe in 1502, with a continuous list from 1747 to the present day. Some of the earlier names might have been town officials calling themselves Portreeve. The full list of names is displayed in St Lawrence Chapel and a short history with names and a potted history of each one is available from the author (*Past Portreeves of Ashburton* by Pete Webb).

In 1898 the Ashburton Urban District Council was formed with a chairman as its head. This was four years after the Local Government Act of 1894. Ashburton was given permission to retain its office of Portreeve for the first time. In 1971 a further reorganisation of local government saw 141 ancient courts abolished. These included six Courts of Record at Exeter, Barnstaple, Bideford, Dartmouth, Great Torrington and Totnes. The Act came into being on 1 April 1974 and again Ashburton was given permission to keep the office of Portreeve due to its continuity, history and function.

At the same time the Urban District Council became the Town Council and the head of the council changed from chairman to a Mayor. The court on Court and Law Day is held on the third Tuesday in November each year and is presided over by the Lord of the Borough of Ashburton. Before 1050 this title and that of Lord of the Manor belonged to the Bishop of Crediton and, from 1050 to 1549, to the Bishop of Exeter. From 1630 the posts were held by separate individuals (Lord of the Borough and Lord of the Manor) until they again amalgamated in 1906. In 1927 the title passed from the last private individual to the Ashburton Urban District Council. The ownership of the title which, from 1774 to 1905, had

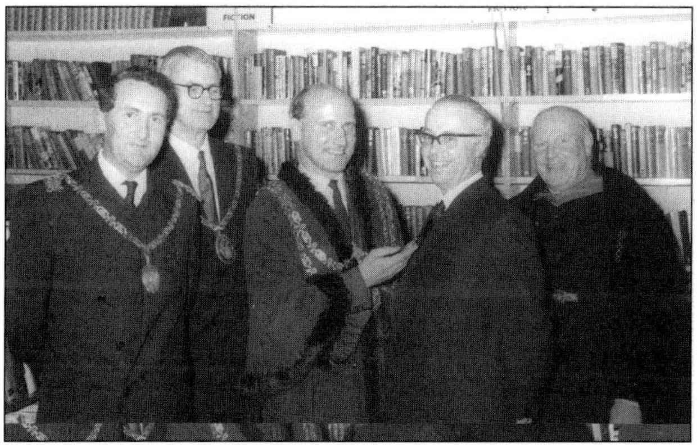

Court and Law Day, 1968. (PETE WEBB COLLECTION)

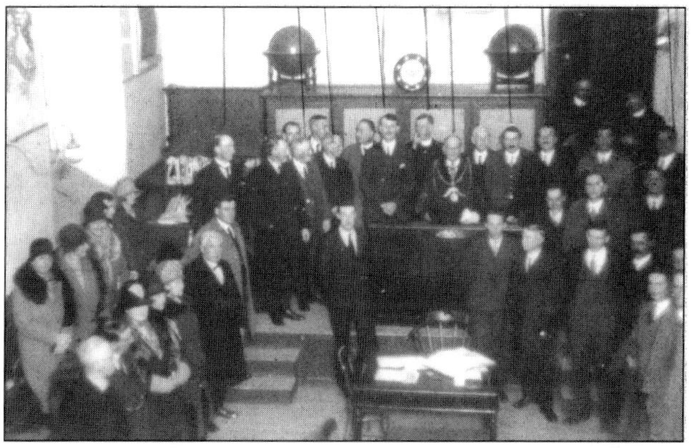

Court and Law Day. (ASHBURTON MUSEUM)

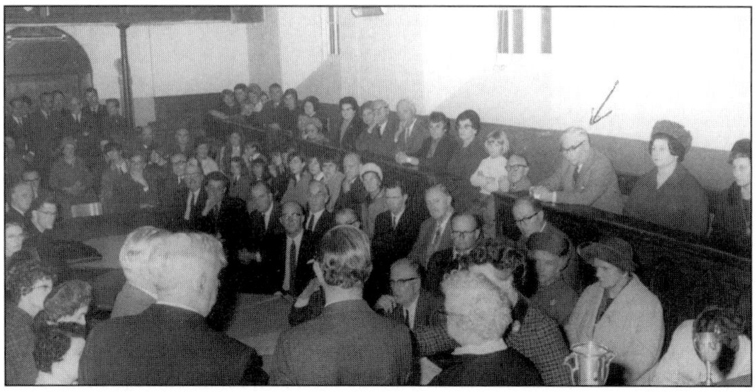

Left: *Court and Law Day in November 1965. Brig. Lyall Grant is seated* (indicated by arrow) *and waiting to be sworn in as Bailiff. Court members are being sworn into office.*
(RIVERS OF NEWTON ABBOT; PETE WEBB COLLECTION)

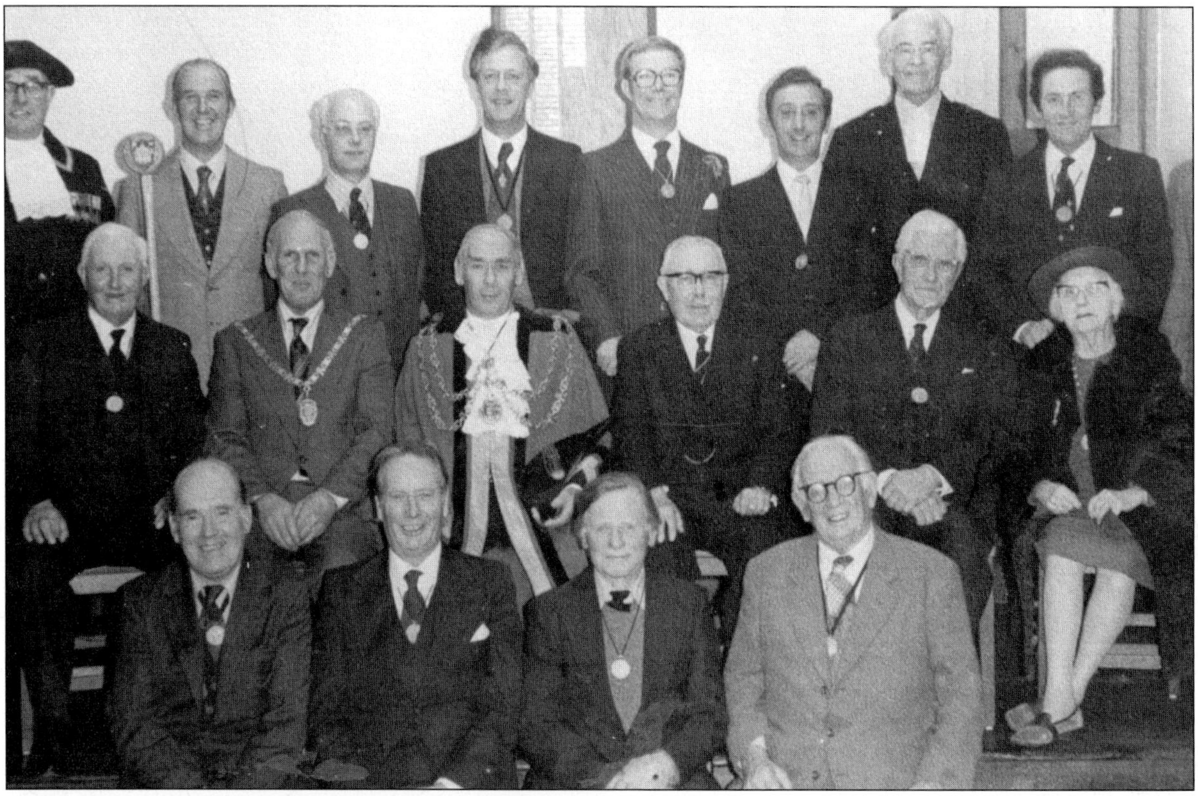

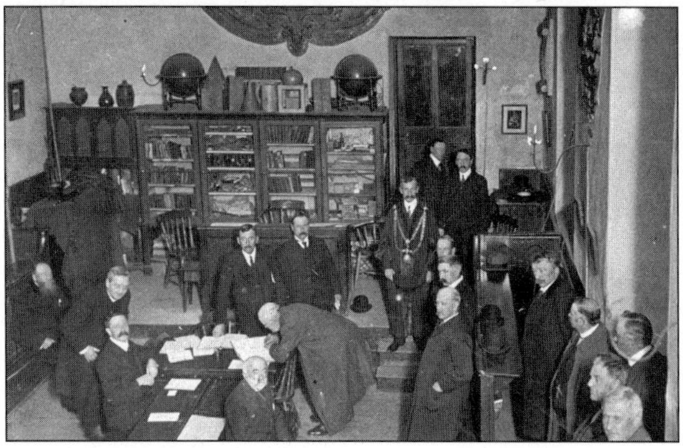

Court Leet, 1913. (ASHBURTON MUSEUM)

Above: *A group photograph of past Portreeves taken on 22 November 1977 in the Chapel of St Lawrence on the occasion of the annual Courts Leet and Baron, following the installation of the 1,157th Portreeve, Bill Pulman, and the unveiling of the past Portreeves' board listing Portreeves since 1900.* Left to right, back row: *Peter N. Smart (Court Crier), Stuart Brooking (Marshall), Fredrick Harris 1967/68, Robert H. West 1973/74, John P. Brown 1975/76, Michael J. Smale 1976/77, John W. Joyner (Steward), Michael C. Webster 1969/70;* centre: *John A. Sawdye 1949/50, Frederick W. Miners (Bailiff), Ernest J. Pulman (Portreeve) 1977/78, Arthur S. Kennard 1953/54, Reginald S. Andrews 1954/55, Amy J. Jones 1963/64;* front: *Henry G. Bradford 1972/73, Gordon A. Dumble 1970/71, Edward le Hunt Ward 1961/62, Ivan T. Barling 1961/62.*

been held by Lord Clinton (17th Baron to 21st Baron) passed to Ashburton Town Council in 1974. They hold the title in the corporate sense. It would be incorrect to call the Town Mayor 'The Lord of the Borough' or for the Town Council to be referred to as 'The Lords of the Borough'. The Town Council appoints a Steward to represent them and conduct normal court proceedings. The Lord of the Borough has by custom been represented at the Annual Court and Law Day rather than attend in person and since 1927 it has been customary for that body to be represented by one of the councillors. This is usually the Mayor and was formerly the chairman of the Urban District Council.

The present Portreeve, Bailiff and other ancient court appointments are keeping alive a tradition stretching back well over 1,000 years when, on the fourth Tuesday in November, a new Portreeve and Bailiff are elected at the Court and Law Day ceremony in St Lawrence Chapel. Other officers elected for a year are elected by the two courts and presentments are made on matters of local interest.

Membership of the courts has an important distinction, essential to the existence of these courts. Qualification for membership of the Leet Jury is that the nominated potential jury member should be a freeholder and have been resident in the town for at least a year. Should they sell their freehold, they are no longer eligible for membership of that court. The Leet Jury elect the Bailiff, Ale Tasters and Bread Weighers as well as the Viewer of the Markets, Inspector of Trees and two constables.

The Baron Jury was originally made up of leaseholders and tenants, with the added qualification of working in the town. As well as making presentments they elected the Pig Drovers, Viewers of the Watercourses, Searcher and Sealer of Leather, Scavengers and two more constables.

The Portreeve's function today is mainly as a social head of the town, attending the many charitable fund-raising events and, in conjunction with the Mayor, leading and representing the town. The elected Mayor is the civic and council head of the town and usually represents the Town Council, members of which are collectively the Lord of the Borough at the Court and Law Day Ceremony.

Some other towns which have a Portreeve include Callington (Cornwall) and Newport (Pembrokeshire), where he is also the Mayor; Holsworthy (Devon), Laugharne (Dyfed) and Watchet (Somerset), where the post is similar to Ashburton; and Hungerford (Berkshire) where the Portreeve is not the head of the court but the equivalent of our constable. Other ancient courts have Reeves, Bailiffs or Sheriffs as their head. Ashburton is the only town in Britain that still holds the office of Portreeve as its head by Act of Parliament. Newton Abbot revived their title in recent years.

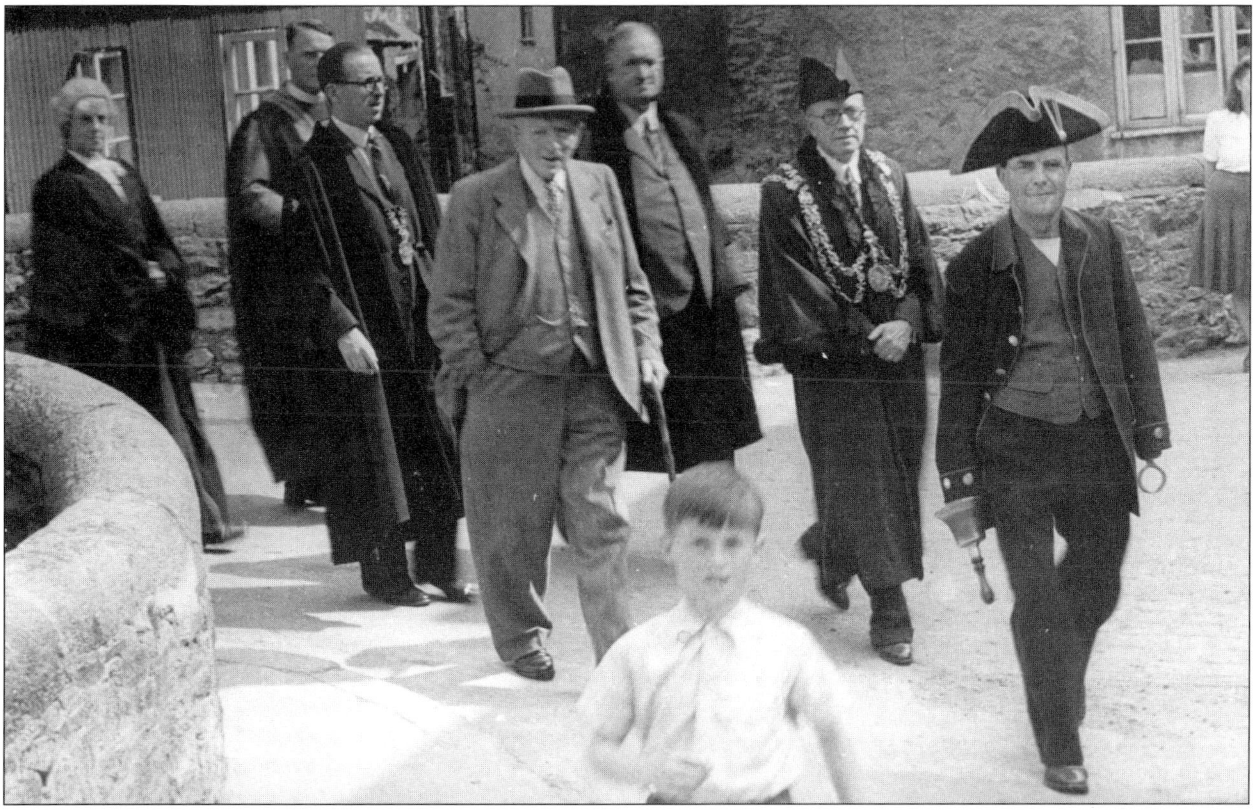

Ale tasting, 1947. Left to right: *Mrs Marjorie Morris (Town Clerk), Revd Gerald Jones, Mr Haydon (Bailiff), Harry Hannaford (Councillor), Brian Baker (Councillor), Mr Truscott (Portreeve), Fred Wills (Town Crier).*

(GARTH GROSE COLLECTION)

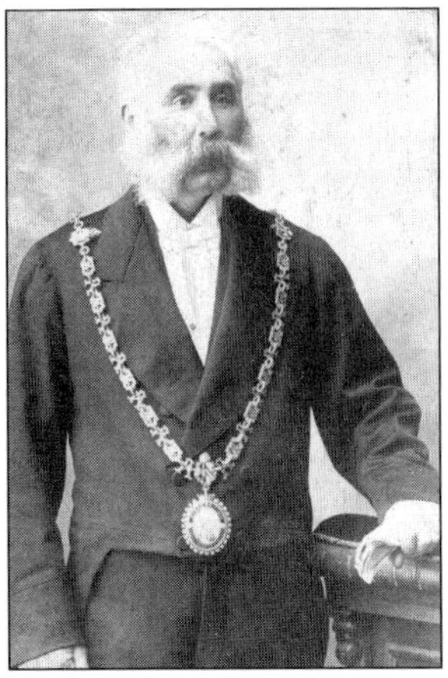

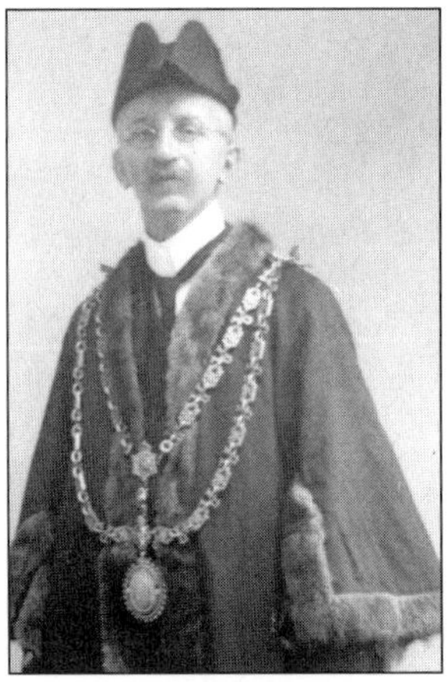

Far left: *John Sawdye, Portreeve, 1896–7.*

Left: *W.T. Butchers, Portreeve, 1918–9.*

Right: *Henry Hannaford, Portreeve 1935–6.*

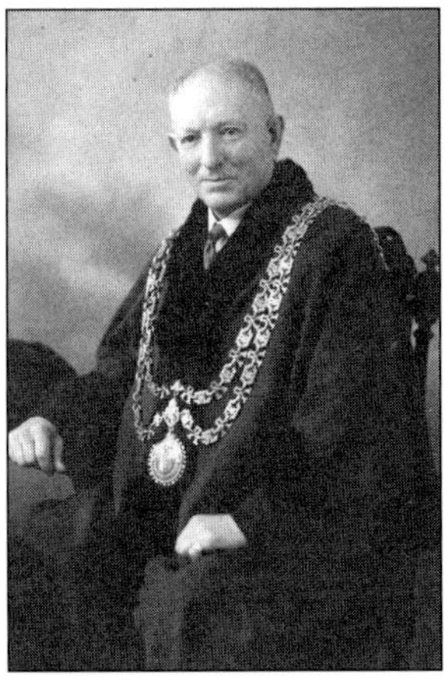

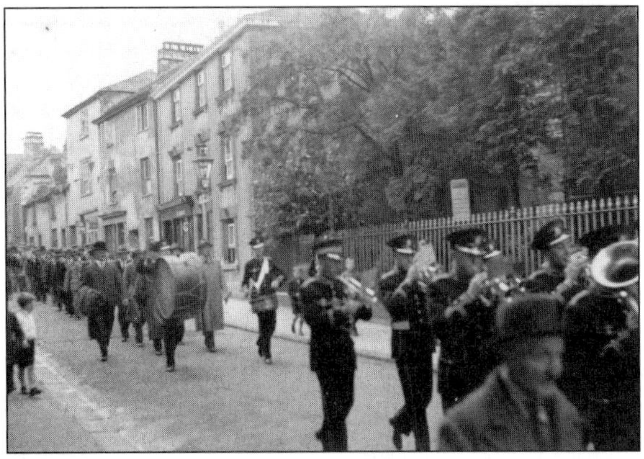

Above: *Carnival parade, 1937.* (PETE WEBB COLLECTION)

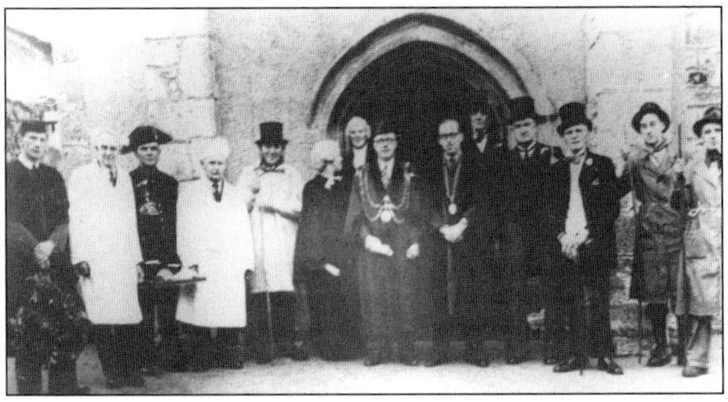

Above: *Carnival Ale Taster procession, 1930. Portreeve Mr Truscott, Mr Haydon (Bailiff), Fred Wills (Town Crier), Brian Baker, Billy Eales and Charlie Paul.* (GARTH GROSE COLLECTION)

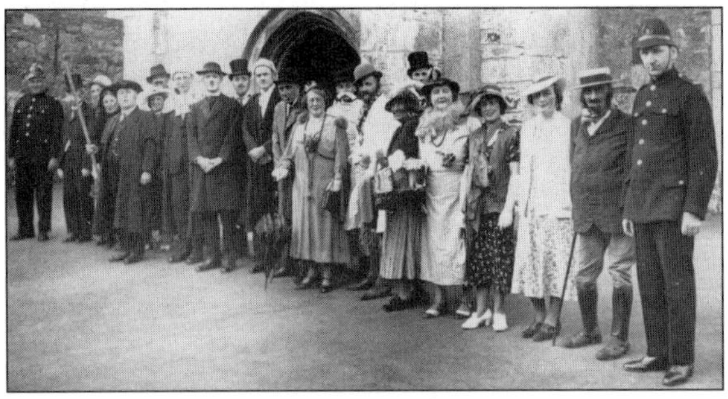

Above: *Portreeve's parade. Dick Stanbury (policeman), lady with fur wrap* (fifth from right) *is Amy Jones, first lady.*

Right: *Mrs Gracey and son Major Tom W. Gracey, Portreeve 1955/6.* (WATERS COLLECTION)

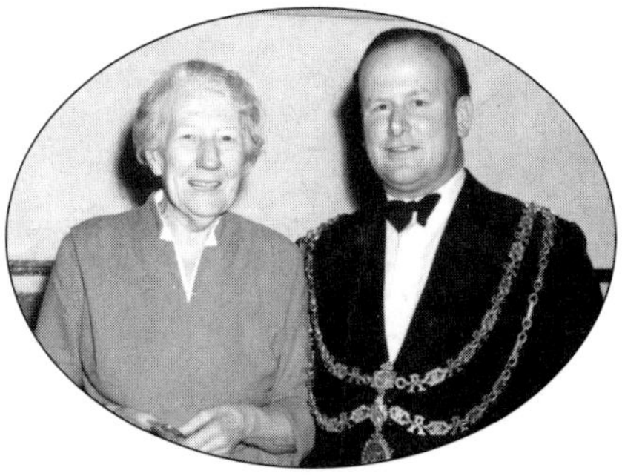

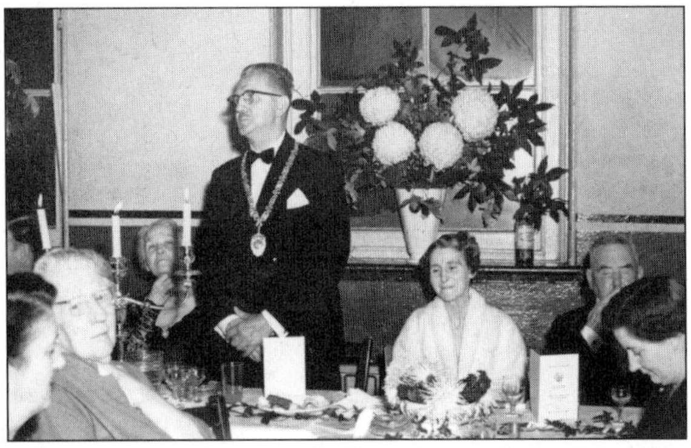

Above: *Portreeve Mr William Underhill giving his inaugural address, November 1956. William was a tobacconist in North Street.* (WATERS COLLECTION)

Below: *Swearing-in, 1956. At the head of the table is Mrs Margorie Morris (Town Clerk and Steward), sitting next to the pew in a light coat is Bill Waters and the last gentleman swearing in on the left is Charles Paul.* (WATERS COLLECTION)

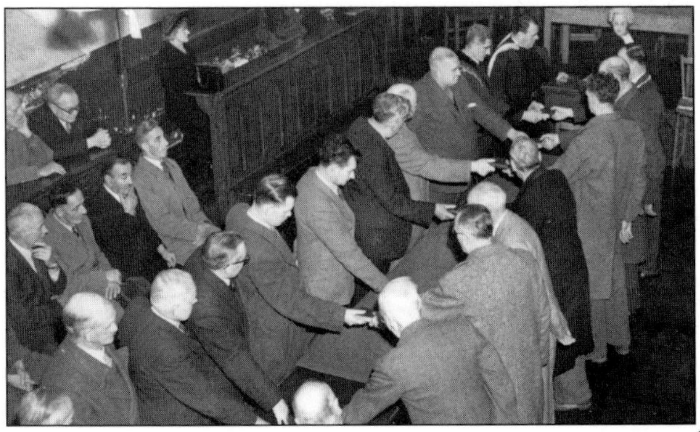

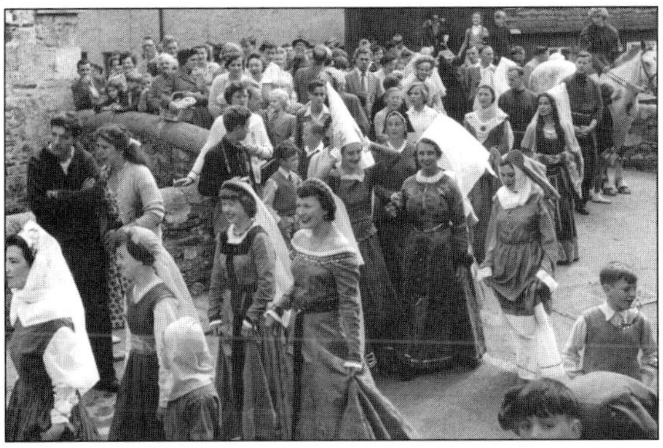

Above: *Ale tasting, 1950s.* (PETE WEBB COLLECTION)

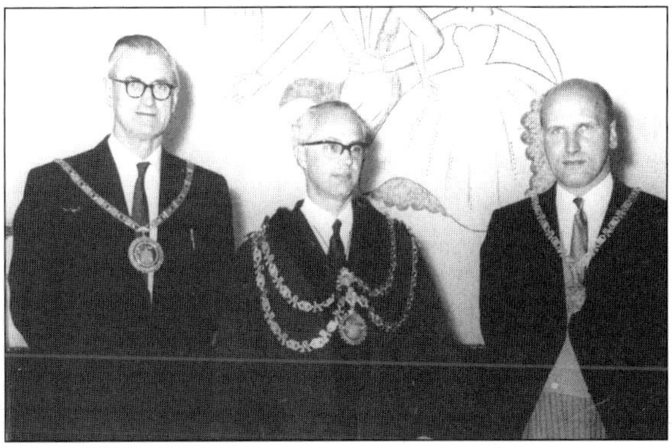

Above: *Councillor N.E. Stacey, Roy Harris (Portreeve), Ken Watson (Bailiff).*

(PETE WEBB COLLECTION)

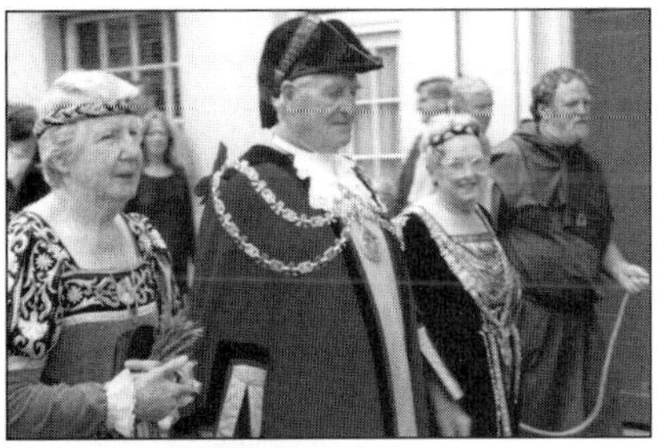

Left: *Mrs Lillian Brown, Portreeve Revd John Brown, Eileen Egbeare (Bailiff), Dave Crook, 1995.*

(JOHN MITCHELL)

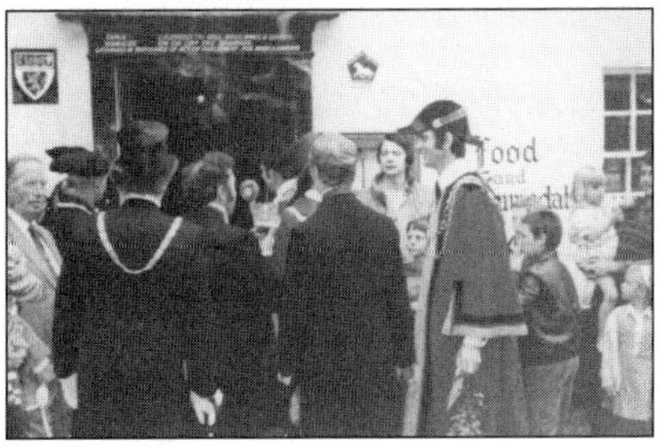

Left: *Portreeve Fred Christophers leading the Ale Tasting and Bread Weighing ceremony, June 1982.*

(PETE WEBB)

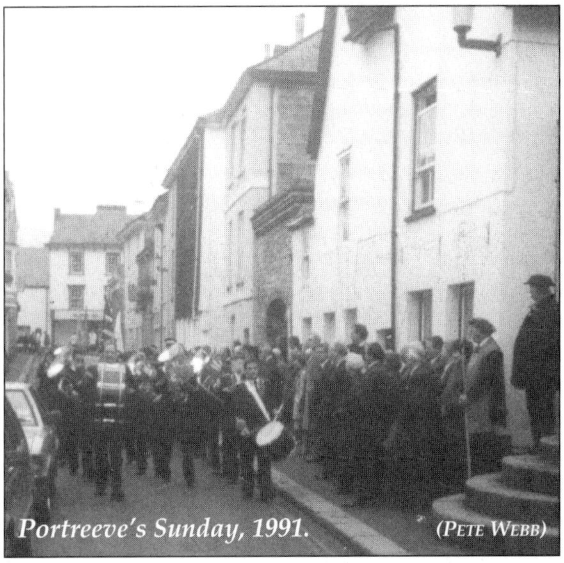

Portreeve's Sunday, 1991. (PETE WEBB)

Below: *Past Portreeves – Past Portreeves dinner in 2001.* Left to right, back row: *Pete Webb (1993–4), Fred Christophers (1981–2);* centre: *Bill Ward (1992–3), Cyril Bowen (1991–2), Adrian Daw (1982–3), Ron Southcombe (1980–1), Phil Poole (1988–9), John Germon (1984–5), Mel Thompson (1985–6), Neil Room–Doubleday (1986–7), David Lewis (1998–9), Ken Connett (1996–7), John Keeling (1997–8);* front: *Michael Smale (1976–7), Bill Pulman (1977–8), Bob West (1973–4), Michael Webster (1969–70), Ken Watson (1968–9), Eileen Egbeare (1995–6), Jim Pearce (1974–5), Revd John Brown (1994–5).*

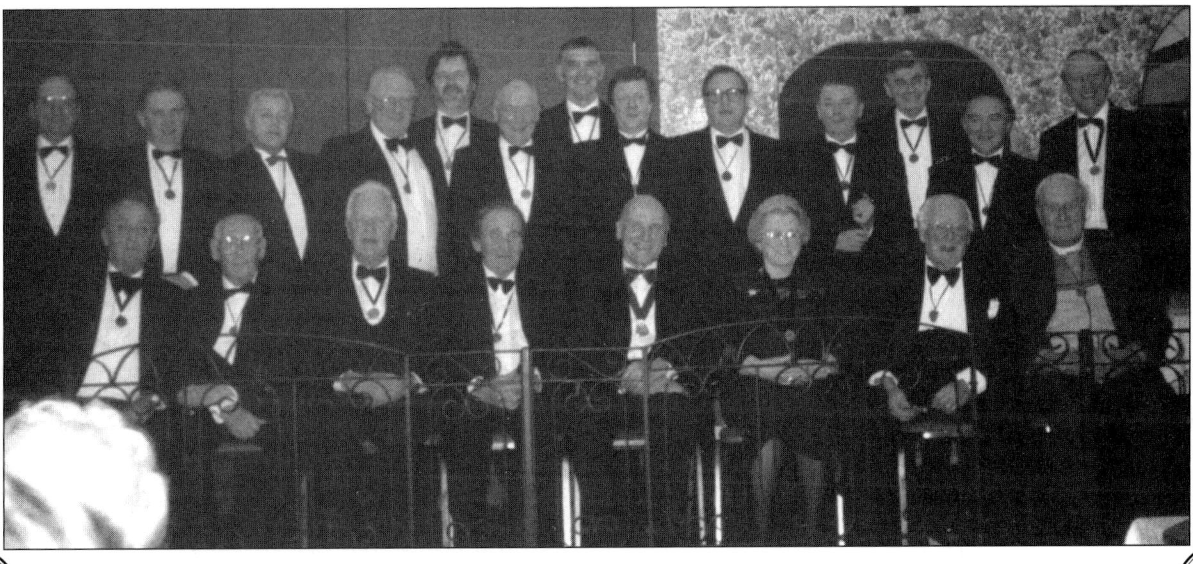

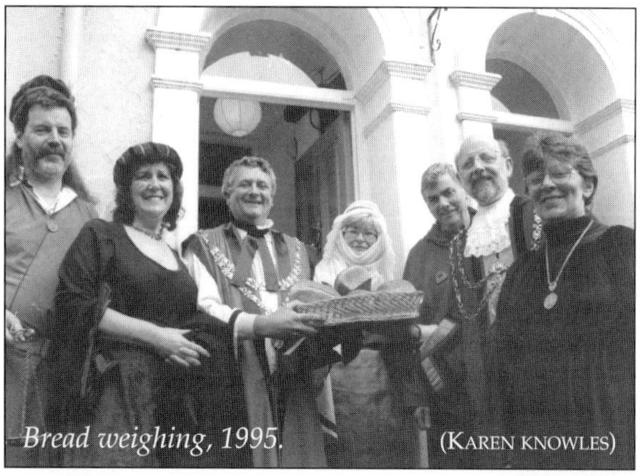

Bread weighing, 1995. (KAREN KNOWLES)

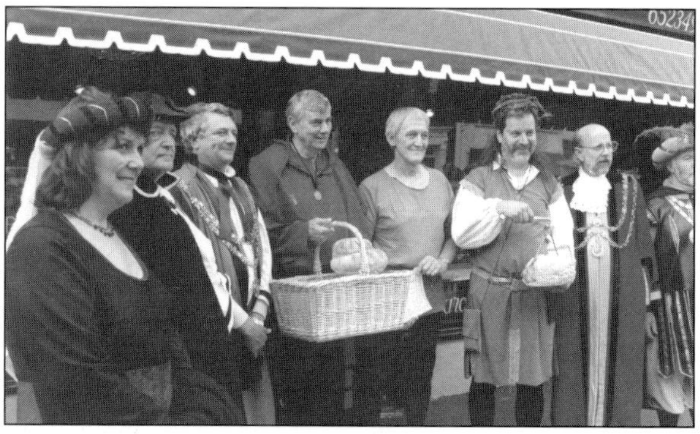

Bread weighing at Bishop's, 1995. (KAREN KNOWLES)

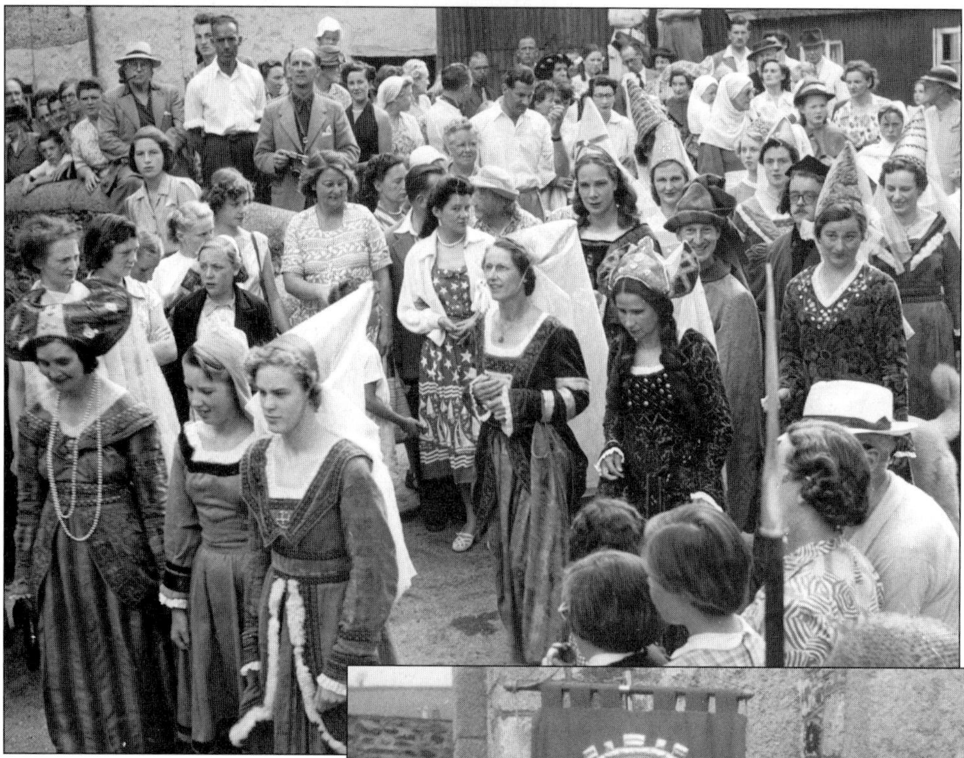

Ale tasting procession in 1955. Two of the front three ladies are Thelma Webber and Roberta Webber (not related). Dee Thurley, behind, has the long (natural) plaits. The parade is crossing King's Bridge.

(PETE WEBB COLLECTION)

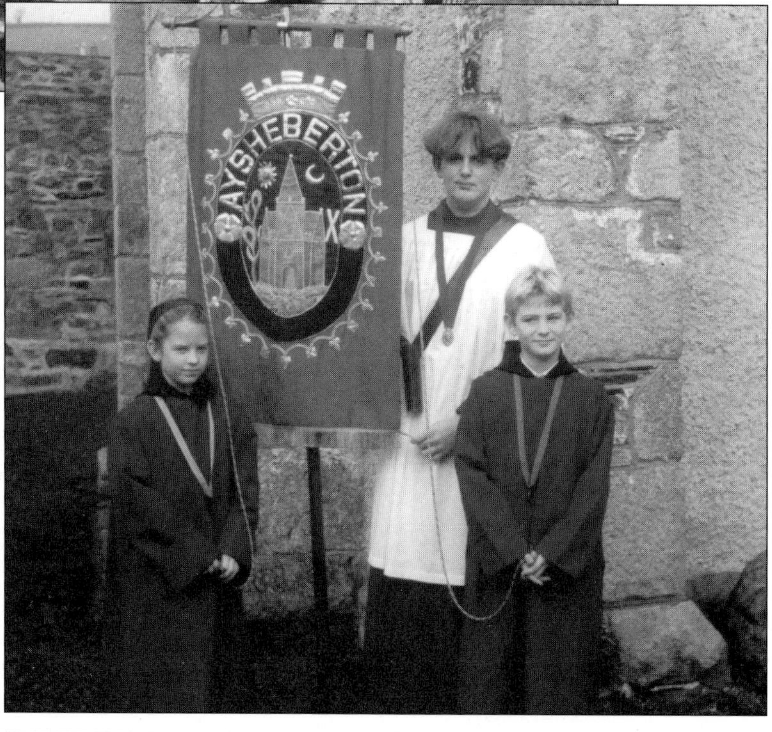

Right: *The Portreeve's banner displayed by members of the choir after the Portreeve's Sunday service, November 1991.*

(PETE WEBB COLLECTION)

CHAPTER 17

Then and Now

The point has been made in this book already that whilst Ashburton has undergone change over the past 130 years, unlike some places, it is still recognisable as the place of yesteryear, particularly in the town centre. Ashburton is reputed to have a larger proportion of Victorian and Edwardian shop-fronts than any town in the country of comparable size. This is something we don't notice unless it is pointed out, as usually when shopping we are intent on getting the job done. Older residents will recognise the places once part of the townscape, newcomers will be able to see that their town is changing to meet modern challenges – traffic comes to mind – yet without destroying the past. Enjoy the tour!

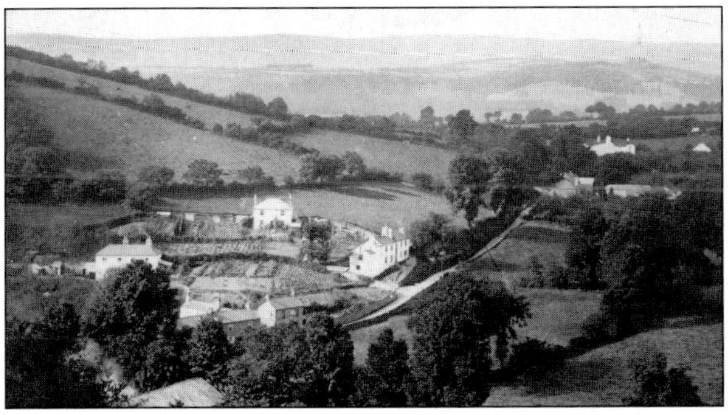

Headborough, c.1910. (PETE WEBB COLLECTION)

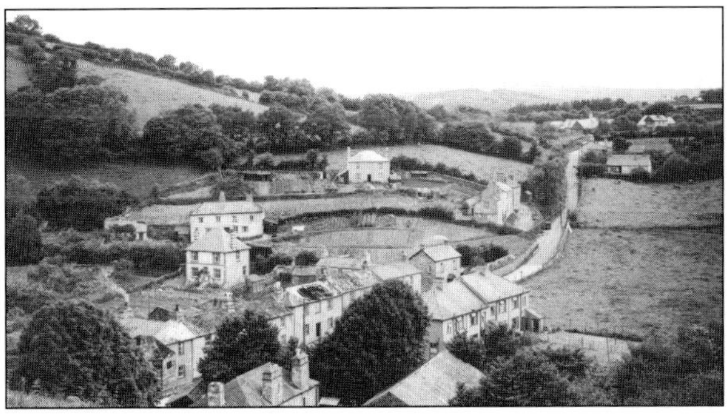

Headborough Road, c.1940, with a few more houses. (PETE WEBB COLLECTION)

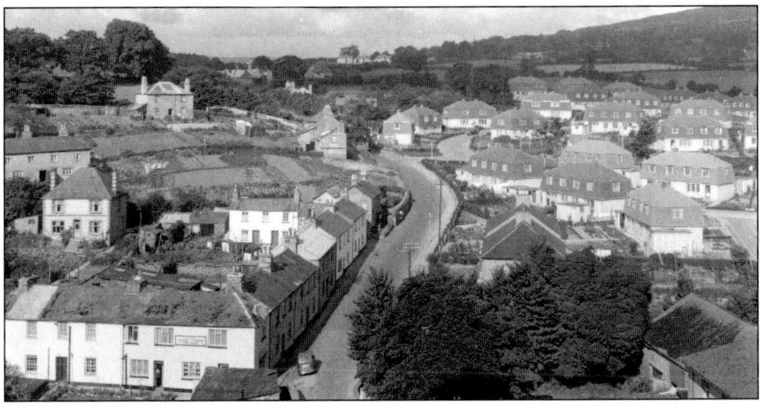

Headborough Road, c.1950, after the estate was built. (PETE WEBB COLLECTION)

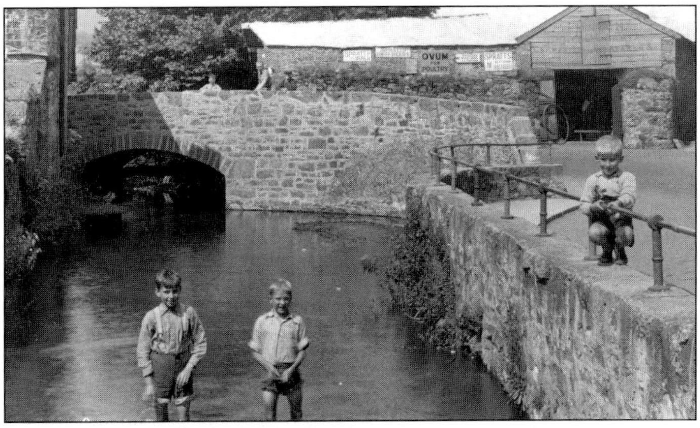

Great Bridge with Hatch's Wheelrights behind. The three lads are, from left: *Bill Mugridge, another Bill (either Brooks or Knowlin) and a young Brich lad. The wheelwright made way for Peter Prouse's garage (later Rex Aucock's who moved to the A38 garage). It is now Bridge Croft Cottages, Rew Road.* (PETE WEBB COLLECTION)

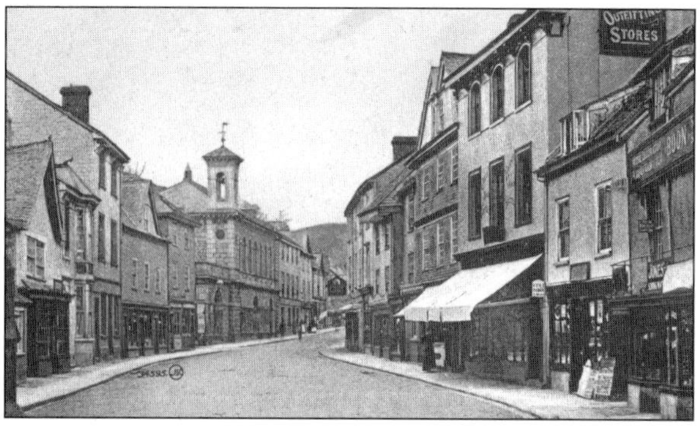

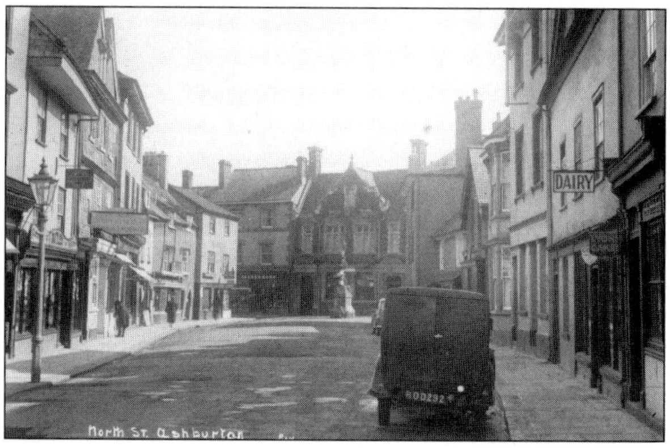

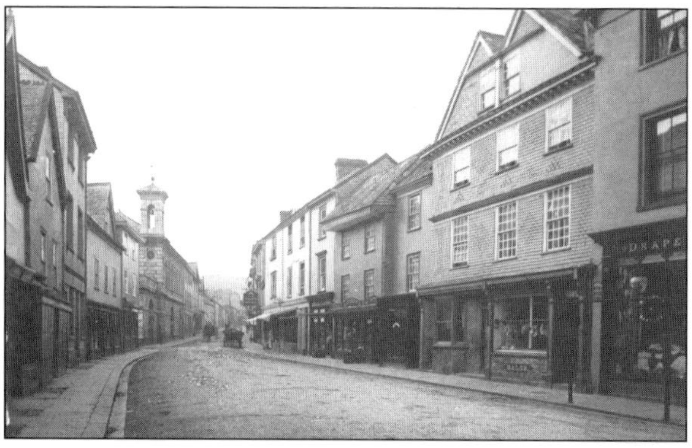

Above left, above and left: *Three early views of North Street.* (PETE WEBB COLLECTION)

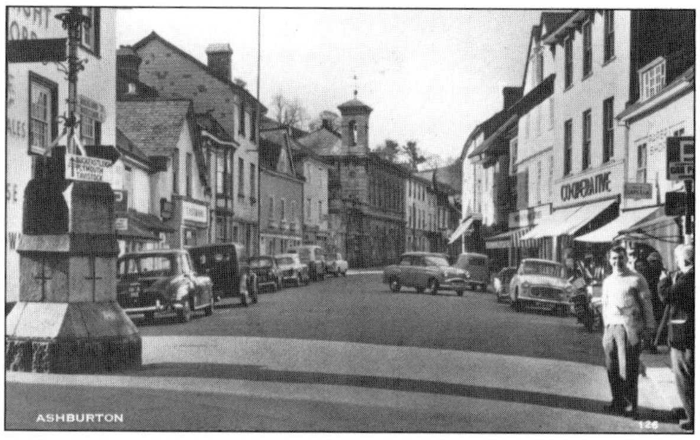

Above: *North Street, 1961, with Brian Horsman on the right looking at the camera. Note also the Co-op, now the chemist (2004), and the 'Bull Ring' (water conduit).* (PETE WEBB COLLECTION)

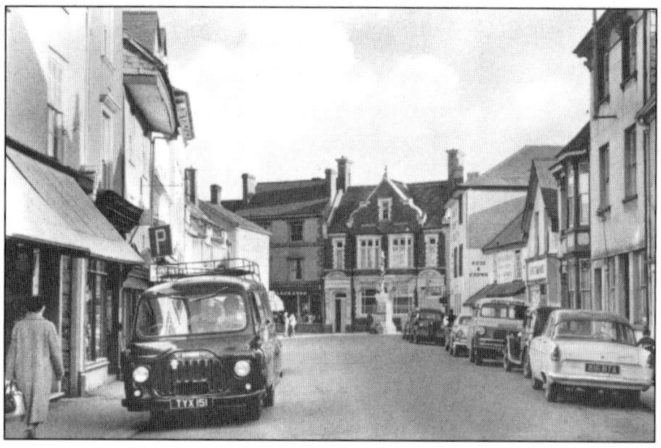

Above: *Looking down North Street, c.1960.* (PETE WEBB COLLECTION)

Right: *Another 1960s view of North street.* (PETE WEBB COLLECTION)

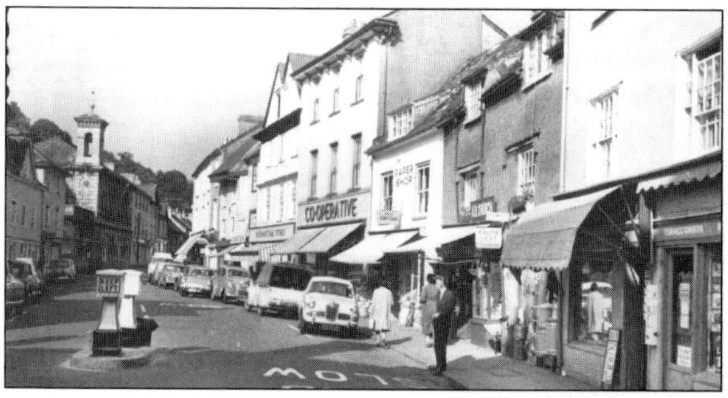

Right: *1970s view of North Street just prior to demolition.* From right to left: *(possibly the entrance to Winsor Court), Badcocks, then shop (Knight's then Dean's), another tumbledown entrance (again possibly Winsor Court – with Mr Northcott in the front and French the blacksmith's in behind), Lang's (bakers) and the Culloden Inn. The next block of a dozen or so houses were owned by Mr Pengelly. All were demolished down to the house with the pedestrian and the Morris Minor with an open door.* (PETE WEBB COLLECTION)

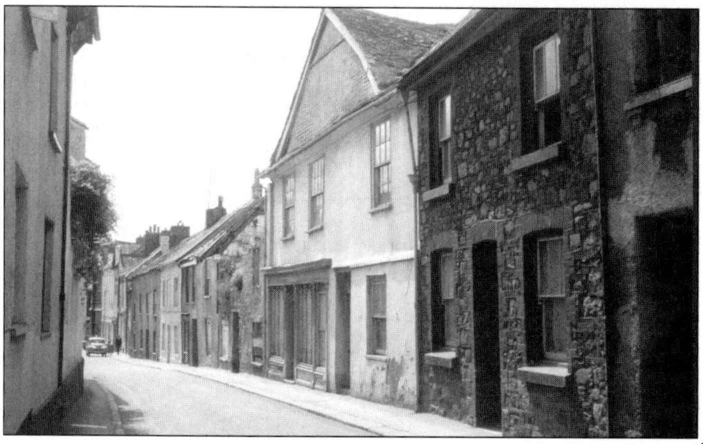

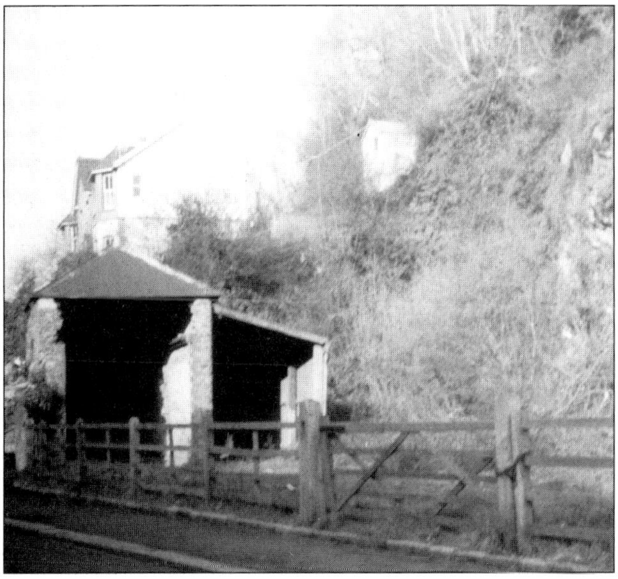

Above: *The old shed in Thornings Quarry in 1984, before the flats were built the following year.* (JEAN ALLEN COLLECTION)

Below: *North Street, c.1905.* (PETE WEBB COLLECTION)

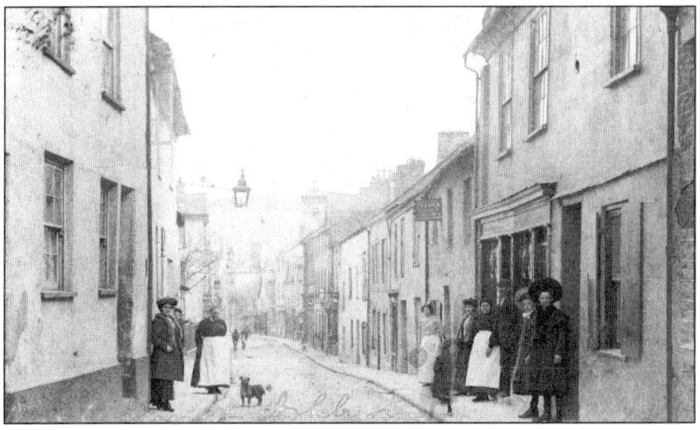

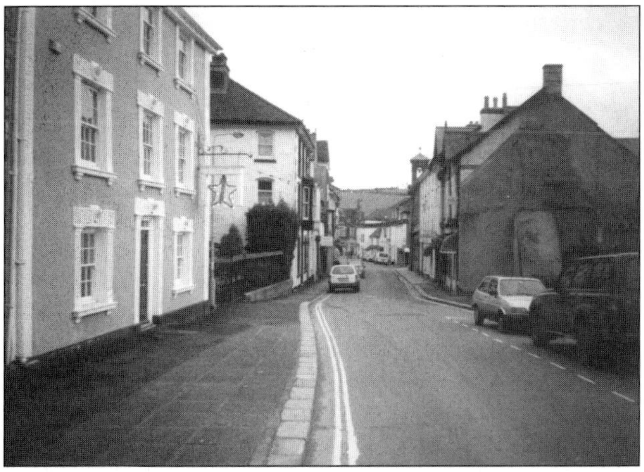

North Street, December 1999. On the left is Ashburton Marbles' premises, housed in the Congregational Chapel. (PETE WEBB)

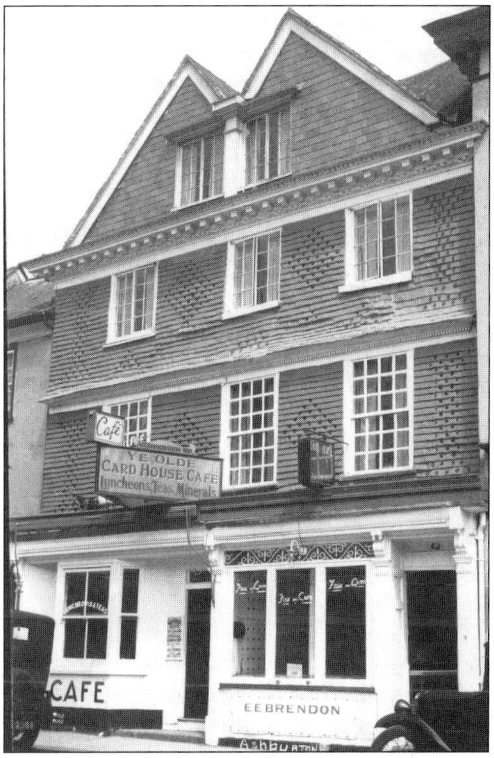

Above: *The Card House Café, North Street, c.1930.* (PETE WEBB COLLECTION)

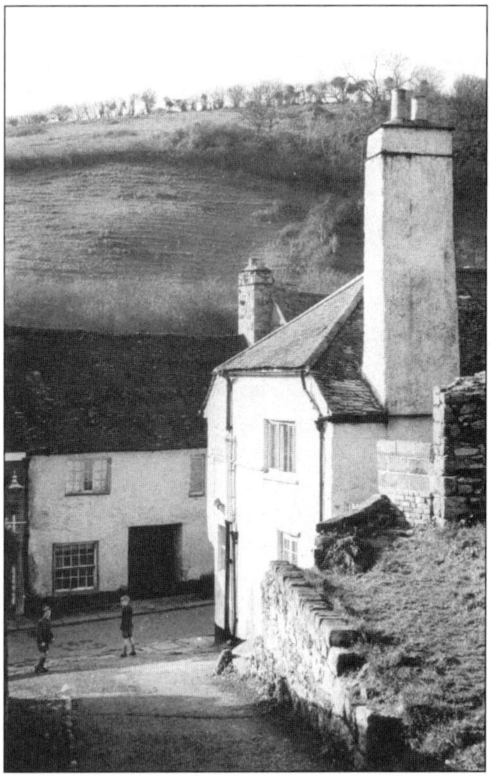

View across North Street from Stapledon Lane in 1959. The boys are Macrae and Mason. (ASHBURTON MUSEUM)

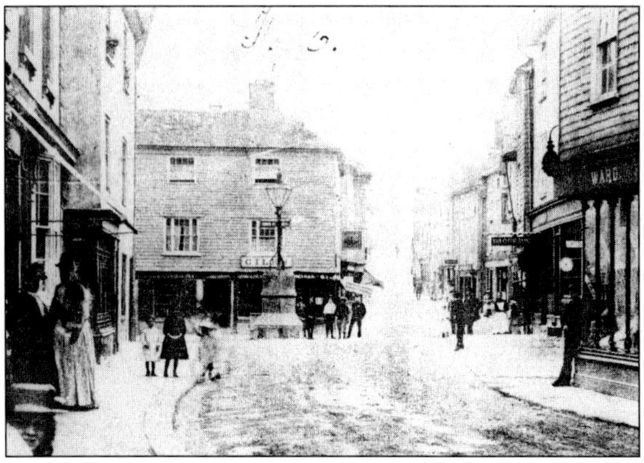

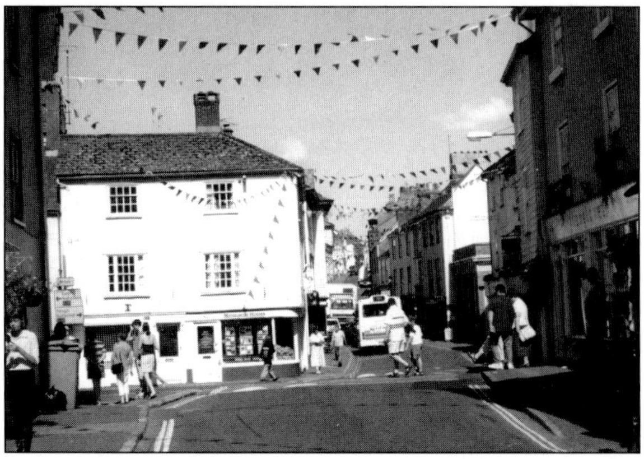

Above left: *The Bull Ring, c.1904, looking from West Street to East Street.* (GARTH GROSE COLLECTION)

Above right: *A similar view in 2002 with carnival bunting.* (GARTH GROSE COLLECTION)

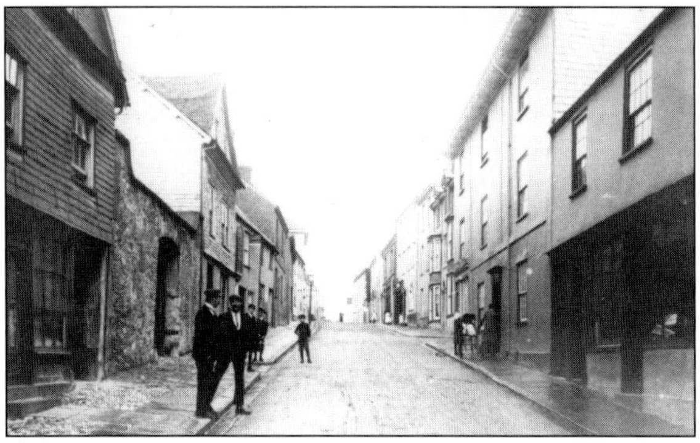

East Street looking down with Tom Lang (butcher) on the left. This 1950s view was taken by one of the Ruth brothers. Note also the Anchor Café sign (formerly the Blue Anchor pub). Taken after the bypass was opened (1935), this shows how quiet the former main Plymouth to Exeter road had become. (PETE WEBB COLLECTION)

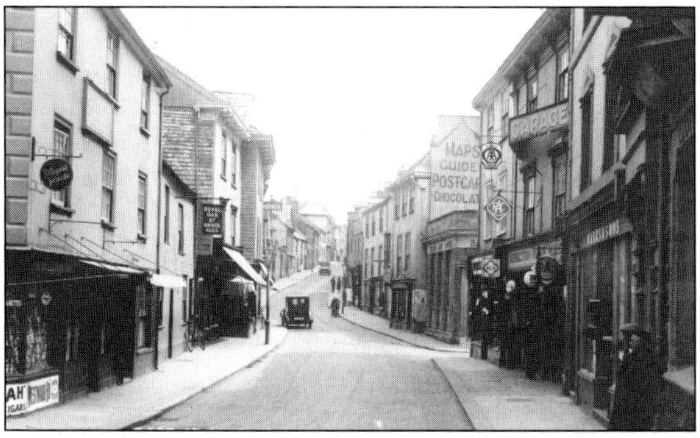

Another view of East Street, looking up from the Bull Ring. This 1920s view shows from the right: *Lloyds Bank, Eales & Sons (saddlers), Ashburton Motor Works (garage), and Frisby's Shoes. After St Lawrence Lane is another bank (later the Midland) and the printers. Opposite is the Royal Oak, then a St Anne's Ales house. Note also the tobacconist on the corner.* (PETE WEBB COLLECTION)

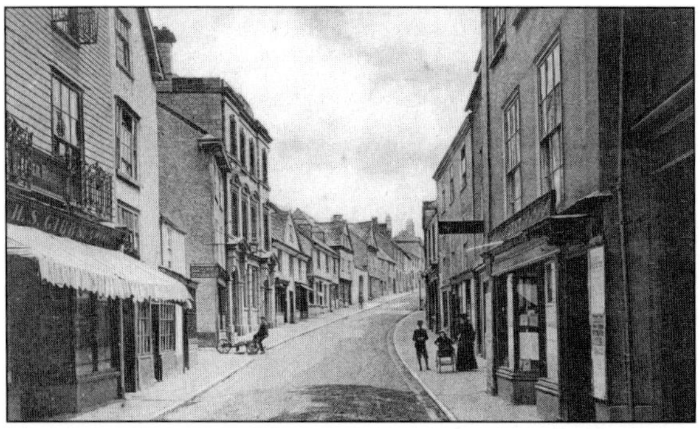

East Street, c.1910 – note the shop (W.B. Palk – confectioner) where there was later a garage. The Midland bank is not yet built but Lloyds is there. Eales the saddlers is there and the Royal Oak has the name 'Browns' in front. Note the few pedestrians and the hand cart. (PETE WEBB COLLECTION)

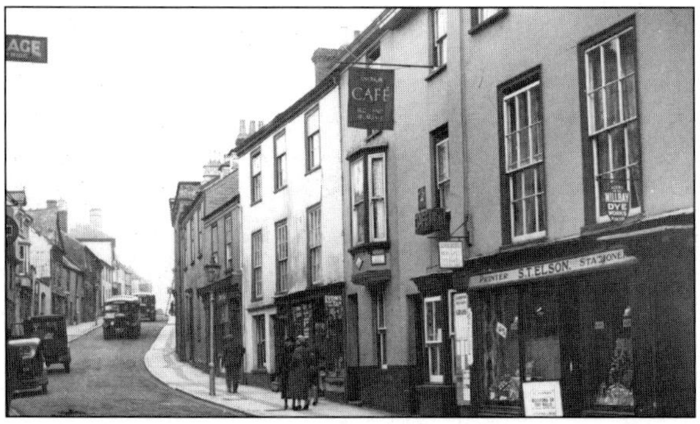

East Street, late 1930s, with two buses coming down the hill. Note Elson the printers and the Anchor Café in what was the Blue Anchor pub. The sign outside the printers refers to the blessing of the bells at St Andrew's. (PETE WEBB COLLECTION)

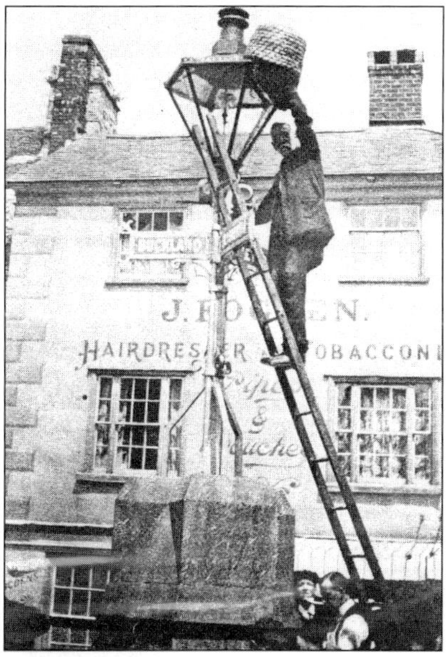

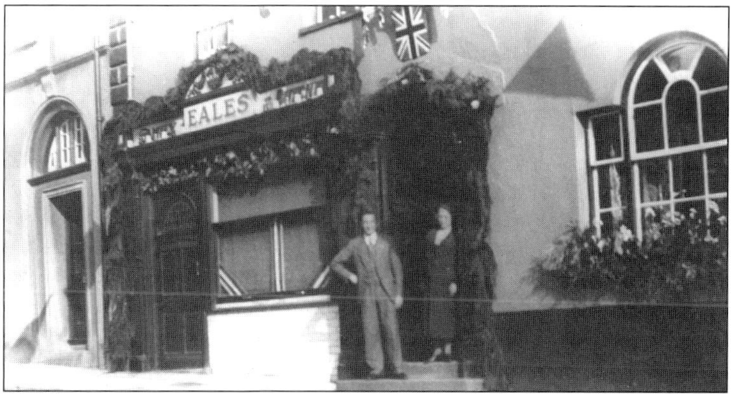

Above: *Eales Butcher's shop (now Smith's), decorated for the Silver Jubilee of George V in 1935.* (PAT ORSMAN COLLECTION)

Left: *A beekeeper catching a swarm of bees in a skep from the lamp in the Bull Ring, c.1912.* (ASHBURTON MUSEUM)

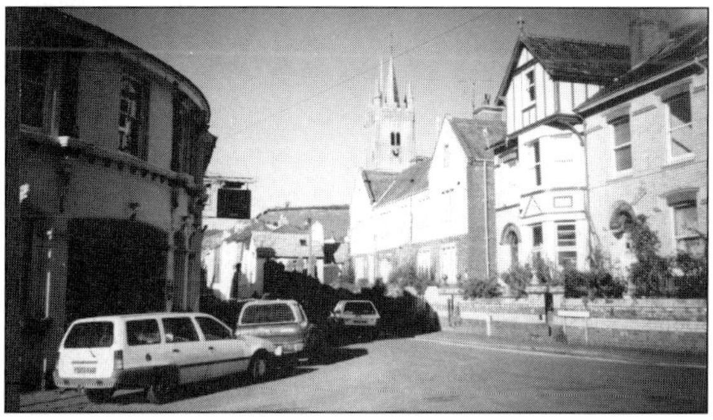

Left: *St Lawrence Lane and Chapel from the south, 1999.* (PETE WEBB)

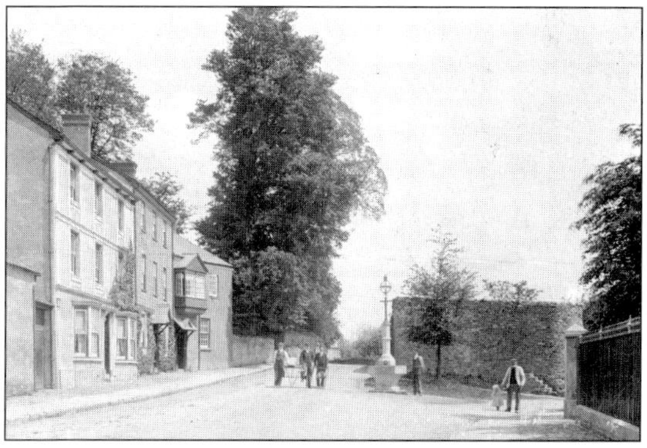

Above: *Bovey Memorial, c.1910, before it was moved and replaced by the War Memorial. It is now next to the Bay Horse, North Street.* (PETE WEBB COLLECTION)

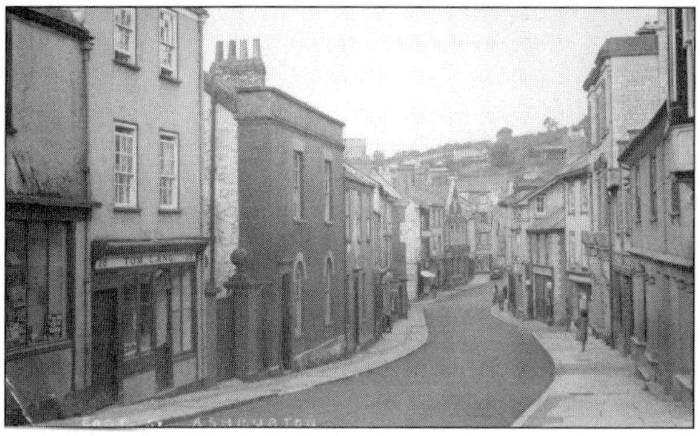

Left: *An early view looking down East Street, c.1905.* (PETE WEBB COLLECTION)

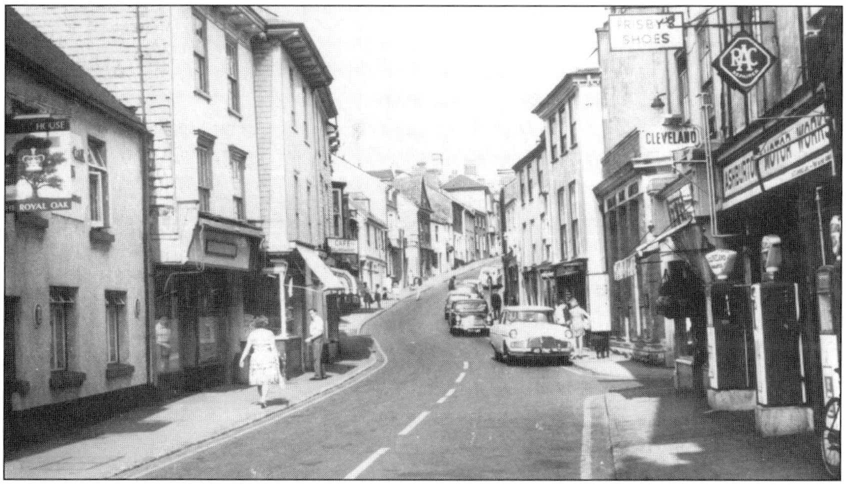

Left: *East Street, early 1960s, given by Mrs Joan Joyner who is pictured walking on the left. Note Ashburton Motor Works, Frisby's Shoes and the Midland Bank, as well as the cars parked where there is no single yellow line.* (PETE WEBB COLLECTION)

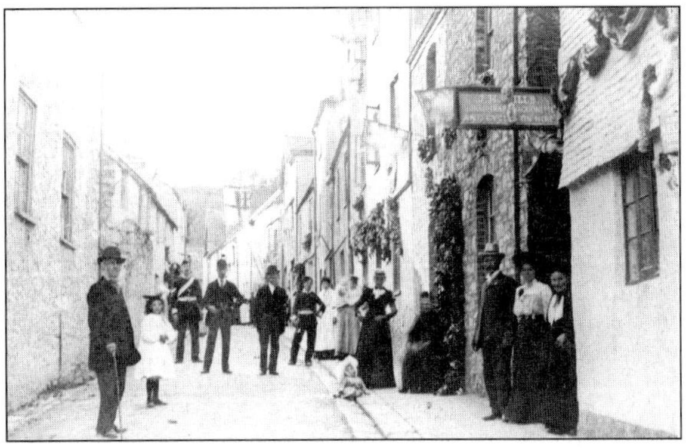

Celebrating Queen Victoria's Diamond Jubilee in Woodland Road, 1897. (GARTH GROSE COLLECTION)

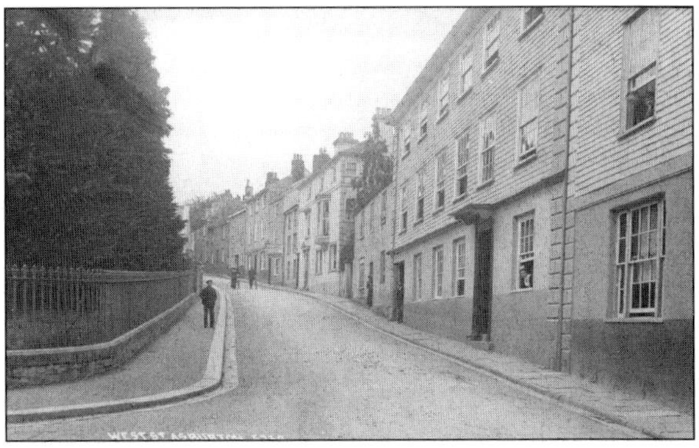

This early (c.1910) view of West Street shows some of the former merchants' houses opposite the church. The photographer would have been outside what is now the Old Coffee House (note the audience!). (PETE WEBB COLLECTION)

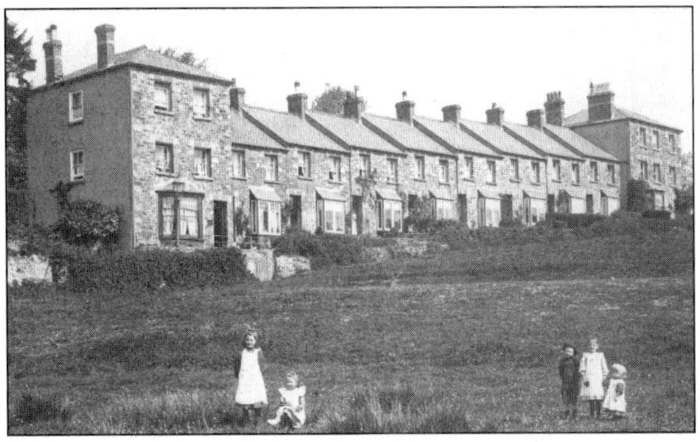

Left: *West End Terrace, c.1910, with children enjoying the fields in front of their houses.* (PETE WEBB COLLECTION)

Right: *West End Terrace with the railway in the foreground, c.1940.* (PETE WEBB COLLECTION)

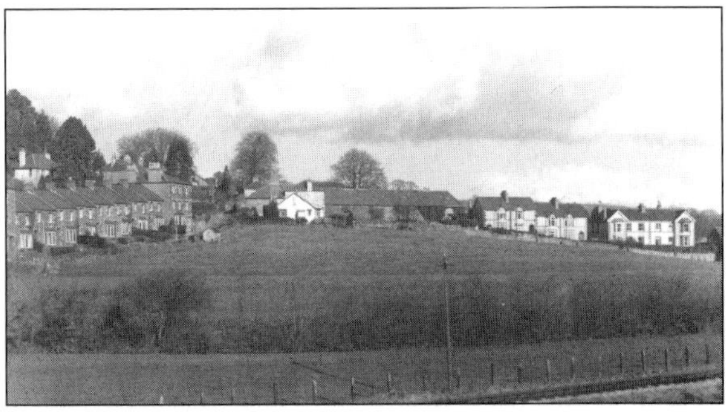

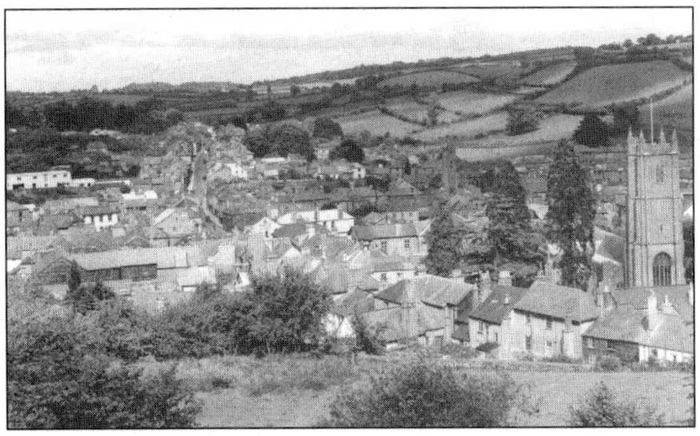

Left: *A general view of Ashburton Railway from Bowden Hill, c.1920* (PETE WEBB COLLECTION)

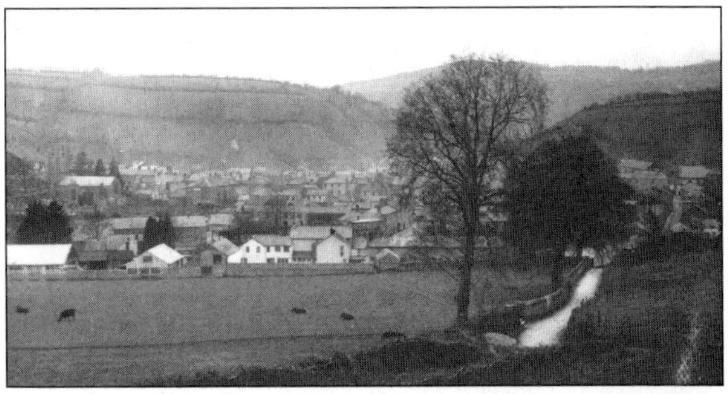

Right: *Ashburton from Yolland Hill – the other side of the A38.* (PETE WEBB COLLECTION)

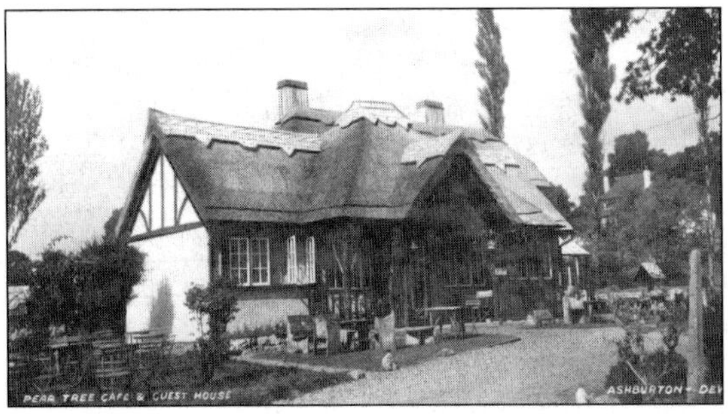

Above: *Pear Tree Café in the 1940s (pre-1948, when a fire destroyed the original thatched building).* (PETE WEBB COLLECTION)

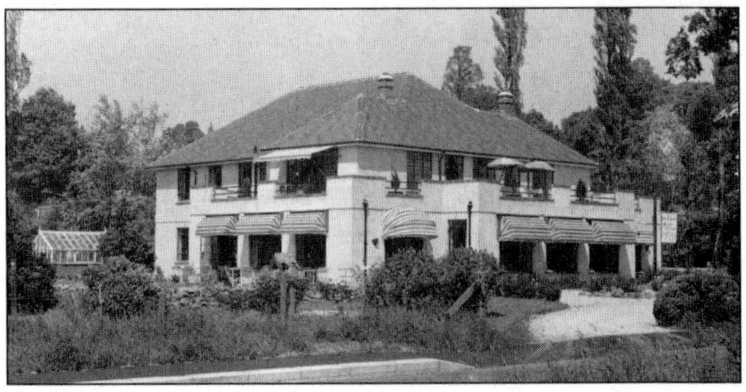

Above: *A 1950s view of the Pear Tree Café, soon after rebuilding.* (PETE WEBB COLLECTION)

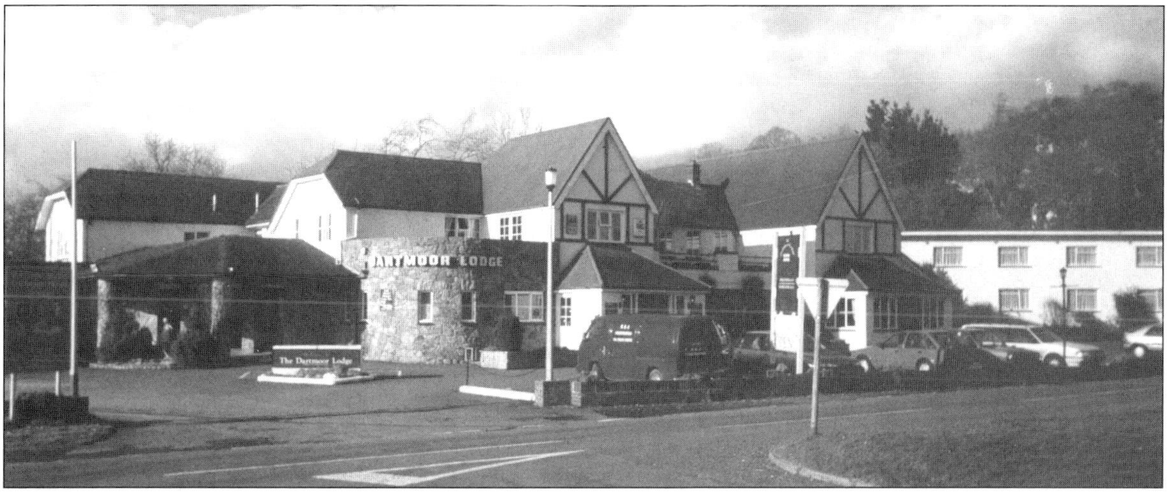

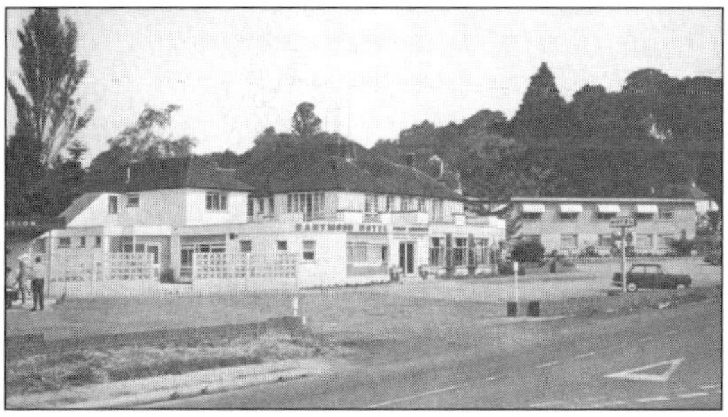

Above: *Pear Tree in 1991 – the Barmy Badger and Dartmoor Motel.* (PETE WEBB)

Left: *Pear Tree in the 1960s – Dartmoor Lodge Motel.* (PETE WEBB COLLECTION)

Below: *Parish Road (now Chuley Road) near the engine shed.* (PETE WEBB COLLECTION)

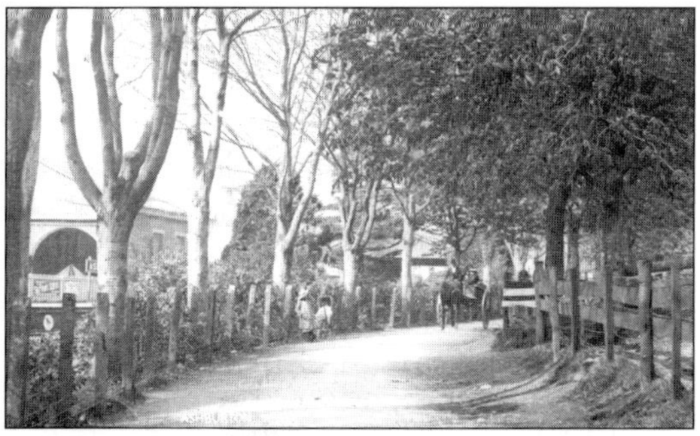

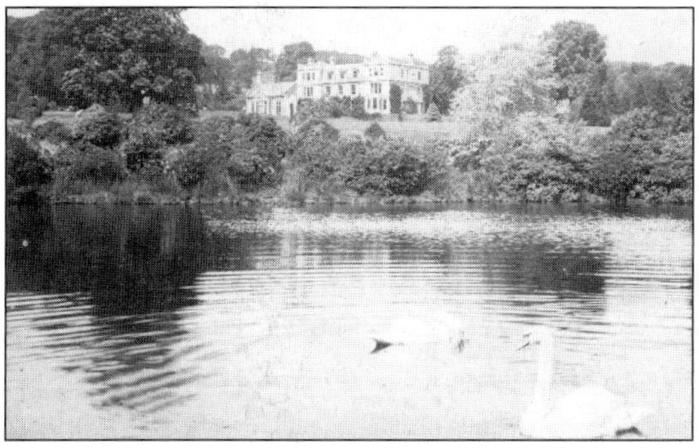

Above: *Holne Park, c.1930. Taken over by the Armed Forces as officer accommodation during the Second World War, it then became an outward bound school and now houses the River Dart Country Park.* (PETE WEBB COLLECTION)

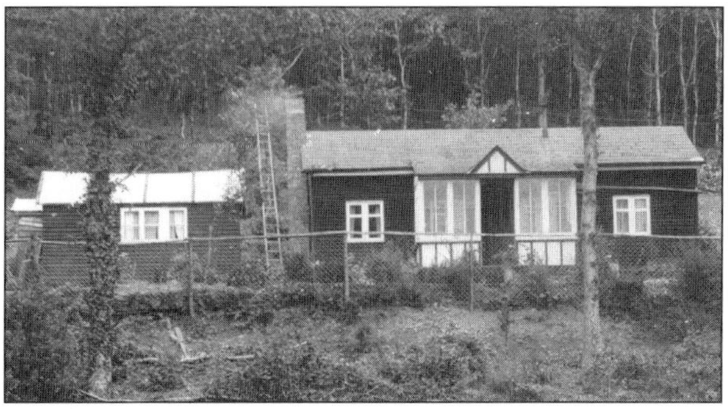

Above: *Lurgecombe Bungalow. This old wooden chalet burnt down in 1982 and the footpath through the bluebell woods (to Waterleat) passes right beside it.* (PETE WEBB COLLECTION)

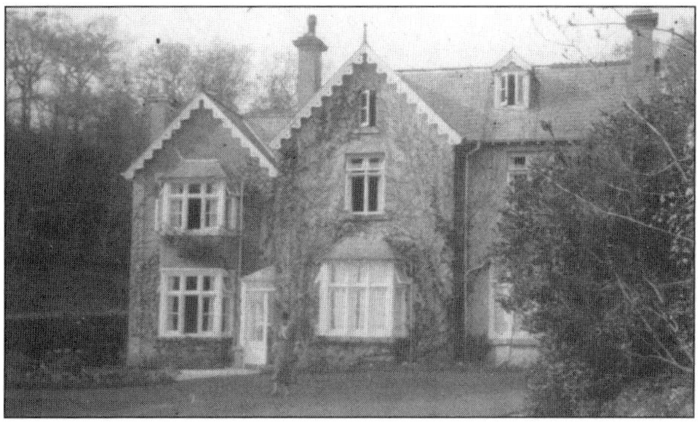

Above: *Dart Vale House on the western edge of town.* (PETE WEBB COLLECTION)

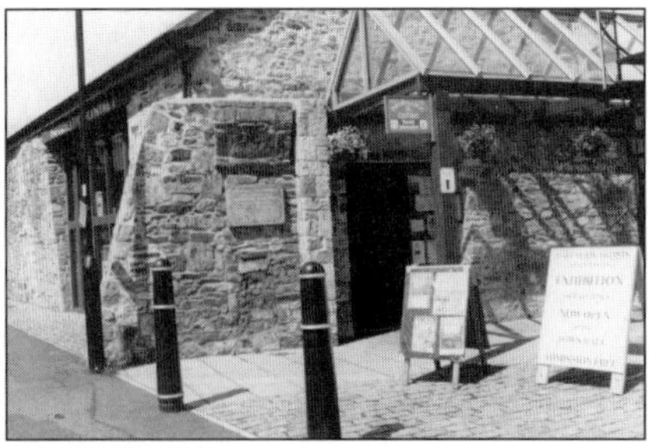

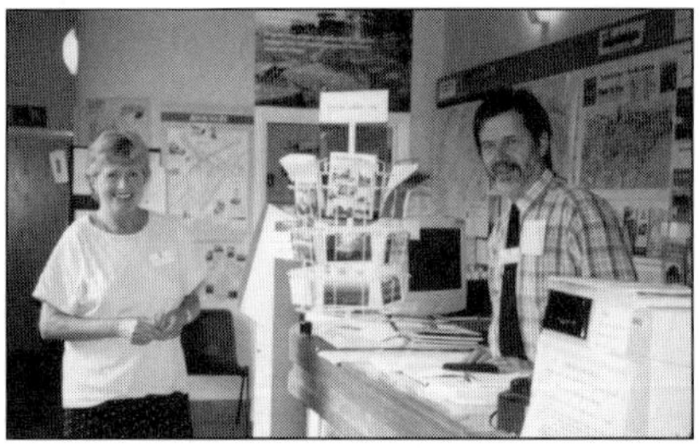

Right: *Ashburton Information Centre, 2002, with the then manager Pete Webb and Barbara Daw – one of the volunteer information assistants.*
(PETE WEBB COLLECTION)

Above: *Exterior of the modern Information Centre (2002).*
(PETE WEBB COLLECTION)

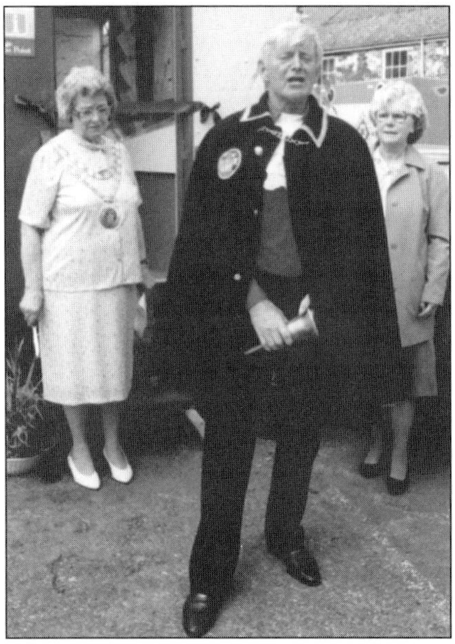

Above: *Town Crier Tony Pugh with Mayor Eileen Egbeare about to open the Information Caravan, 1992.*
(JOHN MITCHELL)

Below: *The opening of the original Information Caravan in July 1992 with John Mitchell and Barbara Pugh taking photos as Tony Pugh 'cries' the opening of the caravan. Paul Clegg is in front of the left doorway. Bill Finney, manager of Lloyd's Bank, is on the far left.* (PETE WEBB)

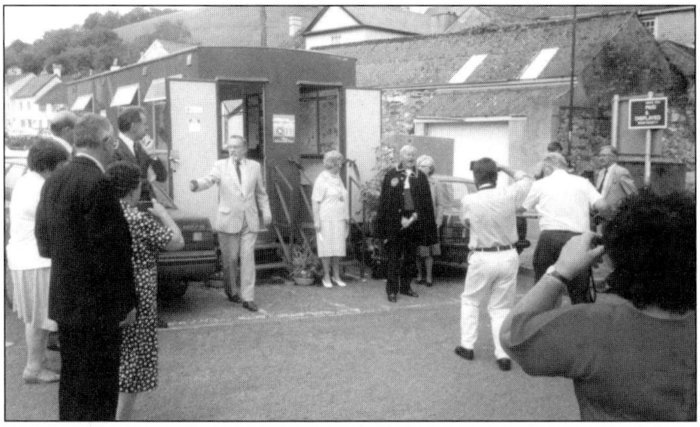

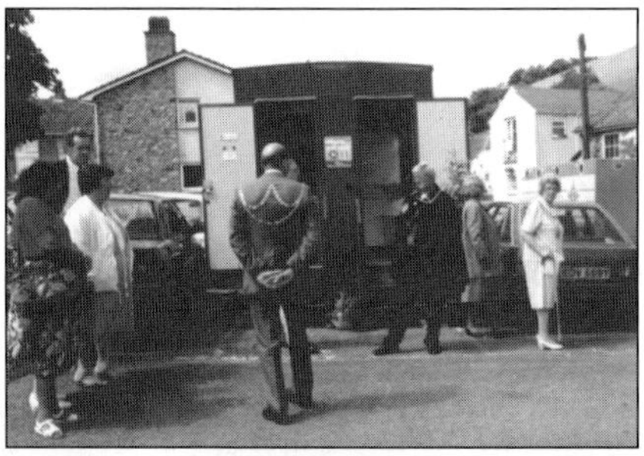

Left: *Another view with* left to right: *Barbara Pugh, Pat Dickenson, ?, Bill Ward (Portreeve), Tony Pugh (Town Crier), Eileen Egbeare (Mayor), ?.*
(JOHN MITCHELL)

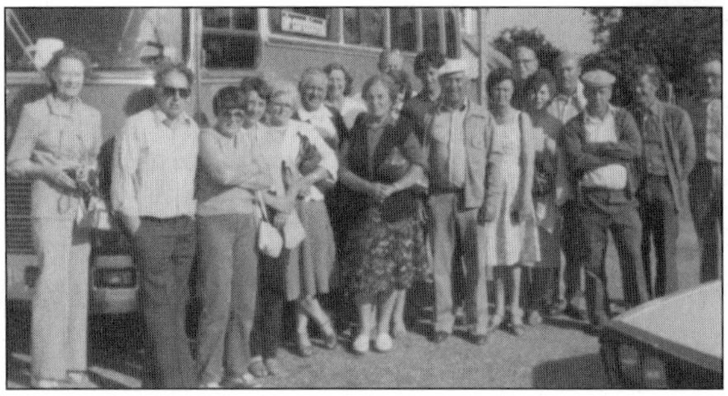

The Twinning Association was founded in 1975 after the Football Club went over the year before. Twinning trip, 1978. Left to right: *Queenie Dumble, Fred Orsman, Claudie Pronost, Danielle Clorec, Madam Pronost, Frank Norwell, Vera Bain, Catherine Clorec, Dan Bain, Phillip Clorec, Matthew Velly, Joan Norwel, ? Gloss, Ben Cartwright, Jean Cartwright, Roger Studdy, François Clorec, Louis Mesguin.*

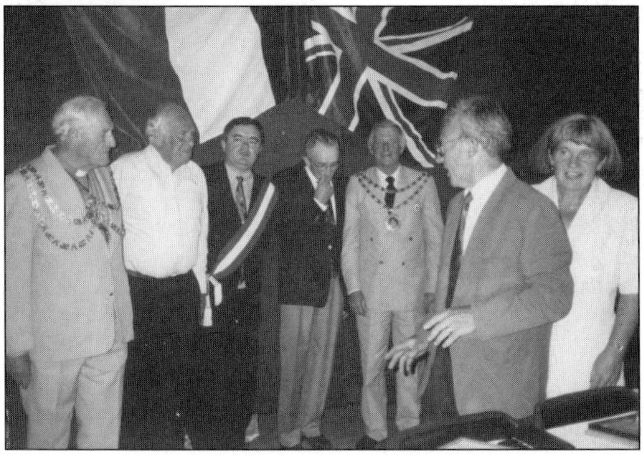

The Twinning Association celebrated its 20th anniversary with a visit to France in 1995. Left to right: *Revd John Brown (Portreeve), Fred Miners, Jean-Luc Uguen (Mayor of Cleder), Louis Mesguin, Tony Pugh (Mayor), Jo Gestin, Odette Quintelle.*

✥ CHAPTER 18 ✥

Sport

Ashburton Cricket Club

Ashburton Cricket Club was founded in 1885 and reformed in 1978.

Little is known of the early days of this club, though included here is a photograph taken between the wars of some of the cricketers of the day. After the Second World War, people such as Bill Waters, Andy Dent and, of course, Vernon (Geoff) Coon were influential in the club. These men enjoyed their cricket. Vernon is a life member of the club so all went well in the end. Fred Christophers, now also a life member, has provided much of the following information. His first recollections date back to 1957. He recalls John Meyrick (from the Royal Signals at Denbury) as being good with both bat and ball – a hard hitter who could also bowl both spin and quickies. Soper, too, was a good bat and a promising wicket keeper. Teams played in those years were Haytor Vale, Torquay Old Grammarians, Dawlish, Old Plymouthians and Centrax.

In 1958 16-year-old David Pedrick gained his first team place. Peter Dand, another member, also played for Etceteras and Plymouth Corinthians.

Bill Waters had by this time 'retired' to ground staff. He used to cut the grass with a three-foot cylinder mower and keep the ground in mint condition. It was devotion such as this that made cricket possible. Younger players were Sid Pugh, Geoff Osborne and Winslow Eggbeare. The highlight of 1958 was a win against South Devon by four wickets, despite their having a professional.

President of the club, Major E. Varwell DSO, gave the field to the club – hence its name, 'Varwell Field'. Les Townsend was Captain and John Merrick Vice Captain. Subscriptions were as follows: over-21 £1.5s.0d. (£1.25); 18-21 12s.6d. (65p); juniors 5s. (25p) and non-playing members 2s.6d. (12.5p). Reports of matches appeared in the local press including the *Western Morning News* and the *Mid Devon Advertiser.* Among members at that time who are still living in 2004 are G.V. Coon (hon. sec.), B. Soper (assistant treasurer), D. Pedrick (team secretary) and R. Vicary (fixture secretary). Umpire Les Luxton's ashes were scattered on the square at the ground in 1998.

John Merrick's farewell game was against Budleigh Salterton (Budleigh 112, Merrick 4 for 58; Ashburton 113 for 6, G.V. Coon 46).

Fred Christophers joined the club in 1960. This was a good season for the club – younger players as well as regulars Dave Pedrick and Peter Dendfield making a good all-round side playing just below

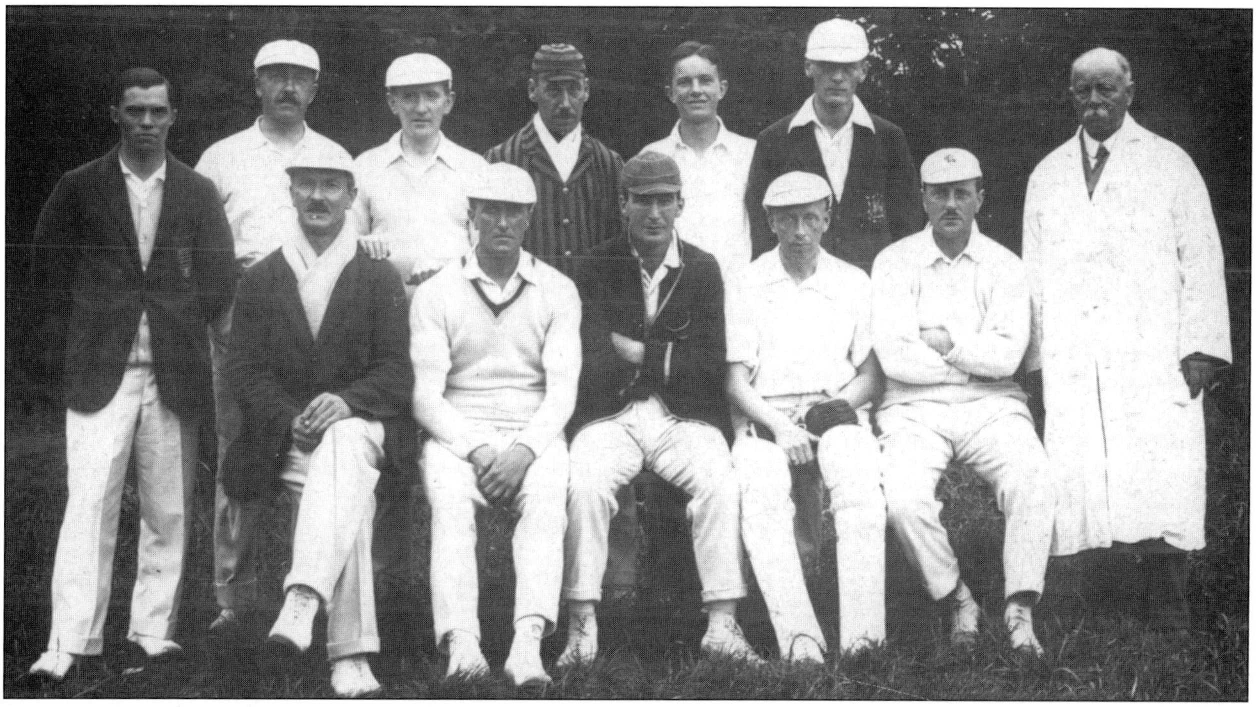

The 1920/30 Ashburton Cricket XI. Photo includes: *A. Whiddon, D.F. Cowls, W.T. Lomax, C. Simpson, H. Edgecombe, A. Goodall, H. Naylor, F.R. Cork, F.C. Bodsman, F. Abbott, H. Arnold.* (WATERS COLLECTION)

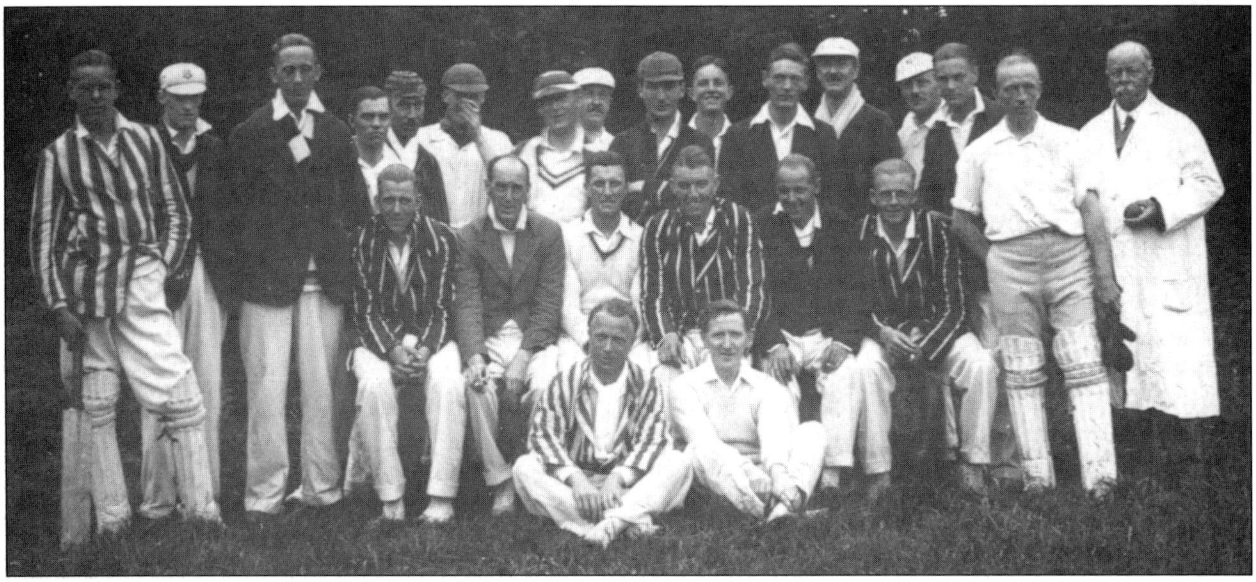

Ashburton XI versus Swansea YMCA, 7 August 1928. (WATERS COLLECTION)

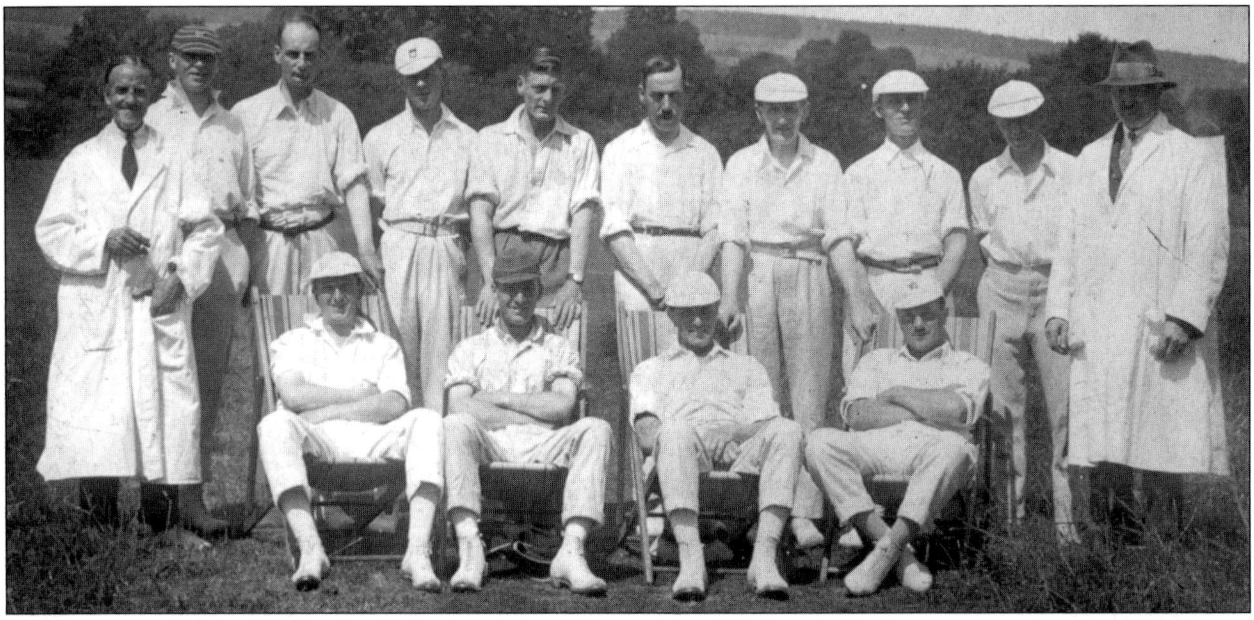

Ashburton XI, 1930s. (WATERS COLLECTION)

Exeter and Torquay in the county structure. Notable victories that season were Buckfastleigh, Exeter St Thomas, Plympton and Plymouth Seconds. Dawlish were bowled out for 21. Among the leading batsmen were Brendan Soper, Leslie Townsend and Geoff Coon, and leading bowlers were Fred Christophers, Alf Goodwin and Andy Dent. However, 1961 was even better – probably the best season in the club's history with only three defeats. Brendan Soper scored 1,000 runs while Fred Christophers, on one occasion, took 7 for 39 all clean bowled against Exeter St Thomas. The highlight of 1963 occurred off the field – the opening of the new pavilion by Brigadier Acland. Money for this project was raised from interest-free loans. The club has a bar with a strong supporters' club.

These years were the most successful for the club and there followed a period of decline. The club was sadly defunct by 1973.

In March 1978, at a meeting at the Victoria Inn, the club was re-formed and received the support of the school. The first match against Dartmouth resulted in a defeat by eight wickets. The newly formed club was made up of young players, the only seniors being Fred Christophers and Colin Rawston. In 1980 the club joined the Coca-Cola Devon League and were league finalists in 1981. On joining the Devon League in 1983 the first match was against Exeter St James at Exeter – Ashburton won by 29 runs. Amongst the younger players were Nigel Bowen, Alan Churchill – top scorer with 69 runs – and Jeremy Christophers. Alan later became club Captain.

Since the re-formation, besides being a finalist in the Coca-Cola League, the club were Mod-Dec League Champions 'E' Division 1985. In 1988 they were runners-up in the same league.

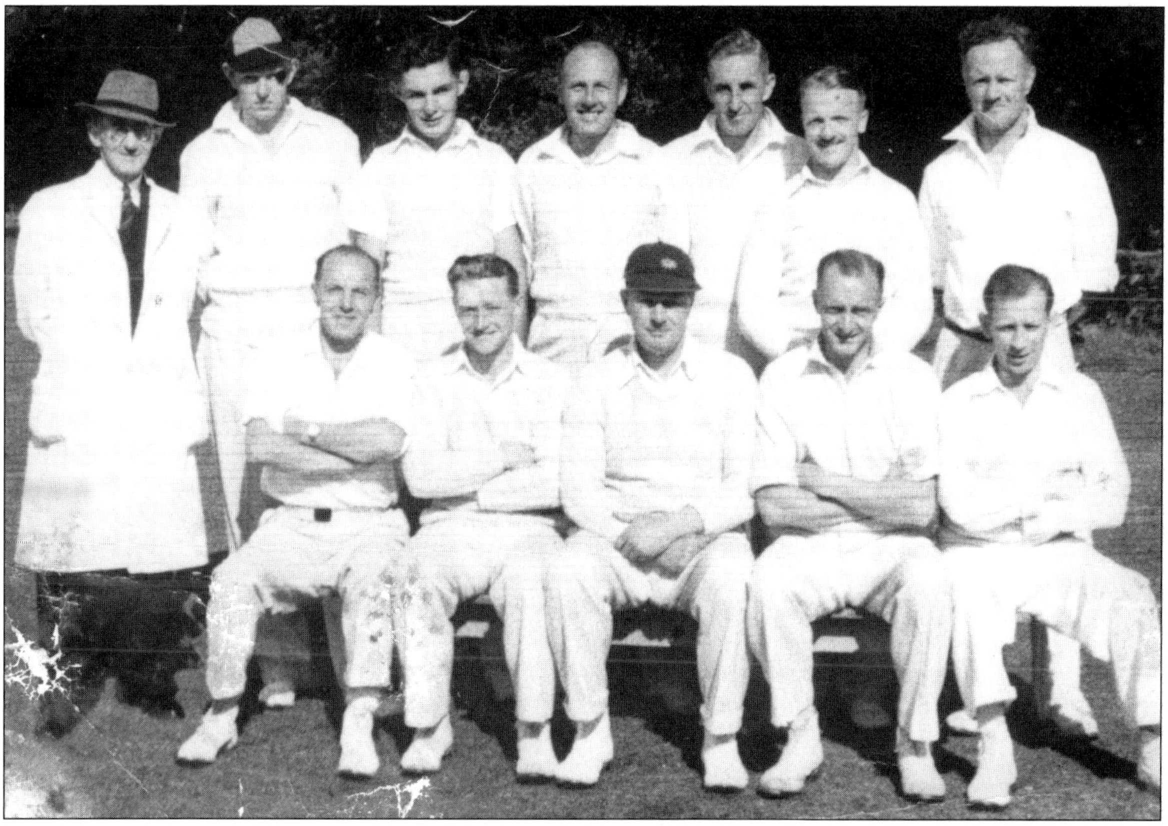

Ashburton Cricket XI, 1950s. Left to right, back row: *Mr Harris (umpire), John Parnell, Fernley Cock, Bill Cotton, Bill Waters, Herbert Owen, Mr Thorogood (head of remand school);* front: *Vernon (Geoff) Coon, Arthur Owen, Tony Caws, Lloyd Matthews, Bert Cowls.*

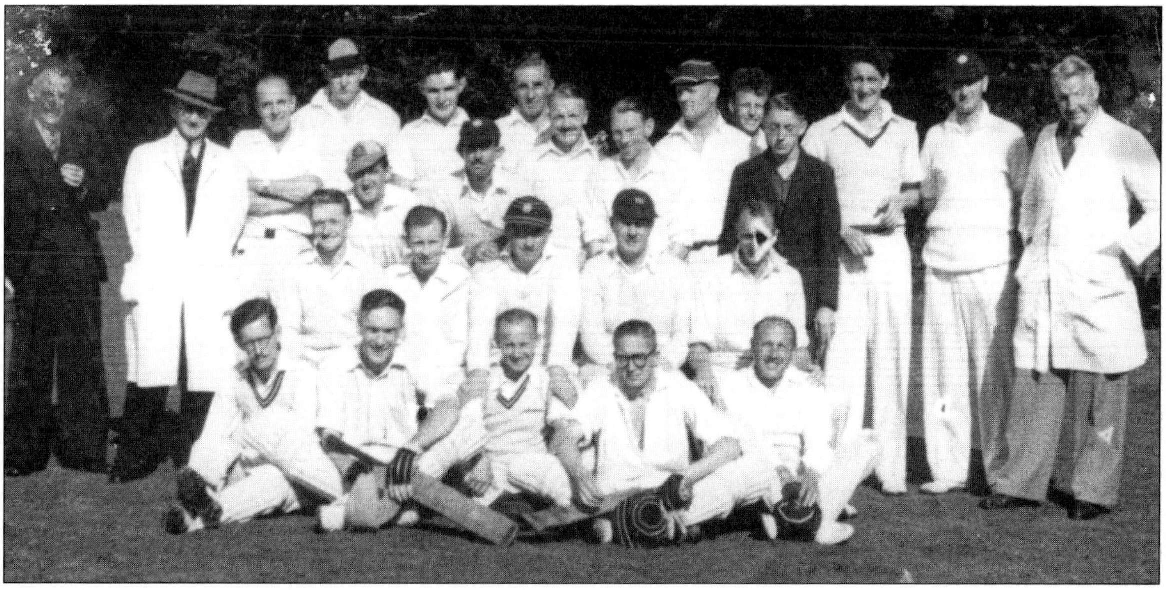

Ashburton Cricket XI, 1950s. (WATERS COLLECTION)

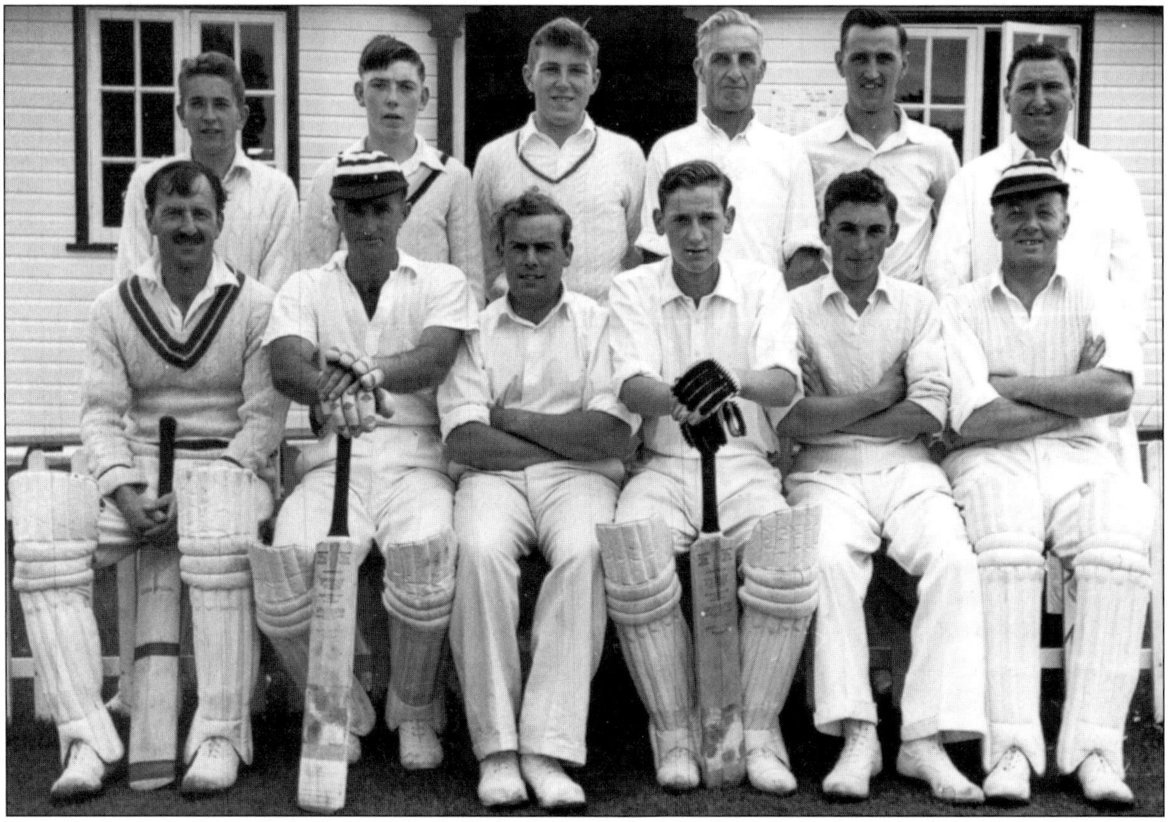

Ashburton cricket team, 1957. Left to right, back row: *Peter Dand, Sid Pugh, Brendan Soper, Bill Walters, John Meyrick, Lewis Russell (umpire);* front: *Andy Dent, Jim Elliot, Leslie Townsend (captain), Dave Pedrick, Bernard Haines, Geoff Coon.* (WATERS COLLECTION)

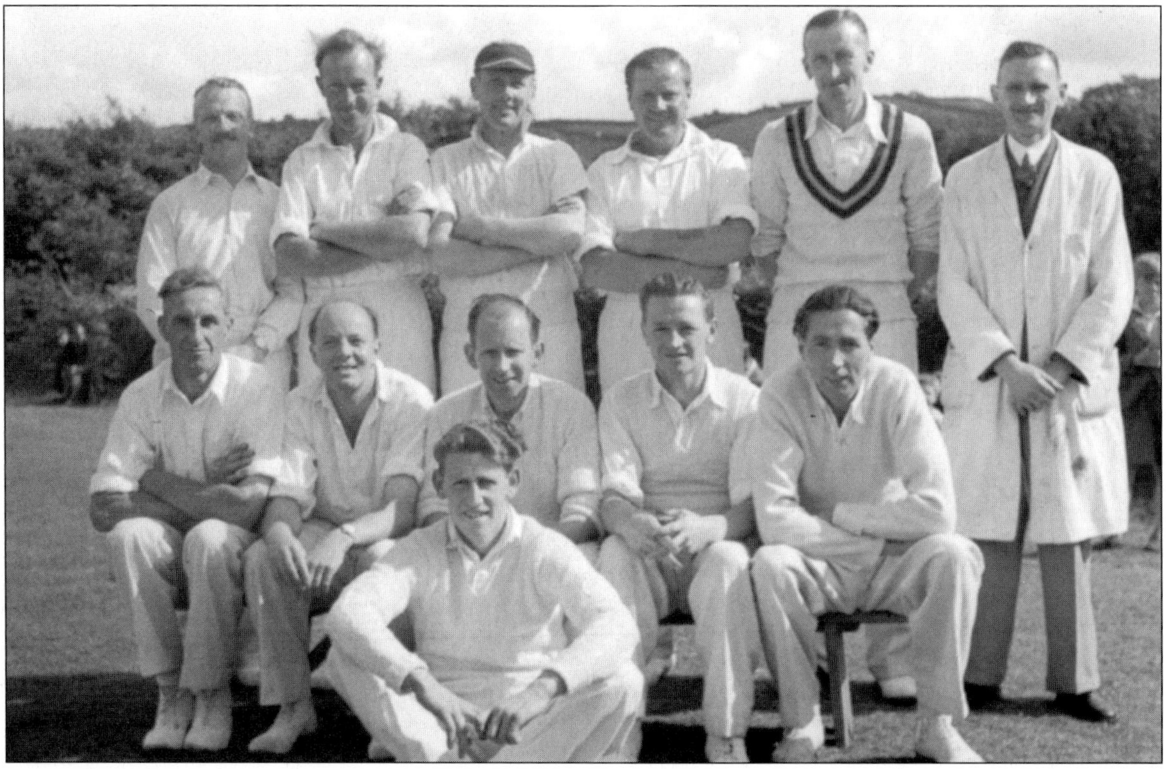

Ashburton Cricket XI, c.1950. Left to right, back row: *Herbert Owen, Cubby Harris, Bill Cotton, Jack Barnett, ? Ashford, Ernie Steer (umpire);* centre: *Bill Waters, Geoff Coon, Bert Cowls, Arthur Owen, Jack Walters;* front: *Alf Goodwin.* (WATERS COLLECTION)

The club has a successful colts team – important to develop young talent for the future success of the club.

Ashburton Football Club

The origins of the football club are lost to us, but it was in existence in 1904 and there are photographs of early teams. Since the Second World War the club has played at a variety of venues. Just after the war matches were played below East End Terrace in a field belonging to Mr Luscombe (now the site of Longpark Estate). In 1950/1 the club played at Linhay Hill, now disappeared into Linhay Quarry. The club then played on the Ashburton Senior School's ground for a number of years. It was the club's ambition to own their own ground in the same way as the cricket club did and in 1980 the club began the long process of obtaining the necessary funds to purchase the site on Chuley Road, which they moved to in that year, and to build new changing rooms. By 1987 the club had received grants totalling £61,525 from the lottery, Teignbridge, the Football League and Ashburton Town Council. The cheque from the lottery was handed over on Sunday 18 May 1987.

Ashburton Football Club has always relied upon local talent to field teams and a glance through the photographs reveals many local names. Perhaps this reliance upon local players, rather than importing and paying footballers from outside the locality, is the reason for success being hard to come by (buying-in talent is not confined to the Premiership!). The club spent one season, just after the Second World War, in the Premier League, but for most of its history has played in the South Devon League Division 1. They were runners up in Division 1 for six successive seasons in the 1960s and in that time reached the semi-final, but sadly never again made the top flight. The club also reached the semi-final of the Herald Cup. Having beaten high-flying Brixham, who at the time were near the top of the Premiership, in the previous round, hopes of reaching the final were high, especially as the semi-final was against Kingsteignton, who were struggling in the league. It was not to be, however; Kingsteignton won 3-2. The romance of 'giant killing' is not confined to the FA Cup. Pride and ambition are just as strongly felt at all levels of the game.

In more recent years the club has won the Devon Intermediate and Ronald cups and, having seen relegation to Divisions 2 and 3, is now in Division 1. Nonetheless a good football club is more than just what happens on the pitch, it is a social activity too. Ashburton have always received good support off the pitch as well as on it. Social functions are always well attended – guest speakers often comment on the support the club has at these occasions. The club has been fortunate throughout the years in having good

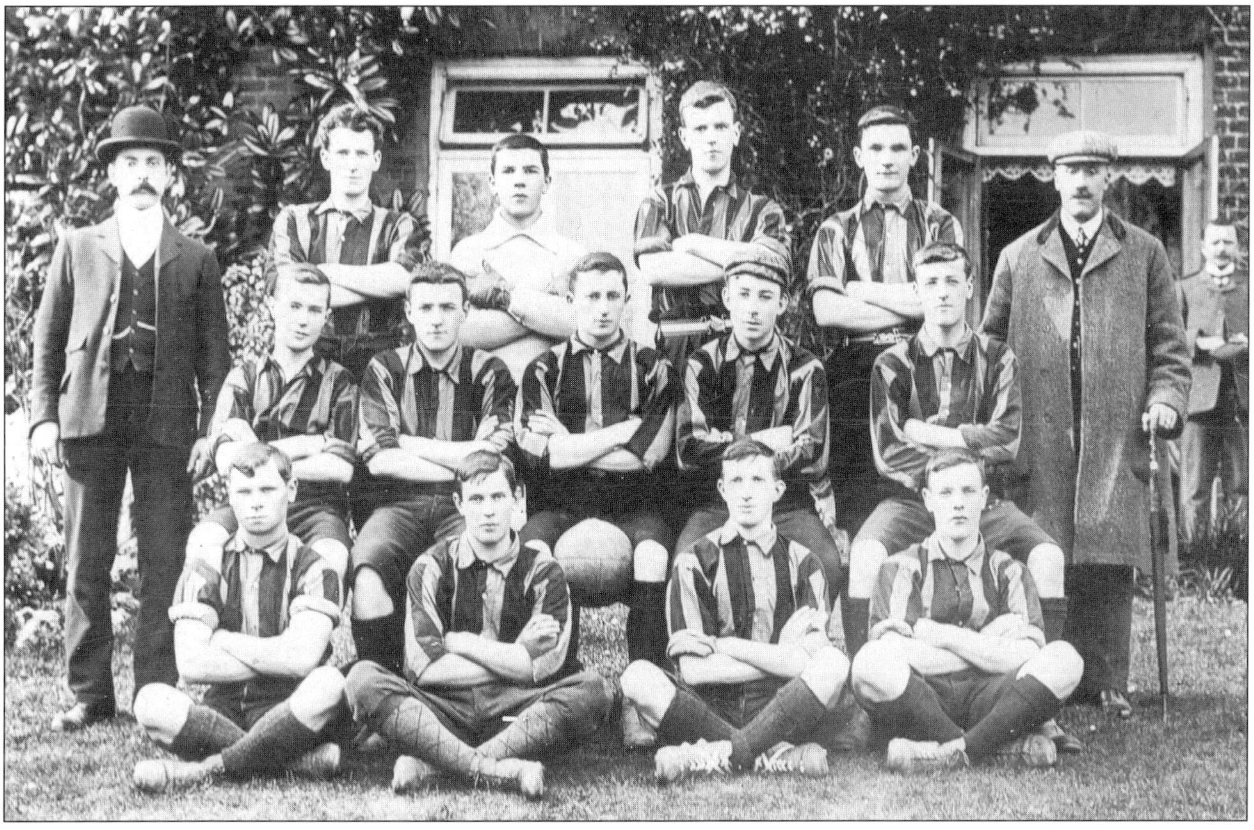

Football Team, 1904–05. Left to right, back row: *Bill Lee (treasurer), W. Waights (vice-captain), C.N. Pascoe, G. Mortimer, A.T. Pascoe, W.C. Paddy Bristol;* centre: *W. Petrie, W.J. Nicks (hon. secretary), C.C. Salisbury (captain), F. Cleaver, E. Nicks;* front: *W. Routley, T.E. Gale, E. Gerry, W. Pengilley.* (PETE WEBB COLLECTION)

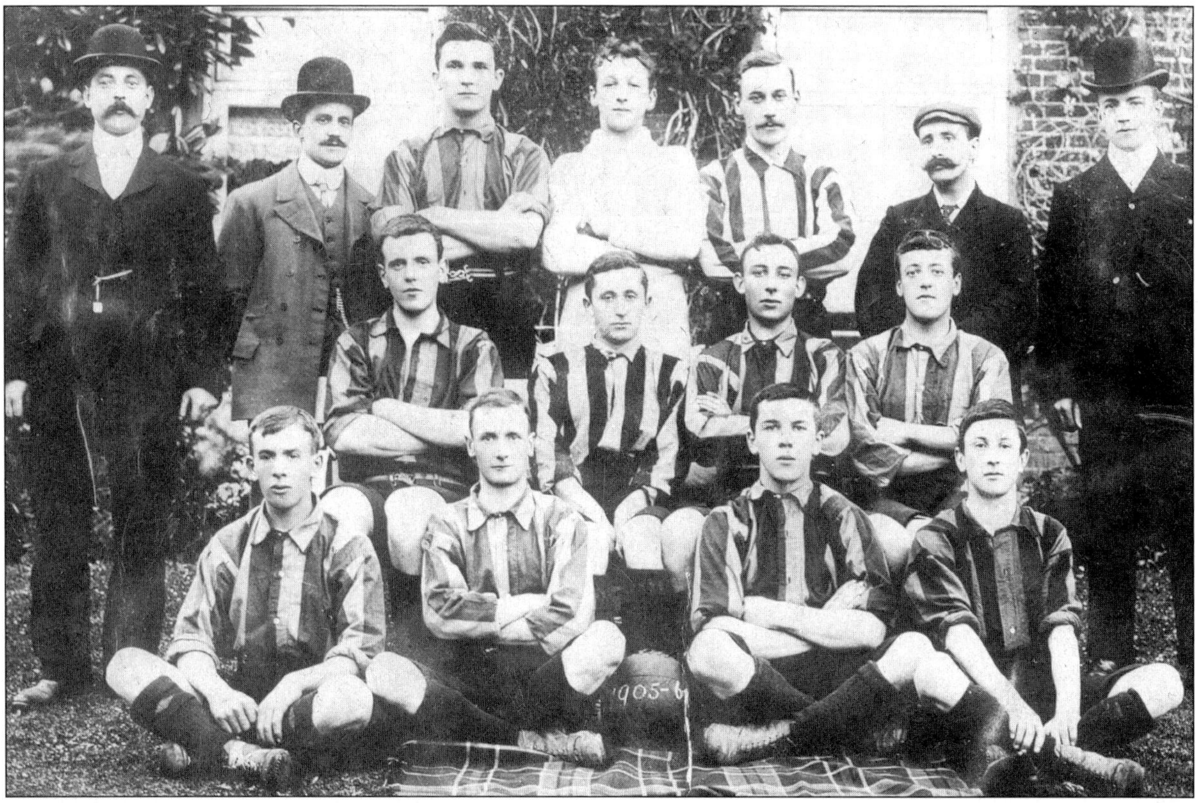

Football Team, 1905–06. Left to right, back row: *H.E. Lee (treasurer), H.E.R. Mallett, A. Pascoe, F. Satterley, W.T. Lomax, C. Woods, J. Wicks;* centre: *G. Mortimore, C.C. Salisbury (captain), F. Cleaver, E. Nicks (vice-captain);* front: *M. Campion, L.W. Messant, C. Pascoe, N. Dent.* (PETE WEBB COLLECTION)

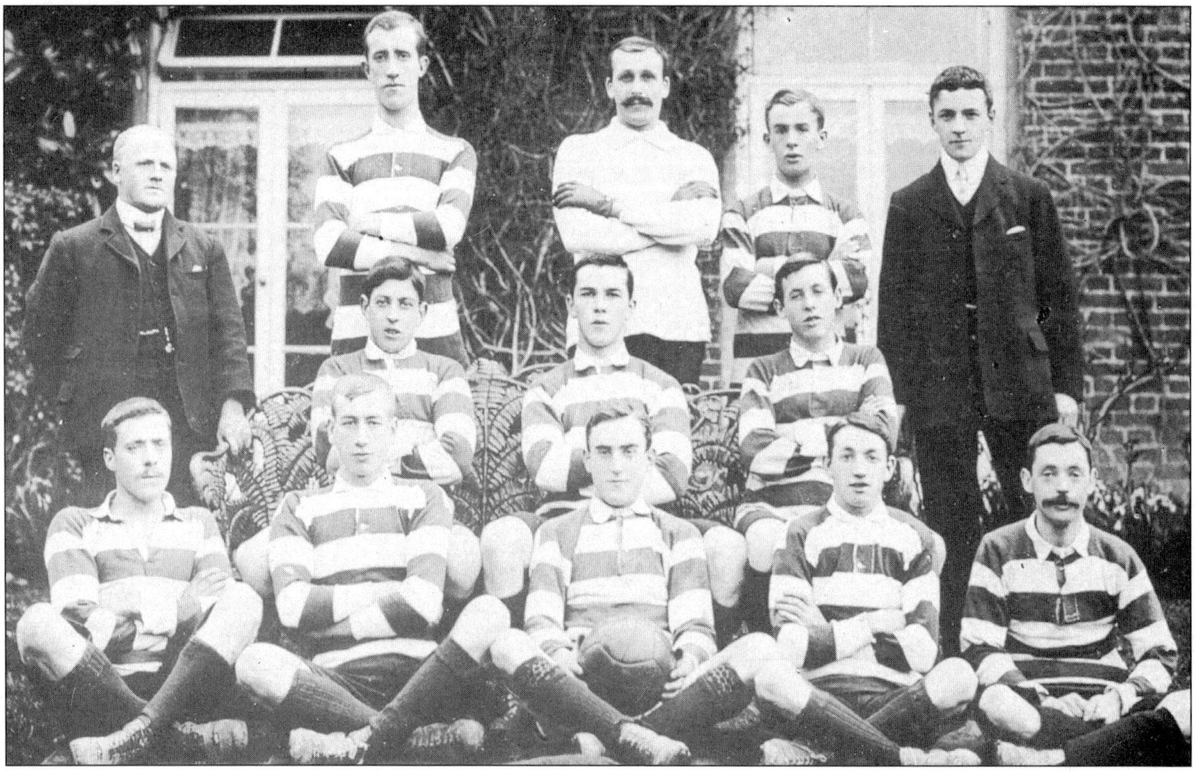

Football Team (reserves), 1907–08. Left to right, back row: *J. Pomeroy, J. Conneybear, W. Peachey (captain), H. Campion (vice-captain), W.J. Hicks (hon. sec.);* centre: *F. Hewings, C. Pascoe, A. Satterley;* front: *G. Crocker, W. Wotton, L. Leveridge, W. Gerry, C. Lone.* (PETE WEBB COLLECTION)

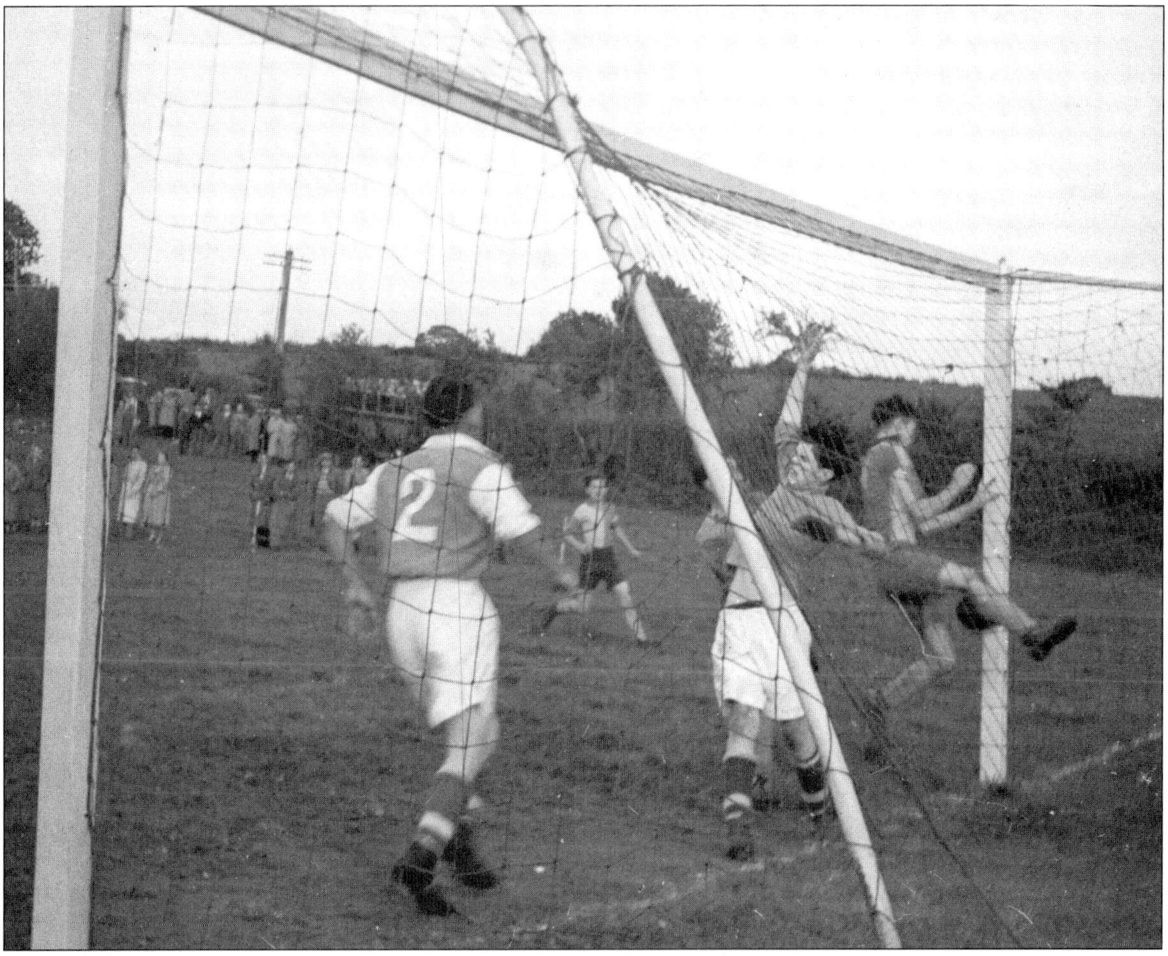

Ashburton, playing away, score against Chudleigh in the 1960s. Paddy Harding is in the centre of the picture with dark shorts. (PADDY HARDING COLLECTION)

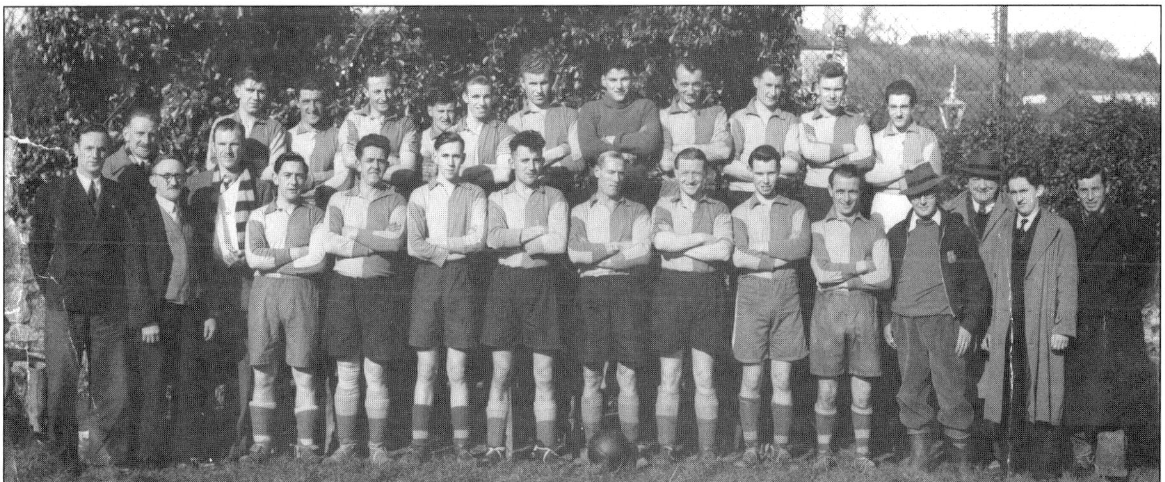

Ashburton Football Club, spring 1955. Left to right, back row: *Tubby Horsman, Garth Grose, Eric Livermore, Bill Campion, Ray Distin, Colin Bowden, Geoff Bassett, Jim Elliot, Tony Thorn, Peter Greenwood, Bill Webb;* front: *Johnny Worthington, Eric Foxworthy, Peter Jennings, Paddy Harding, Jacky Porter, Arthur Owen, David Eales, David Knowles.* Others, on left: *Bill Wright, Jim Morrish, Mr Ruth* (with glasses), *Derek James;* on right: *Charlie Harding, Mr Hayward, Arthur Ruth, Reg Lorrimer.*

(PADDY HARDING COLLECTION)

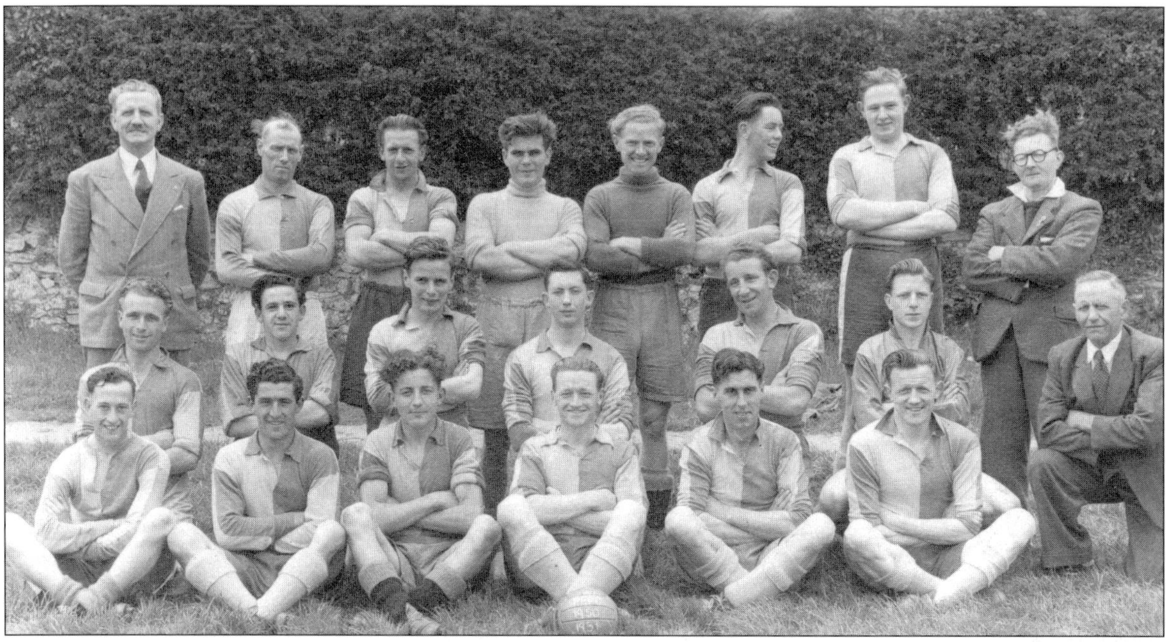

Football Team, 1949/50. Left to right, back row: *Mr Underhill (chairman), J. Porter, J. Desland, J. Fowler, J. Warren, J. Bray, J. Parnell, C. Harding (committee);* centre: *D. Knowles, M. Endacott, Mac Pengilly, R. Laity, H. Knowles, T. Woodgate;* front: *R. Foot, G. Grose, P. Harding, A. Owens, R. Cummings, J. Underhill, B. Pengilly (committee).* (GARTH GROSE COLLECTION)

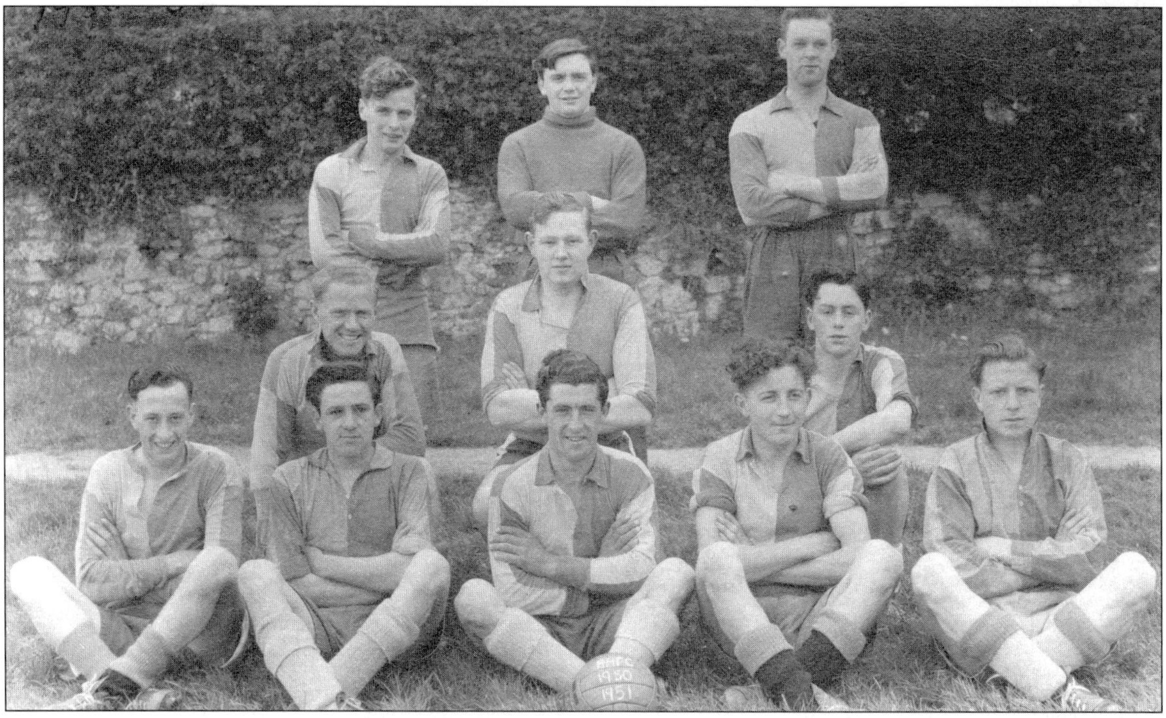

Ashburton Football Team, 1950/1. Left to right, back row: *Mac Pengilly, C. Dowric, R. Webber;* centre: *J. Warren, J. Parnell, J. Bray;* front: *R. Foot, M. Endacott, G. Grose, P. Harding, T. Woodgate.* (GARTH GROSE COLLECTION)

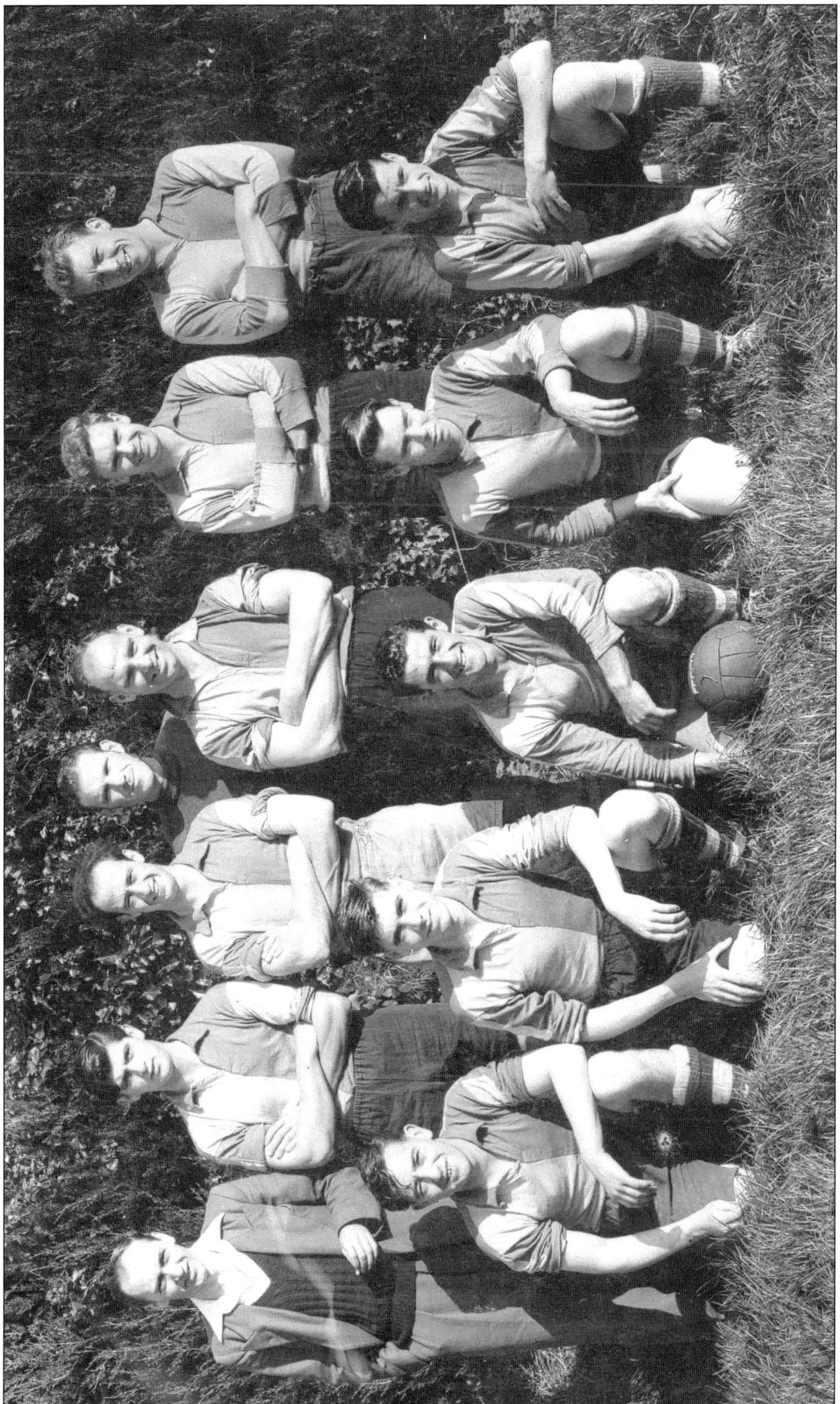

Ashburton Football Team, 1951. Left to right, back row: P. Dennis, T. Baker, R. Foot, D. Dodd, J. Brixey, P. Greenwood, H. Study; front: J. Worthington, M. Eastleigh, G. Grose, D. Eales, T. Thorn.

(GARTH GROSE COLLECTION)

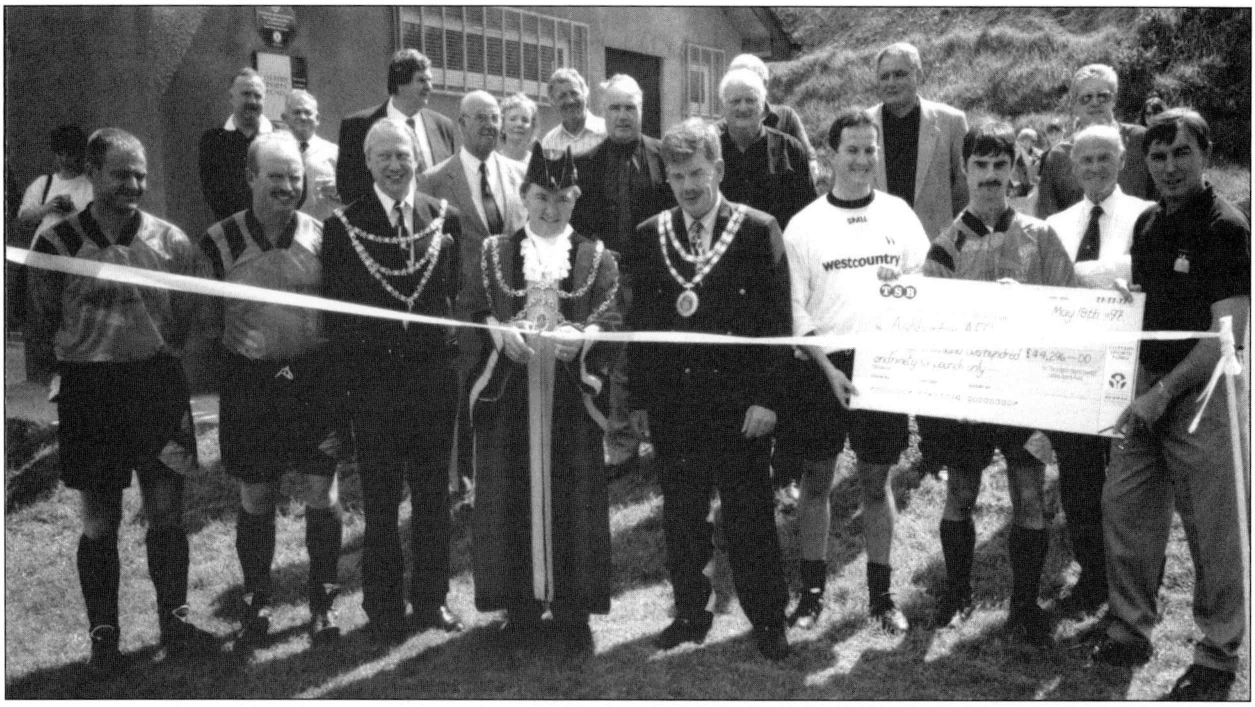

Opening of new changing rooms funded with lottery money, May 1987. Portreeve Ken Connett cuts the tape with Bailiff John Keeling and Mayor Brian Miller. Photo also includes: *Vernon Coon (referee), Roger Parker, Stuart and Pam Brooking, Paddy Harding, Graham Westlake, Peter Wotton, Ray Ford, Adrian Daw, Martin Brooks, Dave White, John K., Ken K., Brian M., Mark Tyler (Westward TV), Andrew Hislop, Cecil Woods, John Brixey.* (PETE WEBB)

secretaries: Paddy Harding, who played for the club for 40 years, from after the war until 1986; Adrian Daw, too, played for the club until into his fifties, 36 years in all. Now (2004) the club has Tony Lewis who, it appears, is following the high standards set by his predecessors. Donald Distin runs the youth team.

In any club there are many jobs which have to be done if the team on the field is to be supported: Vernon Coon, Treasurer for 26 years; Jonny Brixey, Chairman for 16 years; also hard-working groundsman Dave White. Over the years help could always be counted on from the Teagues, Distins, Wottons, Hardings and Daws, not to mention Cecil Woods who kept the changing rooms spick and span. Dave White the groundsman has the sponsorship of Fine Turf. The club has been fortunate in having sponsors such as the Exeter Inn, Glendinnings, Ashburton Motor Works, the town lottery and local businessmen.

The ethos of the club is summed up in the words of Garth Grose, who played for many years. 'We enjoyed our football, of course we wanted to win, but it was the friendships we all made which make Ashburton Football Club what it is.'

CHAPTER 19

Personalities

All places have people who are well known for one reason or another; Ashburton is no exception. This is a portrait gallery of some of these folk.

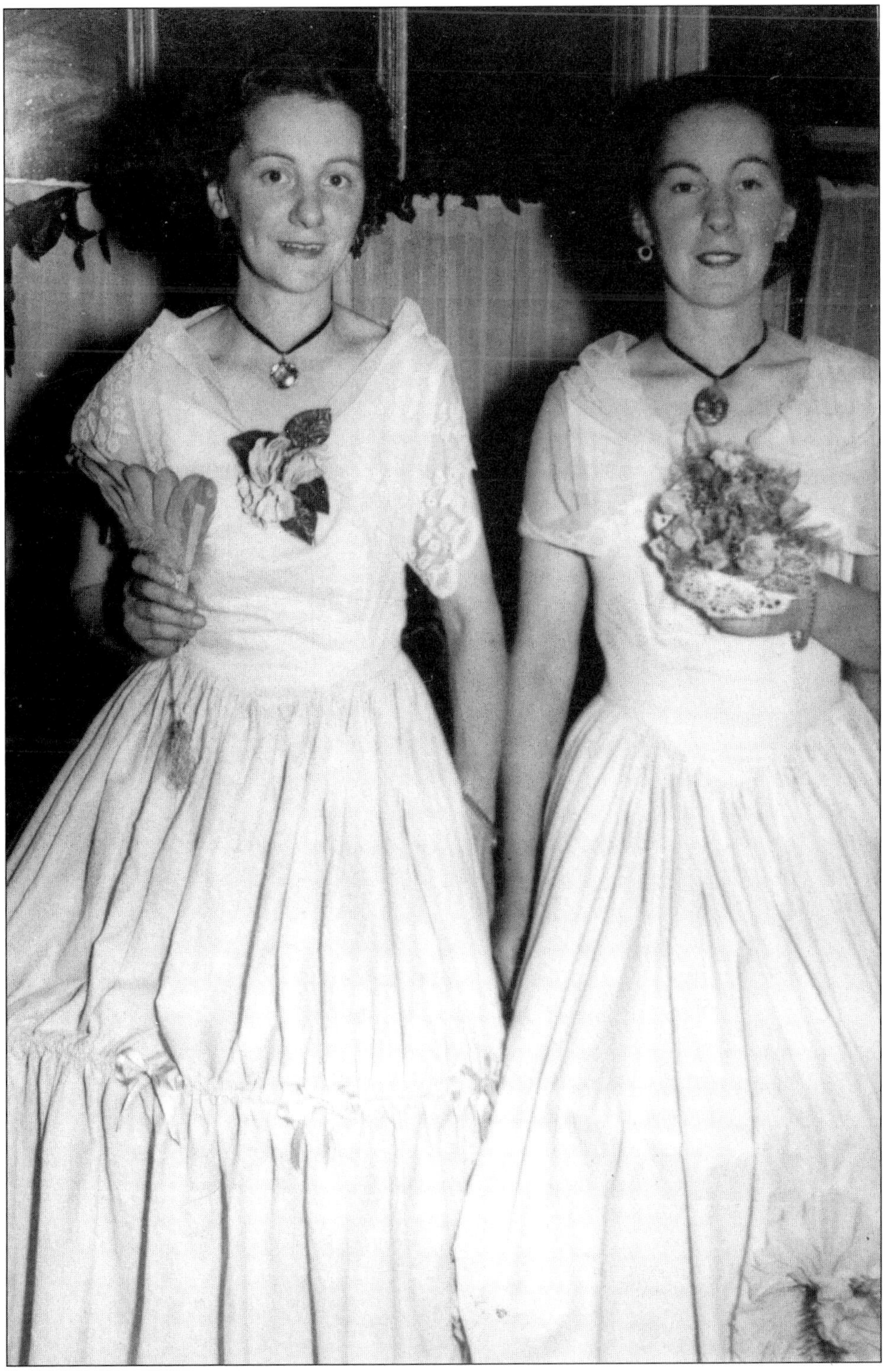

Margery Vooght and Lillian Long (née Vooght), c.1950. (HENRY LANG COLLECTION)

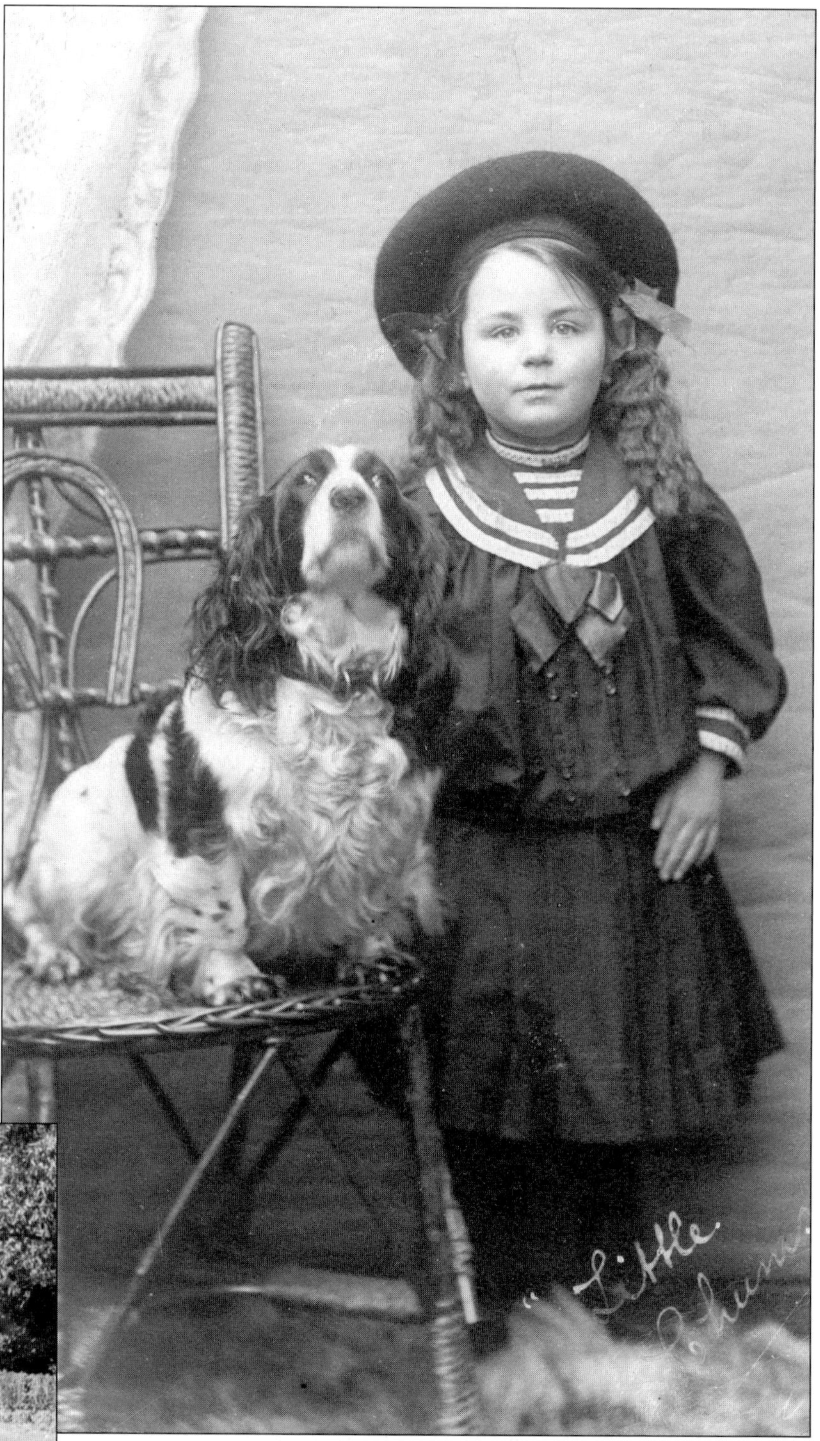

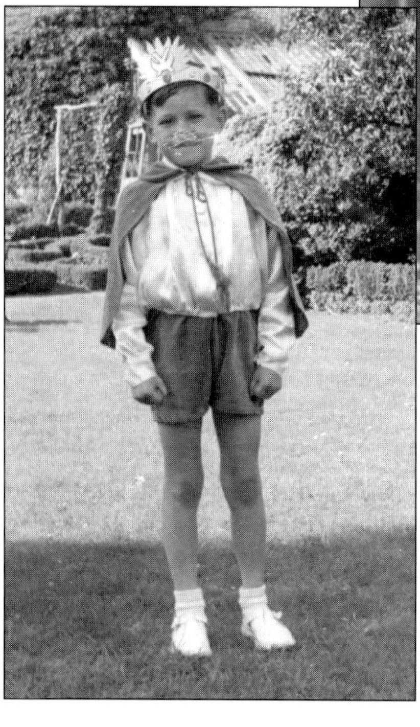

Above: *Lillian Maud Eales (later Smith), c.1905.*
(AMY SATTERLEY; PAT ORSMAN COLLECTION)

Left: *Adrian Daw, 1950.* (PAT ORSMAN COLLECTION)

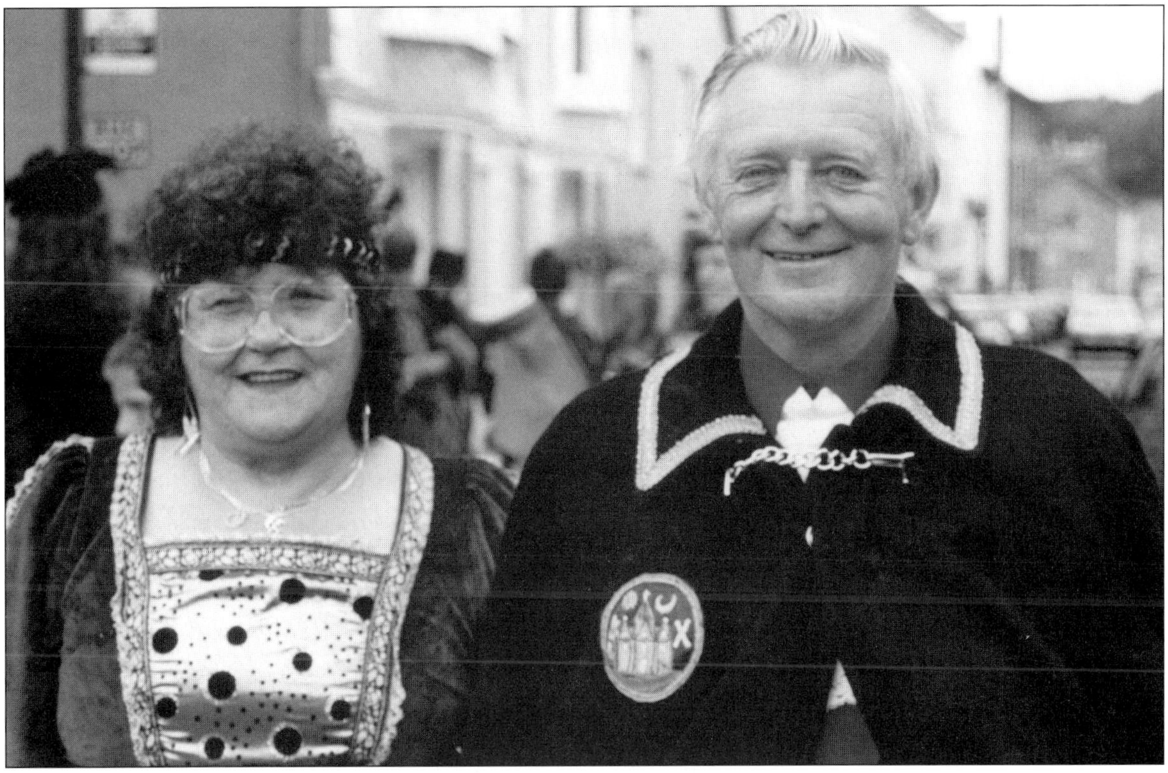

Tony and Barbara Pugh at the 1995 Ale Tasting and Bread Weighing ceremony. Tony was Town Crier for over 25 years and retired recently (2004). (JOHN MITCHELL)

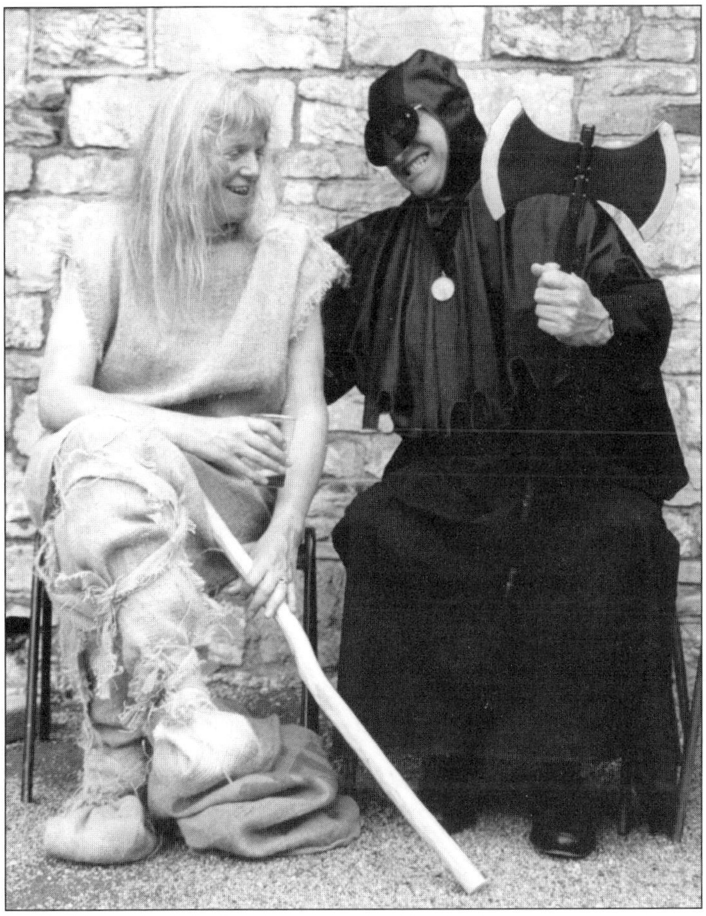

Linda Germon and Bill Ward dressed for the Ale Tasting and Bread Weighing ceremony, 1995. (JOHN MITCHELL)

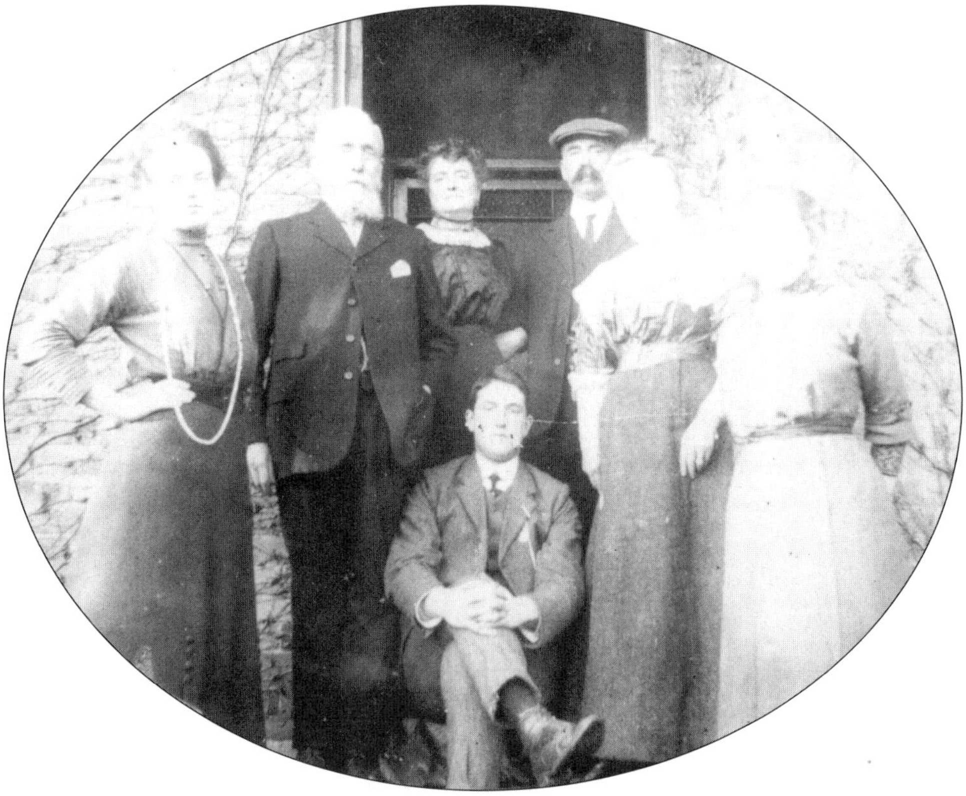

John Fitz Baker (with moustache and cloth cap*) and family, Christmas 1911. Picture from a scrap book kept by him and now in Ashburton Museum.*

(ASHBURTON MUSEUM)

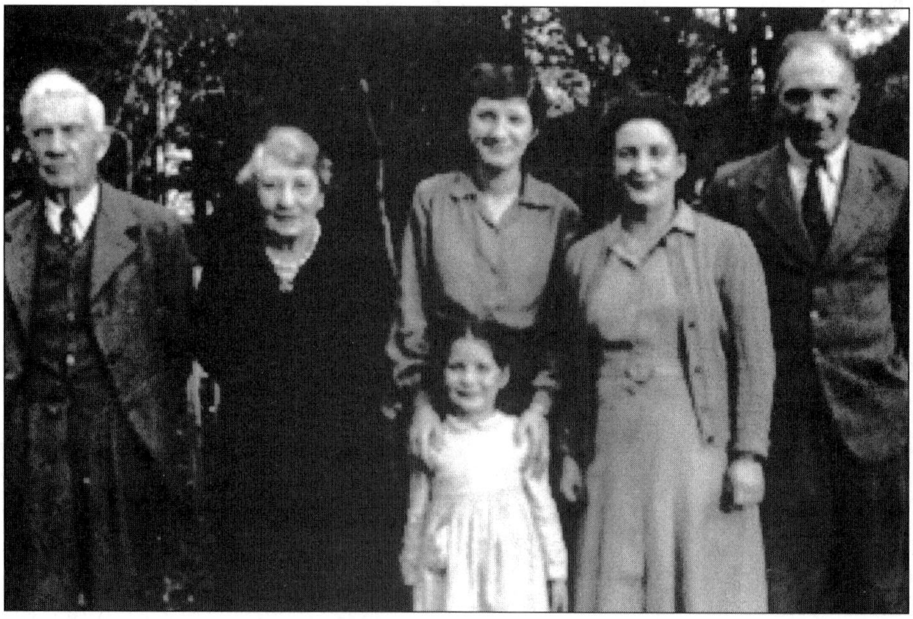

The Grose family at Owlacombe Cottages, c.1947. Back row, left to right: *Pharoah Grose, Annie Grose, Shirley Grose (later Bates), Joan Grose, Hubert Grose;* front: *Joan's daughter, Judy.*

(GARTH GROSE COLLECTION)

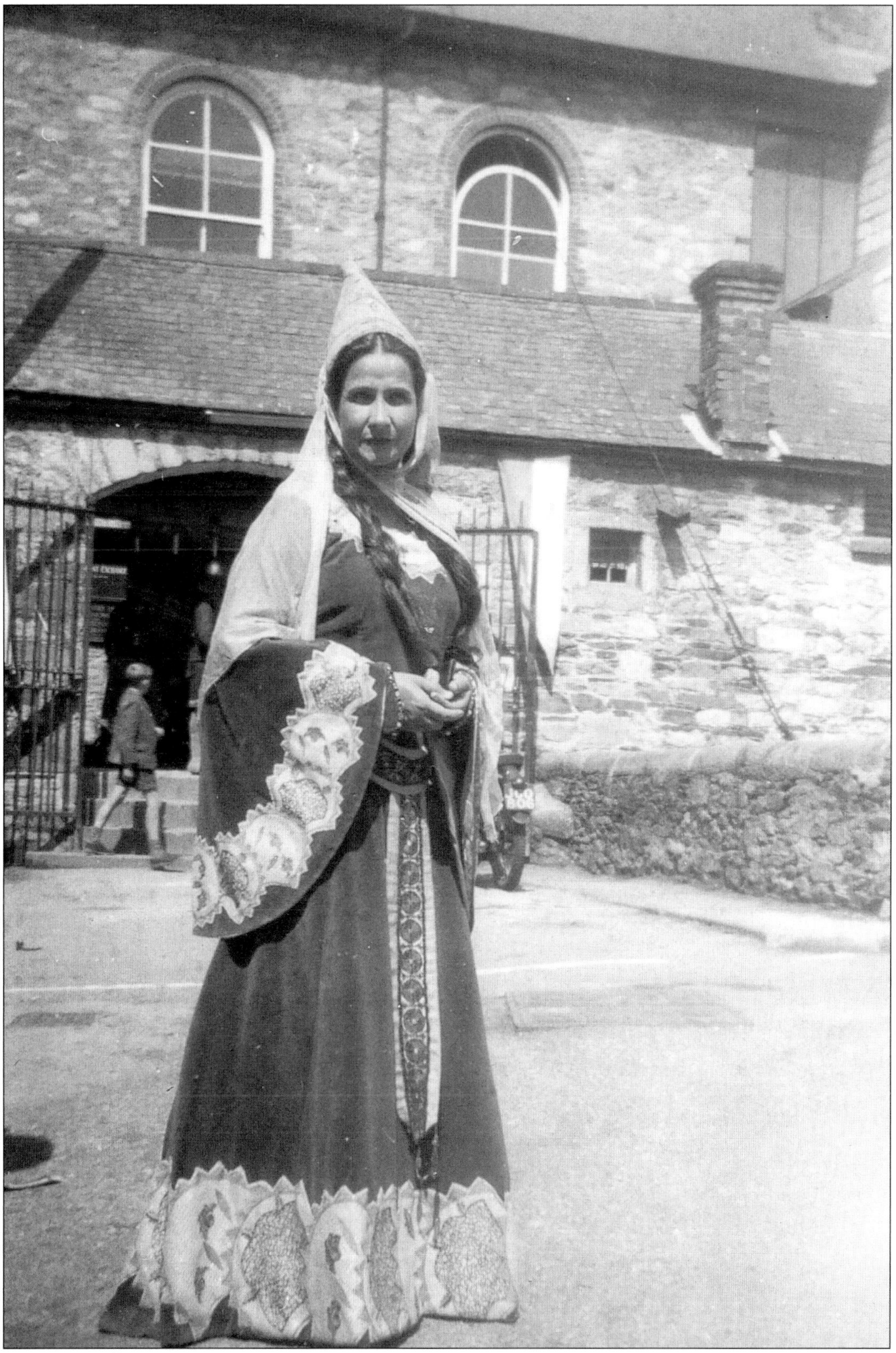

Doreen (Dee) Thurley in medieval costume in 1957 outside the Town Hall. (PETE WEBB COLLECTION)

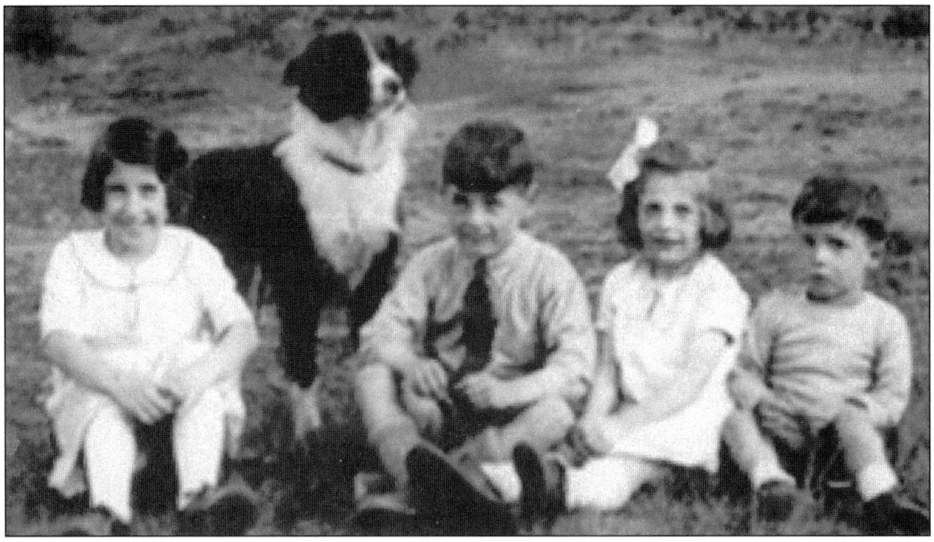

The Grose children: Jill, Alan, Joyce and Garth with Ted the dog, c.1940.
(GARTH GROSE COLLECTION)

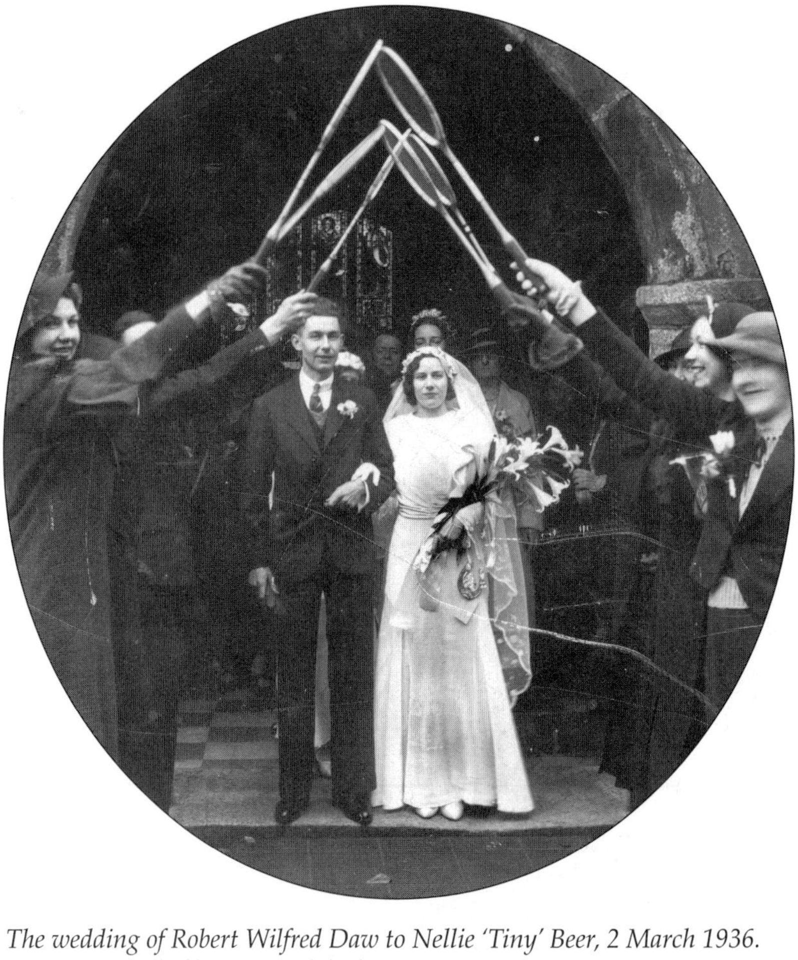

The wedding of Robert Wilfred Daw to Nellie 'Tiny' Beer, 2 March 1936.
Note the guard of honour with badminton racquets. (PAT ORSMAN COLLECTION)

✥ CHAPTER 20 ✥

Stan Gill, Custodian of the Past, 1914–86

The last chapter of *The Book of Ashburton* is dedicated to Stan Gill, who contributed much to conserve the history of the place. Included in this chapter are a series of photographs which Stan took and used as a quiz to see how well people knew their town. Have a go at recognising these pictures. For those unable to visit Ashburton and to enlighten those who can find these unusual views, the answers are available on p.160.

Born in Ashburton in 1914, Stan Gill was an apprentice carpenter-joiner. He worked for Newton Abbot RDC until retirement in 1974. His antiquarian interests and his knowledge of and collections of historic and prehistoric artefacts were vast.

He was a founder member of both the Ashburton and District Amenity Society and of Ashburton Museum. By his own hand, in his spare time over a six-month period, he restored the former brush factory near the Bull Ring which is now the home of the museum. He had previously put together a collection of old artefacts in both the tower room of St Lawrence Chapel and, when it outgrew that, in the old blacksmith's workshop behind the chapel.

He was a staunch member of the St John Ambulance Association from June 1927 until June 1977. He was made a serving brother of St John on the 16 July 1959 and spent many months renovating the present hall. He was a great collector of flints picked up on his beloved Dartmoor during walks.

He died on 2 January 1986.

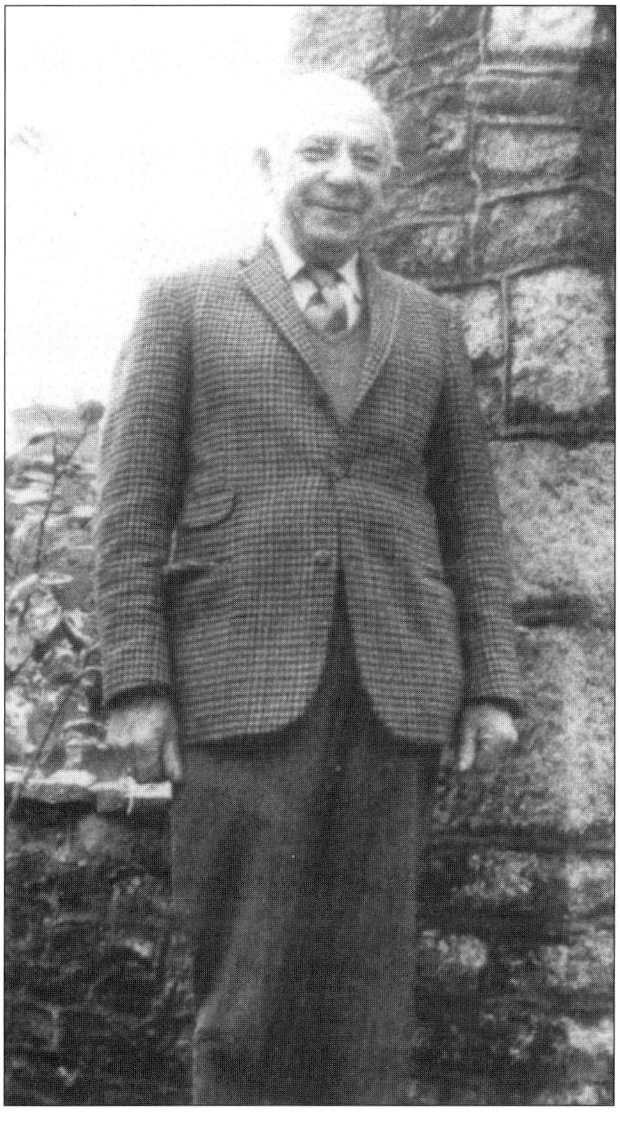

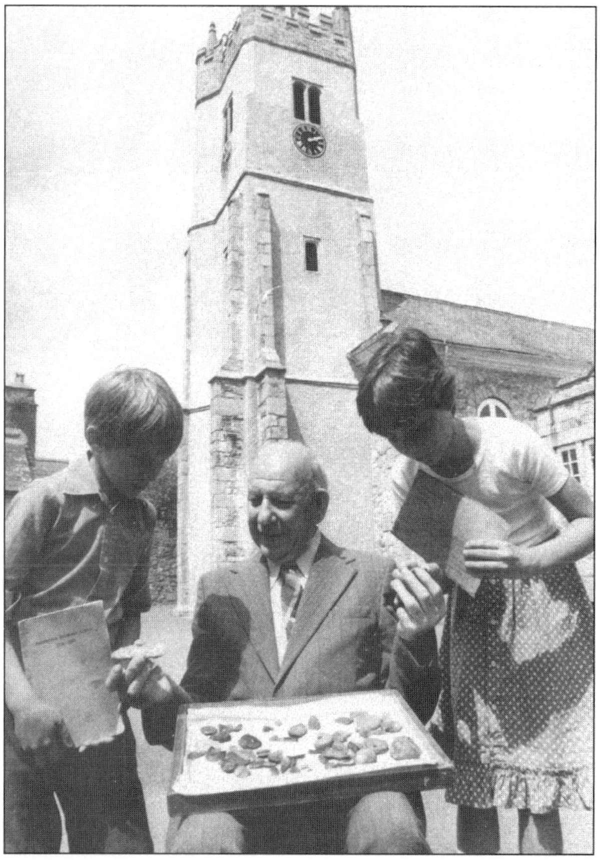

Above and left: *Stan Gill.* (WENDY GILL COLLECTION)

How well do you know Ashburton? Can you identify the following 17 places?

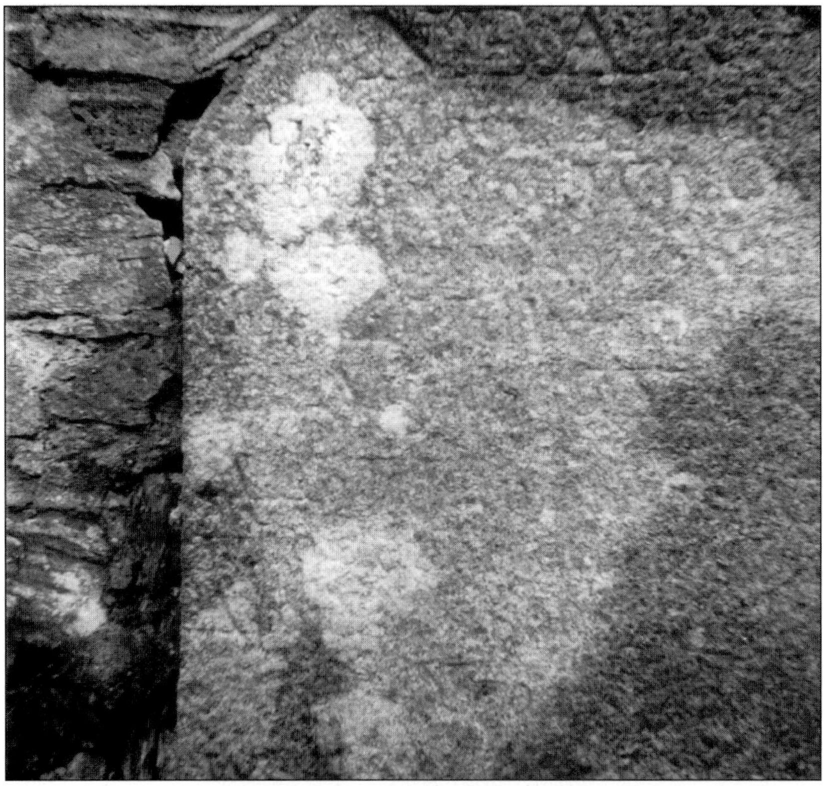

1.

2.

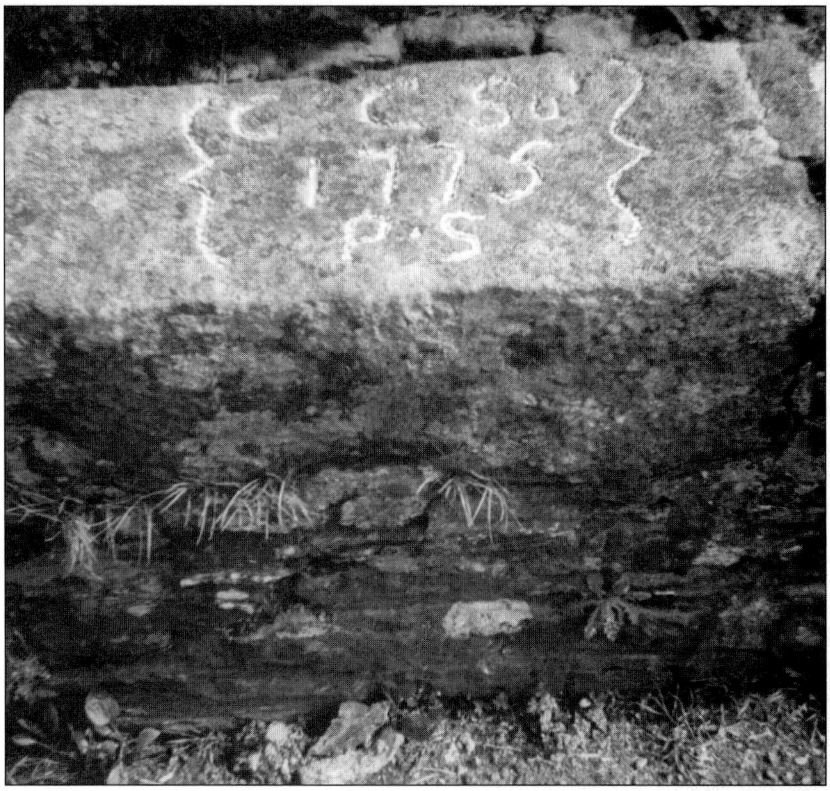

3.

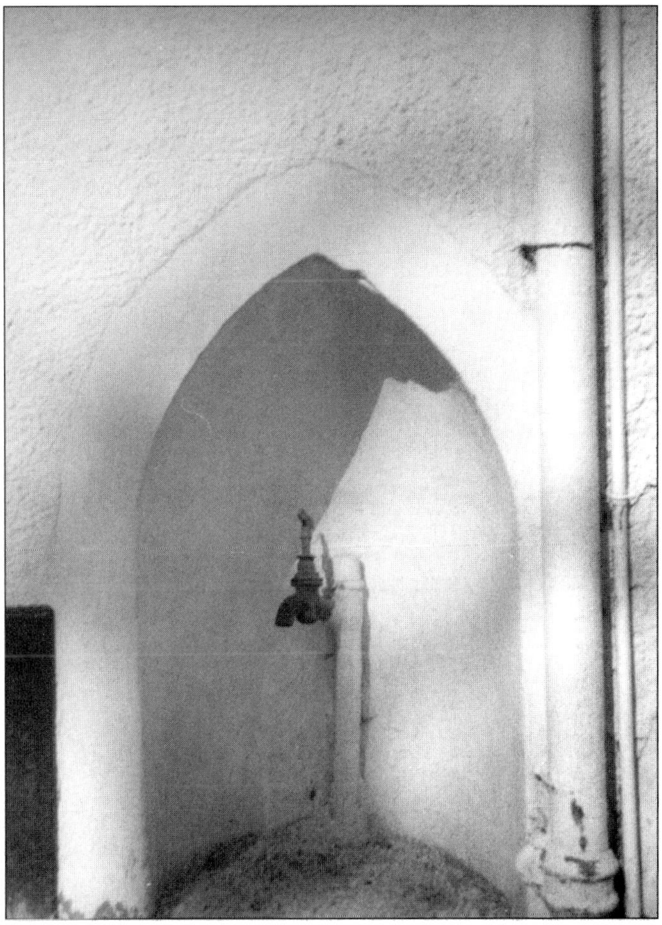

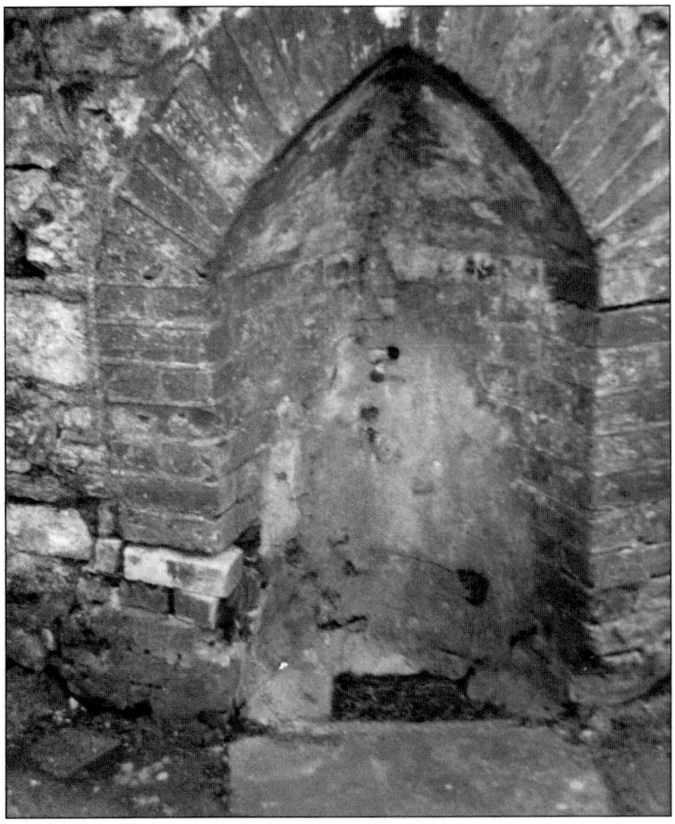

4.

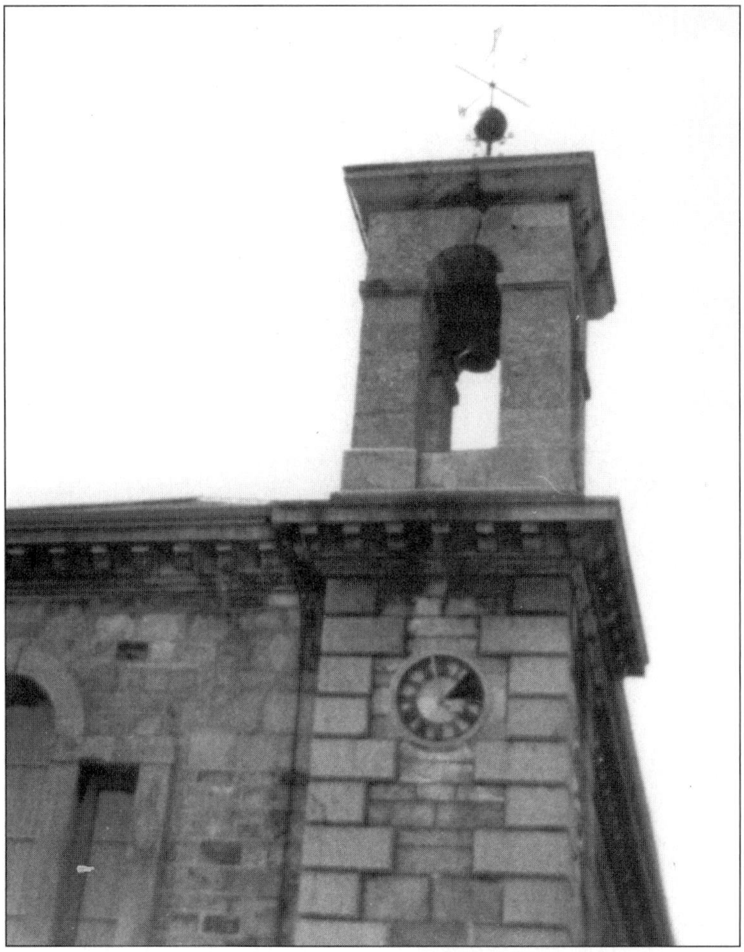

5.

6.

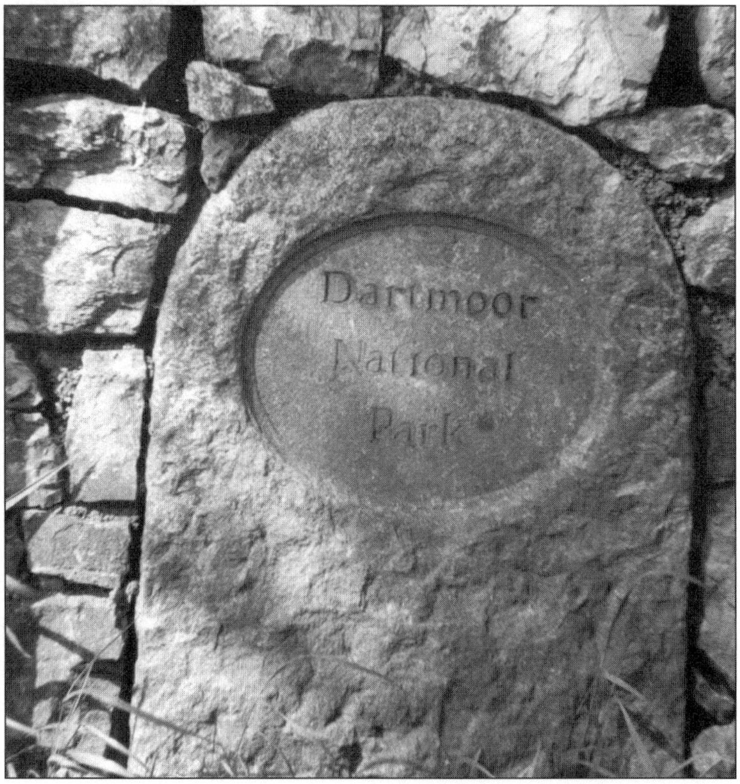

7.

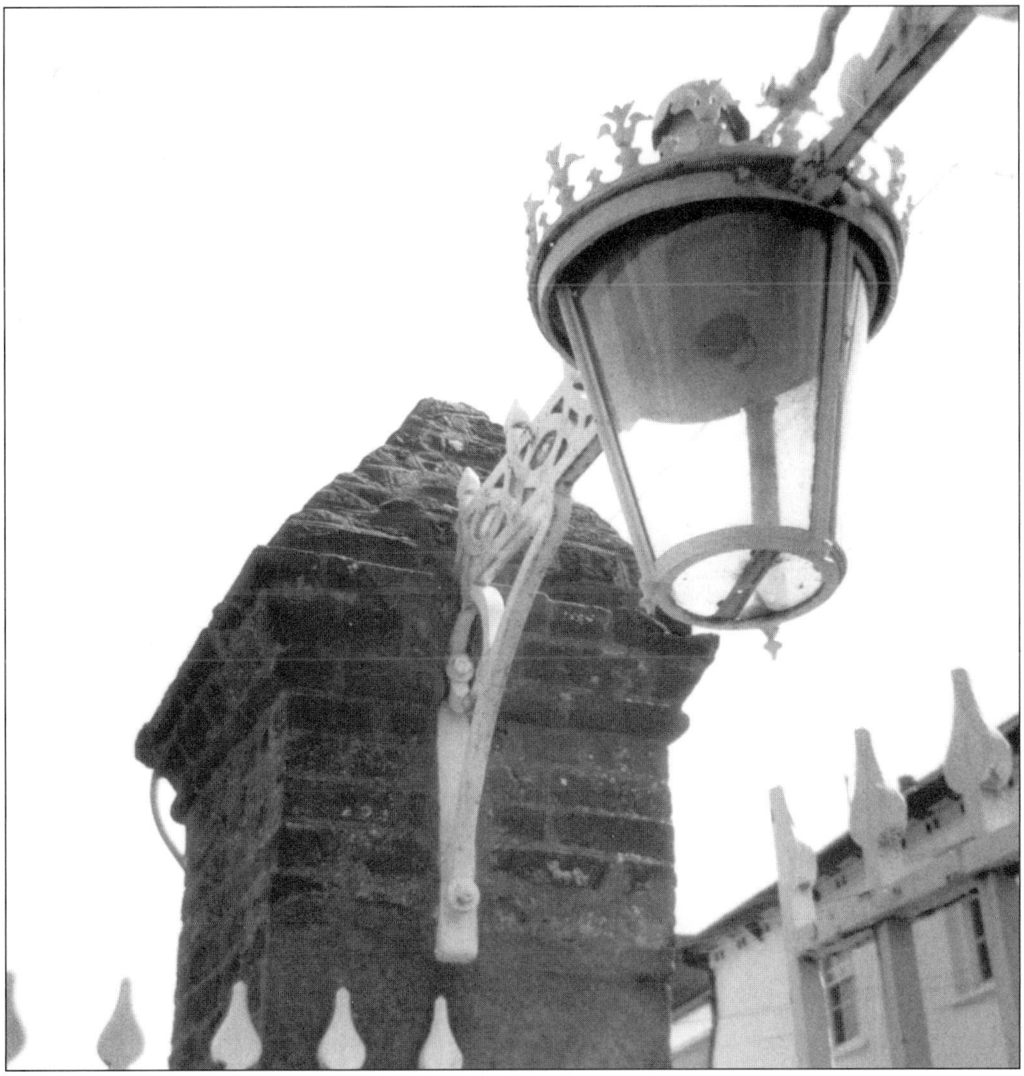

8.

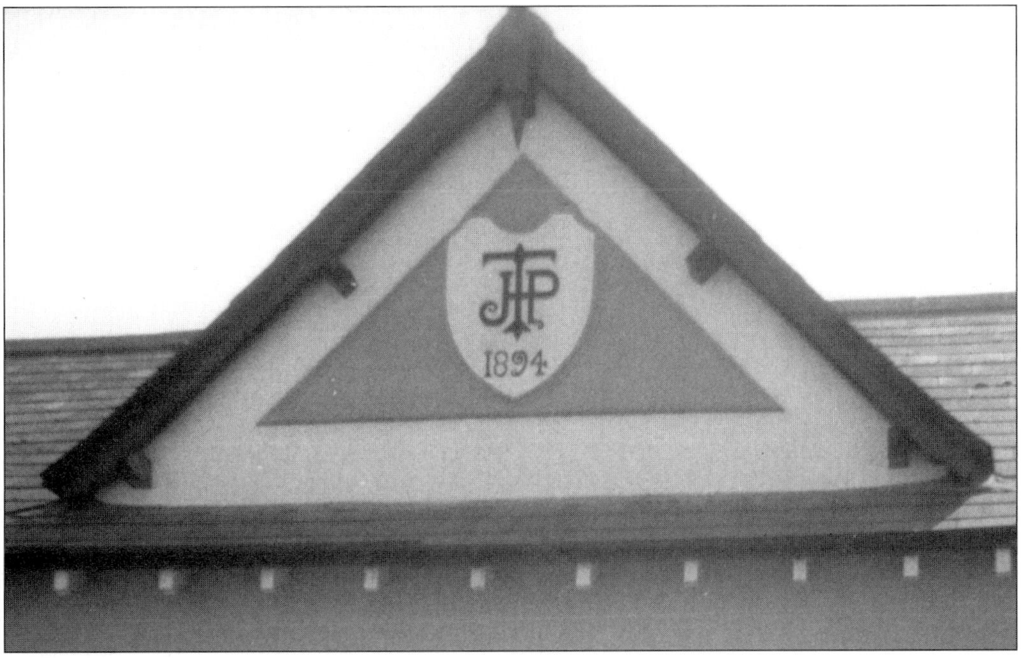

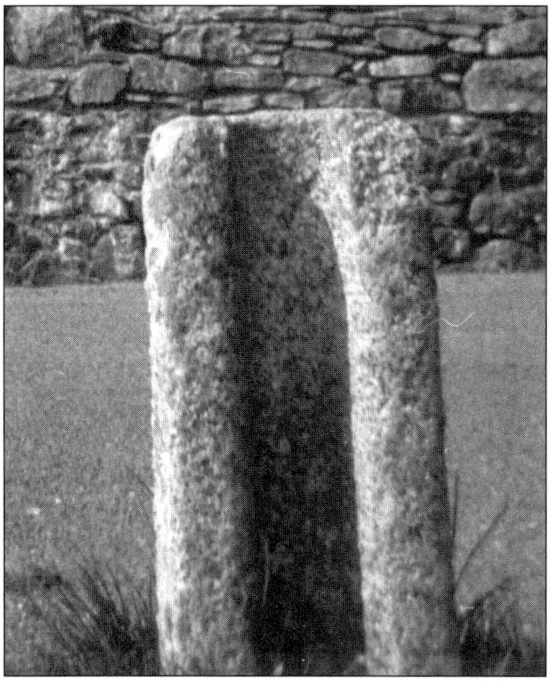

9.

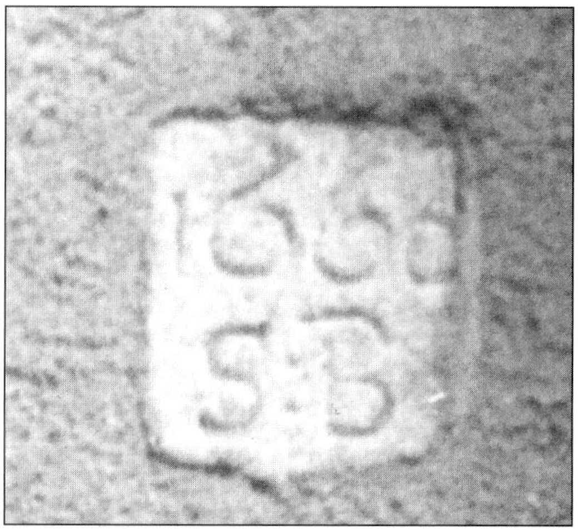

10.

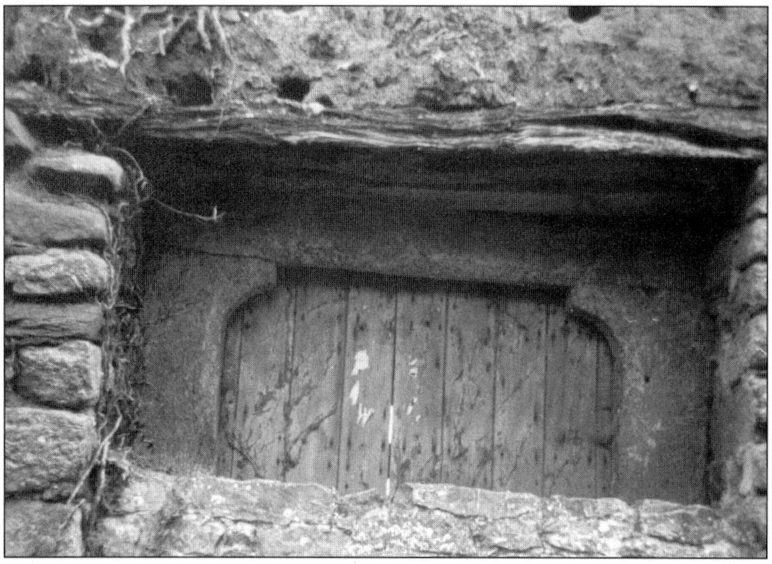

11.

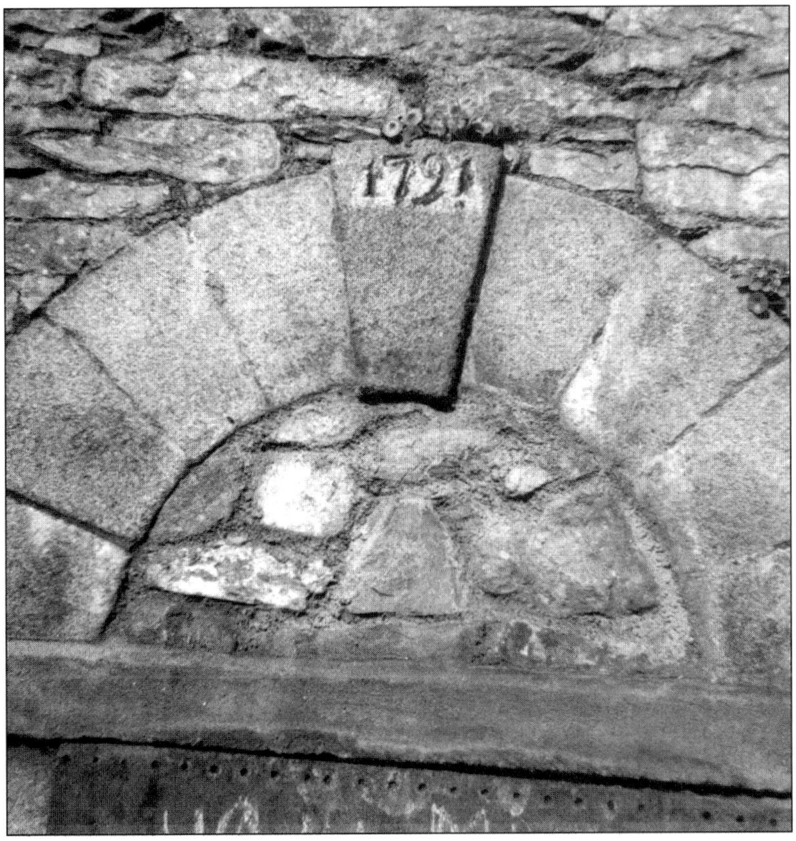

12.

13.

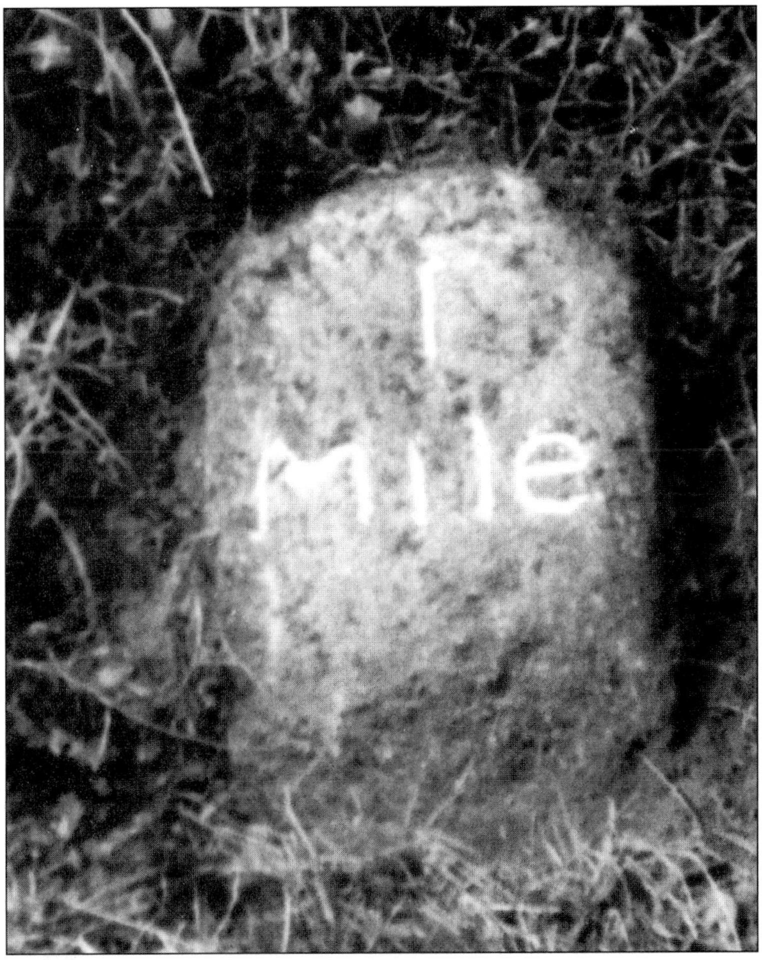

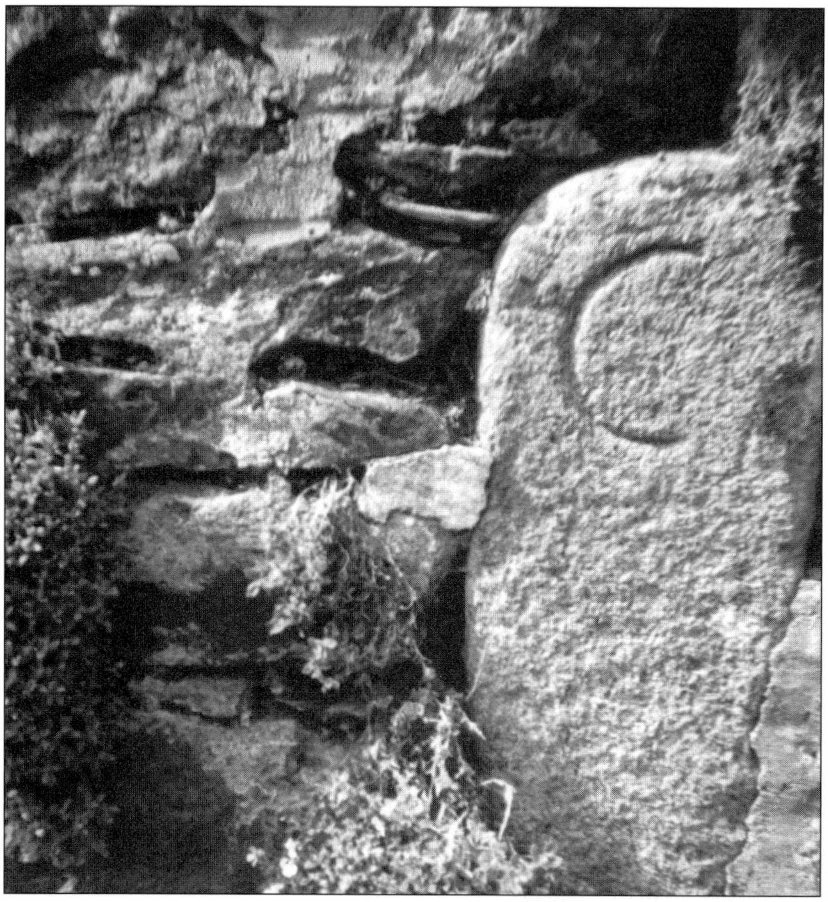

14.

15.

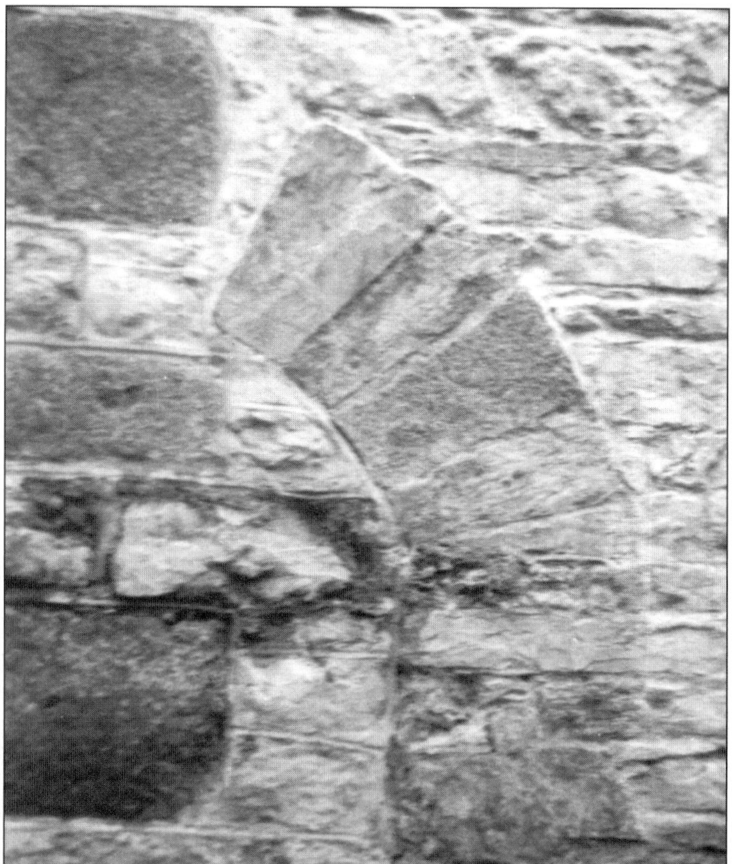

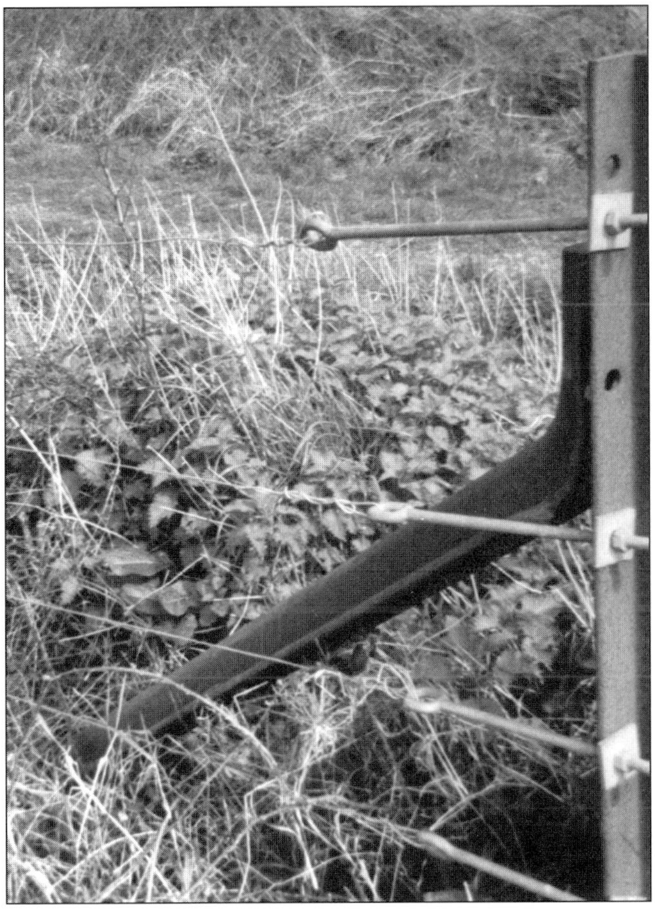

16.

17.

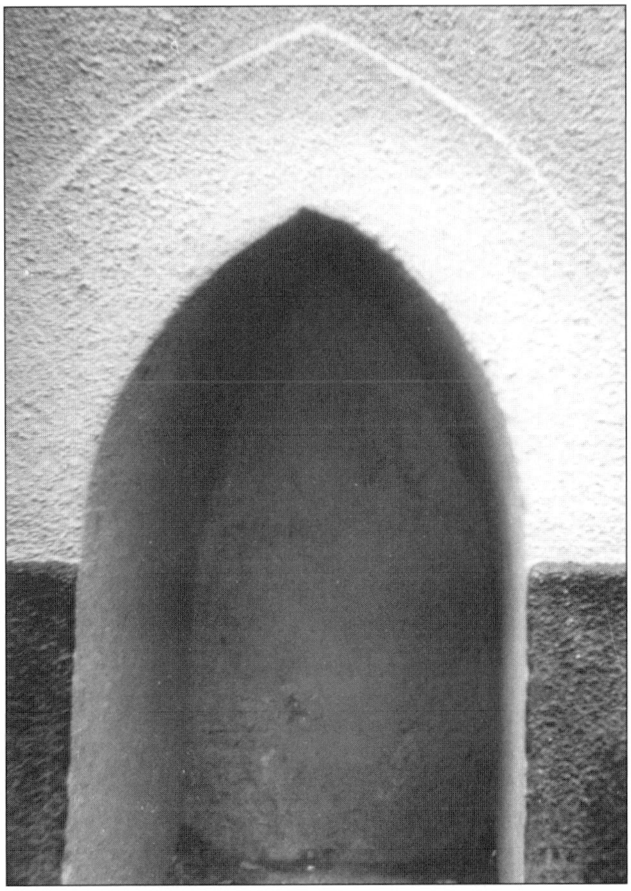

Bibliography

Amery, J.S., 'Presidential Address', *Transactions of the Devonshire Association LVI (pp.43–102)*, Devonshire Association, 1924
Amery, R.F., 'Unrecorded hill fortresses near Ashburton', *Transactions of the Devonshire Association V (pp.261–265)*, Devonshire Association, 1873
Brewer, D., 'Frederick Foot and Dartmoor', *Dartmoor Magazine (*Autumn edition), Halsgrove, 1995
Burt, R. (ed.), *Industry and Society in the SW*, Exeter University, 1970
Deacon, A. (ed.), *Ashburton School 1958–1983*, Ashburton School, 1983
Delderfield, E., *Cradle of the Sea Dogs*, Raleigh Press, 1951
Dell, S., *Policing the Peninsula*, Forest Publishing, 2000
Dines, H.G., *The Metalliferous Mining Region of South-West England*, HMSO, 1994
Donaldson, W., *Great Disasters of the Stage*, Arthur Baker Ltd, 1984
Dymond, R., 'John Ford, Dramatist', *Transactions of the Devonshire Association VIII (pp. 420–425)*, Devonshire Association, 1876
Garner, *Rules of Ashburton's Courts Leet & Baron Jury*, Private Printing, 1950
Gerrish, Tricia, 'Ashburton (Devon's Market Towns)', *Devon Life, 1999*
Gover, J.E.B., Mawer, A. and Stenton, F.M. (eds.), *Place Names of Devon I*, English Place Name Society, 1931
Gover, J.E.B., Mawer, A. and Stenton, F.M. (eds.), *Place Names of Devon II*, English Place Name Society, 1932
Graf, W.S., *Ashburton Grammar School 1314–1938*, Ashburton Grammar School, 1938
Greeves, T.A.P., 'The Great Courts or Parliaments of Devon Tinners 1474–1786', *Report and Transactions of the Devonshire Association for the Advancement of Science 119 (pp.145–167)*, Devonshire Association, 1987
Grimley, R., *Motor Buses of Ashburton, Buckfastleigh and Holne*, Grimley, R., undated
Halsbury, *Laws of England*, HMSO, 1976
Hamilton Jenkin, A.K., *Mines of Devon – North and East of Dartmoor*, Devon Library Service, 1981
Hanham, H.J., 'The suppression of the chantries in Ashburton', *Transactions of the Devonshire Association XCIX (pp.139–146)*, Devonshire Association, 1967
Harker, Frank, *Ashburton Grammar School*, Mid Devon Advertiser, 1914
Hawkins, M., *Devon Roads, an illustrated survey*, Devon Books, 1988
Homer, R.F., 'The Whiddon Tin Mine, Ashburton', *Transactions of the Devonshire Association 128 (pp.155–170)*, Devonshire Association, 1996
Humphries, J., *Life and Works of Sydney Endacott*, Private Printing (USA), 1977
Kain, R. and Ravenhill, W. (eds.), *Historical Atlas of South West England*, Exeter Press, 1999
Karau, P., *Great Western Branch Line Termini*, Oxford Pub. Co., 1977
Karkeek, Paul Q., 'Fairfax in the West 1645–46', *Transactions of the Devonshire Association VIII (pp.117–147)*, Devonshire Association, 1876
Kennerley, A., *The Making of the University of Plymouth*, Plymouth University, 2000
Kingdom, A., *The Ashburton Branch*, Oxford Pub. Co., 1977
Le Messurier, B., *Dartmoor Artists*, Halsgrove, 2002
Lewis, G.R., *The Stannaries – A Study of the English Tin Miner*, Harvard University Press, 1924
Mitchell, V. and Smith, K., *Branch Line to Ashburton*, Middleton Press, 1977
Oliver, Revd G., *Lives of the Bishops of Exeter*, Roberts, *1861*
Pennington, R.E., *Stannary Law – A History of the Mining Law of Cornwall and Devon*, David & Charles, 1973
Pilkington, *The Dartmoor Town*, Devon Books, 1989
Rice, I., *Devon Firefighter*, Halsgrove, 2000
Satterley, J., 'Memories of Ashburton in Late Victorian Days', *Transactions of the Devonshire Association 84 (pp. 20–51)*, Devonshire Association, 1952
Stephan, J., 'Some notes on Ashburton Grammar School', *Transactions of the Devonshire Association XCIX (pp.126-130)*, Devonshire Association, 1967
Webb, P., *Ashburton & Buckfastleigh Cottage Hospital*, South Devon Healthcare Trust, 1998
Webb, P., 'An Ashburton Lady Photographer', *Dartmoor Magazine (*Spring edition), Halsgrove, 1998
Webb, P., *Past Portreeves of Ashburton*, Private Printing, 1998

Webb. P., *The Pubs and Inns of Ashburton*, Obelisk, 1995
Worlt, R.M, *Peter Fabyan Sparke Amery & John Sparke Amery*, English Church, 1934
Worthy, L.C., 'A memoir of Bishop Stapledon', *Transactions of the Devonshire Association VIII (pp.442–452)*, Devonshire Association, 1876

Other sources include:
Ashburton Museum
Ashburton School prospectus for parents, 1980s.
Ashburton School website
Buckfast & Western Gazette, 10 October, 1963
Carnival programmes (various)
Devon Fire Brigade website
History of the Methodist Church, produced by Methodist Church
Notes from St Lawrence Chapel, courtesy of St Lawrence Guild
Research for 50th Anniversary of VE Day exhibition (information provided by local people).
Souvenir programme of the St John's Ambulance headquarters' opening, April 1939
St Andrew's Church Guide, produced by St Andrew's Church PCC
Trade Directories by various publishers (1780–1939)

Answers to quiz, pages 148–155

1. *Gravestone in wall, church path*
2. *Parapet on bridge on Old Totnes Road*
3. *Water point, West Street*
4. *Water point, church*
5. *Bell Turret, Town Hall*
6. *Dartmoor National Park Marker, Pear Tree*
7. *Gas lamp, St Lawrence Chapel*
8. *Gable end, Tugela House*
9. *Market channel, St Gudula's Well, Old Totnes Road*
10. *Date stone, Woodland Road*
11. *Medieval carved doorway, Headborough Farm*
12. *Water chamber, Roborough Lane*
13. *Mile marker, Druid*
14. *Arch, Woodland Road, St Mary's Well*
15. *C stone, Old Totnes Road*
16. *Railway track, Old Bulliver's Way*
17. *Waterpoint, Constitutional Club, St Lawrence Lane*

Subscribers

Jeanne Allen
Philip E.J. Allen, Ashburton, Devon
Miss Allison Atney and Mr Anthony Hrycyszyn, Ashburton, Devon
Steve and Lori Bagnall, Ashburton, Devon
Shirley Baty (née Grose), Kings Pyon, Herefordshire
Mrs Vera M. Beck, Charlton, London
E.D. Bligh and Family
Mr Raymond Edward Bray, Ashburton, Devon
Philip Brimblecombe, Ashburton, Devon
Doreen and Keith Bryant, Goodstone, Bickington, Devon
Elizabeth S. Burge, Ashburton, Devon
K.J. Burrow, Bucks Cross, Devon
Kathleen Vera Burton (née Batten), Torquay, Devon (great-granddaughter of Joseph Batten, Portreeve)
Peter C. Coleby, Ashburton, Devon
Kenneth G. Collins, Ashburton, Devon
Adeline Rose Elizabeth Cook
Miss C.M. Crabb
Doug Creagh, South Guildford, Western Australia
David and Patricia Crook, Ashburton, Devon
John, Anne, Robert, James and Becky Cross, Ashburton, Devon
Preb. Philip W. Darby, Vicar of Ashburton
Allen N. Dent, Ashburton
Mary, Adrian and Susan Dent
Christine Dickens (née Lawrence), In Memory Of
Margaret Dodd (née Pitts)
Kevin and Glenda Down, Melbourne, Australia
The Family of William Frazier Down, San Diego, California
Dave and Margaret Downie, The Red Mullet, Ashburton
Bob and Jen Edwards, Durban, South Africa
Eileen Egbeare, Ashburton
Jack Elliott, Ashburton, Devon
Mr R. Evans, Boscombe, Bournemouth, Dorset
John and Laura Ewen, Christchurch, New Zealand
Trevor William French, Auckland, New Zealand
Stephen and Isobel German
Christine Gibbons (née Pitts)
Stella M. Goss
Dr and Mrs Clive Graymore and Family
Dora C. Guest
John Hallett, Ashburton, Devon
Mr Victor Hamm, Ashburton, Devon
John Hands, London
Mary J. Hands, Reading

Mrs Moira Hands, Ashburton, Devon
Jane Harding (née Harvey), London (great-granddaughter of Joseph Batten, Portreeve)
D. Harvey, Ashburton
Lorna E. Harvey, Ashburton, Devon
Susan Heasman, Belmont Cottage
Gayle Heuer, St Paul, Minnesota, USA
Mrs G.M. Hext, Yeovil, Somerset
Alan Hope, Ashburton Town Mayor 1998–2000, Yateley, Hampshire
The late Charles Gordon Howis, Scarborough, Ontario, Canada
Rowan James, Ashburton, Devon
Saffi James, Ashburton, Devon
Cynthia Jonas (née Leaman)
The Joyner Family, East Street, Ashburton
Len Jury, New Plymouth, New Zealand
Sarah and Chris Kehaya, Ashburton, Devon
The Keywood Family, Ashburton, Devon
Sandra Lloyd (née Hext, Totnes, Devon
Maurice J. Mann, Ashburton, Devon
Warrick Matthew and Olivia Jane Lang
M. McElheron, Kingskerswell
Seath Millar, Ashburton, Devon
Arch and Audrey Mortimore, Widecombe-in-the-Moor
Chris J. Nancarrow, Newton Abbot, Devon
The Rev. M.H. and Mrs Needham, late of Hele House, Ashburton
Mrs Barbara J. Nichol, Ashburton, Devon
Nellie, Dick and Rene Northway
Richard Palk, Halshanger Manor, Ashburton
George Pedrick, Ashburton, Devon
Doreen F. Pengilley, Ashburton
Professor John and Mrs Jennifer Perrin
Mr and Mrs R.M. Perry, Plymouth, Devon
Mr Robert and Mrs Linda Phillips
Mr and Mrs D.W. Puttick, Eastbourne, East Sussex
The Rangeley Family
Daniel J. Ravenscroft, Ashburton, Devon
Ken Rickard, Lydford, Devon
Mrs Doris Ronan (née Hext), Totnes
Hedy and Latifa Sadoc, Ashburton
Gordon Sanders
Sawdye and Harris, Chartered Surveyors & Auctioneers, Ashburton, Devon
Stella Scholes (née Johnson), Durham
Rachel Anne Scott, Stormsdown, Devon
Lynette Shapland (née Egbeare), Yelverton, Devon
Joyce Shilan, Ashburton, Devon
Miss Dorothea F. Sibeth
South Dartmoor Community College Library
Sarah J.P. Southcombe, Bickington
Sylvia Spence
Yvonne Spence
Mr and Mrs W.H. Spry, Ashburton, Devon
Maurice H.J. Steer, Ashburton

Samuel John Steer
Margaret Stocker, Ashburton, Devon
J. and N. Stranex
John R. Topping, Ashburton, Devon
Mr and Mrs Philip Trewin, Ashburton
Gordon and Kathleen Tucker and Family, Midford
Mr and Mrs R.A. Vane, Lincoln
John F.W. Walling, Newton Abbot, Devon
Peggy and Iris Waters
Richard and Jennifer Wells, Ashburton
William H.A. West, Ashburton, Devon
R. Westall, Ashburton
Marianne, David and Tom Weymouth, Ashburton
May Williams, Ashburton, Devon
James Henry Wills Family, Sudbury, Ontario
Ms Jan Wood, Ide, Devon
Geraldine and Chris Woodwark, Dartmouth
Peter Wotton, Ashburton, Devon
Peter Yolland, Bromley, Kent
Bill Yolland, Roborough Lane, Ashburton

In order to include as many historical photographs as possible in this volume, a printed index is not included. However, the Devon titles in the Community History Series are indexed by Genuki.

For further information and indexes to various volumes in the series, please visit: http://www.cs.ncl.ac.uk/genuki/DEV/indexingproject.html